NIEUWE ZIJDE
Pages 70–85

OUDE ZIJDE
Pages 56–69

Nieuwe Zijde

Oude Zijde

D1052253

Eastern Canal Ring

EASTERN CANAL RING
Page 114–123

PLANTAGE
Pages 138–147

0 metres   500

0 yards   500

EYEWITNESS TRAVEL

AMSTERDAM

EYEWITNESS TRAVEL

AMSTERDAM

MAIN CONTRIBUTORS:
ROBIN PASCOE
CHRISTOPHER CATLING

LONDON, NEW YORK,
MELBOURNE, MUNICH AND DELHI
www.dk.com

PROJECT EDITOR Heather Jones
ART EDITOR Vanessa Hamilton
EDITORS Peter Adams, Sasha Heseltine,
Fiona Morgan, Alice Peebles, Nichola Tyrrell
US EDITOR Mary Sutherland
DESIGNERS Emma Hutton, Erika Lang, Malcolm Parchment

CONTRIBUTORS
Paul Andrews, Hedda Archbold, Marlene Edmunds,
Pip Farquharson, Adam Hopkins, Fred Mawer, Alison Melvin,
Kim Renfrew, Catherine Stebbings, Richard Widdows

PHOTOGRAPHERS
Max Alexander, Rupert Horrox, Kim Sayer

ILLUSTRATORS
Nick Gibbard, Maltings Partnership,
Derrick Stone, Martin Woodward

Film outputting bureau Cooling Brown, London
Reproduced by Colourscan, Singapore

Printed and bound in China by L. Rex Printing Company Limited

First American edition 1995
11 12 13 14 10 9 8 7 6 5 4 3 2 1
Published in the United States by DK Publishing,
375 Hudson Street, New York, New York 10014.

**Reprinted with revisions 1996, 1997, 1999, 2000, 2001,
2002, 2003, 2004, 2005, 2006, 2007, 2009, 2010, 2011**

Copyright 1995, 2011 © Dorling Kindersley Limited, London

PUBLISHED IN GREAT BRITAIN BY DORLING KINDERSLEY LIMITED.

A CATALOG RECORD FOR THIS BOOK IS AVAILABLE FROM THE LIBRARY OF CONGRESS.

ISSN 1542-1554
ISBN: 978-0-7566-6954-6

THROUGHOUT THIS BOOK, FLOORS ARE REFERRED TO IN ACCORDANCE WITH
EUROPEAN USAGE; I.E., THE "FIRST FLOOR" IS THE FLOOR ABOVE GROUND LEVEL.

Front cover main image: Canals in the Singel district

MIX
Paper from
responsible sources
FSC FSC™ C018179
www.fsc.org

**The information in this
DK Eyewitness Travel Guide is checked regularly.**

Every effort has been made to ensure that this book is as up-to-date
as possible at the time of going to press. Some details, however,
such as telephone numbers, opening hours, prices, gallery hanging
arrangements and travel information are liable to change. The
publishers cannot accept responsibility for any consequences arising
from the use of this book, nor for any material on third party
websites, and cannot guarantee that any website address in this
book will be a suitable source of travel information. We value the
views and suggestions of our readers very highly. Please write to:
Publisher, DK Eyewitness Travel Guides, Dorling Kindersley, 80 Strand,
London, WC2R 0RL, Great Britain, or email: travelguides@dk.com

◁ **Boats lining Prinsengracht, with Westerkerk in the background**

CONTENTS

Model boat at Scheepvaart Museum

INTRODUCING
AMSTERDAM

AMSTERDAM AREA
BY AREA

Traditional lift bridge

Children in Dutch costume outside a church in the Zuiderzee Museum

SURVIVAL GUIDE

Wheels of Gouda cheese

Café terrace in Artis zoo

TRAVELLERS' NEEDS

Façade of the Rijksmuseum

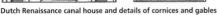
Dutch Renaissance canal house and details of cornices and gables

HOW TO USE THIS GUIDE

This guide helps you get the most from your stay in Amsterdam. It provides expert recommendations as well as detailed practical information. *Introducing Amsterdam* maps the city and sets it in its historical and cultural context. *Amsterdam Area by Area* describes the important sights, with maps, pictures and illustrations. *Further Afield* looks at sights outside the city centre and *Beyond Amsterdam* explores other places near Amsterdam. Suggestions on food, drink, where to stay and what to do are made in *Travellers' Needs*, and *Survival Guide* has tips on everything from travel to Dutch telephones.

AMSTERDAM AREA BY AREA

The centre of the city has been divided into seven sightseeing areas. Each area has its own chapter, which opens with a list of the sights described. All the sights are numbered and plotted on an *Area Map*. The detailed information for each sight is presented in numerical order, making it easy to locate within the chapter.

Sights at a Glance lists the chapter's sights by category: Churches, Museums and Galleries, Historic Buildings, Streets and Canals.

Each area of central Amsterdam has colour-coded thumb tabs.

A locator map shows where you are in relation to other areas of the city centre.

1 Area Map
For easy reference, the sights are numbered and located on a map. The sights are also shown on the Amsterdam Street Finder on pages 280–87.

2 Street-by-Street Map
This gives a bird's-eye view of the heart of each sightseeing area.

A suggested route for a walk covers the more interesting streets in the area.

Stars indicate the sights that no visitor should miss.

3 Detailed information on each sight
All the sights in Amsterdam are described individually. Addresses and practical information are provided. The key to the symbols used in the information block is shown on the back flap.

BEYOND AMSTERDAM

Amsterdam is at the heart of a region known as the Randstad, the economic powerhouse of the Netherlands. The city is a haven for tourists: within easy reach are the ancient towns of Leiden and Utrecht, as well as Den Haag and Haarlem with their exceptional galleries and museums. The Randstad extends south as far as Rotterdam, a thriving modern city full of avant-garde architecture.

4 Introduction to Beyond Amsterdam
Beyond Amsterdam has its own introduction, which provides an overview of the history and character of the region around Amsterdam and outlines what the region has to offer the visitor today. The area covered by this section is highlighted on the map of the Netherlands shown on page 165. It covers important cities, such as Den Haag, Haarlem and Rotterdam, as well as attractive towns and places of interest in the Dutch countryside.

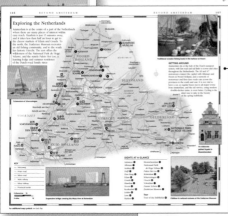

5 Regional Map
This gives an illustrated overview of the whole region. All the sights covered in this section are numbered, and the network of major roads is marked. There are also useful tips on getting around the region by bus and train.

6 Detailed information on each sight
All the important cities, towns and other places to visit are described individually. They are listed in order, following the numbering given on the Regional Map. Within each town or city, there is detailed information on important buildings and other sights.

Stars indicate the best features and works of art.

The Visitors' Checklist
provides a summary of the practical information you will need to plan your visit.

7 The top sights
These are given two or more full pages. Historic buildings are dissected to reveal their interiors; museums and galleries have colour-coded floorplans to help you locate the most interesting exhibits.

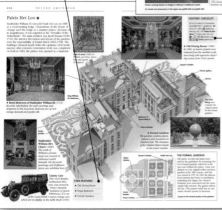

INTRODUCING AMSTERDAM

FOUR GREAT DAYS IN AMSTERDAM

Despite its compact size, Amsterdam is a city with many different aspects and offers a range of attractions to suit all tastes and budgets. The city is home to some of the world's finest art galleries, there are bustling markets for those in search of street life and for kids, there is also a great choice of things to see and do. Here are four themed days out to explore four different sides of the city. Many of the places have cross-references so you can look up more details and tailor the days to suit you. Price guides include transport, meals and admission charges.

Anne Frank statue, Westerkerk

Rembrandt's studio in the Rembrandthuis

TWO GREAT ARTISTS

- At home with Rembrandt
- Lunch by the canal
- Van Gogh's greatest works

TWO ADULTS allow at least €100

Morning

Of all the great painters that Amsterdam claims as its own, two stand head and shoulders above the rest: Rembrandt van Rijn and Vincent van Gogh. Rembrandt's home from 1639 to 1658 is now the **Museum Het Rembrandthuis** *(see pp62–3)* and has been restored to look as it might have when he lived here, at the height of his wealth and fame. The atmosphere is such that one can clearly imagine the great artist and his family roaming these rooms. The museum houses an exhibition of Rembrandt's etchings and sketches, as well as paintings by his contemporaries, notably his teacher Pieter Lastman.

Equally interesting is the recreation of the artist's studio, complete with chalks, charcoal, easels and brushes, and his wonderful "cabinet of curiosities" – a room cluttered with statues, stuffed birds and small beasts, arms and armour, all of which Rembrandt would have used as props in his portraits and still-lives. A great spot for lunch after the Rembranthuis is Dantzig, the café next to the **Muziektheater** *(see p248)*, just a minute's walk away. In summer its sunny terrace has a fine view of the Amstel, while in winter there is a cosy indoor restaurant.

Afternoon

The **Van Gogh Museum** *(see pp134–5)* houses the world's largest collection of the Dutch painter's work, with almost 800 paintings and drawings along with the painter's own collection of glorious Japanese prints and an array of paintings by his contemporaries. It is a dazzling collection, and you should allow two to three hours to take it in at leisure.

HIDDEN HISTORIES

- **Explore life in hiding**
- **A vanished community**
- **Living history**
- **Secret churches**

TWO ADULTS allow at least €115

Morning

The **Anne Frank Huis** *(see pp90–91)* receives up to 1,000 visitors a day, so try to get there early. In a tiny secret apartment above Otto Frank's warehouse, the Jewish Frank and van Pels families hid from the Nazis from 1942 until 1944, when they were betrayed and deported to concentration camps. The 13-year-old Anne Frank began recording life in hiding in her diary in July 1942 and it was published in 1947, two years after her death in Bergen-Belsen. There is a touching statue of Anne outside the **Westerkerk** *(see p90)*. Completed in 1631, the Westerkerk's tower is the tallest in the city at 85 m (278 ft) and the climb to the top offers a breathtaking view.

View of Prinsengracht from the tower of the Westerkerk

The Waterlooplein area was the heart of a Jewish community who were drawn to the city in the 17th century because of its tolerance. The **Joods Historisch Museum** *(see pp64–5)* is housed in four former synagogues built in the 17th and 18th centuries and contains a collection of religious artifacts as well as documents relating to the Holocaust. The museum has a fine restaurant serving both Dutch and Jewish food.

Afternoon
A short walk away, the huge **Portugees-Israëlitische Synagogue** *(see p66)*, with its candle-lit interiors, is still in use by the city's Sephardic Jews. Protestant Amsterdam in the 17th century, however, was less tolerant of Catholic worship. The **Museum Ons' Lieve Heer op Solder** *(see pp84–5)* is a perfectly restored "clandestine" church which was built at this time.

A FAMILY DAY

- **Messing about in boats**
- **Ice cream, jugglers and fire-eaters**
- **Hi-tech hands-on fun**

FAMILY OF FOUR allow at least €140

Morning
Parental pedal-power provides the impetus for the first part of this day out. Amsterdam's **canal bikes** *(see p277)* are four-seater pedal boats that move at a gentle pace, passing old canalside houses, houseboats and nesting waterfowl. They can be rented in winter too, but for families this is really a summer activity. A good option is to pick up your vessel at the **Westerkerk** mooring and paddle around the picturesque Keizersgracht, then drop it off at **Leidsestraat**. This should take no more than an hour. Then stroll down to Leidseplein *(see p108)* with its many outdoor cafés and street entertainers for well-earned coffee and ice cream.

Hands-on exhibits at the Nemo Science Center Amsterdam

Afternoon
Take a tram to the **Nemo Science Center Amsterdam** *(see p150)*. This spectacular building looks like a giant futuristic ship and is full of hands-on, state-of-the-art interactive exhibits for children of all ages. Allow at least a couple of hours to explore the possibilities of the themed technology, energy, science and humanity zones before heading for the centre's pleasant waterside terrace café-restaurant.

COLOURFUL MARKETS

- **Antiques and collectables**
- **Ethnic eating**
- **Vibrant street life**
- **Legendary nightlife**

TWO ADULTS allow at least €50

Morning
You can buy just about anything in Amsterdam's markets. The **Waterlooplein** *(see p63)* open-air market still has the definite feel of the hippie era, with stalls selling tie-dyed clothing, exotic statuettes, vintage leather coats, army-surplus equipment and ceramics. Dive further into this open-air labyrinth to find 19th- and 20th-century collectables, from classic rock albums to psychedelic posters, pipes and cigarette holders, china, glassware, and more. A short walk and tram ride from Waterlooplein, the **Albert Cuypmarkt** *(see p122)* is the heart and soul of de Pijp, the most cosmopolitan part of Amsterdam. It is an ideal place for lunch – there are many ethnic restaurants on and around Albert Cuypstraat, including Moroccan, Surinamese and Turkish.

Afternoon
There are more than 100 shops and 300 street-stalls along Albert Cuypstraat, selling everything from exotic fruit and spices to Dutch cheese, chocolates, sausage and seafood, flowers, clothes and household goods. This is authentic Amsterdam street life at its best. You could easily spend an afternoon here, before taking a 10-minute stroll back to the **Leidseplein** *(see p108)* and a night out at one of its top night-time venues.

Eclectic stalls lining the length of the Albert Cuypmarket

Putting Amsterdam on the Map

Although the Netherlands' seat of government is at Den Haag, Amsterdam is the nominal capital. It is the country's largest city, with a population of almost 750,000, and the most visited, receiving over 7.5 million foreign visitors a year. It stands on precariously low-lying ground at the confluence of the Amstel and IJ rivers near the IJsselmeer and, like much of the Netherlands, would flood frequently but for land reclamation and sea defences. This position places Amsterdam at the heart of the Randstad, a term used to describe the crescent-shaped conurbation covering much of the provinces of Noord Holland, Zuid Holland and Utrecht, and encompassing the cities of Utrecht, Rotterdam, Den Haag, Leiden and Haarlem.

Satellite photograph showing the north-west Netherlands and the IJsselmeer

Western Europe

Amsterdam has a first-class international airport, as well as good road and rail links to all parts of the Netherlands and beyond.

AMSTERDAM AND ENVIRONS

Castricum
Markermeer
Heemskerk
Purmerend
Volendam
Beverwijk
IJmuiden
Haarlem
Almere Stad
Zandvoort
IJmeer
Almere Haven
Gooimeer
Hillegom
Schiphol
Weesp
Huizen
Bussum
Noordwijk
Sassenheim
Uithoorn
Hilversum
Mijdrecht

Amsterdam and its Environs
The sights in central Amsterdam are covered in detail on pages
54–147 and a Street Finder *is provided on pages 278–91.*
Sights outside the centre are covered in Further Afield *on*
pages 148–55. Places of interest elsewhere in the Netherlands
are explored in Beyond Amsterdam *on pages 162–207.*

Groningen
GRONINGEN
Leeuwarden
Assen
FRIESLAND
DRENTHE
Hoogeveen
Meppel
OVER
IJSSEL
Zwolle

NETHERLANDS

Rheine
Mittelland Kanal
Osnabrück
Apeldoorn
Enschede
Münster
Arnhem
GELDERLAND
Nijmegen
GERMANY
Dortmund
Essen
Bochum
Duisburg
Mülheim
Ruhr
Hagen
Krefeld
Düsseldorf
BRABANT
LIMBURG
Mönchengladbach
Maastricht
Aachen

KEY

	Greater Amsterdam
	Area below sea level
✈	Airport
⛴	Ferry port
═	Motorway
▬	Major road
—	Railway
– –	Country boundary

0 kilometres   20

0 miles   20

A flooded polder outside Utrecht

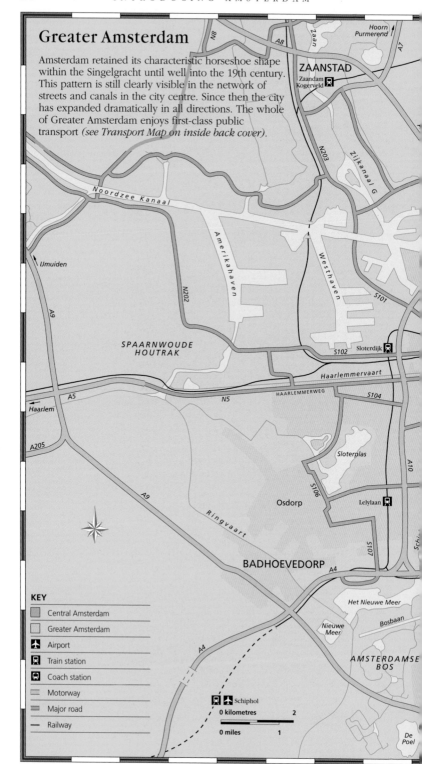

Greater Amsterdam

Amsterdam retained its characteristic horseshoe shape within the Singelgracht until well into the 19th century. This pattern is still clearly visible in the network of streets and canals in the city centre. Since then the city has expanded dramatically in all directions. The whole of Greater Amsterdam enjoys first-class public transport *(see Transport Map on inside back cover)*.

KEY

	Central Amsterdam
	Greater Amsterdam
✈	Airport
🚉	Train station
🚌	Coach station
	Motorway
	Major road
	Railway

0 kilometres   2

0 miles   1

Central Amsterdam

This guide divides central Amsterdam into seven distinct areas, each of which has its own chapter. Most city sights are contained in these areas. The Oude Zijde and Nieuwe Zijde make up the two halves of medieval Amsterdam, while the Museum Quarter was developed in the 19th century and has the three most important national museums. In between lies the Canal Ring, which retains many fine buildings from Amsterdam's Golden Age, while the Plantage *(see pp138–47)*, once an area of green space outside the city, is today best known for the zoological and botanical gardens.

A street musician on Waterlooplein

Houses along the Singel
The Singel was the first concentric canal to be cut in Amsterdam. It forms the border between the medieval centre and the newer Western and Central Canal Rings (see pp86–113).

Vondelpark
This attractive park in the Museum Quarter (see pp124–37) is a good place to relax after a visit to one of Amsterdam's museums.

WESTERN CANAL RING

CENTRAL CANAL RING

MUSEUM QUARTER

EASTERN CANAL RING

Nieuwe Kerk

Amsterdams Historisch Museum

Rijksmuseum

Van Gogh Museum

Stedelijk Museum

VONDELPARK

| 0 metres | 500 |
| 0 yards | 500 |

Spires of Nieuwe Kerk and the Magna Plaza
The Nieuwe Zijde's skyline (see pp70–85) is pierced by the Neo-Gothic spire of Magna Plaza (the former Postkantoor), the steeples of the Nieuwe Kerk and the statues on the Koninklijk Paleis.

House on the Oudezijds Voorburgwal
This attractive residential canal, which now runs through the Red Light District, was first cut in front of the ramparts protecting the Oude Zijde (see pp56–69).

Flowers at the Bloemenmarkt
A fragrant, floating flower market, the Bloemenmarkt is situated beside the Munttoren on the Singel in the Eastern Canal Ring (see pp114–23).

KEY

	Major sight
🚆	Train station
Ⓜ	Metro
🅿	Parking
ℹ	Tourist information
	Police station
	Church
	Synagogue
Ⓒ	Mosque

THE HISTORY OF AMSTERDAM

Amsterdam, the greatest planned city of northern Europe, is today one in which beauty and serenity co-exist happily with a slightly seamy underside. Both parts of this split personality continue to draw visitors. Most of the racier aspects of Amsterdam spring directly from the city's long tradition of religious and political tolerance. The notion of individual freedom of conscience was fought for, long and hard, during the struggles against Spanish domination in the 16th century. This belief stands firm today, with the caveat that no-one should be harmed by the actions of others – a factor that sparked off the riots involving squatters in the 1970s.

Amsterdam's coat of arms on the Munttoren

The city was founded as a small fishing village in an improbable position on marsh at the mouth of the Amstel river. The waters around the village were controlled by a system of dykes and polders, and the young township expanded prodigiously to become the chief trading city of northern Europe, and ultimately, in the 17th century, the centre of a massive empire stretching across the world. The construction of the canals and gabled houses in the 16th and 17th centuries coincided with a period of fine domestic architecture. The result is a city centre of unusually consistent visual beauty. By the 18th century, Amsterdam was a major financial centre, but internal unrest and restrictions imposed under Napoleonic rule led to a decline in her fortunes.

The city quietly slipped into a period of obscurity, and industrialization came late. In the 20th century, however, the city entered the mainstream again. Now, the start of a new millennium has marked a period of urban growth for Amsterdam:ambitious architectural projects have given a new lease of life to former derelict areas such as the Eastern Docklands, while Zuidas, the area south of the ring road, is fast becoming a major business hub, complemented by top-notch cultural facilities.

Plan of Amsterdam (c. 1725) showing the Grachtengordel and Plantage *(see pp138–47)*

◁ *The Maid of Amsterdam Receiving the Homage of her People (c. 1685) by Gérard de Lairesse*

The Origins of Amsterdam

Amsterdam emerged from the mists of the Low Countries in about 1200, on a watery site at the mouth of the Amstel river. It was a settlement of fisherfolk before turning to trade. The first permanent dwellings were built on terps, man-made mounds high enough to provide protection from flood water. As the settlement grew, it was fashioned by dynastic and religious combat, with feudal struggles between the Lords van Amstel and the counts of Holland, who had the backing of the all-powerful bishops of Utrecht *(see p202)*. This rivalry continued into the next century.

Windmills drained the land

EXTENT OF THE CITY

■ *1100*   □ *Today*

Farming on polders outside the village walls

Dam

Cooking Pot
Sturdy earthenware pots were used for cooking communal meals over an open fire in the kitchen area of 13th-century houses.

Wooden defence walls

Lord Gijsbrecht
The 19th-century etching shows Gijsbrecht van Amstel IV being marched into Utrecht as a prisoner by Guy of Hainaut, brother of the Count of Holland, in 1298.

Livestock grazed on reclaimed land called polder.

THE VILLAGE OF AMSTERDAM IN 1300
This medieval artist's impression shows the first tiny settlement on polders along the Damrak. The village was protected by wooden walls, and it is thought that the castle of the Van Amstels may have been located in the area around today's Dam square *(see pp72–3)*.

TIMELINE		
1000 Fishermen float down Rhine in hollow pine logs		

Small wooden cog ship used for fishing

1000	**1050**	**1100**

Primitive boat dating from c. 6000 BC

1015 Local feudal leader repels attack by German tribes and declares himself Count of Holland

c. 1125 Fishermen build huts at mouth of the Amstel river

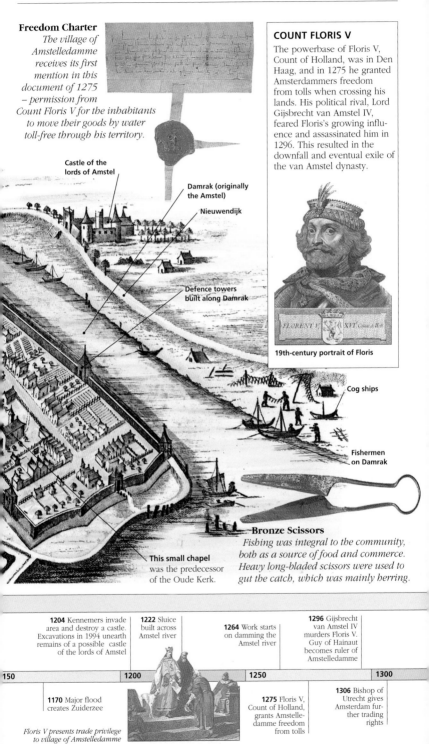

Freedom Charter
The village of Amstelledamme receives its first mention in this document of 1275 – permission from Count Floris V for the inhabitants to move their goods by water toll-free through his territory.

COUNT FLORIS V

The powerbase of Floris V, Count of Holland, was in Den Haag, and in 1275 he granted Amsterdammers freedom from tolls when crossing his lands. His political rival, Lord Gijsbrecht van Amstel IV, feared Floris's growing influence and assassinated him in 1296. This resulted in the downfall and eventual exile of the van Amstel dynasty.

FLORENT V. XVI. Comte de Holl.

19th-century portrait of Floris

Castle of the lords of Amstel

Damrak (originally the Amstel)

Nieuwendijk

Defence towers built along Damrak

Cog ships

Fishermen on Damrak

Bronze Scissors
Fishing was integral to the community, both as a source of food and commerce. Heavy long-bladed scissors were used to gut the catch, which was mainly herring.

This small chapel was the predecessor of the Oude Kerk.

1204 Kennemers invade area and destroy a castle. Excavations in 1994 unearth remains of a possible castle of the lords of Amstel

1222 Sluice built across Amstel river

1264 Work starts on damming the Amstel river

1296 Gijsbrecht van Amstel IV murders Floris V. Guy of Hainaut becomes ruler of Amstelledamme

150 — 1200 — 1250 — 1300

1170 Major flood creates Zuiderzee

Floris V presents trade privilege to village of Amstelledamme

1275 Floris V, Count of Holland, grants Amstelledamme freedom from tolls

1306 Bishop of Utrecht gives Amsterdam further trading rights

Medieval Amsterdam

The little town at the mouth of the Amstel fortified itself against both its enemies and the surrounding water. Amsterdam grew rich quickly after the discovery of a method of curing herring in 1385, which preserved the fish longer, enabling it to be exported. The town became a port for handling beer from Hamburg. Elaborate waterside houses with warehouses attached were used to service the trade. The Low Countries were under the rule of the Dukes of Burgundy, and control passed by marriage to the Austrian Habsburgs.

Medieval leather boot (c. 1500)

EXTENT OF THE CITY

■ 1300   □ Today

CANALSIDE HOUSE

Early canal houses were simple structures, built of wood with a thatched roof. From a single-storey design with the front and back on different levels, the layouts grew more complex. At the front, side rooms became separated off from the main room, and the back house was similarly divided up. The family slept on the first floor and goods were stored under the roof.

Miracle of Amsterdam
This tapestry cushion depicts a miraculous event. A dying man was given the Sacrament which he regurgitated. Thrown on the fire, the Host would not burn.

The wooden façades had simple spout gables *(see pp96–7)*.

Flour, beer and other foodstuffs were stored under the sloping roof.

Philip of Burgundy and Isabella of Portugal
Philip was the ruler of the Low Countries after 1419. He married Isabella of Portugal in 1430.

Timber structure

TIMELINE

1304 Lord Gijsbrecht van Amstel exiled		*Misericord in the Oude Kerk*	**1385** Willem Beukelszoon discovers method of curing herring
Early 1300s Work starts on Oude Kerk *(see pp68–9)*		**c.1380** Work begins on Nieuwe Kerk *(see pp76–7)*	

1300	1325	1350	1375	1

1301 Guy of Hainaut made Bishop of Utrecht

1323 Count of Holland designates Amsterdam a toll port for beer

1345 Miracle of Amsterdam

1350 Amsterdam becomes a beer and grain entrepôt

Stained-glass window in the Nieuwe Kerk

Making Beer
The brewing industry expanded after 1323, when the Count of Holland permitted Amsterdam to become a toll port for beer. Hops were introduced early in the century.

Thatched roof

The Great Fire of 1452
After Amsterdam's second dev-astating blaze, which destroyed the Nieuwe Kerk, legislation was passed preventing the use of wood as a building material.

Access to canal at rear

Stone side walls

Wooden support piles were driven into the first stable layer of sand.

Warehouse space

Amsterdam's Seal
The seal shows the diagonal crosses of St Andrew, the coat of arms of the Habsburgs and the cog ship that brought wealth through trade.

WHERE TO SEE MEDIEVAL AMSTERDAM

Few buildings remain from this period, as fire destroyed two-thirds of the city. The Oude Kerk *(see pp68–9)* dates from the early 14th century and the Nieuwe Kerk *(pp76–7)* from 1380. The Agnieten-kapel *(p61)* was built in 1470 and is one of very few Gothic chapels to survive the Alter-ation of 1578 *(pp24–5)*.

The Waag (p60)
Built in 1488, this was origin-ally a gateway in the city wall.

No. 34 Begijnhof (p75)
The oldest wooden house in the city, it dates from about 1420.

Maximilian marries Maria of Burgundy	**1477** Charles' daughter Maria marries Maximilian Habsburg of Austria	**1480** Defensive walls built around Amsterdam	**1494** Maximilian is Holy Roman Emperor. Power passes to his son, Philip, who marries the daughter of Isabella of Spain
	1452 Second Great Fire of Amsterdam		
1425	**1450**	**1475**	**1500**
1421 First Great Fire of Amsterdam	**1467** Charles the Bold succeeds Philip of Burgundy	**1482** Maria dies and Maximilian Habsburg rules the Netherlands	**1500** Birth of Philip's son, the future Emperor Charles V and king of Spain
1419 Philip the Good of Burgundy begins to unify the Low Countries	*Charles the Bold*		

The Age of Intolerance

By 1500, Amsterdam had outpaced rivals to become the main power in the province of Holland. Trade in the Baltic provided wealth and the city grew rapidly. Spain's Habsburg rulers tried to halt the Protestant Reformation sweeping northern Europe. Dutch resistance to Philip II of Spain resulted in 80 years of civil war and religious strife. Amsterdam sided with Spain but switched loyalties in 1578 – an event known as the Alteration – to become the fiercely Protestant capital of an infant Dutch Republic.

EXTENT OF THE CITY

▦ *1500*   ▢ *Today*

Anabaptists' Uprising *(1535)*
An extremist Protestant cult of Anabaptists seized the Stadhuis. Many were executed after eviction.

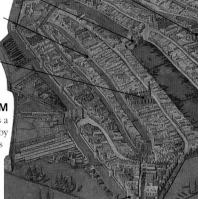

Nieuwe Kerk
(1395)

Rokin

Dam square

Oudezijds
Voorburgwal

Oude
Kerk
(1306)

Schreiers-
toren

PERSPECTIVE OF AMSTERDAM
This painted woodcut is a bird's-eye view of Amsterdam by Cornelis Anthonisz (1538). It is a critically important, detailed and precise map, heralding a centuries-long tradition of world-class map making in the city *(see p146).*

William of Orange
William, portrayed in 1555 by Anthonius Mor, led the Dutch against the Spanish until his assassination in Delft (see p195).

Much of the farmland in the Netherlands is below sea level.

TIMELINE

1502 Population of Amsterdam 12,000			**1535** Anabaptists demonstrate on Dam square. Mass executions follow. Start of 40 years of religious strife		**1550** Edict of Blood decrees death for Protestant heretics
	1516 Charles becomes king of Spain				
1500	**1510**	**1520**	**1530**	**1540**	**15**
	1506 Charles rules over the 17 provinces of the Netherlands			**1543** Charles V unifies Low Countries	
			Charles V, Holy Roman Emperor, king of Spain and ruler of the Netherlands		**1551** Population of Amsterdam about 30,000
	1519 Charles becomes Holy Roman Emperor, Charles V				

The Guild of St George *(1533)*
Guilds set up to keep order in the growing city later formed the Civic Guard (see pp82–3). Map-maker Cornelis Anthonisz painted this guild at supper.

WHERE TO SEE 16TH-CENTURY AMSTERDAM

Few buildings of early 16th-century provenance remain, but No. 1 Zeedijk *(see p67)* was built mid-century as a hostel for sailors. The Civic Guards' Gallery at the Amsterdams Historisch Museum *(pp80–83)* contains a series of splendid group portraits of 16th-century militia companies and guilds.

Montelbaanstoren
The lower section of the tower was built in 1512 (see p66), forming part of the city defences.

Nieuwezijds
Voorburgwal

Singel

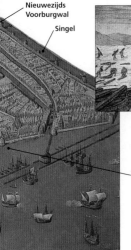

The Third Expedition
Gerrit de Veer's copper engraving (1597) shows Willem Barentsz on his search for a passage to the Arctic Sea.

Damrak

Wind-powered pump

Sea

Silver Drinking Horn
As the guilds grew richer, ceremony played a larger part in their lives. This ornate rinking horn shows St George defending the hapless maiden maiden against the dragon.

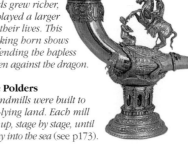

Draining the Polders
"Gangs" of windmills were built to drain the low-lying land. Each mill scooped water up, stage by stage, until it drained away into the sea (see p173).

The Golden Age of Amsterdam

The 17th century was truly a Golden Age for Amsterdam. The population soared; three great canals, bordered by splendid houses, were built in a triple ring round the city; and scores of painters and architects were at work. Fortunes were made and lost, and this early capitalism produced paupers who were cared for by charitable institutions – a radical idea for the time. In 1648, an uneasy peace was formalized with Catholic Spain, causing tension between Amsterdam's Calvinist burgomasters and the less religious House of Orange, dominant elsewhere in the country.

EXTENT OF THE CITY

▨ 1600   ☐ Today

Livestock and grain trading

Self-Portrait as the Apostle Paul *(1661)*
Rembrandt (see p62) was one of many artists working in Amsterdam in the mid-17th century.

Nieuwe Kerk (1395)

The new Stadhuis (now the Koninklijk Paleis) was being constructed behind wooden scaffolding.

The Love Letter *(1666)*
Genre painting (see p194), such as this calm domestic interior by Jan Vermeer, became popular as society grew more sophisticated.

DAM SQUARE IN 1656
Money poured into Amsterdam at this time of civic expansion. Jan Lingelbach (c. 1624–74) painted Dam square as a busy, thriving and cosmopolitan market, full of traders and wealthy merchants.

Delft Tiles
Delicate flower paintings were popular themes on 17th-century Delft tiles (see p195), used as decoration in wealthy households.

TIMELINE

Prince Frederick Henry of Orange

1625 Frederick Henry of Orange is stadholder. Plans to control navy from Den Haag fail

1614 Work finishes on Zuiderkerk *(see p62)*

1642 Rembrandt paints *The Night Watch (see p131)*

1631 Rembrandt comes to live in Amsterdam *(see p62)*

1600	1610	1620	1630	164

1609 Plan for triple ring of canals round heart of Amsterdam

1613 Work starts on first phase of canals

17th-century botanical drawing of a tulip

1634 Tulip mania begins

1637 The great tulip crash

Flora's Bandwagon *(1636)*
Many allegories were painted during "tulip mania". This satirical oil by HG Pot symbolizes the idiocy of investors who paid for rare bulbs with their weight in gold, forcing prices up until the market collapsed.

Commodities weighed at the Waag *(see p60)*

Ships sailing up the Damrak

WHERE TO SEE 17TH-CENTURY AMSTERDAM

Many public buildings sprang up as Amsterdam grew more wealthy. The Westerkerk *(see p90)* was designed by Hendrick de Keyser in 1620, the Lutherse Kerk *(p78)* by Adriaan Dortsman in 1671. Elias Boum built the Portugese Synagoge *(p66)* in 1675 for members of the immigrant Sephardic Jewish community *(p64)*.

Apollo *(c. 1648)*
Artus Quellien's statue is in the South Gallery of the Koninklijk Paleis (see p74).

Cargo unloaded by cranes   **Turkish traders**

Giving the Bread
The painting by Willem van Valckert shows the needy receiving alms. A rudimentary welfare system was introduced in the 1640s.

Rembrandthuis *(1606)*
Jacob van Campen added the pediment in 1633 (see p66).

---

huis (Koninklijk Paleis)

1650 eath of adholder lliam II

1665 New Stadhuis completed

1672 William III is stadholder. De Witt brothers killed by mob in Den Haag *(see p186)*

1685 Huguenot refugees reach Amsterdam after Louis XIV abolished Edict of Nantes

| 1650 | 1660 | 1670 | 1680 | 1690 |

1652 Stadhuis burns down

1669 Death of Rembrandt

1677 William III marries Mary Stuart, heiress to the English throne

William and Mary

1648 Amsterdam achieves supremacy over Antwerp on the maritime trade routes

1663 Second phase of canal building

The Golden Age Overseas

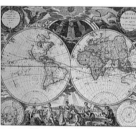

Coat of arms of the VOC

Supremacy in the Netherlands led to success overseas for Amsterdam. The Dutch colonized the Indonesian Archipelago, establishing a profitable empire based on spice trading in the East. The Dutch East India Company (VOC) thrived, using vast wooden ships called East Indiamen. In the New World, the Dutch ruled large parts of Brazil and bought Manhattan from its native owners, naming it New Amsterdam. However, war with England radically trimmed Dutch sea-power by the end of the 17th century.

Purchase of Manhattan
In 1626, explorer Pieter Minuit bought the island of Manhattan from the Native Americans for $24.

Salvaged Silverware
The Batavia *sank off the coast of western Australia in 1629. This bedknob, ewer and plate were salvaged in 1972.*

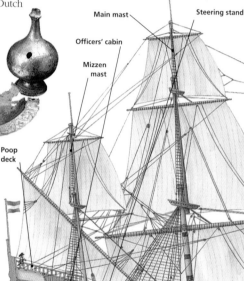

Main mast · Steering stand · Officers' cabin · Mizzen mast · Poop deck

World Map (1676)
Joan Blaeu's map charted the known world, with parts of Asia and Australia missing.

THE BATAVIA
Owned by the VOC, the *Batavia* was an East Indiaman, with three main masts. She was 45 m (148 ft) in length and carried a complement of about 350, including crew, soldiers and families.

TIMELINE OF EXPLORATION

Peter Stuyvesant

1602 Dutch East India Company (VOC) founded

1620 Pilgrim Fathers depart for the New World (*see p185*)

1642 Abel Tasman discovers Tasmania

| 1600 | 1610 | 1620 | 1630 | 16 |

1595 First voyage to Indonesia via Cape of Good Hope

VOC logo

1609 Hugo Grotius advocates freedom of trade at sea

1621 Dutch West India Company founded

1626 Peter Minuit buys Manhattan and founds New Amsterdam

Dutch Battle Ships *(1683)*
*Ludolf Backhuysen (1631–1708) painted the
Dutch battle fleet routing the rival Portuguese
navy off the coast of northern Spain.*

THE DUTCH EAST INDIA COMPANY

Founded in 1602, the VOC had a monopoly on all profits from trade east of the Cape of Good Hope. It became a public company and many a Dutch merchant's fortune was made. By 1611, it was the leading importer of spices into Europe, with ships ranging as far as China, Japan and Indonesia. For nearly 200 years the VOC ran a commercial empire more powerful than some countries.

The Nederlands Scheepvaart Museum *(see pp146–7) has a
hall devoted to the VOC. A replica of the East Indiaman, the
Amsterdam, is moored outside.*

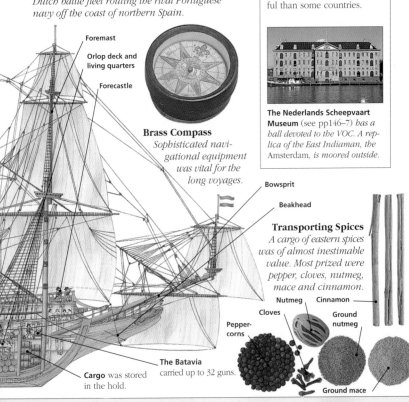

Foremast

Orlop deck and
living quarters

Forecastle

Brass Compass
*Sophisticated navi-
gational equipment
was vital for the
long voyages.*

Bowsprit

Beakhead

Transporting Spices
*A cargo of eastern spices
was of almost inestimable
value. Most prized were
pepper, cloves, nutmeg,
mace and cinnamon.*

Nutmeg   Cinnamon

Cloves   Ground
nutmeg

Pepper-
corns

The Batavia
carried up to 32 guns.

Cargo was stored
in the hold.

Ground mace

1647 Peter Stuyvesant made governor of New Amsterdam		**1665** Admiral de Ruyter *(see p77)* becomes commander-in-chief of the Dutch navy	**1672** *Rampjaar* (year of disaster). France, under Louis XIV, attacks Holland. War with England breaks out once more	*King Louis XIV*
1648 Treaty of Munster ends war with Spain. Dutch Republic recognized	**1664** British take possession of New Amsterdam			

1650	1660	1670	1680	1690

1652 First maritime war with England

*Dutch fleet in river
Medway in 1667*

1667 Dutch sign
Breda Peace Treaty
with England

1666 Dutch navy wins
battle against British fleet

1688 William III
(see p27), invited to
take over English
throne, becoming
King William III

The Age of Consolidation

Though the Dutch Empire declined, the Netherlands remained wealthy. Amsterdam's ships became commercial cargo carriers and by the mid-18th century, the city was the world's financial capital. Tolerance prevailed and the city was flooded with immigrants, including Jews from all across Europe. Dissatisfaction with the ruling House of Orange intensified; although Prussian troops crushed a Patriot uprising in 1787, the Patriots established a short-lived republic, with French backing, only to see Napoleon take over, making his brother Louis king of the Netherlands.

Silver Torah finials *(see p64)*

EXTENT OF THE CITY

▨ *1700*   ▢ *Today*

Drying room with Japanese screen

Bathroom

Receiving Visitors *(c. 1713)*
Amsterdam was cosmopolitan and decadent; in Cornelis Troost's satire, the ladies of a brothel parade before Prince Eugène of Savoy.

Drawing room

DOLLS' HOUSE

Costly dolls' houses were designed for show rather than play, and are a fitting symbol of the extravagance of the age. This example is a miniature replica of the house of an Amsterdam merchant. Now in the Frans Hals Museum in Haarlem *(see pp178–9)*, it was made around 1750 for Sara Rothé.

Wintertime in Amsterdam *(c. 1763)*
Petrus Schenk's print shows people skating on the frozen canals. The ice-breaking barges in the background are bringing fresh water to the city.

TIMELINE

1702 Death of William III. Second stadholderless period begins in the Netherlands

1713 Treaty of Utrecht signed. Dutch Republic becomes isolated

French musketeer

1748 Tax collector riots

1744 France invades Southern Provinces

1700	1710	1720	1730	1740

1697 Tsar Peter the Great of Russia visits Amsterdam to study shipbuilding

Portrait of Tsar Peter the Great (1727) on gold snuff box

1716 Second meeting of the Grand Assembly meets in Den Haag *(see p186)* Radical government reforms imposed

1747 Stadholdership becomes hereditary under William IV

1751 Death of William IV. Start of 40 years of political strife

Prussian Troops Enter Amsterdam *(1787)*
A lithograph by an unknown artist shows Prussian troops entering the city on 10 October 1787, coming to the aid of the House of Orange after pro-French Patriot upheavals.

WHERE TO SEE 18TH-CENTURY AMSTERDAM

De Gooyer windmill *(see p144)* produced corn for the growing city from 1725. A clandestine church was opened in 1735 in today's Museum Amstelkring *(pp84–5)*, in response to the Alteration *(pp24–5)*. Fine canal houses include No. 465 Herengracht *(p112)* and the Felix Meritis Building *(p113)*, designed by Jacob Otten Husly in 1787. Museum van Loon was renovated in 1752 *(p122)*.

Pavilioned bed with green canopy

Museum Willet-Holthuysen
The elaborate, gilded staircase *(see p121)* was built in 1740.

Florin *(1781)*
By 1750, Amsterdam posessed the most sophisticated and successful banking and broking system in the world.

Lying-in room

Library

Tax Collector Riots *(1748)*
This print by Simonsz Fokke shows an angry mob raiding the house of a tax collector in June 1748.

Ceramic Plate *(c. 1780)*
The wealthy lived in great style, sparing no expense. This hand-painted plate is decorated with mythological figures and ornate gold leaf.

1760	1770	1780	1790	1800	1810

1763 Freezing winter

1791 VOC *(see pp28–9)* goes into liquidation

1795 Provinces unite briefly into republic, ruled jointly by Patriots and French

1806 Napoleon Bonaparte takes over republic

1766 William V comes of age

1780–84 War with England, whose navy destroys Dutch fleet

1768 William V marries Wilhelmina of Prussia

1787 Patriots' upheaval ends with Prussian army entering Amsterdam

Louis Napoleon (1778–1846)

1808 Louis Napoleo crowned king of the Netherlands

The Age of Industrialization

By the end of Louis Napoleon's rule, Amsterdam had stagnated. The decline continued, with little sign of enterprise and scant investment. Industrialization came late and attempts to revive the city's fortunes by digging a canal to the North Sea were less than effective. Politically, the country regrouped round the House of Orange, bringing the family back from exile and declaring a monarchy in 1813. The mid-century saw growth of the liberal constitution; by 1900 the Socialist tradition was well established.

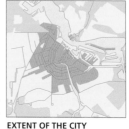

EXTENT OF THE CITY

	1800		Today

CENTRAAL STATION

The station *(see p79)* was completed in 1889. It became a symbol of the emergent industrial age – a sign that Amsterdam was finally moving towards the future rather than looking back to the Golden Age.

Cocoa Trading
Cocoa was one of Amsterdam's main exports in the 1890s.

Dutch Renaissance-style façade

The gilded "clock" shows the wind direction, acknowledging Amsterdam's earlier reliance on the wind to power her sailing ships.

Main concourse

The Sweatshop by H Wolter
As industrialization increased, sweatshops, with their attendant poverty, became commonplace.

Diamond Cutting
The diamond trade thrived in the late 19th century, when precious stones were imported from South Africa.

TIMELINE

1813 House of Orange returns from exile

1824 Noordhollands-kanaal is dug but proves ineffective

1845 Rioters in Amsterdam call for social reform

1839 Amsterdam-to-Haarlem railway opens *(see p177)*

Johan Rudolf Thorbecke

1850 Population 245,000

1820	1830	1840	1850	186

1815 William becomes king of the Netherlands

1831 Low Countries split into north and south. Southern provinces become Belgium

King William I at Waterloo (1815)

1840 William I abdicates. Succeeded by William II

1848 New constitution devised by Thorbecke

1860s Jews begin to arrive in Amsterdam from Antwerp

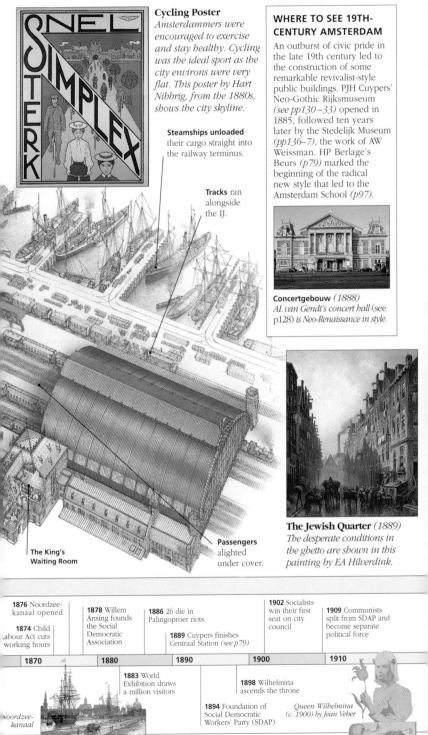

Cycling Poster
Amsterdammers were encouraged to exercise and stay healthy. Cycling was the ideal sport as the city environs were very flat. This poster by Hart Nibbrig, from the 1880s, shows the city skyline.

Steamships unloaded their cargo straight into the railway terminus.

Tracks ran alongside the IJ.

WHERE TO SEE 19TH-CENTURY AMSTERDAM

An outburst of civic pride in the late 19th century led to the construction of some remarkable revivalist-style public buildings. PJH Cuypers' Neo-Gothic Rijksmuseum *(see pp130–33)* opened in 1885, followed ten years later by the Stedelijk Museum *(pp136–7)*, the work of AW Weissman. HP Berlage's Beurs *(p79)* marked the beginning of the radical new style that led to the Amsterdam School *(p97)*.

Concertgebouw *(1888)*
AL van Gendt's concert hall (see p128) is Neo-Renaissance in style.

The Jewish Quarter *(1889)*
The desperate conditions in the ghetto are shown in this painting by EA Hilverdink.

The King's Waiting Room

Passengers alighted under cover.

1876 Noordzee-kanaal opened

1874 Child Labour Act cuts working hours

1878 Willem Ansing founds the Social Democratic Association

1886 26 die in Palingoproer riots

1889 Cuypers finishes Centraal Station *(see p79)*

1902 Socialists win their first seat on city council

1909 Communists split from SDAP and become separate political force

1870	1880	1890	1900	1910

1883 World Exhibition draws a million visitors

1898 Wilhelmina ascends the throne

1894 Foundation of Social Democratic Workers' Party (SDAP)

Queen Wilhelmina (c. 1900) by Jean Veber

Noordzee-kanaal

Amsterdam at War

The Netherlands remained neutral in World War I. After the war, political unrest was rife and the city council embarked on a programme of new housing projects and, in the 1930s, the Amsterdamse Bos was created to counter unemployment. When World War II broke out, the Netherlands again opted for neutrality – only to be invaded by Germany. The early 1940s were bitter years, and many died of starvation in the winter of '44–5. During this time, most of the Jewish population was deported; many, like Anne Frank, tried to avoid detection by going into hiding.

EXTENT OF THE CITY

■ 1945 □ Today

"Vote Red" Poster *(1918)*
The Social Democrats (Labour Party) were responsible for the introduction of a welfare state after World War II.

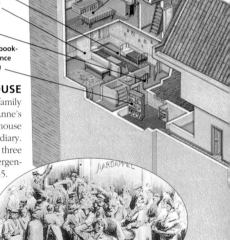

Attic

The van Pels' room

Anne's bedroom

The Franks' bedroom

Bathroom

Revolving book-case (entrance to hideout)

ANNE FRANK'S HOUSE

In July 1942, 13-year-old Anne Frank, her family and the van Pels (renamed van Daans in Anne's diary) went into hiding at the rear of this house *(see p90)*. Anne had already begun her diary. She made her last entry in August 1944, three days before being arrested. She died in Bergen-Belsen concentration camp in March 1945.

Potato Riots *(1917)*
Daan Bout's drawing shows desperate women fighting for vegetables during World War I. Rioting followed and the army was brought in to quell the uprising.

TIMELINE

1917 Potato riots in the Jordaan

1920 Air service from Schiphol to London inaugurated

Detail on façade of ABN Bank

1926 ABN Bank built on Vijzel-straat

1915 SDAP have majority on city council and shape housing policy

1910	1915	1920	1925

1914 World War I begins. Holland remains neutral

Cartoon satirizing the Netherlands' rejection of Germany's offer of friendship in 1915

1928 Olympic Gan held in Amsterd

1920s "Ring" built round southern part of the city. Many canals filled in but work is halted after considerable opposition

Het Schip by Michel de Klerk
At the end of World War I, Amsterdam School architects (see p97) designed new housing projects such as "the ship", to replace the slums in the west of the city.

Amsterdamse Bos
In 1930, as part of a job-creation scheme, 5,000 unemployed Dutch citizens were drafted in to help develop a woodland and leisure area to the southwest of the city.

Offices at the front of the building

Façade of No. 263 Prinsengracht

Dockworker Statue
The statue (see p53) by Mari Andriessen commemorates the February 1941 protest by dockers and transport workers against the Nazis' treatment of Jews.

The Deportation of Jews
Pamphlets were distributed by the Resistance vilifying those who stood by and let the Nazis round up the Jews.

WHERE TO SEE EARLY-20TH-CENTURY AMSTERDAM

Innovative Amsterdam School architecture is found to the south of the city. HP Berlage, PL Kramer and Michel de Klerk collaborated on De Dageraad *(see p151)* and were largely responsible for the Nieuw Zuid *(p154)*. Much of this was built in the run up to the 1928 Olympics; it boasts spectacular housing developments and civic buildings.

Tuschinski Theater *(1921)*
The interior of this exotic complex is awash with colour.

1930 Population 750,000. Unemployment worsens. Work on public project of Amsterdamse Bos begins

1939 Outbreak of World War II. The Netherlands chooses neutrality

1935 Work parties sent to Germany

1942 Deportation of Jews begins

1944 D-Day Landings. "Hunger Winter"

1945 Germany surrenders and western part of the Netherlands finally liberated

1930	1935	1940	1945

1934 Riots in Jordaan over reduction in social security. Seven die

1940 Germany bombs Rotterdam. The Dutch surrender

1932–7 Rise of Dutch Nazi Party under Anton Mussert

1941 450 Jews arrested. Dockworkers strike

Yellow Star of David, which Jews had to wear during Nazi Occupation

Amsterdam Today

Amsterdam tram

After World War II, Amsterdam suffered a series of social problems: its tolerance made it a haven for the 1960s hippy culture, it became a centre of drug use and trafficking, and the left-wing Provos challenged social order. In the 1970s, riots over squatting and urban redevelopment led to measures that alleviated the social issues. Now Amsterdam is again a tranquil city for all to visit. Programmes of urban expansion and sympathetic architectural developments have made the city an exciting hub of modernity.

EXTENT OF THE CITY

▣ 1950   ☐ Today

Football
The fans were ecstatic when the Dutch national team beat England 3:1 in 1988 in the European Championships.

Het Lieverdje
The statue of the Little Urchin *by Carel Kneulman is in Spui. It became a symbol for the Provos in the 1960s.*

The "normal water level" (NAP) of Amsterdam's canals

Lighthouse

Haarlem *(see p174–79)*

Sand dunes (7–20 m/ 23–65 ft in height)

Ringvaart Haarlemmer-meer

Schiphol airport *(see p266–7)*

North Sea

Actual sea level

Sand

LOCATOR MAP

30 km (19 miles) ● AMSTERDAM

Normaal Amsterdams Peil
The city's water level (NAP), set in 1684, is on display near the Stopera (see p63).

Bulbfields *(see p180–81)*

Ringdijk

Haarlemmermeer (4.5 m/15 ft below sea level)

SECTION OF NOORD HOLLAND

This cross-section shows Holland's polders *(see pp24–5)* lying below sea level. Without the protection of dykes and tide barriers, Amsterdam would be inundated. Its buildings are supported by piles which pass through layers of clay and peat into firm sand.

TIMELINE

1948 Queen Wilhelmina abdicates after 50 years. Juliana becomes queen	**1957** The Netherlands signs Treaty of Rome, joining European Community	**1965** Provos win seats on city council for first time	**1966** Provos demonstrate at wedding of Princess Beatrix to German aristocrat Claus von Amsberg		**1981** Amsterd is recog as capita Holland
		1963 The population peaks at 868,000	**1971** Ajax wins European Cup	**1975** Nieuwmarkt riots erupt against destruction of Jewish Quarter	

1950	1955	1960	1965	1970	1975	1980

1967 Hippies arrive in Amsterdam

1952 Completion of the Amsterdam-Rhine Canal allows increased trade

1968 First residents move to the vast Bijlmermeer housing estate

1949 Indonesia officially independent from the Netherlands

Abdication speech by Queen Juliana

1980 Que Juliana abdicates favour of Beatrix

Queen Beatrix
Born in 1938, Beatrix was crowned in the Nieuwe Kerk (see pp76–7) in 1980 following the abdication of her mother Juliana.

House on the Singel
17th-century canal houses often subside as their foundations are shallow. Traditionally they were propped up by wooden support beams, but now technology allows for the replacement of rotten support piles without demolition.

WHERE TO SEE MODERN AMSTERDAM

Amsterdam has many superb new buildings, particularly in the Eastern Docklands and along the Zuidas (South Axis). But Cees Dam's and Wilhelm Holzbauer's Stadhuis-Muziektheater *(see p63)*, completed in 1988 amid much controversy, was built in the old Jewish Quarter.

ING House *head office (2002) on the Zuidas was designed by Meyer & Van Schooten and is nicknamed "the ice-skate".*

Headquarters of IBM
West Amsterdam (2.1 m/7 ft below sea level)
Vondelpark *(see p129)*
Central Amsterdam (2.1 m/7 ft above sea level)
Oude Kerk *(see pp68–9)*
Overground transport system
East Amsterdam (5.5 m/18 ft below sea level)
Rijnkanaal
Oranje Sluizen tide barrier

Layers of clay and peat — **Wooden piles** — **Metro system** — **Frankendael** *(see p150)* — **IJmeer** *(see p15)*

Concrete piles

Hippies
In the late 1960s, Amsterdam was known for its tolerance of sub-cultures. It became a haven for hippies, who gathered in the Vondelpark (see p129).

1989 Centre-right comes to power in Dutch Parliament
1994 For first time since 1918, Christian Democrats do not form part of governing coalition
2000 Law passed legalizing euthanasia
2002 Death of Prince Claus, Beatrix's husband

| 1990 | 1995 | 2000 | 2005 | 2010 | 2015 | 2020 |

1993 Schiphol Airport *(see pp266–7)* modernized
2011 Stedelijk Museum *(see pp136–7)* reopens after an extensive renovation project
1986 Opera House *(see p63)* opens in Stopera

KLM – the Dutch national airline

AMSTERDAM AT A GLANCE

There are more than 100 places of interest described in the *Area by Area* section of this book. The broad spectrum of entries covers recreational as well as cultural sights and ranges from sublime buildings, such as the Oude Kerk, to oddities like the Hash Marihuana Museum *(see p61)* . The Golden Bend *(see p112)* and other impressive canalscapes also feature,

along with suggested walks past some of Amsterdam's finest architecture and notable sights, such as Anne Frank Huis. To help you make the most of your stay, the following 10 pages are a time-saving guide to the best Amsterdam has to offer. Museums, canals, and cafés and bars all have their own sections. Below is a selection of attractions that no visitor should miss.

AMSTERDAM'S TOP TEN ATTRACTIONS

Nederlands Scheepvaartmuseum
See pp146–7

Van Gogh Museum
See pp134–5

Oude Kerk
See pp68–9

Begijnhof
See p75

Koninklijk Paleis
See p74

Rijksmuseum
See pp130–33

Stedelijk Museum
See pp136–7

Ons' Lieve Heer op Solder *See pp84–5*

Magere Brug
See p119

Anne Frank Huis
See pp34–5 & 90–91

◁ Stained-glass coats of arms in the Lady Chapel of the Oude Kerk

Amsterdam's Best: Museums

For a fairly small city, Amsterdam has a
surprisingly large number of museums
and galleries. The quality and variety of
the collections are impressive and
many are housed in buildings of historical or architectural interest.
The Rijksmuseum, with its Gothic
façade, is a city landmark, and
Rembrandt's work is exhibited in his
original home. For more information
on museums see pages 42–3.

Anne Frank Huis
*Anne Frank's photo is
exhibited in the house
where she hid during
World War II.*

**Amsterdams
Historisch Museum**
*A wealth of historical
information is on display
here. Once an orphan-
age, it is depicted in*
Governesses at the Bur-
gher Orphanage *(1683)
by Adriaen Backer.*

*Western
Canal
Ring*

Rijksmuseum
*An extensive collection
of paintings by Dutch
masters, including Jan
van Huysum's* Still Life
with Flowers and
Fruit *(c.1730), is held
at the Rijksmuseum.
The main building is
closed for renovation
until 2013 (see p130).*

*Central
Canal Ring*

Museum Quarter

**Stedelijk
Museum**
*Gerrit Rietveld's simple Steltman
chair (1963) is one of many
exhibits at this ever-changing
contemporary art museum.*

**Van Gogh
Museum**
*Van Gogh's Self-
portrait with Straw
Hat (1870) hangs
in this large, stark
museum, built in
1973 to house the
bulk of his work.*

Museum Ons' Lieve Heer op Solder

Three 17th-century merchant's houses conceal Amsterdam's only remaining clandestine church, restored as the Museum Ons' Lieve Heer op Solder (Our Lord in the Attic).

Nederlands Scheepvaartmuseum

This national maritime museum is decorated with reliefs relating to the city's maritime history. Moored alongside is a replica of the East Indiaman, Amsterdam.

Tropenmuseum

On display here are exhibits from former Dutch colonies in the tropics, including this wooden Nigerian fertility mask portraying a mother and twins.

uwe
jde

Oude Zijde

Eastern
nal Ring

Plantage

| 0 metres | 500 |
| 0 yards | 500 |

Museum Willet-Holthuysen

An impressive collection of furniture, silverware and paintings is housed in this beautifully preserved 17th-century canalside mansion.

Joods Historisch Museum

Four adjoining synagogues are linked to form this museum. The Holy Ark in the Grote Synagogue is the centrepiece of an exhibition on Judaism in the Netherlands.

Exploring Amsterdam's Museums

Wall plaque in St Luciensteeg

The richness of Amsterdam's history and culture is reflected by its wide range of museums, which cover everything from bibles, beer and African masks to shipbuilding and space travel. Its national art galleries house some of the world's most famous paintings, including Rembrandt's *The Night Watch*. The Nederlands Scheepvaart Museum has the largest collection of model ships in the world, while the Anne Frank Huis is a stark reminder of the horrors of World War II.

View of a French-style garden from the Museum van Loon

PAINTING AND DECORATIVE ARTS

The world's most important collection of Dutch art is on display at the **Rijksmuseum**. This vast museum contains approximately 5,000 paintings, including works by Rembrandt, Vermeer, Frans Hals and Albert Cuyp as well as a significant collection of sculptures, prints, artifacts and Asiatic art. The main building is undergoing renovation until 2013.

A short stroll across Museumplein will bring you to the **Van Gogh Museum**. Besides a large collection of Van Gogh's paintings and drawings, which traces his entire career, you can see hundreds of his original letters to his brother Theo and the artist's private collection of Japanese prints. Works by other 19th-century Dutch painters are also displayed here.

Modern art is the focus of the **Stedelijk Museum**. While the collection features works by artists such as Henri Matisse and Vassily Kandinsky, the emphasis is on paintings, sculptures, drawings, graphics and photographs completed after 1945. Andy Warhol, Edward Kienholz and the Dutch Cobra artist Karel Appel are all represented.

The house where Rembrandt lived for 20 years opened as the **Museum Het Rembrandthuis** in 1911. As well as providing an insight into the artist's life, it contains an important collection of his work, including a series of self-portraits.

The **Museum van Loon**, housed in a beautiful 17th-century mansion, is based on the outstanding private collections of the wealthy van Loon family.

Other wonderful collections of art can also be enjoyed by travelling from Amsterdam to the **Frans Hals Museum** in Haarlem, the **Mauritshuis** in Den Haag and the **Museum Boijmans Van Beuningen Rotterdam**.

Indonesian mask at the Tropenmuseum

HISTORY

Various aspects of Amsterdam's absorbing history are documented in several of the city's museums. The **Amsterdams Historisch Museum** covers the growth of Amsterdam from its origins as a fishing village in the 13th century, by means of maps, paintings and archaeological objects. The city's glorious maritime history is recalled at the **Nederlands Scheepvaartmuseum**. Its vast collection of model ships includes a life-size replica of an 18th-century sailing ship. The mechanics of more modern boats is the focus of the **Museum 't Kromhout**, which is housed in one of the few working shipyards left in the city. In the **Museum Willet-Holthuysen**, the richly decorated rooms, Dutch paintings, Venetian glass, silverware and furniture reflect the wealth of Amsterdam in the Golden Age. Catholic ingenuity is revealed at the **Museum Ons' Lieve Heer op Solder**, where a secret church is preserved in the attic of a 17th-century merchant's home. The history of the Dutch trade unions is documented at the **De Burcht**.

Jewish life in the city is remembered in the fascinating **Joods Historisch Museum**. The famous **Anne Frank Huis** provides a poignant reminder that Amsterdam's Jewish

Rembrandt's *The Jewish Bride* (1663) in the Rijksmuseum

community was almost wiped out in World War II, and its secret annexe shows what life was like for those living in hiding. Displays on the activities of the Dutch Resistance at the **Verzetsmuseum Amsterdam** provide more fascinating insights on life in the Netherlands during the Nazi occupation.

Outside the city, the **Zuiderzeemuseum** recreates the life and traditions of the people who once fished these waters.

SPECIALIST MUSEUMS

Mummies, sarcophagi and effigies of ancient Egyptian gods are just a few of the displays at the **Allard Pierson Museum**. The **Bijbels Museum**, in adjoining canal houses, also focuses on the archaeology of Egypt and the Middle East, and contains the oldest Bible ever printed in the Netherlands.

The **Eye Film Institute** screens more than 1,000 films a year, and **Foam** is a lively and welcoming photography museum, covering documentary, history and fashion.

The **Heineken Experience** offers a history of beer-making as part of a tour of this former brewery and free samples at the end. More facts can be absorbed at the **Hash Marijuana Hemp Museum**, which shows the many uses this product has had through the ages.

The sounds and sights of a North African village to an Indonesian rainforest are recreated at the **Tropenmuseum**, devoted to cultures from around the world.

The open-air reconstruction village at the Zuiderzeemuseum

TECHNOLOGY AND NATURAL HISTORY

A hands-on approach is encouraged by **Nemo**, Holland's national science centre, to explain, for instance, how photography works or how computers process information. The centre is housed in a striking modern building.

Along with hundreds of live animals, the **Artis** complex (the oldest zoo in the Netherlands, founded in 1838) contains a variety of museums. Rock collectors will be tempted by a huge range of minerals, rocks, fossils and helpful models in the Geologisch Museum. There is also a collection of skulls, skeletons and stuffed animals in the Zoölogisch Museum, which is housed in the zoo's Aquarium, and a Planetarium. The Hortus Botanicus is a tranquil botanical garden with a three-climate greenhouse and a stunning collection of trees.

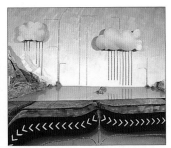

Model showing the process of precipitation in the Geologisch Museum at Artis

Amsterdam's Best: Canals and Waterways

From the grace and elegance of the waterside mansions along the *Grachtengordel* (Canal Ring) to the rows of converted warehouses on Brouwersgracht and the charming houses on Reguliersgracht, the city's canals and waterways embody the very spirit of Amsterdam. They are spanned by many beautiful bridges, including the famous Magere Brug *(see p119)*, a traditionally styled lift bridge. You can also relax at one of the many canalside cafés or bars and watch an array of boats float by.

Brouwersgracht
The banks of this charming canal are lined with house-boats, cosy cafés and warehouses.

Western Canal Ring

Bloemgracht
There is a great variety of archi-tecture along this lovely, tree-lined canal in the Jordaan, in-cluding a row of houses with step gables (see p91).

Central Canal Ring

Prinsengracht
The best way to see all the beautiful buildings along Amsterdam's longest 17th-century canal is by bicycle.

Museum Quarter

Keizersgracht
A view of this canal can be had from any of its bridges. For an overview of the Canal Ring go to Metz & Co at Leidsestraat 34–36 (see p112).

Leidsegracht
Relax at a pavement café along the exclusive Leidsegracht (see p111).

Singel

The Poezenboot, *a boat for stray cats, is just one of the many sights to be found along the Singel, whose distinctive, curved shape established the horseshoe contours of the Canal Ring.*

Entrepotdok

The warehouses on the Entrepotdok (see p144) were redeveloped in the 1980s. The quayside is now lined in summer with lively café terraces that overlook an array of houseboats and pleasure craft.

Herengracht

○ *Known as "the twin brothers", these matching neck-gabled houses at Nos. 409–411 are two of the prettiest houses on the city's grandest canal.*

Reguliersgracht

Many crooked, brick buildings line this pretty canal, which was cut in 1664. The statue of a stork, located at No. 92, is symbolic of parental responsibility and commemorates a 1571 by-law protecting this bird.

Amstel

This river is still a busy commercial thoroughfare, with barges carrying grain and coal to the city's port.

Map labels: Nieuwe Zijde, Onde Zijde, Plantage, Eastern Canal Ring. 0 metres 500, 0 yards 500.

Amsterdam's Best: Cafés and Bars

Amsterdam is a city of cafés and bars, about 1,500 in all. Each area has something to offer, from friendly and relaxed brown cafés to lively and crowded designer bars. The cafés and bars vary and each has some special attraction: a large range of beers, live music, canalside terraces, art exhibitions, board games and pool tables or simply a brand of *gezelligheid*, the unique Dutch concept of "cosiness". Further details of Amsterdam's cafés and bars are given on pages 48–9. Addresses are given in the directory on page 237.

De Tuin
This large brown café in the Jordaan is always crowded with regular customers, often local artists.

Western Canal Ring

Central Canal Ring

Van Puffelen
A smart and fashionable clientele is attracted to this intimate canalside café, with its impressive 19th-century interior, reading room and restaurant.

Vertigo
The café terrace of the Nederlands Filmmuseum has a splendid view across Vondelpark.

Museum Quarter

Café Americain
The American Hotel's grand café has a beautiful Art Deco interior, and is the place to go to be seen.

Café Dulac
The interior of this quirky grand café, situated on Haarlemmerstraat, mixes Art Deco style with Gothic-kitsch fixtures and fittings.

In De Wildeman
There are more than 80 beers from around the world on offer at this modern proeflokaal (see p48).

De Jaren
Popular with students, this trendy two-storey café has a superb view of the Amstel and a wide selection of newspapers.

't Doktertje
This is the ultimate brown café, steeped in cobwebs and atmosphere. It is a dark, friendly and timeless place, tucked away in a tiny side street.

De Kroon
Tastefully restored, this grand café has DJs Thursday to Sunday.

| 0 metres | | 500 |
| 0 yards | | 500 |

Exploring Amsterdam's Cafés and Bars

Wherever you go in this vibrant city, you are never far from a café or bar. Amsterdammers are at their most friendly over a beer or a Dutch gin, so exploring the city's drinking establishments is an easy way to meet the locals. Table service is standard in most cafés and bars, though not universal. Instead of paying for each drink, bars keep a running total which you settle as you leave. The exception is outdoor terraces, where you pay as you order. Most places are open from about 11am until 1am, but some around the Leidseplein and Rembrandt-plein stay open until 4 or 5am at the weekends.

Sportcafé Ajax-Arena, decorated with football memorabilia

BROWN CAFÉS

The traditional Dutch "local pub", the brown café, is characterized by dark wooden panelling and furniture, low ceilings, dim lighting and a fog of tobacco smoke. It is a warm and friendly place and often a social focus for the neighbourhood. Some of the best brown cafés are found in old 17th-century canal houses or tucked away on side streets. The tiny and characterful **'t Doktertje**, just off the Kalverstraat shopping street, is worth a visit, as is the cheap and cheerful **Pieper**, close to

Leidseplein. **De Tuin**, in the heart of the Jordaan, is popular with the local artistic community. Most brown cafés are more than just places to drink at and many serve good, reasonably priced food (see pp236–7).

PROEFLOKALEN AND MODERN TASTING BARS

Literally meaning "tasting houses", *proeflokalen* go back to the Dutch Golden Age of the 17th century. In order to increase sales, wine and spirit importers would invite merchants to taste their wares. Today, *proeflokalen* denote bars specializing in either wine, spirits or beer. One of the oldest tasting bars, **De Drie Fleschjes**, dates from 1650, and *jenever* (Dutch gin) is its speciality. **Mulliner's** offers a superb range of vintage wines and ports, while **In De Wildeman** serves beers from around the world, many of them on draught. See the directory on page 237 for other good *proeflokalen*.

Sampling the wide range of beers in the popular modern tasting bar, Gollem

WHAT TO DRINK

The Dutch national drink is beer. A standard *pils* (a lager-like beer) is served in bars and cafés – the main brands are Heineken and Grolsch. Darker beers like De Kon-inck have a stronger flavour, and the wheat-brewed *witbiers* like Hoega-arden are white and cloudy. Beers from Amsterdam's 't IJ brew-ery, such as Columbus, are widely available. The most popular spirit, *jenever*, is the slightly oily Dutch gin. There is either the sharp tasting *jonge* (young), or the smoother *oude* (old) variety. For the complete Dutch experience, drink *jenever* in a single gulp or order a refreshing *pils* with a *jenever* chaser.

Bottle of *jonge* jenever

Traditional *oude* jenever

Hoegaarden, brewed in Belgium

Tarwebok, strong typ of Heineke

GRAND CAFÉS AND DESIGNER BARS

Grand cafés first emerged in the 19th century. Today, these large and opulent venues are the haunts of the upwardly mobile and fashion-conscious. **Café Luxembourg** has a street terrace for people-watching, while **Café Schiller** is more intimate and has a beautiful Art Deco interior. Designer bars cater for a similar clientele, but they are modern, stark and bright in style. Some of the best are the chic **Het Land Van Walem**, **De Balie**, **Vertigo** and the trendy **De Jaren**.

Café Schiller, one of Amsterdam's Art Deco grand cafés

SMOKING COFFEESHOPS

Smoking coffee shops are ones where cannabis is openly sold and smoked. Although technically illegal, the sale of soft drugs is tolerated by the Dutch authorities if it remains discreet (see p261). Many of these cafés are recognizable by their loud music and often

The beautifully restored De Jaren

psychedelic decor. Smoking coffeeshops appeal to a surprising range of people – old and young alike (under 16s are not permitted) from every social and professional background. **Rusland** and **Siberië** are two of the smaller, more relaxed places, while **The Bulldog Palace** is commercial and tourist-filled. As well as coffee, soft drinks and snacks are generally available. **Abraxas** has a psychedelically colourful interior. If tempted to smoke in a coffeeshop, ask for the menu listing what is on sale. The cannabis is strong, especially the local "skunk". Be wary of hash cakes and cookies as there is no way to gauge their strength. See the directory on page 237 for other good smoking coffeeshops.

COFFEESHOPS AND SALONS DE THÉ

The more conventional type of coffeeshop is where well-to-do ladies go for a chat over coffee and cake. A number of these places use the Dutch spelling, *koffieshop*, or the French *salons de thé* to distinguish themselves from the many smoking coffeeshops, although the differences are obvious. Many, such as **Arnold Cornelis** and **Pompadour**, are attached to confectioners, patisseries or delicatessens, and have a tempting range of cakes and sweets on offer. Several of the city's

larger stores and hotels also have tearooms, ideal places to sit down in comfort and relax after a busy day sightseeing or shopping. **Metz & Co** has a comfortable sixth-floor café that offers one of the most impressive canal views in Amsterdam (see p112). Another canalside experience not to be missed is **Tazzina**, which serves excellent coffee, Italian sandwiches and sweets. For something slightly different, try **Back Stage**, a wonderfully offbeat café run by an eccentric former cabaret artist called Mr. Christmas.

e Koninck, a dark elgian beer

Amstel Bockbier, a dark winter beer

Columbus, brewed in Amsterdam

WHERE TO FIND THE BEST CAFÉS

All the cafés and bars described on these pages are listed in the directory on page 237. The best, as shown on pages 46–7, are also listed below.

Café Americain
American Hotel, Leidsekade 97.
Map 4 E2.
Tel 556 3000.

Café Dulac
Haarlemmerstraat 118.
Map 1 C3. **Tel** 624 4265.

't Doktertje
Rozenboomsteeg 4. **Map** 7 B4.
Tel 626 4427.

In de Wildeman
Kolksteeg 3. **Map** 7 C1.
Tel 638 2348.

De Jaren
Nieuwe Doelenstraat 20.
Map 7 C4.
Tel 625 5771.

De Kroon
Rembrandtplein 17. **Map** 7 C5.
Tel 625 2011.

De Tuin
2e Tuindwarsstraat 13 (near Anjeliersstraat). **Map** 1 B3.
Tel 624 4559.

Van Puffelen
Prinsengracht 377. **Map** 1 B5.
Tel 624 6270.

Vertigo
Nederlands Filmmuseum, Vondelpark 3. **Map** 4 D2.
Tel 612 3021.

AMSTERDAM THROUGH THE YEAR

Although there is no guarantee of good weather in Amsterdam, the cosmopolitan ambience of this 700-year-old city and the congeniality of the Dutch make it an appealing place to visit whatever time of year you go. Most tourists flock into the city from April to September, when temperatures are mild. Amsterdammers, however, are undaunted by the weather and maintain

Herons nest on the canals

an active programme of festivals and outdoor pursuits throughout the year. Crisp autumn days invite long walks along the city's stately canals, followed by a cosy chat in one of Amsterdam's brown cafés. About twice a decade, the winter temperatures drop so low that the canals freeze over. When this occurs a skating race is held between 11 Dutch cities.

SPRING

Spring begins in late March when daffodils and crocuses blossom overnight all over the city. Flower lovers descend on Amsterdam, using it as a base for day trips to Keukenhof, the Netherlands' 28-hectare (69-acre) showcase for Dutch bulb growers (*see pp180–81*).

MARCH

Stille Omgang (*second or third Sat*), Rokin. Silent night-time procession celebrating the Miracle of Amsterdam (*see p22*).

Opening of Keukenhof (*21 Mar*). One of the world's largest flower gardens (*see p181*).

APRIL

National Museum Weekend (*second weekend of Apr*). Cut-price or free admission to many state-run museums.
Koninginnedag (*30 Apr*). Amsterdam becomes the world's biggest flea market-cum-street party as the Dutch celebrate Queen Beatrix's official birthday. Transport grinds to a halt as more than 2 million people throng the streets during the day and

Revellers celebrating in the streets to commemorate Koninginnedag

dance the night away. **World Press Photo** (*end Apr–early Jun*), Oude Kerk. Exhibition of the very best press photographs from around the world.

MAY

Herdenkingsdag (*4 May*). Commemorations throughout the city for the victims of World War II. Largest in Dam square.
Bevrijdingsdag (*5 May*). Concerts and speeches around the city celebrate the end of the German occupation.
Art Amsterdam (*see p151*) (*second week*). A massive exhibition of contemporary art held in Amsterdam RAI.
Nationale Molendag (*second Sat*). Windmills all over the Netherlands are opened to the public and their sails unfurled.
Boeken op de Dam (*third or fourth Sun of May until September*). Dam square fills with book stalls, and sometimes along the Amstel at Muziektheater (*see p63*) – Boeken aan de Amstel.

Tulip fields in bloom near Alkmaar

AVERAGE DAILY HOURS OF SUNSHINE

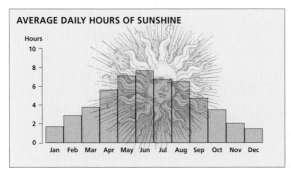

Sunshine Chart
The summer months are the sunniest, but this is no guarantee of good weather. Amsterdammers will often carry an umbrella even on the hottest of July days as summer rain in the morning often precedes the arrival of bright sunshine later.

SUMMER

Summer, which starts with the three week-long Holland Festival, is a hectic cultural roller-coaster ride. As well as the events listed below, classic European drama is staged in the Amsterdamse Bos *(p155)*, and open-air concerts are held in the Vondelpark *(pp128–9)*. This is the best time for people-watching in one of Amsterdam's street-side cafés and bars.

A rower training on the Bosbaan in the Amsterdamse Bos

JUNE

Open Garden Days *(third weekend in Jun)*. For one weekend, Amsterdam's most elegant private gardens open

their gates to the public. Visit www.canalmuseums.nl for more information.
Open Air Theatre in Vondel-park *(early Jun–end Aug)*. Theatre, music and children's shows *(see p128)*.
Holland Festival *(3 weeks of June)*. In venues throughout Amsterdam and in other major cities in the Netherlands, a varied programme of concerts, plays, operas and ballets.
Amsterdam Roots Festival *(late June)*, De Melkweg *(pp110–11)*, Tropenmuseum *(pp152–3)*, Oosterpark, and Concertgebouw *(p128)*. An ethnic programme of music, dance, film and theatre from Africa and other non-Western countries.

JULY

North Sea Jazz Festival *(mid-Jul)*, the Ahoy Exhibition Centre. Weekend of jazz ranging from Dixieland to jazz rock a short train ride away in Rotterdam.
Summer Concerts *(Jul–Aug)*, Concertgebouw *(see p128)*. Annual showcase of classical music.

Orchestral performance at the Prinsengracht Concert

AUGUST

Uitmarkt *(mid-Aug)*. A week-end of music and theatre performances at Leidseplein and Museumplein launches the start of the cultural season.
Grachtenfestival *(Wed–Sun, around third Sat)*. Classical concerts on Herengracht, Keizersgracht and Prinsengracht. The main concert is on Saturday on a barge in front of the Pulitzer Hotel *(see p220)*.

Café-goers relaxing and soaking up the sun at de Jaren Terrace

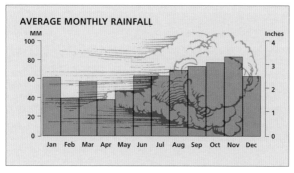

AVERAGE MONTHLY RAINFALL

Rainfall Chart
Expect rain all year round in Amsterdam. The pattern, however, is broadly seasonal. Visit the city in spring to enjoy the driest weather of the year. The heaviest rainfall occurs in autumn, reaching a peak in the windy and wet month of November.

AUTUMN

Temperatures drop quickly at the end of August, but the cultural heat is maintained with the diary of music, dance, opera and drama promoted in the Uitmarkt *(see p51)*. The Autumn is also a busy time for more sporting types. There is a range of spectator sports to watch, and it is a good time of year to enjoy brisk walks in one of the city's many parks or along the Amstel. By November, many Amsterdammers retreat indoors on rainy evenings to cafés like Schaakcafé Het Hok in the Lange Leidsedwarsstraat.

SEPTEMBER

Open Monumentendagen
(first or second weekend). A chance to see inside some historic, listed buildings which are normally closed to the public.

Car-Free Sunday
(second Sun). No cars are allowed in the historic centre, so hire a bike or walk around soaking up the beauty of traffic-free Amsterdam.

Jordaan Festival
(third weekend, including Fri). Festivals are held near Westerkerk and elsewhere in this picturesque district, with fairs, street parties, talent contests and music.

Dam tot Damloop *(third Sun)*. The biggest running event in the Netherlands, with around 30,000 athletes taking part. The 16-km (10-mile) course starts in Amsterdam and ends on the Dam in Zaandam. There's also a mini event in Zaandam for children.

Barges moored along an Amsterdam waterfront in autumn

OCTOBER

Roeisloepengrachtentocht
(second Sat), Oosterdok. One of many rowing competitions.
ING Amsterdam Marathon
(third Sun). Some 1,500 runners circle the city before converging on the Olympic stadium in this 42-km (26-mile) run. A further 10,000 people join in for a 10-km (6-mile) stretch of the race.
Camping and Caravan RAI
(end Oct), Amsterdam RAI *(p151)*. Annual fair for open-air holiday enthusiasts.

NOVEMBER

PAN *(Nov–Dec)*. Art and antiques fair in RAI *(see p151)*.
Museumnacht *(first Sat)*. Many museums stay open during the night. There are often theatrical and musical events, too, as well as a special guided tour.
Sinterklaas' Parade *(second or third Sat)*. The Dutch equivalent of Santa Claus arrives by boat near St Nicholaaskerk *(see p79)* accompanied by *Zwarte Piet* (Black Peter) and distributes sweets to Amsterdam's waiting children.

Sinterklaas parading through Amsterdam

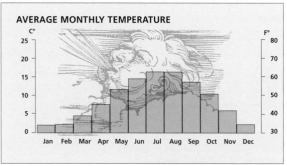

AVERAGE MONTHLY TEMPERATURE

Temperature Chart
The chart shows the average temperature for each month in Amsterdam. Summer is often cooled by the North Sea wind, both spring and autumn can be chilly, and temperatures in winter are frequently freezing.

WINTER

Christmas is a busy tourist season, with visitors and residents thronging to watch Christmas trees being hawked from barges on the main canals. Barrows appear throughout the city, tantalizing passers-by with the smell of freshly fried *oliebollen* and *appelflappen,* two sugary treats not to be missed. After Christmas, the talk of the town is whether or not it will be cold enough for the city authorities to permit skating on the city's canals. If the green light is given – which is rare – whole neighbourhoods turn out to skate under the stars.

DECEMBER

Sinterklaasavond *(5 Dec).*
The traditional Dutch gift-giving day when Sinterklaas and his Moorish helpers visit Dutch children to leave a sack of presents. Friends give poems caricaturing each other.

Amsterdammers ice skating on the Keizersgracht

The Dokwerker Monument in JD Meijerplein

Christmas Day *(25 Dec).*
Increasingly accepted as the main gift-giving day.
New Year's Eve *(31 Dec).*
Firework celebrations throughout the city with an organized display over the Amstel.

JANUARY

Jumping Amsterdam *(Jan–Feb),* Amsterdam RAI *(p151).*
International indoor show-jumping competitions.
Chinese New Year *(Jan or Feb),* Nieuwmarkt. Traditional lion dance, fireworks, Chinese exhibitions and stage art.

FEBRUARY

Februaristaking *(25 Feb),* JD Meijerplein. Commemoration of dockworkers' action against the deportation of Jewish residents during World War II.

PUBLIC HOLIDAYS

New Year's Day (1 Jan)
Tweede Paasdag (Easter Monday) *
Koninginnedag (30 April)
Bevrijdingsdag (5 May)
Hemelvaartsdag (Ascension Day) *
Pinksteren (Whitsun) *
Eerste Kerstdag (Christmas Day) (25 Dec)
Tweede Kerstdag (26 Dec)
* Dates change in accordance with church calendar.

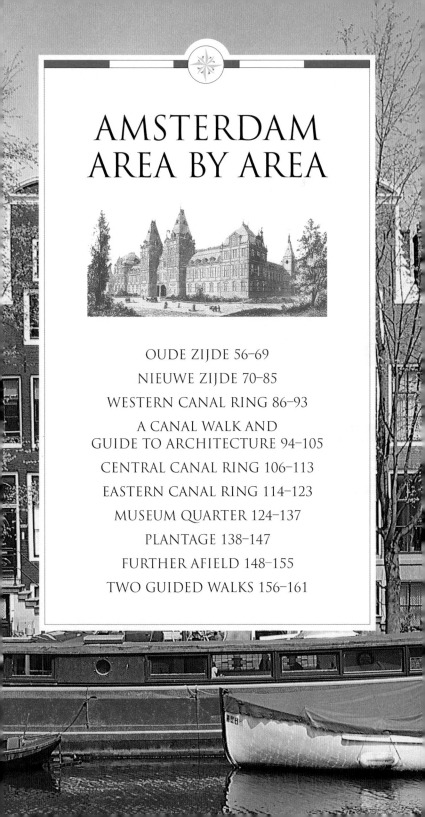

AMSTERDAM AREA BY AREA

OUDE ZIJDE

The eastern half of Amsterdam became known as the Oude Zijde (Old Side). Originally it occupied a narrow strip on the east bank of the Amstel river, running between Damrak and the Oudezijds Voorburgwal *(see pp44–5)*. At its heart was built the Oude Kerk, the oldest church in the city. In the early 1400s the Oude Zijde began an eastward expansion which continued into the 17th century. This growth was fuelled by an influx of Jewish refugees from Portugal. The oldest of the four synagogues, now containing the Joods Historisch Museum, dates from this period. These were central to Jewish life in the city for centuries. During the Golden Age *(see pp26–9)*, the Oude Zijde was an important commercial centre. Boats could sail up the Geldersekade to Nieuwmarkt, where goods were weighed at the Waag before being sold at the market.

Aäron from Mozes en Aäronkerk

SIGHTS AT A GLANCE

Historic Buildings and Monuments
Agnietenkapel ❺
Montelbaanstoren ⓱
Oostindisch Huis ❼
Oudemanhuispoort ❻
Pintohuis ⓰
Scheepvaarthuis ⓲
Schreierstoren ⓳
Trippenhuis ❽
Waag ❷

Opera Houses
Stadhuis-Muziektheater ⓫

Museums
Hash Marijuana Hemp Museum ❹
Joods Historisch Museum pp64–5 ⓮
Museum Het Rembrandthuis ❿

Churches and Synagogues
Mozes en Aäronkerk ⓭
Oude Kerk pp68–9 ㉑
Portugees-Israëlitische Synagoge ⓯
Zuiderkerk ❾

Streets and Markets
Nieuwmarkt ❸
Red Light District ❶
Waterlooplein ⓬
Zeedijk ⑳

GETTING THERE
The best way to reach the Oude Zijde is to get a tram to the Dam (trams 4, 9, 14, 16, 24 and 25) and then walk along Damstraat. Alternatively, take tram 9 or 14 directly to Waterlooplein, or the metro to Nieuwmarkt.

KEY
Street-by-Street map See pp58–9
Tram stop
Metro station
Museum boat boarding point

0 metres   250
0 yards   250

◁ **Some of the many exotic items to be found at the Waterlooplein flea market**

Street-by-Street: University District

The University of Amsterdam, founded in 1877, is predominantly located in the peaceful, southwestern part of the Oude Zijde. The university's roots lie in the former Atheneum Illustre, which was founded in 1632 in the Agnieten-kapel. Beyond Damstraat, the bustling Red Light District meets the Nieuw-markt, where the 15th-century Waag evokes a medieval air. South of the Nieuwmarkt, Museum Het Rembrandt-huis gives a fascinating insight into the life of the city's most famous artist.

★ **Red Light District**
The sex industry brings billions of euros to Amsterdam every year ⓐ

Hash Marijuana Hemp Museum
Marijuana through the ages is the theme here ④

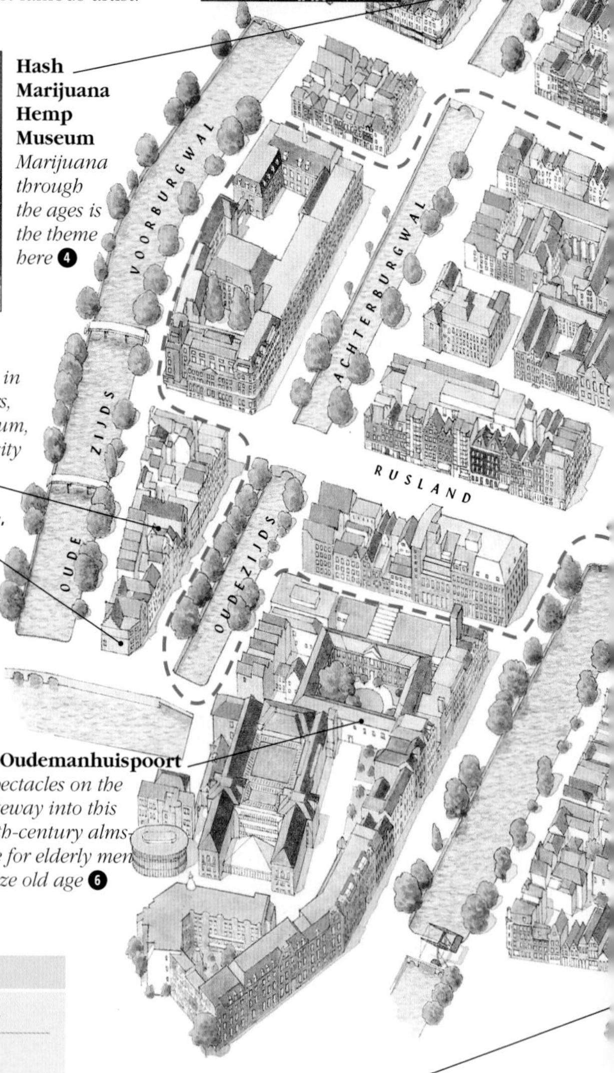

Agnietenkapel
Like many buildings in this area, the cloisters, which house a museum, belong to the University of Amsterdam ⑤

House (1610), unusually, facing three canals

VOORBURGWAL

ACHTERBURGWAL

OUDE ZIJDS

OUDEZIJDS

RUSLAND

Oudemanhuispoort
Spectacles on the gateway into this 18th-century alms-house for elderly men symbolize old age ⑥

STAR SIGHTS

★ Red Light District

★ Museum Het Rembrandthuis

Lift bridge over Groenburgwal

Trippenhuis
Although it appears to be a single 17th-century mansion, this building is in fact two houses, the middle windows being false to preserve the symmetry **8**

Nieuwmarkt
Despite redevelopment southeast of this once-important market square, the Nieuwmarkt itself is still bordered by many fine 17th- and 18th-century gabled houses **3**

LOCATOR MAP
See Street Finder maps 7 and 8

Waag
Amsterdam's only remaining medieval gatehouse now houses a restaurant **2**

Oostindisch Huis
Now part of the University of Amsterdam, this former Dutch East India Company (VOC) building has a fine example of an early 17th-century façade **7**

Zuiderkerk
This prominent city landmark now houses the city's planning information centre **9**

0 metres 50
0 yards 50

KEY

– – – Suggested route

★ **Museum Het Rembrandthuis**
Hundreds of Rembrandt's etchings, including many self-portraits, are on display in the artist's former home **10**

Red Light District ❶

Map 8 D2. 🚊 4, 9, 14, 16, 24, 25.

Barely clad prostitutes bathed in a red neon glow and touting for business at their windows is one of the defining images of modern Amsterdam. The city's Red Light District, referred to locally as de Walletjes (the little walls), is concentrated on the Oude Kerk *(see pp68–9)*, although it extends as far as Warmoesstraat to the west, the Zeedijk to the north, the Kloveniersburgwal to the east and then along the line of Damstraat to the south.

Prostitution in Amsterdam dates back to the city's emergence as a port in the 13th century. By 1478, prostitution had become so widespread, with increasing numbers of sea-weary sailors flooding into the city, that attempts were made to contain it. Prostitutes straying outside their designated area were marched back to the sound of pipe and drum.

A century later, following the Alteration *(see pp24–5)*, the Calvinists tried to outlaw prostitution altogether. Their attempts were half-hearted, and by the mid-17th century prostitution was openly tolerated. In 1850, Amsterdam had a

Entrance to one of the clubs in the Red Light District

population of 200,000, and more than 200 brothels. The most famous of these, like the luxurious Madame Traese's, catered for rich clients.

Today, the area is crisscrossed by a network of narrow lanes. By day, hordes of visitors crowding in generate a festive buzz, and among the sleaze there are interesting cafés, bars, restaurants and beautiful canalside houses. The city council is trying to make this area more culturally attractive by reducing the number of window-prostitutes, closing the seediest clubs and encouraging entrepreneurs outside the sex industry to open up shops here.

Waag ❷

Nieuwmarkt 4. **Map** 8 D3. **Tel** 422 7772. 🚊 9, 14. Ⓜ Nieuwmarkt. ⬤ upper rooms closed to the public.

The multi-turreted Waag is Amsterdam's oldest surviving gatehouse. Built in 1488, it was then, and often still is, called St Antoniespoort. Public executions were held here, and prisoners awaited their fate in the "little gallows room". In 1617, the building became the public weigh house *(waaggebouw)*. Peasants had their produce weighed here and paid tax accordingly. Various guilds moved into the upper rooms of each tower. From 1619 the Guild of Surgeons had their meeting room and anatomy theatre here. They added the central octagonal tower in 1691. Rembrandt's *Anatomy Lesson of Dr Tulp*, now in the Mauritshuis *(see pp188–9)*, and *The Anatomy Lesson of Dr Jan Deijman*, in the Amsterdams Historisch Museum *(see pp80–1)*, were commissioned by the guild and hung here.

After the weigh house closed in the early 1800s, the Waag served as a fire station and two city museums. It is now home to the café-restaurant In de Waag *(see p228)*.

The 15th-century Waag dominating the Nieuwmarkt, with an antique market on the left

Part of the commemorative photo display in Nieuwmarkt metro

Nieuwmarkt ❸

Map 8 D3. 🚇 9, 14.
Ⓜ *Nieuwmarkt.* **Antiques market**
◯ *May–Sep: 9am–5pm Sun.*
Organic market ◯ *9am–4pm Sat.*

An open, paved square, the Nieuwmarkt is flanked to the west by the Red Light District. With the top end of the Geldersekade, it forms Amsterdam's Chinatown. The Waag dominates the square, and construction of this gateway led to the site's development in the 15th century as a marketplace. When the city expanded in the 17th century (*see pp26–7*), the square took on its present dimensions and was called the Nieuwmarkt. It retains an array of 17th- and 18th-century gabled houses. True to tradition, an antiques market is held on Sundays during the summer.

The old Jewish Quarter leads off the square down St Antoniesbreestraat. In the 1970s, many houses were demolished to make way for the metro, sparking off clashes between protesters and police. The action of conservationists persuaded the city council to renovate rather than redevelop old buildings. In tribute to them, photographs of their protests decorate the metro.

Hash Marijuana Hemp Museum ❹

Oudezijds Achterburgwal 148.
Map 7 C3. **Tel** 624 8926. 🚇 4, 9, 14, 16, 24, 25. Ⓜ *Nieuwmarkt.*
◯ *10am–10pm daily.* 🎟 📷 🚻
www.hashmuseum.com

This museum is the only one in Europe to chart the history of hemp (marijuana). Exhibits refer back 8,000 years to early Asiatic civilizations, which used the plant for medicines and clothing. It was first used in the Netherlands, according to a herbal manual of 1554, as a cure for earache.

Until the late 19th century, however, hemp was the main source of fibre for rope, and was therefore important in the Dutch shipping industry. Other exhibits relate to the psychoactive properties of this plant. They include an intriguing array of pipes and bongs (smoking devices), along with displays that explain smuggling methods. The museum also has a small cultivation area where plants are grown under artificial light. Police sometimes raid and take away exhibits, so there may be occasional gaps in displays.

Agnietenkapel ❺

Oudezijds Voorburgwal 231.
Map 7 C4. 🚇 4, 9, 14, 16, 24, 25.
◉ *closed to the public.*

Previously home to the University Museum, the Agnietenkapel was part of the convent of St Agnes until 1578, when it was closed after the Alteration (*see pp24–5*). In 1632, the Athenaeum Illustre, the precursor of the University of Amsterdam, took it over and by the mid-17th century it was a centre of scientific learning. It also housed the municipal library until the 1830s.

The Agnietenkapel, dating from 1470, is one of the few Gothic chapels to have survived the Alteration. During restoration from 1919 to 1921, elements of Amsterdam School architecture were introduced (*see p97*). Despite these changes and long periods of secular use, the building still has the feel of a Franciscan chapel.

The large auditorium on the first floor is the city's oldest, and is used for university lectures. It has a lovely ceiling, painted with Renaissance motifs and a portrait of Minerva, the Roman goddess of wisdom and the arts. A series of portraits of scholars – a gift from local merchant Gerardus van Papenbroeck in 1743 – also adorns the walls.

The chapel is currently used as a conference centre and is not open to the public.

Entrance to Agnietenkapel, part of the University of Amsterdam

Oudemanhuispoort ❻

Between Oudezijds Achterburgwal and Kloveniersburgwal. **Map** 7 C4.
🚇 4, 9, 14, 16, 24, 25. **Book market** ◯ *10am–6pm Mon–Sat.*

The Oudemanhuispoort was once the entrance to old men's almshouses (Oudemannenhuis), built in 1754. Today the building is part of the University of Amsterdam. The pediment over the gateway in the Oudezijds Achterburgwal features a pair of spectacles, a symbol of old age. Trading inside this covered walkway dates from 1757 and today there is a market for second-hand books. Although the building is closed to the public, visitors may enter the 18th-century courtyard via the arcade.

Crest of Amsterdam, Oudemanhuispoort

The spire of the Zuiderkerk, a prominent city landmark

Oostindisch Huis **❼**

Oude Hoogstraat 24 (entrance on Kloveniersburgwal 48). **Map** 7 C3. 🚋 *4, 9, 14, 16, 24, 25.* Ⓜ *Nieuwmarkt.* ◯ *9am–5pm Wed, unless there is a graduation ceremony.*

The Oostindisch Huis, former headquarters of the Dutch East India Company or VOC *(see pp28–9)*, is now part of the University of Amsterdam. Built in 1605, it is attributed to Hendrick de Keyser *(see p90)*. The premises have been expanded several times, in 1606, 1634 and 1661, to house spices, pepper, porcelain and silk from the East Indies.

The VOC was dissolved in 1800 *(see p31)*, and for a while the Oostindisch Huis was taken over by the customs authorities. Later, the state tax offices also moved in, and the VOC medallion carved in the stone gate was replaced with a lion, the traditional heraldic symbol of the Netherlands.

Major restyling in the 1890s destroyed much of the interior decoration, but the façade has remained

largely intact, and the former meeting room of the VOC lords has been restored to its 17th-century state.

Trippenhuis **❽**

Kloveniersburgwal 29. **Map** 8 D3. 🚋 *4, 9, 14, 16, 24, 25.* Ⓜ *Nieuwmarkt.* ⬤ *to the public.*

Justus Vingboons designed this ornate Classical mansion, completed in 1662. It appears to be one house: it is in fact two. The façade, outlined by eight Corinthian columns, features false middle windows. The house was designed for the wealthy arms merchants Lodewijk and Hendrick Trip, and hence the chimneys look like cannons. The city's art collection was housed here

Ornate balustrade of the Oostindisch Huis

from 1817 to 1885, when it moved to the Rijksmuseum *(see pp130–33)*. The Trippenhuis now houses the Dutch Academy. Opposite at No. 26 is the Kleine Trippenhuis, built in 1698. It is only 2.5 m (7 ft) wide and has very detailed cornicing, which includes two carved sphinxes.

Zuiderkerk **❾**

Zuiderkerkhof 72. **Map** 8 D4. **Tel** *552 7987.* 🚋 *9, 14.* Ⓜ *Nieuwmarkt.* ◯ *9am–5pm Mon–Fri, noon–4pm Sat.* ◙ ♿ **Tower** 🎫 🎵 *Apr–Sep: 1–3:30pm Mon–Sat.*

Designed by Hendrick de Keyser in 1603, the Renaissance-style Zuiderkerk was the first Calvinist church to open in Amsterdam after the Alteration *(see pp24–5)*. The spire, with its columns, decorative clocks and onion dome, is a prominent city landmark.

The Zuiderkerk ceased to function as a church in 1929. Restored in 1988, it is now a public housing exhibition centre. The surrounding community housing includes Theo Bosch's modern apartment building, the "Pentagon", completed in the mid-1980s.

Museum Het Rembrandthuis **❿**

Jodenbreestraat 4. **Map** 8 D4. **Tel** *520 0400.* 🚋 *9, 14.* Ⓜ *Nieuwmarkt.* ◯ *10am–5pm daily.* ⬤ *1 Jan.* 🎫 ◙ 🔲 ▢ 🎥 www.rembrandthuis.nl

Rembrandt worked and taught in this house from 1639 until 1656. He lived in the ground-floor rooms with his wife, Saskia, who died here in 1642, leaving the artist with a baby son, Titus *(see p200)*.

Many of Rembrandt's most-famous paintings were created in the first-floor studio.

A fine collection of Rembrandt's drawings includes various self-portraits in different moods and guises. The interior has been restored to its former glory, and

Façade of Museum Het Rembrandthuis

furnished with objects and art works using the original inventory drawn up when Rembrandt sold the house in 1656. Printing and paint-making demonstrations take place regularly, as do tempo-rary exhibitions.

Stadhuis–Muziektheater ⓫

Waterlooplein 22. **Map** 8 D4.
🚊 *9, 14.* Ⓜ *Waterlooplein.*
Stadhuis Tel *14020.*
◯ **offices** *8:30am–4pm Mon–Fri (free concerts Sep–May: 12:30pm Tue).* **Muziektheater Tel** *625 5455. See* **Entertainment** *pp246–51.*
♿ 🖥 **www.**hetmuziektheater.nl

Few buildings in Amsterdam caused as much controversy as the new Stadhuis (city hall) and Muziektheater (opera house). Nicknamed the "Stop-era" by protesters, the scheme required the destruction of dozens of medieval houses, which were virtually all that remained of the original Jew-ish quarter. This led to run-ning battles between squatters and police *(see pp36–7).*

The building was completed in 1988, a massive confection of red brick, marble and glass. A mural illustrating the Normaal Amsterdams Peil *(see pp36–7)* is shown on the arcade linking the two parts of the complex. The Stopera has the largest auditorium in the country, with a seating capacity for 1,689

people, and it is now home to the Netherlands' national opera and ballet companies. There are guided backstage tours.

Waterlooplein ⓬

Map 8 D5. 🚊 *9, 14.* Ⓜ *Waterloo-plein.* **Market** ◯ *9am–5pm Mon–Fri, 8:30am–5pm Sat.*

The Waterlooplein dates from 1882, when two canals were filled in to create a large mar-ket square in the heart of the Jewish quarter. The site was originally known as Vlooyen-burg, an artificial island built in the 17th century to house the Jewish settlers *(see p64).*

The original market disap-peared during World War II when most of the Jewish resi-dents of Amsterdam were rounded up by the Nazis and transported to concentration camps *(see pp34–5).* After the war, a popular flea market grew up in its place.

Despite encroachment by the Stadhuis-Muziektheater,

the northern end of the Water-looplein still operates a lively market, selling anything from bric-a-brac and army-surplus clothing to Balinese carvings.

Mozes en Aäronkerk ⓭

Waterlooplein 205. **Map** 8 E4.
Tel *622 1305.* 🚊 *9, 14.*
Ⓜ *Waterlooplein.* ◯ *to the public except for exhibitions.*

Designed by the Flemish architect T. Suys the Elder in 1841, Mozes en Aäronkerk was built on the site of a hidden Catholic church. The later church took its name from the Old Testament figures of Moses and Aaron depicted on the gable stones found on the original building. These are now set into the rear wall.

The church was restored in 1990, when its twin wooden towers were painted to look like sandstone. It is now used for exhibitions, public meet-ings, concerts and celebrations.

Clothes on offer at the Waterlooplein market

Joods Historisch Museum ⑭

This complex of four synagogues was built by Ashkenazi Jews in the 17th and 18th centuries and opened as a museum in 1987. The synagogues were central to Jewish life in Amsterdam, until the devastation of World War II left them empty. They were restored in the 1980s and connected by internal walkways. Displays of art and religious artifacts depict Jewish culture and the history of Judaism in the Netherlands.

The Star of David, worn by all Jews in the Nazi occupation

The Nieuwe Synagoge was built in 1752.

Galleries of the Nieuwe Synagoge
The side galleries of the Nieuwe Synagoge house part of the permanent collection, while the downstairs area hosts regular temporary exhibitions.

JEWS IN AMSTERDAM

The first Jew to gain Dutch citizenship was a member of the Portuguese Sephardic community in 1597. The Ashkenazi Jews from eastern Europe came to Amsterdam later, in the 1630s. They were restricted to working in certain trades, but were granted full civil equality in 1796. With the rise of Zionism in the 19th century, Jewish identity re-emerged, but the Nazi occupation decimated the community *(see pp34–5)*.

18th-century Torah scroll finial in the shape of the Westerkerk tower

★ Festival Prayer Book
Presented to Amsterdam's Jewish community by printer Uri Phoebus ha-Levi in 1669, this Festival Prayer Book was one of the few to survive the late Middle Ages.

MUSEUM GUIDE

Temporary exhibitions are shown in the Nieuwe Synagoge and in the print room in the basement. The Grote Synagoge has a permanent collection illustrating the religion, culture and history of the Jews in the Netherlands. Younger visitors will enjoy exploring the Children's Museum.

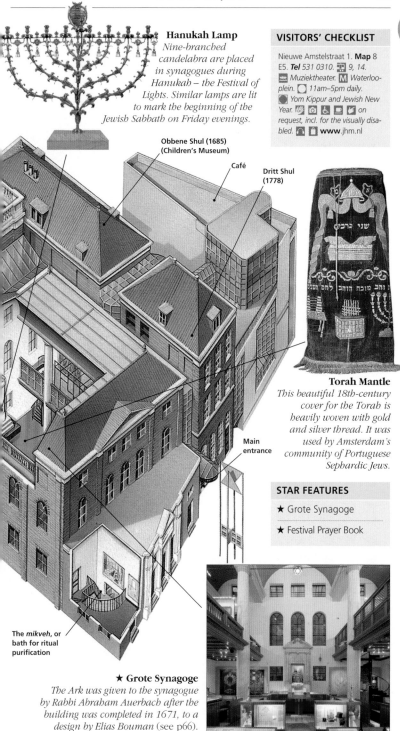

Hanukah Lamp
Nine-branched candelabra are placed in synagogues during Hanukah – the Festival of Lights. Similar lamps are lit to mark the beginning of the Jewish Sabbath on Friday evenings.

VISITORS' CHECKLIST

Nieuwe Amstelstraat 1. **Map** 8 E5. *Tel* 531 0310. ▭ 9, 14. ▭ Muziektheater. Ⓜ Waterlooplein. ☐ 11am–5pm daily. ● Yom Kippur and Jewish New Year. 🎧 ⦿ ♿ ▭ ▭ on request, incl. for the visually disabled. ☎ 🎫 **www**.jhm.nl

Obbene Shul (1685)
(Children's Museum)

Café

Dritt Shul
(1778)

Main entrance

Torah Mantle
This beautiful 18th-century cover for the Torah is heavily woven with gold and silver thread. It was used by Amsterdam's community of Portuguese Sephardic Jews.

STAR FEATURES

★ Grote Synagoge

★ Festival Prayer Book

The *mikveh*, or bath for ritual purification

★ Grote Synagoge
The Ark was given to the synagogue by Rabbi Abraham Auerbach after the building was completed in 1671, to a design by Elias Bouman (see p66). The Neo-Classical entrance was added during renovations in 1822–3.

Portugees-Israëlitische Synagoge ⓯

Mr Visserplein 3. **Map** 8 E5.
Tel 624 5351. 🚊 *9, 14.*
Ⓜ *Waterlooplein.* ◐ *Apr–Oct:
10am–4pm Sun–Fri; Nov–Mar:
10am–4pm Sun–Thu, 10am–2pm Fri.*
◗ *Jewish hols.* 🎑 ♿ 🚻
✆ *phone 531 0380.*
www.esnoga.nl

Elias Bouman's design for this synagogue was inspired by the architecture of the Temple of Solomon in Jerusalem. Built for the Portuguese Sephardic community of Amsterdam *(see p64)* and inaugurated in 1675, the huge building has a rectangular ground plan with the Holy Ark in the southeast corner facing Jerusalem, and the *tebah* (the podium from which the service is led) at the opposite end.

The wooden, barrel-vaulted ceiling is supported by four Ionic columns. The interior of the Synagoge is illuminated by more than 1,000 candles and 72 windows.

Italianate façade of the 17th-century Pintohuis

Pintohuis ⓰

Sint Antoniesbreestraat 69. **Map**
8 D4. *Tel 624 3184.* 🚊 *9, 14.*
Ⓜ *Nieuwmarkt.* ◐ *2–8pm Mon &
Wed, 2–5pm Fri, 11am–4pm Sat.*

Isaac de Pinto, a wealthy Portuguese merchant, bought the Pintohuis in 1651 for the then enormous sum of 30,000 guilders. He had it

remodelled over the next decades to a design by Elias Bouman, and it is one of the few private residences in Amsterdam to follow an Italianate style. The exterior design was reworked from 1675 to 1680. Six imposing pilasters break up the severe, cream façade into five recessed sections, and the cornice is topped by a blind balustrade concealing the roof.

In the 1970s, the house was scheduled for demolition because it stood in the way of a newly planned main road. However, concerted protest saved the building, which now houses a library. Visitors can still admire the painted ceiling, which is decorated with birds and cherubs.

Montelbaanstoren ⓱

Oude Waal/Oudeschans 2.
Map 8 E3. 🚊 *9, 14.* Ⓜ
Nieuwmarkt. ◐ *to the public.*

The lower portion of the Montelbaanstoren was built in 1512 and formed part of Amsterdam's medieval fortifications. It lay just beyond the city wall, protecting the city's wharves on the newly built St Antoniesdijk (now the Oudeschans) from the neighbouring Gelderlanders.

The octagonal structure and open-work timber steeple were both added by Hendrick de Keyser *(see p90)* in 1606. His decorative addition bears a close resemblance to the spire of the Oude Kerk, designed by Joost Bilhamer, which was built 40 years earlier *(see pp68–9)*. In 1611, the tower began to list, prompting Amsterdammers to attach ropes to the top and pull it right again.

Sailors from the VOC *(see pp28–9)* would gather at the Montelbaanstoren before being ferried in small boats down the IJ to the massive East Indies-bound sailing ships, anchored further out in deep water to the north.

The building appears in a number of etchings by Rembrandt, and is still a popular subject for artists. It now houses the offices of the Amsterdam water authority.

One of many stone carvings on the Scheepvaarthuis façade

Scheepvaarthuis ⓲

Prins Hendrikkade 108. **Map** 8 E2.
Tel 552 0000 (Hotel Amrâth).
🚊 *1, 2, 4, 5, 9, 13, 16, 17, 24, 25.*
🚌 *22, 59.* Ⓜ *Centraal Station.*
www.amrathamsterdam.com

Built as an office complex in 1916, the Scheepvaarthuis (Shipping House) is regarded as the first true example of Amsterdam School architecture *(see p97)*. It was designed by Piet Kramer (1881–1961), Johan van der May (1878–1949) and Michel de Klerk (1884–1923) for a group of shipping companies which no longer wanted to conduct business on the quay.

The imposing triangular building has a prow-like front and is crowned by a statue of Neptune, his wife and four

The medieval Montelbaanstoren, with its decorative timber steeple

female figures representing the four points of the compass. No expense was spared on the construction and internal decoration of the building, and local dock workers came to regard the building as a symbol of capitalism. The doors, stairs, window frames and interior walls are festooned with nautical images, such as dolphins and anchors. Beautiful stained-glass skylights are also decorated with images of sailing ships and compasses.

The Scheepvaarthuis is now a luxury hotel, the Grand Hotel Amrâth (*see p216*), with a magnificent hallway and an impressive marble staircase.

Schreierstoren ⓳

Prins Hendrikkade 94–95. **Map** 8 E1. 🚋 *1, 2, 4, 5, 9, 13, 16, 17, 24, 25.* Ⓜ *Centraal Station.* 🚫 *to the public.* **VOC Café *Tel*** *428 8291.* ⏰ *10am–11pm.*

The Schreierstoren (Weepers' Tower) was a defensive structure forming part of the medieval city walls, and dates from 1480. It was one of the few fortifications not to be demolished as the city expanded beyond its medieval boundaries in the 17th century. The building now houses a nautical equipment shop.

Popular legend states that the tower derived its name from the weeping (*schreien* in the original Dutch) of women who came here to wave their men off to sea. It is more likely, however, that the title has a less romantic origin and comes from the tower's position on a sharp (*screye* or *scherpe*), 90-degree bend in the old town walls. The earliest of four wall plaques, dated 1569, adds considerably to the confusion by depicting a weeping woman alongside the inscription *scrayer bovck*, which means sharp corner.

In 1609, Henry Hudson set sail from here in an attempt to discover a new and faster trading route to the East Indies. Instead, he unintentionally "discovered" the river in North America which still bears his name. A bronze plaque, laid in 1927, commemorates his voyage.

The Schreierstoren, part of the original city fortifications

Zeedijk ⓴

Map 8 D2. 🚋 *1, 2, 4, 5, 9, 13, 16, 17, 24, 25.* Ⓜ *Centraal Station.*

Along with the Nieuwendijk and the Haarlemmerdijk, the Zeedijk (sea dyke) formed part of Amsterdam's original fortifications. Built in the early 1300s, some 30 years after Amsterdam had been granted its city charter, these defences took the form of a canal moat with piled-earth ramparts reinforced by wooden palisades. As the city grew and the boundaries expanded, the canals were filled in and the dykes became obsolete. The paths that ran alongside them became the streets and alleys which bear their names today.

One of the two remaining wooden-fronted houses in Amsterdam can be found at No. 1. It was built in the mid-16th century as a hostel for sailors and now houses Café In 't Aepjen (Tel 626 8401). Opposite is St Olofskapel, built in 1445 and named after the first Christian king of Norway and Denmark.

By the 1600s, the Zeedijk had become a slum. The area is on the edge of the city's Red Light District, and in the 1960s and 1970s it became notorious as a centre for drug-dealing and street crime. Following a clean-up campaign in the 1980s, the Zeedijk is now much improved.

Plaques on the gables of some of the street's cafés reveal their former use – the red boot at No. 17 indicates that it was once a cobbler's.

Plaque on the Café 't Mandje (Little Basket), a gay bar at No. 63 Zeedijk

Oude Kerk ㉑

Carving on 15th-century choir misericord

The Oude Kerk dates from the early 13th century, when a wooden church was built in a burial ground on a sand bank *(see pp20–21)*. The present Gothic structure is 14th-century and has grown from a single-aisled church into a basilica. As it expanded, it became a gathering place for traders and a refuge for the poor. Its paintings and statuary were destroyed after the Alteration *(see pp24–5)* in 1578, but the gilded ceiling and stained-glass windows were undamaged. The Great Organ was added in 1724. The church floor is being restored until 2012, and part of the building is screened off.

The spire of the bell tower was built by Joost Bilhamer in 1565. François Hemony added the 47-bell carillon in 1658.

Tomb of Saskia, wife of Rembrandt *(see pp62–3)*

The Oude Kerk Today
The old church, surrounded by shops, cafés and houses, remains a calm and peaceful haven at the heart of the frenetic Red Light District.

Christening Chapel

Tomb of Admiral Abraham van der Hulst (1619–66)

★ Great Organ *(1724)*
Christian Vater's oak-encased organ has eight bellows and 4,000 pipes. Marbled-wood statues of biblical figures surround it.

TIMELINE

1412 North transept completed		**1462** First side chapel demolished to build south transept		**1658** Carillon installed		**1979** Church reopens to public
1330 Church consecrated to St Nicholas			**1552** Lady Chapel added	**1724** Great Organ installed		**1951** Church closes
1300	**1400**	**1500**	**1600**	**1700**	**1800**	**1900**
1300 Small stone church built	**1500** Side chapels added		**1578** Calvinists triumph in the Alteration		**1912–14** Partial restoration of northwest corner	
	1390 Pseudo-basilica replaced by three-nave		*Stained-glass coats of arms in Lady Chapel*		**1955** Restoration of church begins	
1250 First wooden chapel	hall	**1565** Spire added to 13th-century tower				

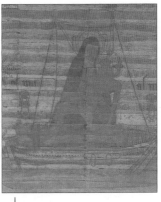

★ Gilded Ceiling
The delicate 15th-century vault paint-ings have a gilded background. They were hidden with layers of blue paint in 1755 and not revealed until 1955.

VISITORS' CHECKLIST

Oudekerksplein (entrance at south side). **Map** 7 C2. **Tel** 625 8284. 4, 9, 16, 24, 25. 11am–5pm daily (from 1pm Sun). 11am Sun. **Tower** call 689 2565. 1 Jan, 30 Apr, 25 Dec. **www**.oudekerk.nl

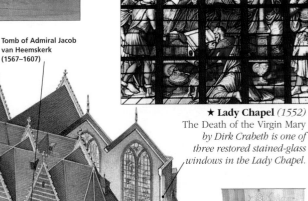

★ Lady Chapel *(1552)*
The Death of the Virgin Mary *by Dirk Crabeth is one of three restored stained-glass windows in the Lady Chapel.*

Tomb of Admiral Jacob van Heemskerk (1567–1607)

Brocaded Pillars
Decorative pillars originally formed niches holding a series of statues of the Apostles, all destroyed by the iconoclasts in 1578.

17th- and 18th-century houses

Former sacristy

The Red Door
The inscription on the lintel above the door into the former sacristy warns those about to enter: "Marry in haste, repent at leisure."

STAR FEATURES

★ Great Organ

★ Gilded Ceiling

★ Lady Chapel

NIEUWE ZIJDE

The western side of medieval Amsterdam was known as the Nieuwe Zijde (New Side). Together with the Oude Zijde it formed the heart of the early maritime settlement. Nieuwendijk, now a busy shopping street, was originally one of the earliest sea defences. As Amsterdam grew, it expanded eastwards, leaving large sections of the Nieuwe Zijde, to the west, neglected and in decline. With its many wooden houses, the city was prone to fires and in 1452 much of the area was burnt down. During rebuilding, a broad moat, the Singel, was cut, along which warehouses, rich merchants' homes

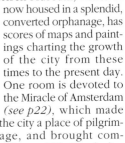

"The calf" emblem on a house in the Begijnhof

and fine quays sprang up. The Amsterdams Historisch Museum, which is now housed in a splendid, converted orphanage, has scores of maps and paintings charting the growth of the city from these times to the present day. One room is devoted to the Miracle of Amsterdam *(see p22)*, which made the city a place of pilgrimage, and brought commerce to the Nieuwe Zijde. Nearby lies Kalverstraat, Amsterdam's main shopping street, and also the secluded Begijnhof. This pretty courtyard is mostly fringed by narrow 17th-century houses, but it also contains the city's oldest surviving wooden house.

SIGHTS AT A GLANCE

Historic Buildings, Monuments and Bridges
Beurs van Berlage ⑮
Centraal Station ⑫
Koninklijk Paleis ②
Magna Plaza ⑩
Nationaal Monument ④
Torensluis ⑨

Streets and Squares
Begijnhof ⑦
Nes ⑤

Churches
Lutherse Kerk ⑪
Nieuwe Kerk pp76–7 ①
St Nicolaaskerk ⑬

Museums
Allard Pierson Museum ⑧
Amsterdams Historisch Museum pp80–83 ⑥
Madame Tussauds Scenerama ③
Museum Ons' Lieve Heer op Solder pp84–5 ⑭

GETTING THERE
The Nieuwe Zijde is easily accessible by public transport. Most tram routes terminate at Centraal Station (1, 2, 4, 5, 9, 13, 16, 17, 24 and 25), as does the metro. Or take a tram (4, 9, 14, 16, 24 and 25) to the Dam. Or 1, 2, 5, 13 or 17 to Magna Plaza.

| 0 metres | 250 |
| 0 yards | 250 |

KEY

	Street-by-Street map *See pp72–3*
	Tram stop
M	Metro station
	Train station
	Museum boat boarding point

◁ **The Fatal Fall of Icarus**, one of the many Classical sculptures in the Koninklijk Paleis

Street-by-Street: Nieuwe Zijde

Although much of the medieval Nieuwe Zijde has disappeared, the area is still rich in buildings that relate to the city's past. The Dam, dominated by the Koninklijk Paleis and Nieuwe Kerk, provides examples of architecture from the 15th to the 20th century. Around Kalverstraat, the narrow streets and alleys follow the course of some of the earliest dykes and footpaths. Here, most of the traditional gabled houses have been turned into bustling shops and cafés. Streets such as Rokin and Nes are now home to financial institutions, attracted by the nearby stock and options exchanges. Nes is also known for its venues which feature alternative theatre.

Kalverstraat, now a busy tourist shopping area, took its name from the livestock market which was regularly held here during the 15th century.

★ **Amsterdams Historisch Museum**
Wall plaques and maps showing the walled medieval city are on display in this converted orphanage that dates from the 16th century ⑥

INDE·OVDE·SCHANS

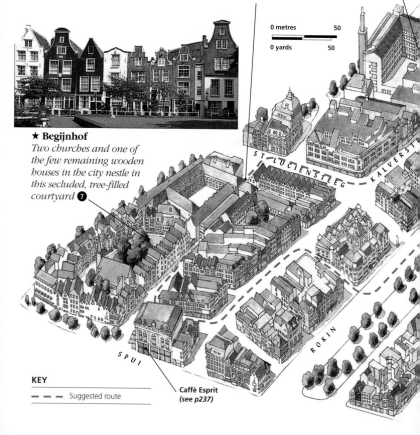

★ **Begijnhof**
Two churches and one of the few remaining wooden houses in the city nestle in this secluded, tree-filled courtyard ⑦

0 metres 50
0 yards 50

ST LUCIENSTEEG

KALVERST

ROKIN

SPUI

Caffè Esprit
(see p237)

KEY

− − − Suggested route

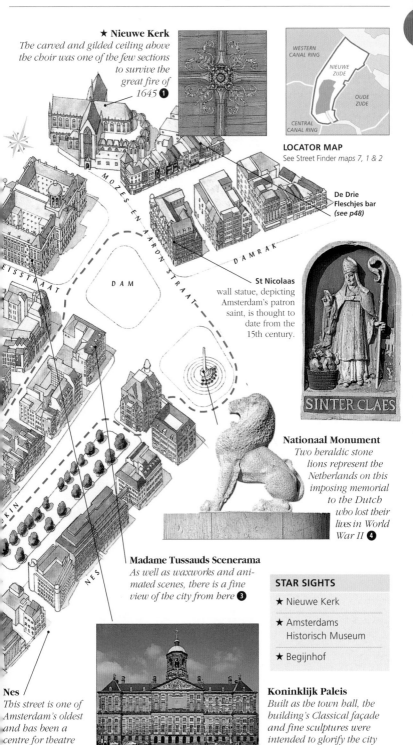

★ **Nieuwe Kerk**
The carved and gilded ceiling above the choir was one of the few sections to survive the great fire of 1645 ❶

LOCATOR MAP
See Street Finder maps 7, 1 & 2

WESTERN CANAL RING

NIEUWE ZIJDE

OUDE ZIJDE

CENTRAL CANAL RING

De Drie Fleschjes bar
(see p48)

St Nicolaas
wall statue, depicting Amsterdam's patron saint, is thought to date from the 15th century.

SINTER CLAES

Nationaal Monument
Two heraldic stone lions represent the Netherlands on this imposing memorial to the Dutch who lost their lives in World War II ❹

Madame Tussauds Scenerama
As well as waxworks and animated scenes, there is a fine view of the city from here ❸

STAR SIGHTS

★ Nieuwe Kerk

★ Amsterdams Historisch Museum

★ Begijnhof

Nes
This street is one of Amsterdam's oldest and has been a centre for theatre for 150 years ❺

Koninklijk Paleis
Built as the town hall, the building's Classical façade and fine sculptures were intended to glorify the city and its government ❷

The vast marble-floored Burgerzaal in the Koninklijk Paleis

Nieuwe Kerk ❶

See pp76–7.

Koninklijk Paleis ❷

Dam. **Map** 7 B2. 🔢 *1, 2, 4, 5, 9, 13, 14, 16, 17, 24, 25.* ⭕ *Usual hours are Jul–Aug: 11am–5pm Tue–Sun; Sep–May: noon–5pm Tue–Sun: check website for up-to-date info.* 🖼️🏠📷♿🚻🎫 *(Tel 620 4060 to reserve a private group tour).* **www**.paleisamsterdam.nl

The Koninklijk Paleis, still used occasionally by the Dutch royal family for official functions, was built as the Stadhuis (town hall). Work began in 1648, after the end of the 80 Years War with Spain *(see pp28–9)*. It dominated its surroundings and more than 13,600 piles were driven into the ground for the foundations. The Classically inspired design by Jacob van Campen (1595–1657) reflects Amsterdam's mood of confidence after the Dutch victory. Civic pride is also shown in the allegorical sculptures by Artus Quellien (1609–68), which decorate the pediments, and in François Hemony's statues and carillon.

The full magnificence of the architecture is best seen in the vast Burgerzaal (citizen's hall). Based on the assembly halls of ancient Rome, this 30-m (95-ft) high room runs the length of the building. It boasts a marble floor inlaid with maps of the eastern and western hemispheres, as well as epic sculptures by Quellien.

Most of the furniture on display, including the chandeliers, dates from 1808, when Louis Napoleon declared the building his royal palace *(see pp30–31)*.

Madame Tussauds Scenerama ❸

Peek & Cloppenburg Building, Dam 20. **Map** 7 B3. **Tel** *523 0623.* 🔢 *4, 9, 14, 16, 24, 25.* ⭕ *Jul–Aug: 10am–8:30pm daily.* ⚫ *30 Apr.* 🖼️📷♿🚻 **www**.madametussauds.nl

Located above the Peek & Cloppenburg department store, Madame Tussauds offers an audiovisual tour of Amsterdam's history, plus projected future developments. Some of the displays, such as the animated 5-m (16-ft)

figure of "Amsterdam Man", are bizarre, but the wax models of 17th-century people give an insight into life in the Golden Age *(see pp26–7)*.

Nationaal Monument ❹

Dam. **Map** 7 B3. 🔢 *4, 9, 14, 16, 24, 25.*

Sculpted by John Raedecker and designed by architect JJP Oud, the 22-m (70-ft) obelisk in the Dam commemorates Dutch World War II casualties. It was unveiled in 1956, and is fronted by two lions, heraldic symbols of the Netherlands. Embedded in the wall behind are urns containing earth from all the Dutch provinces and the former colonies of Indonesia, the Antilles and Surinam.

Nes ❺

Map 7 B3. 🔢 *4, 9, 14, 16, 24, 25.*

This quiet, narrow street is home to several theatres. In 1614, Amsterdam's first bank was opened in a pawnshop at No. 57. A wall plaque marks the site, and pawned goods still clutter the shop window. At night, Nes can be dangerous for the unguarded visitor.

De Engelenbak, one of several theatres located along Nes

Amsterdams Historisch Museum ❻

See pp80–83.

Begijnhof ⓐ

Spui (entrance at Gedempte Begijnensloot). **Map** 7 B4. 🚋 1, 2, 5, 9, 14, 16, 24, 25. **Gates** 🕙 9am–5pm daily.

The Begijnhof was originally built in 1346 as a sanctuary for the Begijntjes, a lay Catholic sisterhood who lived like nuns, although they took no monastic vows. In return for lodgings within the complex, these worthy women undertook to educate the poor and look after the sick. Nothing survives of the earliest dwellings, but the Begijnhof still retains a sanctified atmosphere. The rows of beautiful houses that overlook its well-kept green include Amsterdam's oldest surviving house at No. 34. On the adjoining wall, there is a fascinating collection of wall plaques with a biblical theme taken from the houses.

The southern fringe of the square is dominated by the Engelse Kerk (English Church), which dates from the 15th century. Directly west stands the Begijnhof Chapel, a clandestine church in which the Begijntjes and other Catholics worshipped in secret until religious tolerance was restored in 1795. It once housed relics of the Miracle of Amsterdam (see pp22–3). Four splendid stained-glass windows and paintings depict scenes of the Miracle. The occupants request that noise be kept to a minimum and no tour groups are allowed.

Plaque on the Engelse Kerk

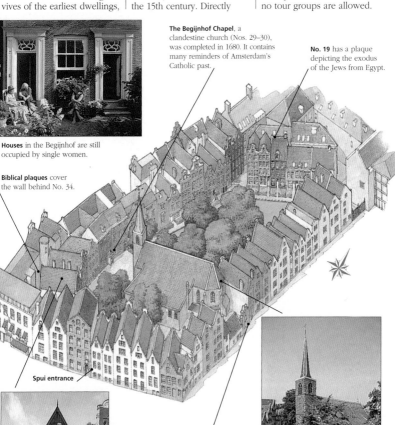

Houses in the Begijnhof are still occupied by single women.

Biblical plaques cover the wall behind No. 34.

The Begijnhof Chapel, a clandestine church (Nos. 29–30), was completed in 1680. It contains many reminders of Amsterdam's Catholic past.

No. 19 has a plaque depicting the exodus of the Jews from Egypt.

Spui entrance

Main entrance from Gedempte Begijnensloot

Het Houten Huis at No. 34 is Amsterdam's oldest house, dating from around 1420. It is one of only two wooden-fronted houses in the city, as timber houses were banned in 1521 after a series of catastrophic fires. Most of the houses in the Begijnhof were not built until after the 16th century.

Engelse Kerk was built around 1419 for the Begijntjes. The church was confiscated after the Alteration (see pp24–5) and rented to a group of English and Scottish Presbyterians in 1607. The Pilgrim Fathers (see p185) may have worshipped here.

Nieuwe Kerk ❶

Dating from the 14th century, Amsterdam's second parish church was built as the population outgrew the Oude Kerk *(see pp68–9)*. During its turbulent history, the church has been destroyed several times by fire, rebuilt and then stripped of its finery after the Alteration *(see pp24–5)*. It reached its present size in the 1650s. Since 1814 all the Dutch monarchs have been crowned here. A cultural centre hosts impressive exhibitions.

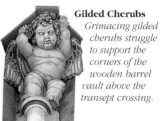

Gilded Cherubs
Grimacing gilded cherubs struggle to support the corners of the wooden barrel vault above the transept crossing.

Baptistry

Box pews around the carved pulpit

The New Stadhuis, Dam Square
The Nieuwe Kerk is in the background, at the corner of Dam square, in this painting by Jan van de Heyden (1637–1712). It shows the newly completed Stadhuis, which is now the Koninklijk Paleis (see p74).

Ornate blind windows

★ Great Organ *(1645)*
Marbled-wood cherubs and angels adorn the elaborate gilded casing of the Great Organ, which was designed by Jacob van Campen.

★ Carved Pulpit *(1664)*
It took Albert Vinckenbrinck 15 years to carve the pulpit, which is unusually flamboyant for a Dutch Protestant church.

STAR FEATURES

★ Great Organ

★ Tomb of De Ruyter

★ Carved Pulpit

Stained-Glass Windows
The lower-right section of the colourful arched window in the south transept was designed by Otto Mengelberg in 1898. It depicts Queen Wilhelmina (see p33) surrounded by courtiers at her coronation.

Apse

Mason's Chapel

Brass Candelabra
Magnificent three-tiered brass candelabra were hung from the ceilings of the nave and transepts during restoration work following the fire of 1645.

Main entrance

Rood screen by Johannes Lutma (c.1650)

Orphans' Gallery

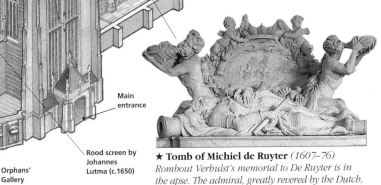

★ Tomb of Michiel de Ruyter *(1607–76)*
Rombout Verhulst's memorial to De Ruyter is in the apse. The admiral, greatly revered by the Dutch, died at sea in battle against the French at Messina.

TIMELINE

Goblet commemorating beginning of renovation of the church (1647)

1350	1450	1550	1650	1750	1850	1950

1421 Fire destroys much of original building

1452 Damaged in the Great Fire

1540 North transept razed

1653 Work on tower halted, reason unclear

1841 First royal investiture in Nieuwe Kerk

1847 Gothic structure built to replace tower

1380 Estimated date of earliest church on site

1578 Church plundered following the Alteration (see pp24–5)

1645 Fire destroys all but façade and walls

1646 Work begins on construction of Jacob van Campen's tower

1783 Part of tower torn down

1907 Large-scale restoration

1959 Restoration begins and lasts 20 years

Allard Pierson Museum **8**

Oude Turfmarkt 127. **Map** 7 B4.
Tel 525 2556. 🚊 4, 9, 14, 16, 24, 25. ⏰ 10am–5pm Tue–Fri, 1–5pm Sat, Sun & pub hols.
⬤ 1 Jan, Easter Sun, 30 Apr, Whitsun, 25 Dec. 🔄 📷 ♿ ✔
www.allardpiersonmuseum.nl

Amsterdam's only specialist archaeological collection is named after Allard Pierson (1831–96), a humanist and scholar. The museum contains Cypriot, Greek, Egyptian, Roman, Etruscan and Coptic artifacts. Look out for a case of rather gruesome Egyptian mummy remains, a computer that enables you to write your name in hieroglyphics, a jointed Greek doll from 300 BC and some fine Roman jewellery. Next door is Amsterdam University's special collections department.

Torensluis **9**

Singel between Torensteeg and Oude Leliestraat. **Map** 7 B2. 🚊 1, 2, 5, 13, 14, 17.

The Torensluis is one of the widest bridges in Amsterdam. It was built on the site of a 17th-century sluice gate and

Allard Pierson Museum's Neo-Classical façade made of Bremer and Bentheimer stone

took its name from a tower that stood on the bridge until demolished in 1829 (its outline is marked in the pavement). A jail was built in its foundations.

In summer, visitors can sit out at café tables on the bridge and enjoy pleasant views down the Singel. The statue dominating the bridge is of Multatuli, the 19th-century Dutch writer who wrote the well-known book *Max Havelaar*.

Magna Plaza **10**

Nieuwezijds Voorburgwal 182.
Map 7 B2. **Tel** 626 9199. 🚊 1, 2, 5, 13, 14, 17. ⏰ 11am–7pm Mon, 10am–7pm Tue, Wed, Fri, Sat, 10am–9pm Thu, noon–7pm Sun.
⬤ 1 Jan, 30 Apr, 25 & 26 Dec. 📷 ♿ www.magnaplaza.nl

A post office building has been sited here since 1748. A wall panel on the current building's façade depicts the original office, which was

taken out of service in 1854. The present building was completed in 1899. CH Peters, the architect, was ridiculed for the extravagance of its Neo-Gothic design. Critics dubbed the Postkantoor's elaborately decorated style and spindly towers "post-office Gothic". It has been redeveloped, and is now a shopping mall, the Magna Plaza. The grand dimensions of Peters' design have been well preserved.

Lutherse Kerk **11**

Kattengat 2. **Map** 7 C1.
🚊 1, 2, 5, 13, 17.
⬤ to the public.

The Lutherse Kerk was designed by Adriaan Dortsman (1625–82) and opened in 1671. It is sometimes known as the Ronde Lutherse Kerk, being the first Dutch Reformed church to feature a circular ground plan and two upper galleries, giving the whole congregation a clear view of the pulpit.

In 1882 a fire started by careless plumbers destroyed everything except the exterior walls. When the interior and entrance were rebuilt in 1883, they were made

An outdoor café on the Torensluis bridge overlooking the Singel canal

squarer and more ornate, in keeping with church architectural style of that time. A vaulted copper dome replaced the earlier ribbed version.

Falling attendances led to the closure and deconsecration of the church in 1935. The building is now used by the Amsterdam Renaissance Hotel *(see p217)* as a conference centre and banqueting chamber.

Centraal Station ⑫

Stationsplein. **Map** 8 D1. *Tel* 0900 9292. 🚊 1, 2, 4, 5, 9, 11, 13, 16, 17, 24, 25. Ⓜ *Centraal Station.* **Information** ◯ 6am–midnight Mon–Fri, 7am–midnight Sat, Sun & public hols. ◉ ♿

Weather vane on Centraal Station

When the Centraal Station opened in 1889, it replaced the old harbour as the symbolic focal point of the city *(see pp32–3)* and effectively curtained Amsterdam off from the sea. The Neo-Renaissance red-brick railway terminus was designed by PJH Cuypers, who was also responsible for the Rijksmuseum *(see pp130–31)* and AL van Gendt, who designed the Concertgebouw *(see p128)*.

Three artificial islands were created, using 8,600 wooden piles to support the structure. In the design of the station's twin towers and imposing central section there are architectural echoes of a triumphal arch. The imposing façade is adorned with elaborate gold and coloured decoration showing allegories of maritime

Decorative brickwork on the façade of the Beurs van Berlage

trade – a tribute to the city's past. Today it is a major meeting point as well as the transport hub of the capital, with 1,400 trains operating daily *(see p268)*, and buses and trams terminating here. The station is currently undergoing major renovation.

Sint Nicolaaskerk ⑬

Prins Hendrikkade 73. **Map** 8 D1. *Tel* 624 8749. 🚊 1, 2, 4, 5, 9,13, 16, 17, 24, 25. Ⓜ *Centraal Station.* ◯ noon–3pm Mon & Sat, 11am–4pm Tue–Fri. ✝ 12:30pm Mon–Sat; 10:30am, 1pm (in Spanish) Sun. ◉ www.nicolaas-parochie.nl

Sint Nicolaas, the patron saint of seafarers, is an important icon in Holland. Many churches are named after him, and the Netherlands' principal day for the giving of presents, 5 December, is known as Sinterklaasavond *(see p53)*.

The Sint Nicolaaskerk was designed by AC Bleys (1842–1912), and completed in 1887. It replaced some clandestine Catholic churches set up in the city when Amsterdam was officially Protestant *(see p84)*.

The exterior is rather grim and forbidding, its twin towers dominating the skyline. The monumental interior was recently enlivened by the replacement of stained-glass windows in the dome.

Museum Amstelkring ⑭

See pp84–5.

Beurs van Berlage ⑮

Damrak 2. **Map** 7 C2. *Tel* 530 4141. 🚊 4, 9, 16, 24, 25. ◉ only during exhibitions. ◉ 1 Jan. 📷 ♿ 🏠 www.beursvanberlage.nl

Hendrik Berlage's stock exchange was completed in 1903. Its clean, functional appearance marked a departure from late 19th-century revivalist architecture. Many of its design features were adopted by the Amsterdam School *(see p97)*. It has an impressive frieze showing the evolution of man from Adam to stockbroker. Now used for concerts and shows, it is home to the Nederlands Philharmonic Orchestra. The Beurs houses a variety of changing exhibitions.

Neo-Renaissance façade of the Sint Nicolaaskerk

Amsterdams Historisch Museum ❻

The Convent of St Lucien was turned into a civic orphanage two years after the Alteration of 1578 (*see pp24–5*). The original red brick convent has been enlarged over the years, with new wings added in the 17th century by Hendrick de Keyser (*see p90*) and Jacob van Campen (*see p76*). The present building is largely as it was in the 18th century. Since 1975 the complex has housed the city's historical museum.

Lecture Room

Muse... Attic

★ **The Anatomy Lesson of Dr Jan Deijman** *(1656)*
In this painting, Rembrandt depicts the dissection of Black Jack, an executed criminal.

Second floor

Orphans' Relief *(1581)*
The relief above the gateway to Kalver-straat is a copy of Joost Bilhamer's original, kept in the main entrance hall. Its inscription asks people to contribute to the upkeep of the orphans.

Library

MUSEUM GUIDE

The permanent exhibitions are housed around the complex's inner courtyards, and a multimedia map offers a concise overview of the site. The museum is in the process of rearranging the rooms and updating the exhibitions, but this should be finished by mid-2011. Check the website for more details. There are also temporary exhibitions.

Kalverstraat main entrance

Goliath *(c.1650)*
This massive statue is one of a trio of biblical figures dominating the Civic Guards' Gallery.

STAR FEATURES

★ The Flower Market and the Town Hall by Gerrit Berckheijde

★ Civic Guards' Gallery

★ The Anatomy Lesson of Dr Jan Deijman

KEY TO FLOORPLAN

- ☐ Civic Guards' Gallery
- ☐ Regents' Chamber
- ☐ Introduction & The First Amsterdammers (Departures)
- ☐ The Young City: 1350–1550
- ☐ The Mighty City: 1550–1815
- ☐ The Modern City: 1815–Today
- ☐ Temporary exhibition space
- ☐ Non-exhibition space

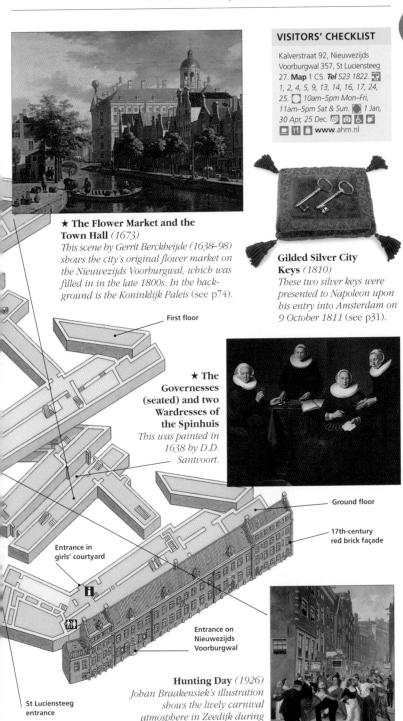

VISITORS' CHECKLIST

Kalverstraat 92, Nieuwezijds
Voorburgwal 357, St Luciensteeg
27. **Map** 1 C5. **Tel** 523 1822.
1, 2, 4, 5, 9, 13, 14, 16, 17, 24,
25. 10am–5pm Mon–Fri,
11am–5pm Sat & Sun. 1 Jan,
30 Apr, 25 Dec.
www.ahm.nl

★ **The Flower Market and the Town Hall** *(1673)*
This scene by Gerrit Berckheijde (1638–98) shows the city's original flower market on the Nieuwezijds Voorburgwal, which was filled in in the late 1800s. In the background is the Koninklijk Paleis (see p74).

Gilded Silver City Keys *(1810)*
These two silver keys were presented to Napoleon upon his entry into Amsterdam on 9 October 1811 (see p31).

First floor

★ **The Governesses (seated) and two Wardresses of the Spinhuis**
This was painted in 1638 by D.D. Santvoort.

Ground floor

17th-century red brick façade

Entrance in girls' courtyard

Entrance on Nieuwezijds Voorburgwal

St Luciensteeg entrance

Hunting Day *(1926)*
Johan Braakensiek's illustration shows the lively carnival atmosphere in Zeedijk during the celebrations for this day, which took place on the third Monday of August.

Exploring the Amsterdams Historisch Museum

The museum charts the development of Amsterdam from its humble origins as a small fishing village at the mouth of the Amstel in the Middle Ages to today's cosmopolitan city. The main focus of the museum is on trade, commerce and culture in Amsterdam's Golden Age during the 17th century, when the city's population and prosperity exploded (see pp26–7). Three main exhibitions cover the various stages of the city's growth, from 1350 through to the present day. A series of Civic Guard group portraits are a highlight of the collection.

CIVIC GUARDS' GALLERY

This covered walkway is accessible to all during museum hours. Queen Juliana opened the gallery in 1975 to house the group portraits which were popular during the 16th century. The Civic Guard comprised three guilds of marksmen, which merged in 1580. This is a rare collection as few portraits were commissioned after 1650. Best-known are Rembrandt's works; highlights are by Dirck Barendsz (see p81) and Cornelis Anthonisz, such as The Meal of the 17 Guardsmen of Company H (1533).

REGENTS' CHAMBER

Built in 1634, this room was the meeting place of the orphanage's directors (regents). Its fine ceiling, added in 1656, shows the orphans receiving charity. Portraits of the regents hang on

17th-century coats of arms on wooden panel

the walls alongside Abraham de Verwer's two paintings of The Battle of Slaak (1633). The long table and cabinets are 17th-century.

DEPARTURES

The museum's introductory room has been completely modernized. It features a 13-m (43-ft) multimedia presentation showing the growth of the city from 1100 right up until the present day, using satellite maps and photographs of familiar places in Amsterdam. In addition, 55 display cases containing a selection of objects from different historical periods introduce visitors to the museum's extensive collections.

Bronze dagger (c. 1500)

THE YOUNG CITY: 1350–1550

Amsterdam's rise to prominence in trade and commerce began at this time (see pp22–3). Scale models and archeological finds such as a cauldron used to soften tar for shipbuilding, and many household items such as shoes and tools, help to explain what the city was like. In addition, there is a huge map on the ground showing where the important areas in the city were. A fervent religious

revival took place during this period, spurred on by the Miracle of Amsterdam in 1345. A dying man was given the Sacrament, which he regurgitated, but when thrown on the fire the Host would not burn. Many churches were built and thousands of pilgrims flocked to the city.

THE MIGHTY CITY: 1550–1815

Between 1500 and 1560 the city's population tripled (in 1502 it had been just 12,000). The Civic Guard became defenders of law and order in the overcrowded city and there is a display of its armour and weaponry shown here. Cornelis Anthonisz's bird's-eye View of Amsterdam (see pp24–5) is the oldest city plan to survive, dated 1538. Many churches and convents are clearly marked. It is during this time that the inner horseshoe of canals was constructed and the Town Hall on the Dam was built. Hendrick Cornelisz Vroom's oil painting (1615) of the fortified Haarlemmerpoort shows how the city defended itself against any outside attack from its political rivals.

The Golden Age (see pp26–9) and the importance of overseas trade and colonial expansion forms a large part of this exhibition and includes the globe of the famous cartographer Willem Blaeu (see p146). A late 18th-century model of an East Indiaman is shown resting on a primitive floating dock known as a "camel". This ingenious piece of marine engineering enabled heavily laden ships to travel through the very shallow waters of the Zuiderzee.

Portraits and busts of a variety of dignitaries abound, as well as a collection of official silverware and a 1648 model of the town hall, designed by Jacob van Campen (1595–1657), now the Koninklijk Paleis (see p74).

The great discrepancy between the rich and poorer

The First Steamship on the IJ (1816) by Nicolaas Baur

inhabitants of the city is shown in a room with walls hung with huge and rather gloomy canvases depicting the wealthy governors of Amsterdam's poor houses.

The patronage of art flourished in the city's Golden Age and artists flooded into the city. Contemporary paintings, often allegorical in nature, portray rich families and their lives such as Jacob de Wit's *Maid of Amsterdam* (1741). This and other paintings by great masters such as Pieter de Hooch and Rembrandt, as well as magnificent sculpture are just a few of the exhibits bringing the rich and varied history of Amsterdam to life.

THE OLD ORPHANAGE

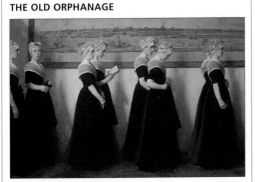

Orphan Girls Going to Church (c. 1880) by Nicolaas van der Waaij

The orphanage moved to St Lucien's convent in 1580. It was open only to the children of burghers, excluding the poorest children. As the city grew, so did the number of orphans. In the 17th century, two wings were built to accommodate more children, and a separate entrance for girls was added on St Luciensteeg. The building was used as an orphanage until 1960, but the formal uniform was abandoned in 1919.

THE MODERN CITY: 1815–TODAY

Decline in trade resulted in poverty in the 19th century and charitable institutions grew up to deal with the problem. Art began to reflect the social problems such as the squalour and slum conditions in the city. Melancholic late Hague School works by George Breitner *(see p133)* and sombre black-and-white photographs reflect the city's demise. A series of unrealized plans for the expansion of Amsterdam highlight this stagnation.

A spectacular presentation, including interactive multimedia exhibits, documents more recent history. The museum shows a series of evocative photographs taken during the Depression of the early 1930s and the war years *(see pp34–5)*, when the city was under Nazi occupation.

Photographs, videos and computers allow modern city life to be explored in detail. One of the main themes is the 'Young in Amsterdam'. Temporary exhibitions cover aspects of 20th-century and contemporary Amsterdam and the Amsterdammers.

Museum Ons' Lieve Heer op Solder ⑭

Wooden viewing gallery of church

A chaplain's tiny box bedroom is hidden off a bend in the stairs. There was a resident chaplain in the church from 1663.

Tucked away on the edge of the Red Light District is a restored 17th-century canal house, with two smaller houses to the rear. The upper storeys conceal a secret Catholic church known as Our Lord in the Attic (Ons' Lieve Heer op Solder), originally built in 1663. After the Alteration *(see pp24–5)*, when Amsterdam officially became Protestant, many such hidden churches were built throughout the city. The whole building became a museum in 1888, and has a fine collection of church silver, religious artifacts and paintings. The museum is currently being restored and expanded into another house, although it will stay open.

Christ and the Dove of Peace in silver

Museum Façade
The house on the canal has a simple spout gable and includes the two smaller houses behind. It was built by bourgeois merchant Jan Hartman in 1661.

Main entrance

House on the canal

Antechamber in late 18th-century style

★ The Parlour
Restored to its former opulence, the Parlour is an unusually fine example of a living room decorated and furnished in the Dutch Classical style of the 17th century.

STAR FEATURES

- ★ Our Lord in the Attic
- ★ Altar Painting by Jacob de Wit
- ★ The Parlour

Sacristy

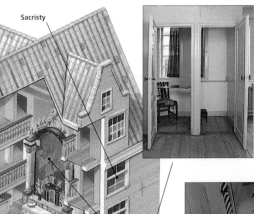

VISITORS' CHECKLIST

Oudezijds Voorburgwal 40. **Map**
8 D2. **Tel** 624 6604. 🚋 4, 9, 16,
24, 25. ⬜ 10am–5pm Mon–
Sat, 1–5pm Sun and public hols.
⬤ 1 Jan, 30 Apr. 🖼 📷 🎞 🚻
www.opsolder.nl

Confessional
*The landing where the tiny
wooden confessional stands
was formerly the living room
of the rear house.*

★ Altar Painting
The Baptism of Christ *(1716) hanging above
the mock marble altar is by Jacob de Wit (1695–
1754). It is one of three altar paintings that
were designed to be interchangeable.*

Rear
house

17th-Century Kitchen
*The kitchen was originally part of
the sacristan's secret living quarters.
The Delft tiles, fireplace and black-
and-white floor are all original.*

ddle
use

★ Our Lord in the Attic
*The original hidden church was
extended in c. 1735 to create more
seating space. It served the Catholic
community until St Nicolaaskerk
(see p79) was finished in 1887.*

WESTERN CANAL RING

At the start of the 17th century, construction of the *Grachten-gordel* began here, just west of the Singel. At the same time, city planner Hendrick Staets laid out the marshy area beyond these fashionable canals as an area for workers whose industries were banned from the town centre. Its network of narrow streets and oblique canals followed the course of old paths and drainage ditches. Immigrants fleeing religious persecution also settled here. It is thought that Huguenot refugees called the district *jardin* (garden), later corrupted to "Jordaan". Historically a poor area, it is famous for its almshouses *(hofjes)*, and the Claes Claesz-hofje is a fine early example. Recently, the Jordaan has taken on a more bohemian air. Further north are the characterful Western Islands, created in the mid-17th century to meet the demand for warehouses.

"Writing hand" emblem on Claes Claeszhofje

SIGHTS AT A GLANCE

Historic Buildings and Monuments
Haarlemmerpoort ⑬
Homomonument ❶
Huis met de Hoofden ❹

Museums
Anne Frank Huis ❸
Pianola en Piano
  Museum ⑪

Canals and Islands
Bloemgracht ❻
Brouwersgracht ⑫
Egelantiersgracht ❺
Western Islands ⑭

Churches
Noorder-
  kerk ❾
Westerkerk ❷

Markets
Noordermarkt ⑩

Hofjes
Claes Claeszhofje ❼
De Star and Zon's Hofje ❽

GETTING THERE
It is a 10–15-minute walk from the Dam and Centraal Station to the Jordaan. Trams 13, 14 and 17 go to Rozengracht; 3 follows Marnixstraat to Haarlemmer-poort and 10 goes halfway.

KEY

	Street-by-Street map *See pp88–9*
	Tram stop
	Museum boat boarding point

0 metres 250

0 yards 250

◁ View of Prinsengracht with its densely packed houseboats and the Westerkerk in the distance

Street-by-Street: Around the Jordaan

West of the *Grachtengordel*, the
Jordaan still retains a network of
narrow, characterful streets and
delightful canals. Among the 17th-
century workers' houses are dozens of
quirky shops, which are well worth a
browse, selling anything from designer
clothes to old sinks, and lively brown
cafés and bars, which spill on to the
pavements in summer. A stroll along
the *Grachtengordel* provides a glimpse
into some of the city's grandest canal
houses, including Huis met de Hoofden.

★ **Anne Frank Huis**
*For two years, the
Frank family and
four others lived in a
small upstairs apart-
ment that was hidden
behind a revolving
bookcase* ❸

Bloemgracht
*This quiet, pretty canal was once
a centre for makers
of paint and
dye* ❻

★ **Westerkerk**
*Hendrick de Keyser's church
is the site of Rembrandt's
unmarked grave, and was
the setting for the wedding
of Queen Beatrix and
Prince Claus in 1966* ❷

Egelantiersgracht
*This charming tree-
lined Jordaan canal
overlooked by an
interesting mixture of
old and new archi-
tecture. Pretty views
are provided from its
numerous bridges* ❺

Huis met de Hoofden
The name "House with the Heads"
refers to the six Classical busts at
the entrance, depicting Apollo,
Ceres, Mars, Minerva,
Bacchus and Diana **4**

LOCATOR MAP
See Street Finder maps 1 & 7

| 0 metres | 75 |
| 0 yards | 75 |

The Eerste Hollandsche Levensverzeker-
ingsbank building, with its fine façade, is
a rare example of Dutch Art Nouveau,
designed by Gerrit van Arkel in 1905.

Homomonument
The pink triangle
used to "brand"
homosexual men
during World War II
influenced the design of
this memorial to
oppressed gay men and
women everywhere. It
was unveiled in
September 1987 **1**

KEY

– – – Suggested route

STAR SIGHTS

★ Westerkerk

★ Anne Frank Huis

Homomonument ❶

Westermarkt (between Westerkerk and Keizersgracht). **Map** 1 B4.
🚋 *13, 14, 17.* 🚤 *Keizersgracht.*
www.homomonument.nl

This monument to the homo-sexual men and women who lost their lives during World War II provides a quiet place of contemplation amid the bustle of the Westermarkt.

The pink triangular badge which gay men were forced to wear in Nazi concentration camps later became an emblem of gay pride, and provided the inspiration for Karin Daan's 1987 design. The monument consists of three large pink granite triangles, one of which bears an engraving from a poem by Jacob Israël de Haan (1881–1924).

Westerkerk ❷

Prinsengracht 281. **Map** 1 B4. **Tel**
624 7766. 🚋 *13, 14, 17.* ⬜ *Easter–Sep: 11am–3pm Mon–Fri & Sat (Jul–Aug only, except during services).* 📷
629 7766. 📷 **Tower** ⬜ *Apr–Sep: 10am–6pm Mon–Sat; Jul–Aug: 10am–8pm; Oct–Nov: 11am–4pm.* 📷 *689 2565.* 📷 **www**.westerkerk.nl

Built as part of the develop-ment of the Canal Ring *(see pp44–5)*, this church has the

Re-creation of Otto Frank's office in the Anne Frank Huis

tallest tower in the city at 85 m (272 ft), and the largest nave of any Dutch Protestant church. It was designed by Hendrick de Keyser, who died in 1621, a year after work began.

Rembrandt was buried here though his grave has never been found. The shutters of the huge organ (1686) were painted, by Gérard de Lairesse, with lively scenes showing King David, the Queen of Sheba and the Evangelists.

The spire, built in tapering sections, is topped by the Imperial Crown of Maximilian *(see pp22–3)*. The panoramic views of Amsterdam from the top of the tower justify the rather gruelling climb.

Anne Frank Huis ❸

Prinsengracht 267. **Map** 1 B4.
Tel *556 7105.* 🚋 *13, 14, 17.*
🚤 *Prinsengracht.* ⬜ *mid-Sep–mid-Mar: 9am–7pm daily; mid-Mar–mid-Sep: 9am–9pm Sun–Fri, 9am–10pm Sat; Jul–Aug: 10am–10pm daily; 1 Jan: noon–7pm; 4 May: 9am–7pm; 25 Dec: noon–5pm; 31 Dec: 9am–5pm.* 📷 *Yom Kippur.* 📷 📷 📷 📷
www.annefrank.org

For two years during World War II, the Frank and van Pels families, both Jewish, hid here until their betrayal to the Nazis. In 1957, the Anne Frank Stichting (founda-tion) took over the house, to carry out "the ideals set

The Westerkerk in the 18th century, a view by Jan Ekels

down in the *Diary of Anne Frank.*" The 13-year-old Anne began her now-famous diary in July 1942. It gives a unique account of growing up under persecution, and of life in confinement *(see pp34–5).* It was first published in 1947 as *Het Achterhuis (The Annexe).*

Visitors to the Anne Frank Huis climb to the second floor and enter the annexe via the revolving bookcase that hid its entrance. Its rooms are now empty, except for the film-star pin-ups in Anne's room, and Otto Frank's model of the annexe as it was during the occupation. At the front of the house, Otto Frank's office has been re-created using period furniture. Original documents concerning the Frank family are on display. Get here early or late in the day – with nearly one million visitors a year, the museum gets very crowded. Avoid queues by ordering tickets online. Last admittance is half an hour before closing time.

Huis met de Hoofden ❹

Keizersgracht 123. **Map** 7 A1.
🚊 *13, 14, 17.*
🚫 *to the public.*

Built in 1622, the Huis met de Hoofden (house with the heads) is one of the largest double houses of the period. It has a fine step gable and takes its name from the six heads placed on pilasters along the façade. Legend has it that they commemorate a housemaid who, when left alone in the house, surprised six burglars and cut off their heads. The sculptures are in fact portrayals of six Classical deities (from left to right): Apollo, Ceres, Mars, Minerva, Bacchus and Diana.

The design of the building is sometimes attributed to Pieter de Keyser (1595–1676), the son of Hendrick de Keyser.

Bikes and boats along the tranquil Bloemgracht

Egelantiersgracht ❺

Map 1 B4. 🚊 *13, 14, 17.*

Many canals in the Jordaan were named after trees or flowers, and this includes the Egelantiersgracht (sweetbrier or eglantine). The canal was cut in the 17th century along a drainage ditch. The houses in this area, built for artisans, are on a more intimate scale than the grand mansions along Herengracht, Keizersgracht and Prinsengracht. As a result, demand for canalside residences in the Jordaan has boomed. Despite some development, the Egelantiersgracht retains much of its original character and one of the most charming spots along the canal is the St Andrieshofje at Nos. 107–114. This

Head of Apollo on the Huis met de Hoofden

hofje was built in 1617, and the passage through to its courtyard is decorated with splendid blue-and-white tiles.

Bloemgracht ❻

Map 1 B4. 🚊 *13, 14, 17.*

The Bloemgracht (flower canal) was a centre for dye and paint manufacture in the 17th century. Today, only one paint maker remains, and this quiet canal is called the Herengracht (gentlemen's canal) of the Jordaan, because of the fine gable houses along its banks.

The most beautiful are the three houses at Nos. 87 to 91. Built in 1642 in the traditional "burgher" style of the period, they feature stepped gables and a strong use of glass. Their gable stones, which served as house names until numbering was introduced in the 19th century, depict a farmer, a townsman and a seaman.

Stone plaque on the *hofje* founded
in 1616 by the merchant Anslo

Claes Claeszhofje **7**

1e Egelantiersdwarsstraat. **Map** 1 B3.
⊞ *3, 10, 13, 14, 17.* ◯ *on & off.*

This is a group of *hofjes*, the
earliest of which was founded
in 1616 by a textile merchant,
Claes Claesz Anslo. They
were renovated by the Stichting Diogenes, a foundation
which now rents out the
houses to art students.

One of the oldest and most
distinctive is the "Huis met de
Schrijvende Hand" (house with
the writing hand), Egelantiersstraat 52. Once the home of a
teacher, it dates from the 1630s.

De Star Hofje and Zon's Hofje **8**

De Star Hofje: Prinsengracht 89–133;
Zon's Hofje: Prinsengracht 159–171.
Map 1 C3. ⊞ *3, 10, 13, 14, 17.* **Star**
◯ *6am–6pm Mon–Fri, 6am–2pm
Sat.* **Zon** ◯ *10am–5pm Mon–Fri.*

These two charming *hofjes* are
within a short walk of each
other. De Star was built on

the site of the Star Brewery in
1804 and is officially known
as Van Brienen *hofje*. Legend
has it that a merchant, Jan
van Brienen, founded this
almshouse ~~in gratitude for~~
his release from a vault in
which he had been acci-
dentally imprisoned. The
peaceful courtyard has a
lovely flower garden.

Zon's *hofje* was built on the
site of a clandestine church,
known as Noah's Ark, now
indicated by a plaque in the
courtyard. The church's original name of Kleine Zon (Little
Sun) gave the *hofje* its name.

Noorderkerk **9**

Noordermarkt 44–48. **Map** 1 C3.
Tel *626 6436.* ⊞ *3, 10, 13, 14, 17.*
◯ *10:30am–12:30pm Mon,
11am–1pm Sat.* ⌂ *10am &
7pm Sun.*

Built for poor settlers in the
Jordaan, the North Church
was the first in Amsterdam to
be constructed in the shape
of a Greek cross. Its layout
around a central pulpit
allowed all in the encircling
pews to see and hear well.

The church was designed
by Hendrick de Keyser *(see
p90)*, who died in 1621, a
year after building began. It
was completed in 1623. The
church is still well attended
by a Calvinist congregation,
and bears many reminders of
the working-class origins of
the Jordaan. By the entrance
is a sculpture of three bound

figures, inscribed: "Unity is
Strength". It commemorates the
Jordaanoproer (Jordaan Riot) of
1934 *(see pp34–5)*. On the
south façade is a plaque recall-
ing the strike of February 1941,
a protest at the Nazis' deportation of Jews.

There are regular concerts
on Saturday afternoons.

Noordermarkt **10**

Map 1 C3. ⊞ *3, 10, 13, 14, 17.*
General Market ◯ *9am–1pm
Mon;* **Boerenmarkt** (organic fruit
and vegetables) ◯ *9am–5pm Sat.*

Visitors to the Saturday morning
fair in Noordermarkt

Since 1627, the square that
surrounds the Noorderkerk
has been a market site. At that
time, it sold pots and pans
and *vodden* (old clothes), a
tradition that continues today
with a flea market. Since the
18th century, the area has
been a centre for bed shops,
and bedding, curtains and
fabrics are still sold on Monday morning along the Westerstraat. On Saturday
mornings, the *vogel-tjes* (small
birds) market sells various
birds and rabbits. Around
10am, the *boerenmarkt* takes
over, selling health foods, ethnic crafts and candles.

Pianola en Piano Museum **11**

Westerstraat 106. **Map** 1 B3.
Tel *627 9624.* ⊞ *3, 10, 13, 14, 17.*
◯ *2–5pm Sun & for concerts.*
▨ www.pianola.nl

Fifteen instruments and some
15,000 piano rolls are on
show here, celebrating the
automatic pianos that were
introduced in 1900. There are
regular performances often
with live pianists.

The lush garden in the courtyard of De Star *hofje*

A flower-filled houseboat on Brouwersgracht

Brouwersgracht 𝟭𝟮

Map 1 B2. 🚋 3.

Brouwersgracht (brewers' canal) was named after the breweries established here in the 17th and 18th centuries. Leather, spices, coffee and sugar were also processed and stored here. Today, most of the warehouses are smart residences that look out on an array of houseboats moored between the canal's picturesque hump-backed bridges.

Prime examples of these functional buildings, with their spout gables *(see pp96–7)* and shutters, can be seen at Nos. 188 to 194. The last distillery in the area, the Ooievaar, is just off Brouwersgracht on Driehoekstraat (Triangle street). The Dutch gin, *jenever*, has been made here since 1782. Visit one of the many *proeflokalen* or tasting houses *(see p48)* around the city to sample it.

Haarlemmerpoort 𝟭𝟯

Haarlemmerplein 50. **Map** 1 B1. 🚋 3. 🚫 to the public.

Originally a defended gateway into Amsterdam, the Haarlemmerpoort marked the beginning of the busy route to Haarlem. The present gateway, dating from 1840, was built for King William II's triumphal entry into the city *(see pp32–3)* and officially named Willemspoort. However, as the third gateway to be built on or close to this site, it is still referred to as the Haarlemmerpoort by Amsterdammers.

Designed by Cornelis Alewijn (1788–1839), the Neo-Classical gatehouse was used as tax offices in the 19th century and was made into flats in 1986. Traffic no longer goes through the gate, since a bridge has been built over the adjoining Westerkanaal. Beyond the Haarlemmerpoort is the peaceful Westerpark *(see p151)*, a pleasant retreat.

Western Islands 𝟭𝟰

Map 1 C1. 🚋 3.

Plaque with shipping motif on a house in Zandhoek, Realeneiland

This district comprises three islands built on the IJ in the early 17th century to provide space for warehouses and shipyards. Some of these are still in use and many of the period houses have survived.

Bickerseiland was bought in 1631 by the merchant Jan Bicker, who then developed it. Today, the island is residential with a mix of colourful apartment blocks on one side of its walkway and a jumble of tugs and houseboats on the other.

Photogenic Realeneiland has one of the city's prettiest spots, the waterside street of Zandhoek. Here, a row of 17th-century houses built by the island's founder, Jacobsz Reaal, overlook the sailboats moored along Westerdok.

Prinseneiland, the smallest island, is dominated by characterful warehouses, many of which are now apartments. The walk on pages 158–9 explores the area in more detail.

DUTCH HOFJES

Before the Alteration *(see pp24–5)*, the Catholic Church usually provided subsidized housing for the poor and elderly, particularly women. During the 17th and 18th centuries, rich merchants and Protestant organizations took on this charitable role and built hundreds of almshouse complexes, which were planned around courtyards and known as *hofjes*. Behind their street façades lie pretty houses and serene gardens. Visitors are admitted to some but are asked to respect the residents' privacy. Many *hofjes* are found in the Jordaan and some still serve their original purpose *(see p75)*.

The "house with the writing hand" (c. 1630) in Claes Claeszhofje

A CANAL WALK AND GUIDE TO ARCHITECTURE

With the increase in wealth and civic pride in Amsterdam during the 17th century, an ambitious plan was formed to build a splendid ring of canals round the city *(see pp26–7)*. Conceived in 1609, and added to in 1664 by Daniel Stalpaert, the scheme grew

Wall plaque, No. 1133 Prinsengracht

to encompass wide canals lined with opulent town houses in a variety of architectural styles *(see pp96–7)*. The houses on the canals of Singel, Keizersgracht, Herengracht, Reguliersgracht and Prinsengracht, illustrated on pp98–105, form a fascinating walk through Golden Age Amsterdam.

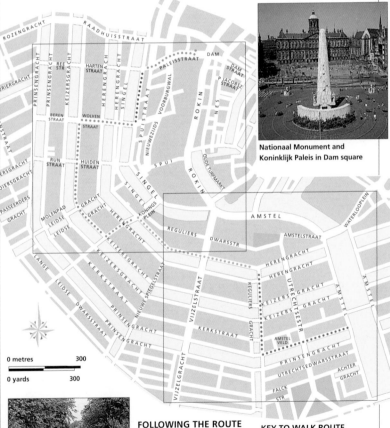

Nationaal Monument and Koninklijk Paleis in Dam square

0 metres 300

0 yards 300

A picturesque stone hump-back bridge on the Reguliersgracht

FOLLOWING THE ROUTE

The walk begins at Dam square and should be followed from left to right across the next two pages, always walking on the left-hand side of the canal. The coloured dots correspond to the stretch of canal illustrated, the grey dots trace interconnecting roads forming part of the route, but are not illustrated.

KEY TO WALK ROUTE

- • • • Singel
- • • • Keizersgracht
- • • • Herengracht
- • • • Reguliersgracht
- • • • Prinsengracht
- • • • Connecting streets

◁ *Keizersgracht (c. 1750) by Hendrick Keun – a scene of beauty and tranquillity*

A Guide to Canal House Architecture

Amsterdam has been called a city of "well-mannered" architecture because its charms lie in intimate details rather than
in grand effects. From the 15th century on, planning laws,
plot sizes and the instability of the topsoil dictated that
façades were largely uniform in size and built of lightweight
brick or sandstone, with large windows to reduce the weight.
Canal house owners stamped their own individuality on the
buildings, mainly through the use of decorative gables and
cornices, ornate doorcases and varying window shapes.

**Broken pedi-
ment and vase**

**"Broken handle"
window surrounds**

Pediment carvings symbolize
the arts and sciences.

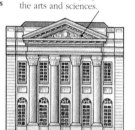

Bartolotti House *(1617)*
*The contrasting brick and
stone, flamboyant step gable,
with its marble obelisk and
scrolls, is typical of the
Dutch Renaissance style
of Hendrick de Keyser.*

Felix Meritis Building *(1778)*
*The Corinthian columns and
triangular pediment are influenced by Classical architecture.
This marks the building (see
p113) by Jacob Otten Husly
as Dutch Classical in style.*

Ground Plans
*Taxes were levied acc⸺
ing to width of façade⸺
canal houses were oft⸺
long and narrow, wit⸺
achterhuis (back anne⸺
used for offices and sto⸺*

CORNICES

Decorative top mould-
ings, called cornices,
became popular from
1690 onwards when
the fashion for gables
declined. By the 19th
century, they had
become unadorned.

**Louis XV-style with
rococo balustrade (1739)**

**19th-century cornice
with mansard roof**

**19th-century dentil
(tooth-shaped) cornice**

GABLES

The term gable refers to
the front apex of a roof. It
disguised the steepness
of the roof under which
goods were stored
(see pp22–3). In
time, gables became
decorated with
scrolls, crests, and
even coats of arms.

**Simple tri-
angular gable**

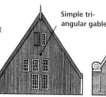

**Warehouse-style
spout gable**

**Dutch Renais-
sance style**

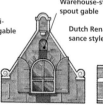

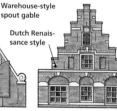

No. 34 Begijnhof (c. 1420) is
one of few remaining
timber houses *(see pp22–3).*

The style of gable on No.
213 Leliegracht (c. 1620)
was used for warehouses.

Step gables like the one o⸺
No. 2 Brouwersgracht we⸺
vogue between 1600–65.

AMSTERDAM SCHOOL ARCHITECTURE

Members of the Amsterdam School, a loose grouping of like-minded and idealistic architects, built many distinctive housing estates between 1911 and 1923 *(see p151)*. They believed in the ability of unusual architecture to enhance residents' lives, many of whom were rehoused from appalling slums. Michel de Klerk's development, Het Schip (1921), is on

Michel de Klerk (1884–1923)

the corner of Zaanstraat Spaarndammerplantsoen in northwest Amsterdam (www.hetschip.nl). It is typical of the lively style of the Amsterdam School.

aning Façades

nal houses were often built
h a deliberate tilt, allowing
ods to be winched up to the
ic without crashing against
• windows. A law dating from
65 restricted this lean to 1:25,
limit the risk of buildings
lapsing into the streets.

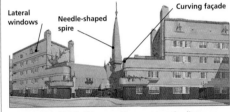

Lateral windows — Needle-shaped spire — Curving façade

Het Schip (the ship), built to resemble an ocean-going liner

tch Hofjes

nshouses (hofjes) were built
roughout the Netherlands by
h benefactors in the 17th and
th centuries. By providing
commodation for the elderly
d infirm (see p93), the hofjes
arked the beginning of the
utch welfare system.

Sign of a sailor's hostel

Symbol of a dairyman

WALL PLAQUES

Carved and painted stones were used to identify houses before street numbering was introduced in the 19th century. Many reflect the owner's occupation.

Noah's Ark – a refuge for the poor

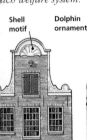

Shell motif — Dolphin ornament

419 Singel has a neck
le, a common feature
n 1640 to around 1840.

No. 119 Oudezijds Voor-burgwal has an ornate 17th-century neck gable.

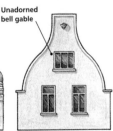

Unadorned bell gable

No. 57 Leliegracht has a plain bell gable, popular from the late 17th century.

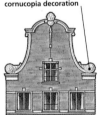

Stonework with cornucopia decoration

No. 298 Oudezijds Voorburg-wal has a bell gable dating from the 18th century.

Dam Square to Herengracht 487

The walk along Amsterdam's finest canals begins in Dam square *(see pp74)*. Following the grey dots on the map, leave the square past the Koninklijk Paleis *(see p74)*, cross Nieuwezijds Voorburgwal and Spuistraat down Paleisstraat, and turn left along the left bank of Singel, marked by purple dots. Further directions are incorporated into the route below.

LOCATOR MAP

SINGEL

No. 239 Singel
AL Van Gendt (see p128) designed this massive stone office block for trader Julius Carle Bunge. Known as the Bungehuis, it was completed in 1934.

The double-fronted 17th-century canal house at No. 265 Singel has been rebuilt several times since it was first constructed.

The step gable at No. 279 Singel dates from the 19th century – most along this canal were built between 1600–65 *(see p96)*.

The three neck gables on Nos. 353–7 Keizersgracht date from the early 18th century *(see pp96–7)*.

Huidenstraat

No. 345a Keizersgracht is a narrow house sharing a cornice with its neighbour.

In 1708, No. 333 Keizersgracht was rebuilt for tax collector Jacob de Wilde. It has been converted into apartments.

The Sower at Arles *(1888)*.
In March 1878, Vincent van Gogh (see pp134–5) visited his uncle, who ran a bookshop and art dealership at No. 453 Keizersgracht.

Nos. 289–293 Singel
These houses stand on an alley once called Schoorsteenvegersteeg (chimney sweeps' lane), home to immigrant chimney sweeps.

Yab Yum Brothel
This famous former brothel, with its opulent interior, was located at No. 295 Singel.

The doorway of No. 365 Keizersgracht was taken from an almshouse on Oudezijds Voorburgwal in the 19th century.

Jacob de Wit
The artist (see p122) bought Nos. 383 and 385 Keizersgracht, living in No. 385 until his death in 1754.

o is an elegant
nt store at No. 34–36
at on the corner
ergracht *(see p112)*.

Gerrit Rietveld
Rietveld (see p136) designed the cupola on Metz & Co, and a line of plain, inexpensive furniture for the store.

De Vergulde Ster (gilded star), at No. 387 Keizersgracht, was built in 1668 by the municipal stonemasons' yard. It has an elongated neck gable *(see p96–7)* and narrow windows.

DIRECTIONS TO HERENGRACHT
Turn left on to Leidsestraat, and walk to Koningsplein, then take the left bank of the Herengracht eastwards towards Thorbeckeplein.

HERENGRACHT

Herengracht *(1790)*
A delicate watercolour by J Prins shows the "gentlemen's canal" from Koningsplein.

Tsar Peter *(see p101)* stayed at No. 527 Herengracht, home of the Russian ambassador, after a night of drunken revelry at No. 317 Keizersgracht in 1716.

The asymmetrical building at Nos. 533–7 Herengracht was built in 1910 on the site of four former houses. From 1968–88 it was the Registry of Births, Marriages and Deaths.

The façades of Nos. 37 and 39 Reguliersgracht lean towards the water, showing the danger caused by subsidence when building on marshland.

Reguliersgrach[t] Bridges
Seven arched sto[ne] bridges cross the [...] which was origi[nally] designed to be a [...]

Keizersgracht

Nos. 1059 and 1061 Prinsengracht have tiny basement entrances, rare amid the splendour of the *Grachtengordel*, where the height of the steps was considered an indication of wealth.

The sober spout-gabled building at No. 1075 Prinsengracht was built as a warehouse in 1690.

My Domestic Companions
Society portraitist Thérèse van Duyl Schwartze painted this picture in 1916. She owned Nos. 1087, 1089 and 1091 Prinsengracht, a handsome row of houses where she lived with her extended family.

The unusual office block at No. 313 Keizersgracht was built in 1914 by CN van Goor.

No. 319 Keizersgracht was built by the architect Philips Vingboons (1608–78) in 1639. It has a rare, highly decorated façade covered with scrolls, vases and garlands.

Peter the Great *(1716) The Russian tsar sailed up Keizersgracht to No. 317, the home of his friend Christoffel Brants. Legend says the tsar got drunk and kept the mayor waiting while at a civic reception.*

Leidsegracht *This canal marked the end of Daniel Stalpaert's city expansion plan of 1664 (see p26). It has a mixture of fine 17th- and 18th-century canal houses.*

The Louis XIV-style house at No. 323 Keizersgracht was built in 1728. It has a raised cornice embellished with two hoisting beams, one functional and the other to provide symmetry.

Art patron Jan Gildemester bought No. 475 Herengracht in 1792. Attributed to Jacob Otten Husly (*see p113*), it has a stuccoed entrance hall.

Jan Corver *Burgomaster of Amsterdam 19 times, Corver built No. 479 Herengracht in 1665.*

Turn over to continue walk at top of page 102

Herengracht 489 to the Amstel

The second half of the walk takes you along Herengracht, winding past grand, wide-fronted mansions. It then follows Reguliersgracht and Prinsengracht down to the Amstel. Many of the fine houses have recently been converted into banks, offices and exclusive apartment blocks.

LOCATOR MAP

HERENGRACHT

The house at No. 491 Herengracht was built in 1671. The façade, rebuilt in the 18th century, is decorated with scrolls, vases and coats of arms.

No. 493 Herengracht
This 17th-century house was given a Louis XV-style façade in 1767 by Anthony van Hemert.

The Kattenkabinet at No. 497 Herengracht was created by financier B Meijer in 1984. It is devoted to exhibits featuring the cat in art.

DIRECTIONS TO REGULIERSGRACHT

At Thorbeckeplein, take the bridge to the right, which marks the beginning of Reguliersgracht. Follow the left bank.

REGULIERSGRACHT

Amstelveld in the 17th Century
This etching shows the construction of a wooden church at Amstelveld, with sheep grazing in front of it.

Restaurant Janvier
The Amstelkerk (see p119) now contains a restaurant and offices, while the square itself is a popular play area for local children.

DIRECTIONS TO PRINSENGRACHT

Turn left by the church, take the left bank of Prinsengracht and walk to the Amstel river.

PRINSENGRACHT

Jan Six II

The façade of No. 495 Herengracht was rebuilt and a balcony added by Jean Coulon in 1739 for burgomaster and art expert Jan Six (see p118).

Riots in 1696

No. 507 Herengracht was home of mayor Jacob Boreel. His house was looted in retaliation for the burial tax he introduced into the city.

Vijzelstraat

…ree houses boasting …pical neck gables, at Nos. …7, 19 and 21 Reguliers-…acht, are now much …ught after as prestigious … addresses.

The Nieuwe Amsterdammer

A weekly magazine aimed at Amsterdam's Bolshevik intelligentsia was published at No. 19 Reguliersgracht from 1914–20.

…e spout-gabled *(see …96–7)* 16th-century ware-…ouses at Nos. 11 and 13 …eguliersgracht are called …e Sun and the Moon.

…fé Marcella, at No. 1047a …nsengracht, is a typical …al bar which has seating …tside in summer.

Houseboats on Prinsengracht

All registered houseboats have postal addresses and are connected to the electricity mains.

Utrechtsestraat

Keizersgracht

This photograph of the "emperor's canal" is taken at dusk, from the corner of Leidsegracht. The Westerkerk (see p90) is in the distance.

Behind the contrasting 18th-century façades at Nos. 317 and 319 Singel are two second-hand bookshops, which are well worth browsing through.

DIRECTIONS TO KEIZERSGRACHT

At Raamsteeg, cross the bridge, take the Oude Spiegelstraat, cross Herengracht and walk along Wolvenstraat to the left bank of Keizersgracht.

KEIZERSGRACHT

No. 399 Keizersgracht dates from 1665, but the façade was rebuilt in the 18th century. Its *achterhuis (see p96)* has been perfectly preserved.

No. 409 Keizersgracht
Built in 1671 on a triangular piece of land, this house contains a newly discovered, highly decorated wooden ceiling.

No. 401 Kaizersgracht houses a museum of photography known as Huis Marseille.

The plain, spout-gabled building *(see pp96–7)* a No. 403 Keizersgracht originally a warehouse rarity in this predomina residential area.

No. 469 Herengracht
The modern office block by KL Sijmons replaced the original 18th-century houses in 1971.

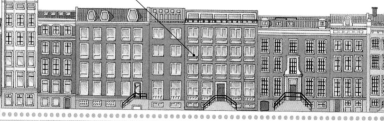

Herengracht (c. 1670)
Berckheijde's etching shows one side of the canal bare of trees. Elms were later planted, binding the topsoil, to strengthen the buildings' foundations.

No. 543 Herengracht was built in 1743 under the supervision of owner About Bollard. It has a double-fronted façade with an ornate balustrade and decorated balcony.

The small houses at the corner of Herengracht and Thorbeckeplein contrast with the grand neighbouring buildings.

Isaac Gosschalk
The architect designed Nos. 57, 59 and 63 Reguliersgracht in 1879. They have ornate stone, brick and woodwork façades.

Reguliers Monastery
This engraving by J Wagenaar (1760) shows the monastery that once stood on the canal.

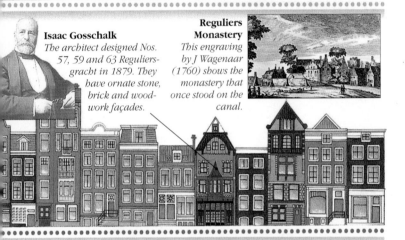

The Amstel
Turn left and follow the broad sweep of the Amstel river, up past the Magere Brug (see p119) on up and back to the Dam, where the walk began.

CENTRAL CANAL RING

The extension of Amsterdam's three major canals continued from the early 17th century *(see pp26–7)*, as the merchant classes sought to escape the overcrowding and industrial squalor in the old city, around the Amstel. They bought plots of land along the new extensions to the Herengracht, Keizersgracht and Prinsengracht, and in the 1660s the wealthiest built opulent houses on a stretch of Herengracht known as the

Pillar decoration on the Felix Meritis Building

Golden Bend. Designed and decorated by the best architects of the day, such as Philips Vingboons *(see p101)*, the mansions built here were often twice the width of standard canal houses *(see p96)*. Today, many of these grand buildings are owned by institutions. Other architectural landmarks include the Neo-Gothic Krijtberg, with its soaring steeples, the imposing Paleis van Justitie and the Art Nouveau American Hotel overlooking the busy Leidseplein.

SIGHTS AT A GLANCE

Historic Buildings and Monuments
American Hotel **2**
Metz & Co **7**
Paleis van Justitie **5**

Museums
Bijbels Museum **10**
Houseboat Museum **13**

Churches
Krijtberg **9**

Markets
Looier Kunst en Antiekcentrum **11**

Clubs and Theatres
Felix Meritis Building **12**
De Melkweg **3**

Stadsschouwburg **4**

Canals and Squares
Golden Bend **8**
Leidsegracht **6**
Leidseplein **1**

GETTING THERE
It takes about 15 minutes to walk from the Dam to Leidseplein via the Leidsegracht. Leidseplein can be reached by trams Nos. 1, 2 and 5 which terminate at Centraal Station; 7 and 10 also cross the square from the north and west going east towards Plantage.

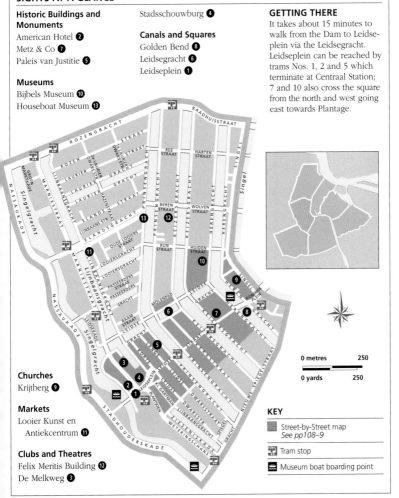

KEY

▨	Street-by-Street map *See pp108–9*
🚋	Tram stop
⛴	Museum boat boarding point

◁ **Cyclist crossing one of the many bridges on Leidsegracht**

Street-by-Street: Leidsebuurt

The area around Leidseplein is one of Amsterdam's busiest nightspots. There are various films to be seen at the many cinemas, plays at the Stadsschouwburg and lively programmes of music at De Melkweg. In contrast, there is fine architecture to admire around the Canal Ring, such as the imposing Paleis van Justitie on Prinsengracht, the lavish De Krijtberg on the Singel and scores of grand houses on the Golden Bend.

Leidseplein street performer

Bijbels Museum
In addition to bibles, there are several archaeological finds from Egypt and the Middle East on display here ❿

Leidsegracht
Cut in 1664, this canal was the main waterway for barges heading for Leiden ❻

Paleis van Justitie
This vast Empire-style building contains Amsterdam's Court of Appeal ❺

Stadsschouwburg
This historic theatre, built in 1894, is the venue for Amsterdam's Holland Festival in June (see p51) ❹

★ **American Hotel**
The hotel's Café Americain has a fine Art Deco interior and is a popular place to while away an afternoon (see p110) ❷

De Melkweg
This converted milk-processing factory and former hippie hang-out survives as one of Amsterdam's key venues for alternative entertainment ❸

Leidseplein
Young people flock to this square to watch street performances and enjoy the vibrant nightlife ❶

SINGEL

HERENGRACHT

KEIZERSGRACHT

KSTRAAT

CHT

LEIDSESTRAAT

DSEDWARSSTRAAT

LOCATOR MAP
See Street Finder maps 4 & 7

★ **De Krijtberg**
This Neo-Gothic church houses an ornate wooden carving of the Immaculate Conception ⑨

★ **Golden Bend**
Classical columns and façades on this part of the Herengracht powerfully recall the city's wealth ⑧

Metz & Co
The post-modern café at the top of this elegant department store offers one of the best views of Amsterdam ⑦

KEY

– – – Suggested route

0 metres   100

0 yards   100

STAR SIGHTS

★ American Hotel

★ Golden Bend

★ De Krijtberg

Leidseplein ❶

Map 4 E2. ⊞ *1, 2, 5, 7, 10.*

Amsterdam's liveliest square, Leidseplein is also a busy tram intersection and centre of night-time transport.

The square developed in the 17th century as a wagon park on the outskirts of the city – farmers and peasants would leave their carts here before entering the centre. It takes its name from the Leidsepoort, the massive city gate demolished in 1862, which marked the beginning of the route out to Leiden.

During the day, the square is buzzing with fire-eaters, buskers and other street performers playing to café audiences. It is also popular with pickpockets. At night, it is the focal point for the city's youth, who hang out in the many bars, cafés, restaurants, nightclubs and cinemas in and around the square.

Street performer in Leidseplein

American Hotel ❷

Leidsekade 97. **Map** 4 E2. *Tel 556 3000.* ⊞ *1, 2, 5, 7, 10.* ▣ ⧉

Leidseplein was fast becoming fashionable entertainment-area when the American Hotel was built overlooking it in 1882. The hotel got its name because its architect, W Steinigeweg, studied hotel design in the United States, and adorned his Neo-Gothic creation with a bronze eagle, wooden figures of native Indians and murals of American landscapes. Within 20 years it was deemed *passé* and the hotel was demolished. The present building is by Willem Kromhout (1864–1940) and was completed in 1902. His design marked a radical departure, interpreting the Art Nouveau style in an angular Dutch fashion. The building's turreted exterior and elaborate brickwork anticipated the progressive Amsterdam School *(see p97)*. A carved stone plaque on the Leidseplein side of the hotel shows the original building.

The Café Americain *(see p46)*, decorated in Art Deco style, remains one of the most elegant in Amsterdam. It retains its period furnishings and stained-glass windows. The rest of the hotel was redecorated in the 1980s. Samples of the original furnishings are in the Rijksmuseum *(see pp130–33)*.

De Melkweg ❸

Lijnbaansgracht 234a. **Map** 4 E2. *Tel 531 8181.* ⊞ *1, 2, 5, 7, 10.* **Box office** ◻ *from 4:30pm daily.* **Performances:** *8:30pm approx.* ▨ ◙ *See Entertainment p249.* **www**.melkweg.nl

De Melkweg (Milky Way) is a multimedia centre situated in a former dairy behind the Stadsschouwburg. It opened in 1970 and soon gained a dazzling reputation as an alternative cultural meeting place. Nowadays, it offers a wide range of entertainment, including live music, film,

The American Hotel seen from Singelgracht

video, theatre, dance and a photographic gallery. The theatre has a stage for new international acts, and De Melkweg's annual Amsterdam Roots Festival *(see p51)* promotes the latest in world music and film.

De Melkweg's star-lit façade

Stadsschouw-burg ❹

Leidseplein 26. **Map** 4 E2. *Tel 624 2311.* 🚊 *1, 2, 5, 7, 10.* **Box Office** ⬚ *noon–6pm Mon–Sat; two hours before performance Sun. See Entertainment p246.* 📷 🚫 ♿ www.stadsschouwburgamsterdam.nl

This Neo-Renaissance building is the most recent of three successive municipal theatres in the city, its predecessors having burned down. The theatre was designed by Jan Springer, whose other credits include the Frascati building on Oxford Street in London, and AL van Gendt, who was also responsible for the Concertgebouw *(see p128)* and for part of the Centraal Station *(see p79)*. The planned ornamentation of the theatre's red-brick exterior was never carried out because of budget cuts. This, combined with a hostile public reaction to his theatre, forced a disillusioned

Springer into virtual retirement. Public disgust was due, however, to the theatre management's policy of restricting use of the front door to patrons who had bought expensive tickets. The whole building has been given a face-lift.

Until the Muziektheater was completed in 1986 *(see p63)*, the Stadsschouwburg was home to the Dutch national ballet and opera companies. Today, the theatre stages plays by local groups such as the resident Toneelgroep Amsterdam, and international companies, including some English-language productions.

A new auditorium has been constructed between the Melkweg and the Stadsschouwburg. It is used by both centres.

Paleis van Justitie ❺

Prinsengracht 434–436. **Map** 4 E1. *Tel 541 2111.* 🚊 *1, 2, 5, 7, 10.* ⬚ *with restrictions.*

Conversion of the former city orphanage into the Empire-style Palace of Justice, designed by the city architect Jan de Greef, was completed in 1829. Balustrades run along the roofline and the monotony of the imposing Neo-Classical façade is broken up by Corinthian-pilasters. The building houses Amsterdam's Court of Appeal, and the courtrooms inside are set around two open yards.

The orphanage opened in 1666 with space for 800

children. By 1811, the building housed more than 2,000, over half of the city's orphans. To control their rising numbers, a royal decree was passed permitting the relocation of orphans to other towns. When this act was implemented in 1822, there was widespread protest from local people and accusations that the authorities had stolen children. Once all the children were relocated, the orphanage was closed.

Leidsegracht ❻

Map 4 E1. 🚊 *1, 2, 5, 7, 10.*

No. 39 Leidsegracht, on the right

The Leidsegracht was for a few years the main route for barges from Amsterdam to Leiden. It was cut in 1664 to a plan by city architect Daniel Stalpaert, and is now one of the city's smartest addresses.

Cornelis Lely, who drew up the original plans for draining the Zuiderzee *(see p165)*, was born at No. 39 in 1854. A wall plaque shows Lely poised between the Zuiderzee and the newly created IJsselmeer.

The elongated Neo-Classical façade of the Paleis van Justitie, converted from the city orphanage

Metz & Co ❼

Leidsestraat 34–36. **Map** 7 A5.
Tel 520 7020. 🚋 1, 2, 5. ⏱ 11am–
6pm Mon, 9:30am–6pm Tue–Sat,
noon–6pm Sun. ⬤ public hols.
🖥 See **Cafés** p49.

On its completion
in 1891, Metz & Co was
the tallest commercial
building in Amsterdam,
measuring 26 m (85 ft)
in height. It was
designed by J van
Looy and was built
for the New York
Life Insurance Com-
pany. Since 1908, it
has housed the luxu-
ry store Metz & Co.
In 1933, a splendid
glass cupola by
Gerrit Rietveld *(see
p136)* was added. Lib-
erty of London, which
bought Metz & Co in 1973,
renovated the building and
commissioned Cees Dam to
design a café on the sixth
floor. The views from the café
across the city are superb.

**The 1891 turret
of Metz &Co**

Golden Bend ❽

Map 7 A5. 🚋 1, 2, 4, 5, 9, 14, 16,
24, 25. *Kattenkabinet Herengracht
497.* **Tel** 626 5378. ⏱ 10am–4pm
Tue–Fri, noon–5pm Sat & Sun.
⬤ 1 Jan, 24–26 Dec, 31 Dec.

The stretch of the Heren-
gracht between Leidsestraat
and Vijzelstraat was first
called the Golden Bend in the
17th century, because of
the great
wealth of the
shipbuilders,
merchants
and poli-
ticians who
originally
lived along
here. Most
of the man-
sions have
been
converted
into offices
or banks, but
their former
elegance
remains. The
majority of the
buildings are
faced with

**Window decor-
ation on No. 475
Herengracht**

sandstone, which was more
expensive than brick and had
to be imported. The earliest
mansions date from the
1660s. One very fine and
largely untouched example,
designed by Philips Ving-
boons in 1664 *(see p99)*,
stands at No. 412. Build-
ing continued into the
18th century, with the
Louis XIV style pre-
dominating. No. 475
is typical of this
trend. Built in 1730,
it is often called
the jewel of canal
houses. Two
sculpted female
figures over the
front door adorn its
monumental sand-
stone façade. The
ornate mansion at
No. 452 is a good
example of a 19th-
century conversion. The Kattenkabinet (cat museum) at
No. 497 Herengracht is one of
the few houses on the Golden
Bend which is accessible to
the public. The museum is
well worth visiting for its
interesting collection of
feline artifacts.

De Krijtberg ❾

Singel 448. **Map** 7 A4. **Tel** 623
1923. 🚋 1, 2, 5. ⏱ half an hour
before the services; 1:30–5pm
Tue–Thu & Sun. ✝ 12:30pm, 5:45pm
Mon–Fri; 12:30 pm, 5:15pm, Sat;
9.30am, 11am, 12:30pm, 5:15pm
Sun. ♿ www.krijtberg.nl

An impressive Neo-Gothic
church, the Krijtberg (or
chalk hill) replaced a clandestine Jesuit chapel *(see p84)* in
1884. It is officially known as
Franciscus Xaveriuskerk, after
St Francis Xavier, one of the
founding Jesuit priests.
Designed by Alfred Tepe,
the church was constructed
on the site of three houses;
the presbytery beside the
church is on the site of two
other houses, one of which
had belonged to a chalk
merchant – hence the
church's nickname. The back
of the church is wider than
the front, extending into the
space once occupied by the
original gardens. The

narrowness of the façade is
redeemed by its two magnificent, soaring, steepled towers.
The ornate interior of the
building contains some good
examples of Neo-Gothic
design. The stained-glass
windows, walls painted
in bright colours and liberal
use of gold are in striking
contrast to the city's austere
Protestant churches. A statue
of St Francis Xavier stands in
front and to the left of the
high altar; one of St Ignatius,
founder of the Jesuits, stands
to the right.
Near the pulpit is an 18th-
century wooden statue of the
Immaculate Conception,
showing Mary trampling the
serpent. It used to be housed
in the original hidden chapel.

**The twin-steepled façade of the
Neo-Gothic Krijtberg**

Bijbels Museum ❿

Herengracht 366–368. **Map** 7 A4.
Tel 624 2436. 🚋 1, 2, 5.
🚊 Herengracht/Leidsegracht.
⏱ 10am–5pm Mon–Sat, 11am–5pm
Sun & public hols. ⬤ 1 Jan, 30 Apr.
📷 ♿ 🚻 www.bijbelsmuseum.nl

Reverend Leendert Schouten
founded the Bijbels Museum
in 1860, when he first put his
private collection of biblical
artifacts on public display. In

1975, the museum moved to its present site, two 17th-century houses in a group of four designed by Philips Vingboons.

The Bible Museum is packed with artifacts that aim to give historical weight to Bible stories. Displays feature models of historical sites, and there are archaeological finds from Egypt and the Middle East. Highlights include a copy of the Book of Isaiah from the Dead Sea Scrolls, and the Delft Bible, dating from 1477. The museum also has a beautiful garden, two ceiling paintings by Jacob de Wit and two well-preserved 17th-century kitchens.

Looier Kunst en Antiekcentrum ⓫

Elandsgracht 109. **Map** 4 D1.
Tel 624 9038. 🚊 7, 10, 13, 14, 17.
⏰ 11am–5pm Sat–Thu. 🔴 public hols. 🅿 🛗 **www**.looier.com

A vast network of ground-floor rooms in a block of houses has been turned into the Looier Antiques Centre. The market, named after its location near the Looiersgracht (tanners' canal), boasts the largest collection of art and antiques in the Netherlands.

It has around 100 stalls selling everything from glassware to dolls. On Saturdays, anyone can rent a stall here and once a month the facility is rent-free. Lively bridge sessions, open to all, are always on the go.

The Palladian façade of the 18th-century Felix Meritis Building

Felix Meritis Building ⓬

Keizersgracht 324. **Map** 1 B5. **Tel** 623 1311. 🚊 1, 2, 5, 10, 13, 14, 17. Box office & enquiries ⏰ 9am–7pm Mon–Fri, if there is an event, 9am–start of event; Sat–Sun 90 mins before start. See **Entertainment** p246. 🎭 🅿 🛗 **www**.felix.meritis.nl

This Neo-Classical building is best viewed from the opposite side of the canal (see p96). Designed by Jacob Otten Husly, it opened in 1787 as a science and arts centre set up by the Felix Meritis society. The name means "happiness through merit". An association of wealthy citizens, the society was founded by watchmaker Willem Writs in 1777, at the time of the Dutch Enlightenment (see pp30–31).

Five reliefs on the façade proclaim the society's interest in natural science and art. The building was fitted out with an observatory, library,

laboratories and a small concert hall. Mozart, Edvard Grieg and Johannes Brahms are among the distinguished musicians who have given performances here.

In the 19th century, it became Amsterdam's main cultural centre, and its concert hall inspired the design of the Concertgebouw (see p128)

The Dutch Communist Party (CPN) occupied the premises from 1946, but cultural prominence was restored in the 1970s when the Shaffy Theatre Company used the building as a theatre and won acclaim for its avant-garde productions.

The building is now used as a European Centre for Arts and Sciences, a place where politics and culture meet.

Houseboat Museum ⓭

Prinsengracht, opposite no. 296.
Map 1 B5. **Tel** 427 0750.
🚊 1, 2, 5, 7, 10, 13, 14, 17.
⏰ Mar–Oct: 11am–5pm Tue–Sun, Nov–Feb: 11am–5pm Fri–Sun.
🔴 Jan, 30 Apr, 25, 26 & 31 Dec.
🎭 📷 **www**.houseboatmuseum.nl

Moored on the Prinsengracht canal on the edge of the Jordaan, the *Hendrika Maria* is a showcase of life aboard an Amsterdam houseboat. Built in 1914, it served as a barge and transported coal, sand and gravel until the 1960s when it was converted into a houseboat. Coffee is served in the spacious living room.

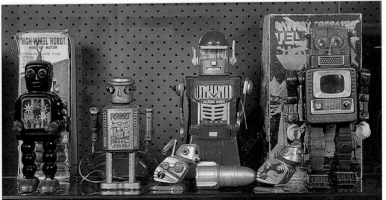

Vintage robots on sale at the Looier Kunst en Antiekcentrum

EASTERN CANAL RING

Stretching south from Munttoren, part of a former city gate, this area lies wholly beyond the line of the medieval city wall. From the 1660s, the *Grachtengordel* was extended further east towards the Amstel. One of Amsterdam's prettiest canals, Reguliersgracht with its seven bridges, was cut at this time. Today, houses on

Sun motif on a café in Reguliersdwarsstraat

the major Canal Ring, such as the Van Loon, with its grand façade and fine interior, convey a sense of life in the Golden Age *(see pp26–9)*. Beyond is the 19th-century De Pijp, a working-class district built to relieve the overcrowded Jordaan. De Pijp is now a lively multicultural area, and home to the Albert Cuypmarkt, the city's biggest street market.

SIGHTS AT A GLANCE

Historic Buildings and Bridges
Amstelkerk **7**
Blauwbrug **3**
Magere Brug **6**
Munttoren **12**
Stadsarchief Amsterdam **5**

Squares and Markets
Albert Cuypmarkt **8**
Bloemenmarkt **13**
Rembrandtplein **1**

Cinemas
Tuschinski Theater **11**

Museums
Foam Museum **4**
Heineken Experience **9**
Museum van Loon **10**
Museum Willet-Holthuysen pp120–21 **2**

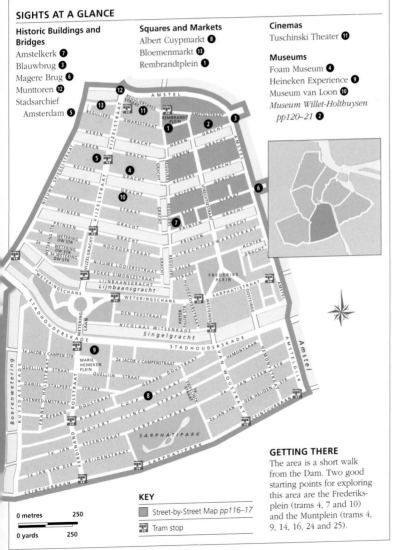

GETTING THERE
The area is a short walk from the Dam. Two good starting points for exploring this area are the Frederiksplein (trams 4, 7 and 10) and the Muntplein (trams 4, 9, 14, 16, 24 and 25).

KEY
▢ Street-by-Street Map *pp116–17*
🚋 Tram stop

0 metres 250
0 yards 250

◁ Colourful display of flowers at the Albert Cuypmarkt, including roses, lilies and sunflowers

Street-by-Street: Amstelveld

The eastern end of the *Grachtengordel* is quiet and largely residential, especially around the Amstelveld, with its pretty wooden church and houseboats. A short walk will take you past shops and numerous cafés, particularly on the bustling Rembrandtplein. As you wander down the broad sweep of the Amstel river, Amsterdam suddenly loses its village atmosphere and begins to feel like a city.

★ Rembrandtplein
Looking on to the former Botermarkt (butter market) and the cast-iron statue of Rembrandt, there are dozens of cafés dating from the 19th century, including the De Kroon at No. 17 (see p47) ❶

Café Schiller
(see p49)

★ Museum Willet-Holthuysen
This double canal house contains a number of period rooms, including the fine 19th-century-style garden room which looks out on to the restored 18th-century formal garden ❷

Amstelkerk
This wooden church was meant to be a temporary structure while money was raised to build a big new church on Rembrandtplein, but the grand scheme fell through. Today, the church houses offices and a restaurant (see p119) ❼

Blauwbrug

This cast-iron and stone bridge, in-spired by the Alexander III bridge in Paris, is adorned with sculptures on nautical and marine themes **3**

At Amstel 216, the walls of the building still show the mysterious scribbles left by former resident Coenraad van Beuningen, city mayor in the mid-1600s.

LOCATOR MAP
See Street Finder maps 5 & 8

| 0 metres | 100 |
| 0 yards | 100 |

KEY

- - - Suggested route

STAR SIGHTS

★ Rembrandtplein

★ Museum Willet-Holthuysen

★ Magere Brug

The Market Crier statue commemorates Professor Kokadorus (1867–1934), one of Amsterdam's most famous street traders.

★ Magere Brug

The current wooden bridge is a 20th-century replica of the 17th-century original, but its mechanical drive was only installed in 1994 **6**

Rembrandtplein ❶

Map 7 C5. 🚃 *4, 9, 14.*

Formerly called the Botermarkt, after the butter market held here until the mid-19th century, this square acquired its present name when the statue of Rembrandt was erected in 1876.

Soon afterwards, Rembrandtplein developed into a centre for nightlife with the opening of various hotels and cafés. The Mast (renamed the Mille Colonnes Hotel) dates from 1889, and the Schiller Karena hotel *(see p220)* and the Café Schiller *(see p49)* both opened in 1892. De Kroon *(see p47)*, which epitomizes a typical grand café, dates from 1898. The popularity of Rembrandtplein has persevered, and the café terraces are packed during summer with people enjoying a pleasant drink and watching the world go by.

Museum Willet-Holthuysen ❷

See pp120–21.

Blauwbrug ❸

Amstel. **Map** 8 D5. 🚃 *9, 14.* Ⓜ *Waterlooplein.*

The Blauwbrug (Blue Bridge) is thought to have taken its name from the colour of the wooden bridge that originally crossed this particular stretch of the Amstel in the 17th

Detail of the ornate stone carving on the Blauwbrug

Outdoor café on Rembrandtplein

century. The present bridge is made of stone. It was built in preparation for the World Exhibition, which attracted thousands of visitors to Amsterdam in 1883.

The Blauwbrug is decorated with sculptures of medieval boats, fish and the imperial crown of Amsterdam and is surmounted by ornate lamps. The design was inspired by the plans for the elaborate Alexander III bridge in Paris.

Foam Museum ❹

Kaizersgracht 609. **Map** 5 A3. **Tel** 551 6500. 🚃 *16, 24, 25.* ⬜ *10am–6pm Sat–Wed, 10am–9pm Thu & Fri.* ⬜ *1 Jan, 30 Apr.* 🈲 ⬜ ⬜ www.foam.nl

Three elegant canal houses have been joined together and renovated to create a labyrinth of rooms filled with photographs. Foam (Fotografiemuseum Amsterdam) is dedicated to exhibiting every form of photography, from historical to journalistic, to cutting-edge and artistic.

The museum holds four major exhibitions a year and 15 smaller ones, showcasing both established figures of the art form and emerging local talent. Some of the most recent exhibitions have included Annie Leibovitz's "American Music", a retrospective on Henri Cartier-Bresson and "50 Years of World Press Photo".

More than just a museum, though, Foam prides itself for being an interactive centre for photography, a place where amateurs can learn more about the art by meeting professionals, attending lectures and taking part in discussion evenings, or just stop for a coffee and a browse of the well-stocked bookshop.

Stadsarchief Amsterdam ❺

Vijzelstraat 32. **Map** 4 F2. **Tel** 251 1510. 🚃 *16, 24, 25.* ⬜ *10am–5pm Tue–Fri, 11am–5pm Sat & Sun.* ⬜ *public hols.* ⬜ ⬜ *(with permission).* 🈲 ⬜ ⬜ www.stadsarchief. amsterdam.nl

The Stadsarchief, which houses the city's municipal archives, has moved from its former location in Amsteldijk to this monumental building. Designed by KPC de Bazel, one of the principal representatives of the Amsterdam school of architecture, the edifice was completed in 1926 for the Netherlands Trading Company. In spite of much renovation work at the end of World War II and in the 1970s, the building retains many attractive original features, such as the colourful floor mosaics (designed by de Bazel himself) and the wooden panelling in the boardrooms on the second floor. There is a permanent display of treasures from the archives in the monumental vaults.

In 1991 the building, affectionately known as "The Bazel", was declared a national monument.

Magere Brug

Amstel. **Map** 5 B3. 🚊 4.

Of Amsterdam's 1,400 or so bridges, the Magere Brug (Skinny Bridge) is undoubtedly the city's best-known, instantly associated with Amsterdam. The original drawbridge was constructed in about 1670. The traditional story has it that it was named after two sisters called Mager, who lived on either side of the Amstel. However, it appears more likely that the bridge acquired the name from its narrow *(mager)* design. At night many lights illuminate the bridge.

The drawbridge was widened in 1871 and most recently renovated in 1969, though it still conforms to the traditional double-leaf style. Since 2003 traffic has been limited to bicycles and pedestrians. The bridge is made from African azobe wood, and was intended to last for at least 50 years. Several times a day, the bridge master lets boats through, then jumps on his bicycle and opens up the Hoge Sluis bridge.

The Amstelkerk, built as a temporary church in the 17th century

Amstelkerk

Amstelveld 10. **Map** 5 A3.
Tel 520 0060. 🚊 4. ◯ 9am–5pm Mon–Fri. ● public hols.

Designed by Daniel Stalpaert in 1668, the wooden Amstelkerk was originally intended to be only a temporary structure, while in the meantime money was going to be raised for a large new church on the Botermarkt (now Rembrandtplein). Unfortunately, the necessary funds for the grand scheme were never forthcoming, and so the temporary Amstelkerk had to be kept and maintained. In 1825, the Protestant church authorities attempted to raise money to renovate the Amstelkerk's plain interior in a Neo-Gothic style. It was not until 1840, however, when Frederica Elisabeth Cramer donated 25,000 guilders to the project, that work could begin. The interior walls, pulpit, pews, and organ, which was made by Jonathan Batz, all date from this period. The windows, however, are older and date from 1821.

In the late 1980s, the Amstelkerk underwent a substantial and radical conversion, which cost some 4 million guilders. Glass-walled offices were installed inside the building. However, services and concerts are still held in the nave, which was preserved in all its Neo-Gothic magnificence. The excellent top-class café-restaurant Nel is housed in a side building.

Magere Brug, a traditional double-leaf Dutch drawbridge

HOW THE MAGERE BRUG WORKS

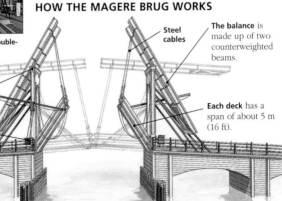

The arched wooden portal provides a pivot for the balance.

Mechanical chain-drive

Steel cables

The balance is made up of two counterweighted beams.

Each deck has a span of about 5 m (16 ft).

Museum Willet-Holthuysen ❷

Statue of Paris on stairway

Named after its last residents, the museum allows the visitor a glimpse into the lives of the merchant class who lived in luxury along the *Grachtengordel* (Canal Ring). The house was built in 1685 and became the property of coal magnate Pieter Holthuysen (1788–1858) in 1855. It passed to his daughter Louisa (1824–95) and her husband, Abraham Willet (1825–88), both fervent collectors of paintings, glass, silver and ceramics. When Louisa died childless and a widow in 1895, the house and its many treasures were left to the city. Room by room, the house is being restored and brought back to the time Abraham and Louisa lived here.

Portrait of Abraham Willet
Painted in 1877 by André Mniszech, a Polish artist, this full-length portrait shows the master of the house dressed in a traditional 17th-century costume.

STAR FEATURES

★ Blue Room

★ Dining Room

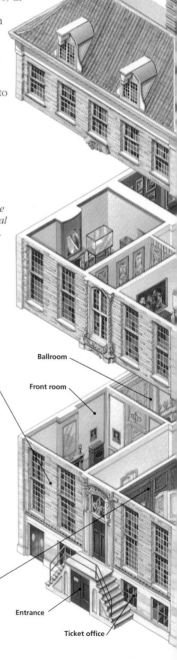

Ballroom

Front room

Entrance

Ticket office

★ Blue Room
Hung with heavy blue damask, the room boasts a chimney piece by Jacob de Wit (see p122), and was the exclusive preserve of the men of the house.

Garden Room

Now repainted in its original green, the Garden Room offers views over the intricate knot garden, laid out in 18th-century French style. It was used by the family to entertain guests to tea.

VISITORS' CHECKLIST

Herengracht 605. **Map** 8 D5.
Tel 523 1822. 🚋 4, 9, 14.
⬜ 10am–5pm Mon–Fri, 11am–
5pm Sat & Sun. ⬤ 1 Jan,
30 Apr, 25 Dec. 📷 🎫 📹 📁
www.willetholthuysen.nl

Bedroom

Staircase

The staircase was built in 1740 and has an elaborate gilded balustrade. The lower walls are painted to look like marble.

Hall

★ Dining Room

The wallpaper is a careful copy of the 18th-century silk original. The elaborate 275-piece Meissen dinner service provided up to 24 places.

The Blue Room porcelain collection includes Chinese vases made during the Kangxi dynasty (1662–1722).

Kitchen

The 18th-century kitchen has been restored using items salvaged from similar houses, including the sink and pump.

Albert Cuypmarkt 🔵

Albert Cuypstraat. **Map** 5 A5.
🚊 4, 16, 24, 25. ◯ 9:30am–5pm
Mon–Sat.

The market running along Albert Cuypstraat began trading in 1904, shortly after the expansion of the city was completed. The wide street, once a canal, is named after the Dutch landscape painter Albert Cuyp (1620–91). It is located in the Pijp district, originally built for workers.

Described by the stallholders as "the best-known market in Europe", it attracts some 20,000 visitors on weekdays and often twice as many on Saturdays. The goods on sale at the 325 stalls range from fish, poultry, cheese, fruit and vegetables to clothes, and prices are among the cheapest in Amsterdam.

Smoked fish in Albert Cuypmarkt

Heineken Experience 🔵

Stadhouderskade 78. **Map** 4 F3. **Tel** 523 9222. 🚊 7, 10, 16, 24, 25. ◯ 10am–7pm daily. **Box office** 10am–5:30pm. ⬤ 1 Jan, 30 Apr, 25 Dec, 26 Dec. 📷 📷
www.heinekenexperience.com

Gerard Adriaan Heineken founded the Heineken company in 1864 when he bought the 16th-century Hooi-berg (haystack) brewery on the Nieuwezijds Voorburgwal.

Formal rose garden at Museum van Loon

The original Stadhouderskade building was erected in 1867. His readiness to adapt to new methods and bring in foreign brewers established him as a major force in Amsterdam's profitable beer industry.

In 1988, the company finally stopped producing beer in its massive brick brewery on Stadhouderskade, as it was unable to keep up with the demand. Production is now concentrated in two breweries, one in Zoeterwoude, near Den Haag, another in Den Bosch. Today, Heineken produces around half of the beer sold in Amsterdam, has production facilities in dozens of countries and exports all over the world.

The Stadhouderskade building now houses the Heineken Experience, where visitors can learn about the history of the company and about beer-making in general. Extensive renovations to the museum in 2008 created a new floor to accommodate the increasing number of visitors. There is also a tasting bar, mini brewery and a "stable walk", offering visitors the oppor-tunity to view Heineken's splendid dray horses. All visitors must be over 18.

Museum van Loon 🔵

Keizersgracht 672. **Map** 5 A3.
Tel 624 5255. 🚊 16, 24, 25.
◯ 11am–5pm Wed–Mon.
⬤ public hols. 📷 📷 📷
www.museumvanloon.nl

Van Loon was the name of one of Amsterdam's foremost families in the 17th century. They did not move into this house on the Keizersgracht, however, until 1884. Designed by Adriaan Dortsman, No. 672 is one of a pair of symmetrical houses built in 1672 for the Flemish merchant Jeremias van Raey. It was redecorated in 1752 when Dr Abraham van Hagen and his wife Catharina Elisabeth Trip moved in.

The house was opened as a museum in 1973, after many years of restoration. It is now a delightful canalside museum, retaining the original charming character of the house. It con-tains a collection of Van Loon family portraits, stretching back to the early 1600s. The period rooms are adorned with fine pieces of furniture, porcelain and sculpture. Some of the upstairs rooms contain sumptuous illusionistic wall paintings, which were popular in the 17th and 18th centuries. Four were painted by the classicist artist Gérard de Lairesse (1641–1711).

Outside, in the formal rose garden, is the original 18th-century coach house, now restored and housing the Van Loon family coaches and livery worn by the servants.

Dray horse and beer wagon at the Heineken Experience

Tuschinski Theater ⑪

Reguliersbreestraat 26–28.
Map 7 C5. **Tel** 0900 1458. 🚊 4, 9, 14. **Box office** 🕐 12:15–10pm.
♿ 📷 📵

Abraham Tuschinski's cinema and variety theatre caused a sensation when it opened in 1921. Until then, Amsterdam's cinemas had been sombre places, but this was an exotic blend of Art Deco and Amsterdam School architecture *(see pp96–7)*. Its twin towers are 26 m (85 ft) in height. Built in a slum area known as the Duivelshoek (Devil's Corner), it was designed by Heyman Louis de Jong and decorated by Chris Bartels, Jaap Gidding and Pieter de Besten. In its heyday, Marlene Dietrich and Judy Garland performed here.

Now converted into a six-screen cinema, the building has been meticulously restored, both inside and out. The carpet in the entrance hall, replaced in 1984, is an exact copy of the original. Visitors may take a guided tour, but the best way to appreciate the opulence of the Tuschinski Theater is to go and see a film. For just a few extra euros, you can take a seat in one of the exotic boxes that make up the back row of the huge semi-circular, 1,472-seater main auditorium.

Detail of Tuschinski Theater façade

Munttoren ⑫

Muntplein. **Map** 7 B5. 🚊 4, 9, 14, 16, 24, 25. **Tower** ⊘ to the public.
Shop 🕐 10am–6pm Mon–Sat.

The polygonal base of the Munttoren (mint tower) formed part of the Reguliers-poort, a gate in Amsterdam's medieval city wall. The gate was destroyed by fire in 1618, but the base survived. In the following year, Hendrick de Keyser *(see p90)* added the clock tower, capped with a

View of the Munttoren at the base of Muntplein

steeple and openwork orb. The carillon was designed by François Hemony *(see p68)* in 1699, and rings every 15 minutes. The tower acquired its name in 1673, during the French occupation of Amsterdam, when the city mint was temporarily housed here. Up-market gift shops are now found in the base of the tower.

Bloemenmarkt ⑬

Singel. **Map** 7 B5.
🚊 1, 2, 4, 5, 9, 14, 16, 24, 25.
🕐 9:30am–5pm daily.

On the Singel, west of Muntplein, is the last of the city's floating markets. In the past, nurserymen sailed up the Amstel from their smallholdings and moored here to sell cut flowers and plants directly from their boats. Today, the stalls are still floating but are permanent. Despite the sellers' tendency to cater purely for tourists, the displays of fragrant seasonal flowers and bright spring bedding-plants are always beautiful to look at.

Florist arranging his display at the Bloemenmarkt

MUSEUM QUARTER

Until the late 1800s, the Museum Quarter was little more than an area of farms and small-holdings. At this time, the city council designated it an area of art and culture and plans were conceived for constructing Amsterdam's great cultural monuments: the Rijksmuseum, the Stedelijk Museum and the Concertgebouw. The Van Gogh Museum followed in 1973, its striking

"Russia" gablestone in Roemer Visscherstraat

extension being added in 1999. The Museumplein has two memorials to the victims of World War II. The *plein* is still used as a site for political demonstrations. To the north and south are turn-of-the-century houses, where the streets are named after artists and intellectuals, such as the 17th-century poet Roemer Visscher. To the west, the Vondelpark offers a pleasant, fresh-air break from all the museums.

SIGHTS AT A GLANCE

Museums and Workshops
Coster Diamonds **2**
Eye Film Institute **9**
Rijksmuseum pp130–33 **1**
Stedelijk Museum pp136–7 **4**
Van Gogh Museum pp134–5 **3**

Concert Halls
Concertgebouw **5**

Historic Buildings
Hollandsche Manege **7**
Vondelkerk **8**

Parks
Vondelpark **6**

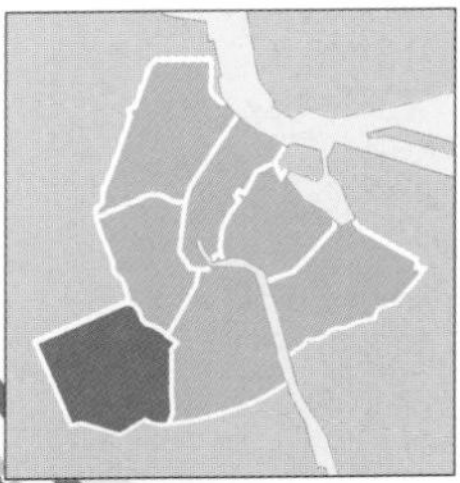

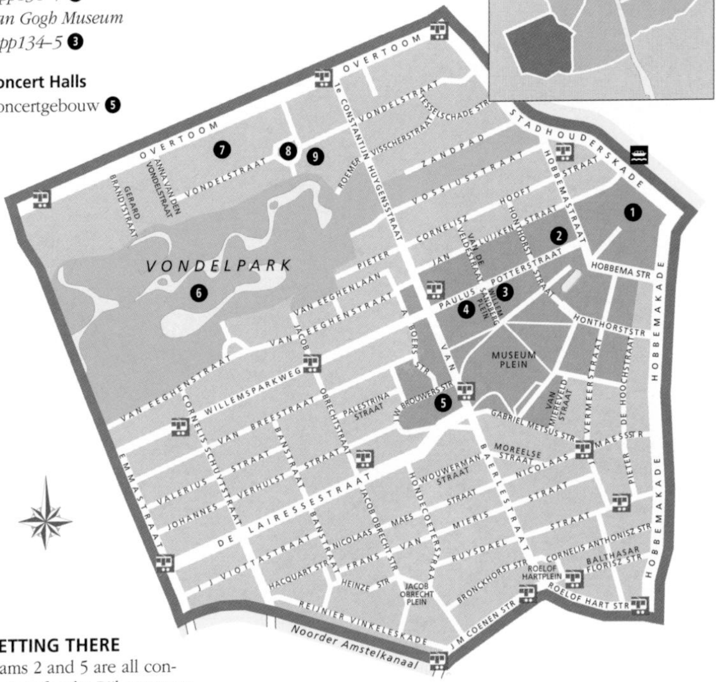

GETTING THERE
Trams 2 and 5 are all convenient for the Rijksmuseum and other museums, while trams 3 and 12 stop outside the Concertgebouw. The area has a mixture of parking areas and meters. The museum boat stops near the Rijksmuseum, on the Singelgracht.

0 metres 250
0 yards 250

KEY
Street-by-Street map
See pp126–7

Tram stop

Museum boat boarding point

Statue of the painter Pieter Aertsen (1509–75) on the façade of the Stedelijk Museum

Street-by-Street: Museum Quarter

Statue on façade of Sttedelijk

The green expanse of Museumplein was once bisected by a busy main road known locally as the "shortest motorway in Europe". But dramatic renovation between 1996 and 1999 has transformed it into a stately park, fringed by Amsterdam's major cultural centres. The district is one of the wealthiest in the city, with wide streets lined with grand houses.

After the heady delights of the museums, it is possible to window-shop at the up-market boutiques along the exclusive PC Hooftstraat and Van Baerlestraat, or watch the diamond polishers at work in Coster Diamonds.

★ Van Gogh Museum
This wing of the museum, an elega[n]t oval shape, was designed by Kisho Kurokawa and opened in 1999. It is dedicated to temporary exhibitions of 19th-century art ❸

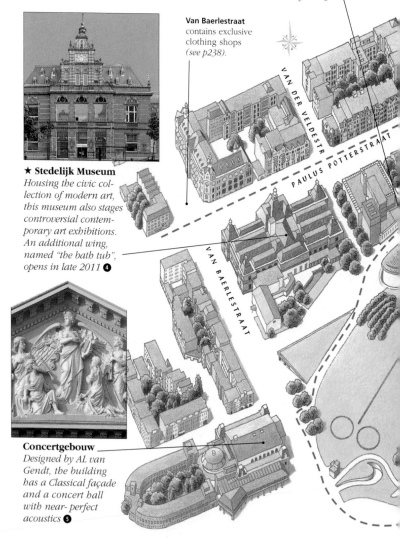

Van Baerlestraat contains exclusive clothing shops (*see p238*).

★ Stedelijk Museum
Housing the civic collection of modern art, this museum also stages controversial contemporary art exhibitions. An additional wing, named "the bath tub", opens in late 2011 ❹

Concertgebouw
Designed by AL van Gendt, the building has a Classical façade and a concert hall with near-perfect acoustics ❺

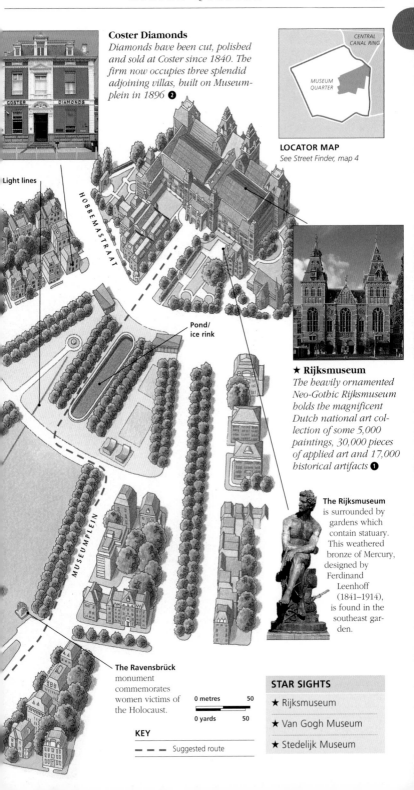

Coster Diamonds
Diamonds have been cut, polished and sold at Coster since 1840. The firm now occupies three splendid adjoining villas, built on Museumplein in 1896 **②**

LOCATOR MAP
See Street Finder, map 4

CENTRAL CANAL RING

MUSEUM QUARTER

Light lines

HOBBEMASTRAAT

Pond/ice rink

★ Rijksmuseum
The heavily ornamented Neo-Gothic Rijksmuseum holds the magnificent Dutch national art collection of some 5,000 paintings, 30,000 pieces of applied art and 17,000 historical artifacts **①**

The Rijksmuseum
is surrounded by gardens which contain statuary. This weathered bronze of Mercury, designed by Ferdinand Leenhoff (1841–1914), is found in the southeast garden.

MUSEUMPLEIN

The Ravensbrück
monument commemorates women victims of the Holocaust.

0 metres   50

0 yards   50

KEY

– – – Suggested route

STAR SIGHTS

★ Rijksmuseum

★ Van Gogh Museum

★ Stedelijk Museum

Rijksmuseum ❶

See pp130–33.

Coster Diamonds ❷

Paulus Potterstraat 2–6.
Map 4 E3. *Tel* 305 5555. 🚋 *2, 5.*
🕐 *9am–5pm daily.* 📷 📹 📶
www.costerdiamonds.com

Coster was founded in 1840.
Twelve years later, Queen
Victoria's consort, Prince Albert,
honoured the company by giving them the task of repolish-
ing the enormous *Koh-i-Noor*
(mountain of light) diamond.
This blue-white stone is one of
the treasures of the British
crown jewels and weighs in at
108.8 carats. A replica of the
coronation crown, with a copy
of the fabulous stone, is found
in Coster's entrance hall.

More than 2,000 people visit
the factory each day to witness
the processes of grading, cutting and polishing the stones.
Goldsmiths and diamond-
cutters work together to
produce customized items of
jewellery, in a range of styles,
which are available over the
counter. For serious diamond-
buyers, such as the jewellers
who come to Amsterdam from
all over the world, there is a
series of private sales rooms
where discretion is assured.
A few doors down is a small
museum, in which the history
of the diamond is traced.

**A potential sale under discussion
at Coster Diamonds**

Van Gogh
Museum ❸

See pp134–5.

Stedelijk Museum ❹

See pp136–7.

Façade of the award-winning Concertgebouw (1881) by AL van Gendt

Concertgebouw ❺

Concertgebouwplein 10.
Map 4 D4. *Tel* 0900 671 8345.
🚋 *2, 3, 5, 12, 16.* Box office
🕐 *1–7pm Mon–Fri, 10am–7pm Sat
& Sun.* 🕐 *Mon 5pm, Sun 12:15pm.*
📹 📶 ♿ *by arrangement.*
www.concertgebouw.nl

Following an open architectural competition held in
1881, AL van Gendt (1835–
1901) was chosen to design a
vast new concert hall for
Amsterdam. The resulting
Neo-Renaissance building
boasts an elaborate pediment
and colonnaded façade, and
houses two concert halls.
Despite Van Gendt's lack of
musical knowledge, he managed to produce near-perfect
acoustics in the Grote Zaal
(main concert hall), which is
renowned the world over.

The inaugural concert at the
Concertgebouw was held on
11 April 1888, complete with
an orchestra of 120 musicians
and a choir of 600.

The building has been renovated several times over the
years, most recently in 1983,
when some serious subsid-
ence threatened the building's
entire foundation. To remedy
this, the whole superstructure
had to be lifted up off the
ground while the original
supporting piles, which rested
on sand 13 m (43 ft) underground, were removed and
replaced by concrete piles
sunk into the ground to a
depth of 18 m (59 ft). A glass
extension and new entrance
were added by Pi de Bruijn in
1988. The original entrance
was relocated round to the
side of the building. Though

primarily designed to hold
concerts, the Concertgebouw
has become multi-functional;
it has played host to business
meetings, exhibitions, confer-
ences, political meetings and
occasional boxing matches.

Bandstand in Vondelpark

Vondelpark ❻

Stadhouderskade. **Map** 4 E2.
🚋 *1, 2, 3, 5, 12.* Park
🕐 *24hrs daily.* Open-air theatre
🕐 *Jun–last week Aug: Wed–Sun.*

In 1864, a group consisting of
prominent Amsterdammers
formed a committee with the
aim of founding a public park,
and they raised enough money to buy 8 hectares (20 acres)
of land. JD and LP Zocher, a
father-and-son team of landscape architects, were then
commissioned to design the
park in typical English landscape style. They used vistas,
pathways and ponds to create
the illusion of a large natural
area, which was opened to
the public on 15 June 1865, as
the Nieuwe Park. The park's
present name was adopted in
1867, when a statue of Dutch
poet Joost van den Vondel

(1586–1679) was erected in the grounds. The committee soon began to raise money to enlarge the park, and by June 1877 it had reached its current dimensions of 47 hectares (110 acres). The park now supports around 100 plant species and 127 types of tree. Squirrels, hedgehogs, ducks and garden birds mix with a huge colony of greedy, bright green parakeets, which gather in front of the pavilion every morning to be fed. Herds of cows, sheep, goats and even a lone llama graze in the pastures.

Vondelpark welcomes more than ten million visitors a year, and is popular with the locals for dog-walking, jogging, or just for the view. Free concerts are given at the *openluchttheater* (open-air theatre) or at the bandstand in the summer.

Hollandsche Manege ❼

Vondelstraat 140. **Map** 3 C2.
Tel *618 0942.* 🚊 *1.* ⭕ *9:30am–11pm Tue–Fri, 9:30am–6pm Sat–Mon.* 📷 🖥️

The Dutch Riding School was originally situated on the Leidsegracht *(see p111)*, but in 1882 a new building was opened, designed by AL van Gendt and based on the Spanish Riding School in Vienna. The riding school was threatened with demolition in the 1980s, but was saved after a public outcry. Reopened in 1986 by Prince Bernhard, it has been restored to its former

Façade of the Hollandsche Manege

glory. The Neo-Classical indoor arena boasts gilded mirrors and moulded horses' heads on its elaborate plasterwork walls. Some of the wrought-iron stalls remain and sound is muffled by sawdust. At the top of the staircase, one door leads to a balcony overlooking the arena, another to the café.

Vondelkerk ❽

Vondelstraat 120. **Map** 3 C2.
🚊 *1, 3, 12.* ⭕ *to the public.*

The Vondelkerk was the largest church designed by PJH Cuypers, architect of the Centraal Station *(see pp32–3)*. Work began on the building in 1872, but funds ran out by the following year. Money gathered from public donations and lotteries allowed the building to be completed by 1880.

When fire broke out in November 1904, firefighters saved the nave of the church by forcing the burning tower to fall away into Vondelpark. A new tower was added later by the architect's son, JT Cuypers. The church was deconsecrated in 1979 and converted into offices in 1985.

Eye Film Institute ❾

Vondelpark 3. **Map** 4 D2. ***Tel*** *589 1400.* 🚊 *1, 3, 12.* Library ⭕ *1–5pm Mon–Fri.* ⭕ *public hols.* Box Office ⭕ *9am–10:15pm Mon–Fri, 1 hour before first screening Sat–Sun.* Screenings: *from 7:30pm daily, and 1:45pm Wed & Sun (for children).* 🎬 *for cinema.* 🚭 🖥️ 🍴 **www**.eyefilm.nl

Vondelpark's pavilion opened in 1881 as a café and restaurant. After World War II, it reopened as a cultural centre. In 1991 the complete Art Deco interior of the Cinema Parisien, Amsterdam's first cinema, built in 1910, was moved into one of the rooms. It is now an important national film museum, showing more than 1,000 films a year. The Institute owns a film poster collection, runs a public film library at Nos. 69–71 Vondelstraat and holds free outdoor screenings during summer.

At the end of 2011, it will move to a new location on the Badhuisweg across the IJ (behind Centraal Station). The building is not yet completed; check the website for details.

The terrace of Café Vertigo at the Eye Film Institute

Rijksmuseum ❶

The Rijksmuseum is a familiar Amsterdam landmark and possesses an unrivalled collection of Dutch art, begun in the early 19th century. The huge museum opened in 1885 to bitter criticism from Amsterdam's Protestant community for its Neo-Gothic style. The main building is undergoing extensive renovation until 2013. However, the highlights from the Golden Age are on show in the Philips Wing during this period.

Second floor

Winter Landscape with Skaters (1618)
Painter Hendrick Avercamp specialized in intricate icy winter scenes.

The Gothic façade
of PJH Cuypers' building is red brick with elaborate decoration, including coloured tiles.

★ **The Kitchen Maid** (1658)
The light falling through the window and the stillness of this scene are typical of Jan Vermeer (see p194).

KEY TO FLOORPLAN

- ▢ Dutch history
- ▢ Dutch painting
- ▢ European painting
- ▢ Sculpture and decorative art
- ▢ Prints and drawings
- ▢ Asiatic art
- ▢ Temporary exhibitions
- ▢ Non-exhibition space

Entrance

STAR PAINTINGS

- ★ The Night Watch by Rembrandt

- ★ St Elizabeth's Day Flood

- ★ The Kitchen Maid by Vermeer

★ **St Elizabeth's Day Flood** (1500)
An unknown artist painted this altarpiece, showing a disastrous flood in 1421. The dykes protecting Dordrecht were breached, and 22 villages were swept away by the flood water.

Entrance

Study collections

VISITORS' CHECKLIST

Jan Luykenstraat 1 (Philips Wing).
Map 4 E3. **Tel** 674 7047. 🚋 2,
5, 7, 10. 🚊 Stadhouderskade.
⬤ 9am–6pm daily (Philips Wing
only). ⬤ 1 Jan. 🖼 📷 ♿ ✓
🅿 🖥 🛍 www.rijksmuseum.nl

★ **The Night Watch** *(1642)*
The showpiece of Dutch 17th-century art, this vast canvas was commissioned as a group portrait of an Amsterdam militia company.

Philips Wing

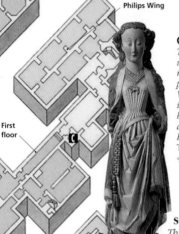

GALLERY GUIDE
The museum is currently undergoing the biggest renovation and rebuilding programme in its history. Whilst the main building is being renovated, all the highlights of the Golden Age are on show throughout the Philips Wing, under the title of The Masterpieces. *More than 400 pieces are on display.*

First floor

St Catherine *(c.1465)*
This sculpture by the Master of Koudewater shows the saint stamping on Emperor Maxentius, who allegedly killed her with his sword.

Philips Wing

GENRE PAINTING

For the contemporaries of Jan Steen (1625–79), this cosy everyday scene was full of symbols that are obscure to the modern viewer. The dog on the pillow may represent fidelity, and the red stockings the woman's sexuality; she is probably a prostitute. Such genre paintings were often raunchy, but nearly always had a moral twist *(see p189)* – domestic scenes by artists such as ter Borch and Honthorst were symbolic of brothels, while other works illustrated proverbs. Symbols like candles or skulls indicated mortality.

Jan Steen's *Woman at her Toilet* was painted in about 1660

Ground floor

Exploring the Rijksmuseum

The Rijksmuseum is almost too vast to be seen in a single visit, though the key pieces can be found in the Philips Wing. It is famous for owning probably the best collection of Dutch art in the world, from early religious works to the masterpieces of the Golden Age. However, the applied art and sculpture sections, and the Asiatic artifacts, are equally wonderful, and the Dutch history section only slightly less rewarding. If time is short, start with the incomparable 17th-century paintings, taking in Frans Hals, Vermeer and scores of other Old Masters, to arrive finally at Rembrandt's *The Night Watch*.

Feeding the Hungry from a series of seven panels by the Master of Alkmaar

DUTCH HISTORY

The turbulent history of the Netherlands is encapsulated in this section. In the opening room is the medieval altar painting of *St Elizabeth's Day Flood (see p130)*. The central room has 17th-century models of ships, artifacts salvaged from shipwrecks and paintings of factories and townscapes from the days of the Dutch Empire. Later displays recall battles in naval history; exhibits from the 18th century deal with the impact of revolutionary France on Amsterdam, ending in 1815 after the Napoleonic Wars.

EARLY PAINTING AND FOREIGN SCHOOLS

Alongside a small collection of Flemish and Italian art, including portraits by Piero di Cosimo (1462–1521), are the

first specifically "Dutch" paintings. These works are mostly religious, such as *The Seven Works of Charity* (1504) by the Master of Alkmaar, Jan van Scorel's quasi-Mannerist *Mary Magdalene* (1528) and Lucas van Leyden's triptych, *Adoration of the Golden Calf* (1530). As the 16th century progressed, religious themes were superseded by pastoral subjects; by 1552, paintings like Pieter Aertsen's *The Egg Dance* were full of realism, by then the keystone of much Dutch art.

17TH-CENTURY PAINTING

By the Alteration in 1578 *(see pp24–5)*, Dutch art had moved away completely from religious to secular themes. Artists turned to realistic portraiture, landscapes, still lifes, seascapes, domestic interiors, including genre work *(see p131)*, and animal portraits.

Rembrandt *(see p62)* is the most famous of many artists who lived and worked around Amsterdam at this time. Examples of his work hanging in the Rijksmuseum include *Portrait of Titus in a Monk's Habit* (1660), *Self Portrait as the Apostle Paul* (1661), *The Jewish Bride (see p42)* and the incredible *Night Watch (see p131)*. Look out too for the work of his many pupils, who included Nicolaes Maes and Ferdinand Bol.

Don't miss Jan Vermeer's (1632–75) serenely light-filled interiors including *The Kitchen Maid, (see p130)*, and *The Woman Reading a Letter* (1662). Of several portraits by Frans Hals *(see pp178–9)* the best known are *The Wedding Portrait* and *The Merry Drinker* (1630). *The Windmill at Wijk* by Jacob van Ruisdael (1628–82) is a great landscape by an artist at the very height of his power. Other artists whose works contribute to this unforgettable collection include Pieter Saenredam, Jan van de Capelle, Jan Steen *(see p131)* and Gerard ter Borch.

18TH- AND 19TH-CENTURY PAINTING

In many ways, 18th-century Dutch painting merely continued the themes and quality of 17th-century work.

The Wedding Portrait (c. 1622) by Frans Hals

This is particularly true of portraiture and still lifes, with the evocative *Still Life with Flowers and Fruit* by Jan van Huysum (1682–1749) standing out. A trend developed later for elegant "conversation pieces" by artists such as Adriaan van der Werff (1659–1722) and Cornelis Troost (1696–1750). Most had satirical undertones, like *The Art Gallery of Jan Gildemeester Jansz* (1794) by Adriaan de Lelie (1755–1820), showing an 18th-century salon whose walls are crowded with 17th-century masterpieces.

HAGUE SCHOOL AND THE IMPRESSIONISTS

The so-called Hague School was made up of a group of Dutch artists who came together around 1870 in Den Haag. Their landscape work, which earned them the alternative title the "Grey" School for their overcast skies, captures the atmospheric quality of subdued Dutch sunlight. One of the prizes of the Rijksmuseum's 19th-century collection is *Morning Ride on the Beach* (1876) by Anton Mauve (1838–88), painted in soft pearly colours. Alongside hangs the beautiful polder landscape, *View near the Geestbrug* by Hendrik Weissenbruch (1824–1903). In contrast, the Dutch Impressionists, closely linked to the French Impressionists, preferred active subjects such as *The Bridge over the Singel at Paleisstraat, Amsterdam* (1890) by George Hendrik Breitner (1857–1923).

SCULPTURE AND APPLIED ARTS

Beginning with religious medieval sculpture, this section moves on to the splendour of Renaissance furniture and decoration. Highlights that capture the wealth of the Golden Age include an exquisite collection of glassware, Delftware *(see p195)* and diamond-encrusted jewellery. A late 17th-century 12-leaf Chinese screen incorporates European figures on one side, a phoenix on the other; and two dolls'

Still Life with Flowers and Fruit (c. 1730) by artist Jan van Huysum (1682–1740), one of many still lifes exhibited in the Rijksmuseum

houses are modelled on contemporary town houses. Some outstanding 18th-century Meissen porcelain and Art Nouveau glass complete the collection.

PRINTS AND DRAWINGS

The Rijksmuseum owns about a million prints and drawings. Although the emphasis is on Dutch works (most of Rembrandt's etchings as well as rare works by Hercules Seghers (c. 1589–1637) are here), there are prints by major European artists, including Dürer, Tiepolo, Goya, Watteau and Toulouse-Lautrec as well as a set of coloured Japanese woodcuts. Small exhibitions are held on the ground floor of the museum, but particular prints can be viewed with special permission from the Study Collection in the basement.

ASIATIC ART

Rewards of the Dutch imperial trading past are on show in this department, which has a separate entrance at the rear of the museum. Some of the earliest artifacts are the most unusual: tiny bronze Tang dynasty figurines from 7th-century China and gritty, granite rock carvings from Java (c. 8th century). Later exhibits include a lovely – and extremely explicit – Hindu statue entitled *Heavenly Beauty*, luscious Chinese parchment paintings of tigers, inlaid Korean boxes and Vietnamese dishes painted with curly-tailed fish. This is a veritable hoard of delights and, above all, a monument to the sophistication and skill of craftsmen and artists in early Eastern cultures.

Late 7th-century Cambodian *Head of Buddha*

Van Gogh Museum ❸

The Van Gogh Museum is based on a design by De Stijl architect Gerrit Rietveld (*see p136*) and opened in 1973. A new, freestanding wing, designed by Kisho Kurokawa, was added in 1999. When Van Gogh died in 1890, he was on the verge of being acclaimed. His younger brother Theo, an art dealer, amassed a collection of 200 of his paintings and 500 drawings. These, with around 850 letters by Van Gogh, and selected works by his friends and contemporaries, form the core of the collection. You can avoid queues by buying tickets online beforehand.

KEY TO FLOORPLAN

- Works by Van Gogh
- Study collection & Print room
- Other 19th-century paintings
- Temporary exhibitions

Third floor

Stairwell

Second floor (study collection)

First floor

19th-century art

★ **Vincent's Bedroom in Arles** (*1888*)
One of Van Gogh's best-known works, this was painted to celebrate his achievement of domestic stability at the Yellow House in Arles. He was so delighted with the colourful painting that he did it twice.

★ **Sunflowers**
(*1888*)
The vivid yellows and greens in this version of Van Gogh's Sunflowers *have been enriched by broad streaks of bright mauve and red.*

STAR PAINTINGS

- ★ Sunflowers

- ★ Vincent's Bedroom in Arles

- ★ Wheatfield and Crows

MUSEUM GUIDE

The museum owns the world's largest Van Gogh collection. Paintings from his Dutch period and from his time in Paris and Provence are on the first floor. The study collection, occasional exhibits of Van Gogh's drawings and other temporary exhibitions are on the second floor. Works by other 19th-century artists are on the ground floor and third floor. The Exhibition Wing houses temporary exhibitions. Every Friday night the central hall is turned into a bar with lounge chairs and DJs.

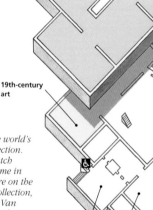

Entrance

Ground floor

Shop

AN ARTIST'S LIFE

Vincent Van Gogh (1853–90), born in Zundert, began painting in 1880. He worked in the Netherlands for five years before moving to Paris, later settling at Arles in the south of France. After a fierce argument with Gauguin, he cut off part of his own ear and his mental instability forced him into an asylum in Saint-Rémy. He sought help in Auvers, where he shot himself, dying two days later.

Van Gogh in 1871

VISITORS' CHECKLIST

Paulus Potterstraat 7. **Map** 4 E3.
Tel 570 5200. 🚋 2, 3, 5, 12
🕙 10am–6pm Mon–Thu, Sat & Sun; 10am–10pm Fri. 🔴 1 Jan. 🎦 🚫 🎥 🔊 ♿ 🖥 📷 🛍
www.vangoghmuseum.com

Pietà (after Delacroix) *(1889)*
Van Gogh painted this work while in the asylum at Saint-Rémy. The figure of Christ is thought to be a self-portrait.

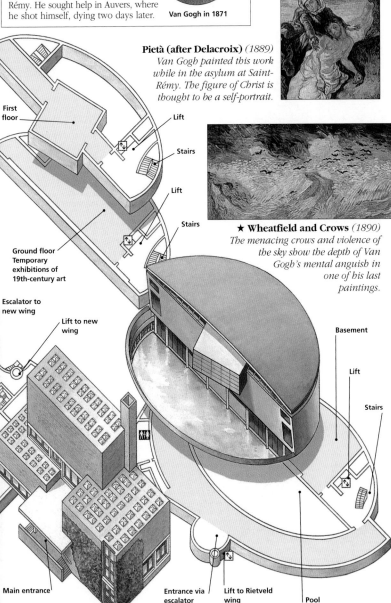

★ Wheatfield and Crows *(1890)*
The menacing crows and violence of the sky show the depth of Van Gogh's mental anguish in one of his last paintings.

First floor

Lift

Stairs

Lift

Stairs

Ground floor
Temporary exhibitions of 19th-century art

Escalator to new wing

Lift to new wing

Basement

Lift

Stairs

Main entrance

Entrance via escalator

Lift to Rietveld wing

Pool

Stedelijk Museum 4

Built to house a collection left to the city by Sophia de Bruyn in 1890, the Stedelijk Museum became the national museum of modern art in 1938, displaying works by artists such as Picasso, Matisse, Mondriaan, Chagall and Cézanne. After years of planning and preparation, the renovated museum and its spectacular wing (nicknamed the "bath tub") will hold collections from present-day artists in a larger exhibition space, with a café-restaurant and a terrace overlooking Museumplein.

Portrait of the Artist with Seven Fingers (1912)

Marc Chagall's self-portrait is heavily autobiographical; the seven fingers of the title allude to the seven days of Creation and the artist's Jewish origins. Paris and Rome, the cities Chagall lived in, are inscribed in Hebrew above his head.

Solidaridad con America Latina (1970)

The Stedelijk's collection of rare posters comprises some 17,000 works, including this graphic image by the Cuban human rights campaigner Asela Perez.

THE MUSEUM BUILDING

The Neo-Renaissance building was designed by AW Weissman (1858–1923) in 1895. The façade is adorned with turrets and gables and with niches containing statues of artists and architects. Inside, it is ultra-modern. The museum has undergone major renovation and reopens in 2011.

Hendrick de Keyser *(1565–1621)*

Jacob Cornelisz van Oostsanen *(1470–1533)*

Pieter Aertsen *(1509–75)*

Joost Jansz Bilhamer *(154...*

Gerrit Rietveld's *Red Blue Chair* **(1918)**

DE STIJL MOVEMENT

The Dutch artistic movement known as De Stijl (The Style) produced startlingly simple designs which have become icons of 20th-century abstract art. These include Gerrit Rietveld's famous *Red Blue Chair* and Pieter Mondriaan's *Composition in Red, Black, Blue, Yellow and Grey* (1920). The movement was formed in 1917 by a group of artists who espoused clarity in their work, which embraced the mediums of painting, architecture, sculpture, poetry and furniture design. Many De Stijl artists, like Theo van Doesburg, split from the founding group in the 1920s, and their legacy can be seen in the work of the Bauhaus and Modernist schools which followed.

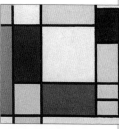

Composition in Red, Black, Blue, Yellow and Grey by Mondriaan

Dancing Woman (1911)
Ernst Ludwig Kirchner (1880–1938) was inspired by the primitive art of African and Asian cultures, and by the natural qualities of the materials he worked with.

Elaborate bell tower

Man and Animals (1949)
Karel Appel (born 1921) was a member of the short-lived, experimental Cobra movement. The human figure, dog fish and mythical creature are painted in the naive style of a child.

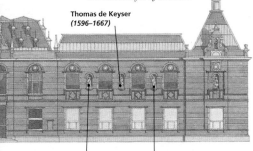

Thomas de Keyser
(1596–1667)

Jan van der Heyden
(1637–1712)

Jacob van Campen
(1595–1657)

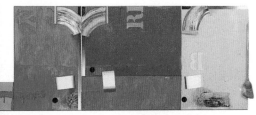

Untitled (1965)
Jasper Johns (born 1930) believed viewers should draw their own conclusions from his work. This huge canvas, with its bold rainbow (red, blue and yellow streaks and slabs), invites the viewer to think about the symbolism of colour.

STAR COLLECTIONS

★ Works by Mondriaan

★ Cobra Collection

★ Works by Malevich

VISITORS' CHECKLIST

Paulus Potterstraat 13.
Map 4 D3. *Tel* 573 29 11.
2, 3, 5, 12. for renovation until 2011 (check website for the latest information).
www.stedelijk.nl

PERMANENT ARTISTS

Works by inventive photographer Man Ray, Russian artist Kazimir Malevich and sculptor Jean Tinguely are usually on show in the museum.

Man Ray (1890–1977)
elevated photography to an art form, and was a major influence on the Surrealists.

Kazimir Malevich (1878–1935) *founded Suprematism, an abstract movement which experimented with colour.*

Jean Tinguely (1925–1991) *created humorous, moving sculptures, welded together from junk and recycled metal.*

PLANTAGE

K nown as the "plantation", this area was once green parkland beyond the city wall, where 17th-century Amsterdammers spent their leisure time. From about 1848, it became one of Amsterdam's first suburbs. The tree-lined streets around Artis and Hortus Botanicus are still popular places to live. In the 19th century, many middle-class Jews prospered in the area, mainly in the

Pillar decoration on Theater Carré

diamond-cutting industry. They formed a large part of the Diamond Workers' Union, whose history is recorded at De Burcht (Vakbondsmuseum). From the Werf 't Kromhout, once a thriving shipyard, there is a fine view of De Gooyer Windmill, one of the few in Amsterdam to survive. The national maritime collection is kept at the Scheepvaart Museum, a former naval storehouse.

SIGHTS AT A GLANCE

Museums
De Burcht ❷
Geologisch Museum ❺
Hermitage Amsterdam ⓰
Hollandsche Schouwburg ❸
Museum 't Kromhout ⓫
Nederlands Scheepvaart-
  museum pp146–7 ⓬
Verzetsmuseum ⓯

Historic Buildings and Structures
Amstelsluizen ⓮
Entrepotdok ❽
De Gooyer Windmill ❿
Muiderpoort ❾

Sights of Scientific Interest
Aquarium ❼
Artis ❹
Planetarium ❻

Botanical Gardens
Hortus Botanicus Amsterdam ❶

Theatres
Koninklijk Theater Carré ⓭

GETTING THERE
Trams 9 and 14 pass Artis and Hortus Botanicus; buses 22 and 32 stop at the Scheepvaartmuseum. Weesperplein metro station is located in the southwest of Plantage. It can be intimidating at night, so use the nearby Waterlooplein station.

KEY

| Street-by-Street map See pp140–41 |
| Bus stop |
| Tram stop |
| Metro station |
| Museum boat boarding point |

0 metres   250
0 yards   250

◁ Replica of the *Amsterdam*, an East Indiaman, moored alongside the Scheepvaart Museum

Street-by-Street: Plantage

Elephant from Artis zoo

With its wide, tree-lined streets and painted, sandstone buildings, the Plantage is a graceful and often overlooked part of the city. Though it seems like a quiet part of town, there is a lot to see and do. The area is dominated by the Artis complex. It has a diverse range of popular attractions which can get very busy on sunny days. The area has a strong Jewish tradition, and several monuments commemorate Jewish history in Amsterdam, including a basalt memorial in the Hollandsche Schouwburg. The cafés of the Entrepotdok offer a pleasant setting for a relaxing coffee, within earshot of the zoo.

De Burcht (Vakbondsmuseum)
Inspired by an Italian palazzo, its museum displays trade-union memorabilia ❷

PLANTAGE PARKLAAN

PLANTAGE KIRKLAAN

Planetarium
Part of the Artis complex, the domed Planetarium explores man's relationship with the stars. Interactive displays show the positions of the planets ❻

Moederhuis,
Aldo van Eyck's refuge for pregnant women, has a colourful, modern façade intended to draw people inside.

★ **Hortus Botanicus Amsterdam**
The old glasshouses have been restored, and this new one put up to hold tropical and desert plants ❶

STAR SIGHTS

★ Artis

★ Hollandsche Schouwburg

★ Hortus Botanicus Amsterdam

★ **Hollandsche Schouwburg**
Little remains of this former theatre, now a sombre monument to the deported Jews of World War II ❸

Entrepotdok
This was the largest warehouse development in Europe during the 19th century. It has been redeveloped and transformed into an attractive quayside housing, office and leisure complex ⑧

LOCATOR MAP
See Street Finder maps 5 & 6

★ **Artis**
More than 5,000 species, including a variety of reptiles, live in the zoo complex, which occupies a beautifully laid out garden site ④

Geologisch Museum
This updated exhibition covers planet earth, dinosaurs and fossils ⑤

Artis restaurant

MIDDENLAAN

St Jacob's incorporates the stone portal from an old peoples' home formerly on this site.

| 0 metres | 100 |
| 0 yards | 100 |

Aquarium
The fine Neo-Classical building is home to thousands of aquatic species, ranging from tiny, fluorescent tropical fish to gigantic, European moray eels ⑦

Tropical plants in the Hortus Botanicus

Hortus Botanicus Amsterdam ❶

Plantage Middenlaan 2. **Map** 6 D2.
Tel 625 8411. 🚋 9, 14.
Ⓜ Waterlooplein. ◯ 9am–5pm
Mon–Fri; 10am–5pm Sat, Sun &
public hols (to 7pm Jul–Aug, to 4pm
Dec–Jan). ● 1 Jan, 25 Dec. 🎥 📷
♿ 📷 in English by arrangement.
🖥 📷 www.dehortus.nl

This botanical garden began
as a small apothecaries' herb
garden in 1682, and now
boasts one of the world's largest botanical collections. Its
range of flora expanded when
tropical plants were brought
back by the Dutch East India
Company *(see pp28–9)*. In
1706, it became the first place
outside Arabia to succeed in
cultivating the coffee plant.

The glass-domed Palm
House, built in 1912, contains
a 400-year-old cycad (palm
fern). Art shows with abotan-
ical theme are held here. The
restored Orangery has a museum, café and terrace and is
open for dinner July to August.

A modern glass and alu-
minium construction, designed
by Moshé Zwarts and Rein
Jansma, was opened in 1993
to make room for the tropical,
sub-tropical and desert plants.
There is also a butterfly house.

De Burcht ❷

Henri Polaklaan 9. **Map** 5 C2.
Tel 624 1166. 🚋 9, 14.
● under restoration. Check website
for information. 🎥 📷 ♿ 🖥 📷
www.deburcht.org

This red-brick crenellated
building, known locally as
"the castle", was designed
by HP Berlage *(see p79)* in
1900. It housed the head-
quarters of the General
Dutch Diamond Workers'

Union (ANDB) and
there is a small exhibi-
tion outlining the history
of the Dutch trade union
movement. Founded in
1894, the ANDB was
the first, largest and
wealthiest union in the
Netherlands.

The building has a
beautiful interior, with
murals by the socialist
artist Richard Ronald Holst of
the Amsterdam School
(see p97), and a spectacular
arched foyer. But the material
on show will be best enjoyed
by Dutch speakers.

Hollandsche Schouwburg ❸

Plantage Middenlaan 24. **Map** 5 C2.
Tel 531 0340. 🚋 9, 14. ◯ 11am–
4pm daily. ● Rosh Hashanah
(Jewish New Year), Yom Kippur. 📷
♿ www.hollandscheschouwburg.nl

Formerly a theatre, this is now
a memorial to the 104,000
Dutch Jewish victims of World
War II. Thousands of them

were detained here before
being deported to concentration camps. After the war, the
building was abandoned until
1962. A basalt column with a
base in the shape of the Star of
David was erected on the site
of the stage and behind it is
written: "To the memory of
those taken from here".

Following its restoration in
1993, the Hollandsche Schouwburg became an education
centre. On the ground floor, a
candle illuminates the names of
the war victims. Upstairs, there
is a permanent exhibition on
the persecution of the Jews in
the Netherlands from 1940–45.

Artis ❹

Plantage Kerklaan 38–40. **Map** 6
D2. **Tel** 0900 278 4796. 🚋 9, 14.
◯ 9am–5pm daily (Apr–Sep: to
6pm, Jul–Aug: till sunset). 🎥 📷 ♿
🍴 📷 11am Sat & Sun (Jun–
Aug: 6:30pm Sat). www.artis.nl

Artis is the oldest surviving
zoological complex in the
Netherlands. Since its inception

Decorative tiles on the staircase of the Vakbondsmuseum

Seals basking in their pool in Artis zoo complex

biologists have worked here and later the general public were allowed in to admire the collection of plants, trees and animals.

The complex has more than 5,000 animal species, as well as three greenhouses, the Planetarium, Geologisch Museum, Aquarium, Amfibarium, Insectarium and Zoölogisch Museum.

The zoo's attractions include big cats, giraffes, penguins, hippos and seals. It also contains a reptile house, nocturnal house, aviary, ape house, butterfly house and flamingo lake. African and South American habitats have been re-created.

Over the coming years, Artis is expanding its space, and the aviary and ape house are closed for restoration until 2011. There are also plans to restore the Groote Museum, a natural history museum currently in disrepair.

Geologisch Museum ❺

Plantage Kerklaan 38–40. **Map** 6 D2. **Tel** 523 3400. 🚊 9, 14. ⬜ 9am–5pm daily (Apr–Sep: to 6pm, Jul–Aug: till sunset). 📷 ♿ 📹

Located at the southwest corner of the Artis complex, the Geologisch Museum offers an entertaining introduction to planet earth. The admission charge is automatically covered by the entry ticket to Artis.

The first gallery on the ground floor is devoted to the evolution of life on earth. Displays trace the gigantic leap from single-cell life forms, via

dinosaurs, to mammals. The second gallery on the ground floor deals imaginatively with the interacting elements of the earth and the forces which control it. The gallery's central attraction is the Earth Machine, which features rotating components to represent the biosphere (the area inhabited by living things), hydrosphere (water), atmosphere (air) and geosphere (the earth's solid crust). Upstairs, there is an extensive display of fossils, minerals and stones.

Ammonite fossil at the Geologisch Museum

Planetarium ❻

Plantage Kerklaan 38–40. **Map** 6 D2. **Tel** 523 3400. 🚊 9, 14. ⬜ 9am–5pm daily (Apr–Sep: to 6pm, Jul–Aug: till sunset); shows every hour. 📷 ♿ 📹

Budding astronomers should not miss the show at the Planetarium, which takes place on the hour every hour. In this large, domed building a powerful projector reproduces the night sky and shows how the planets constantly change positions in relation to the constellations. Adult and children's programmes are shown alternately and, although the commentary is in Dutch, there are summaries in English, French and German.

Around the edge of the Planetarium, stellar and planetary systems are mapped out using

models, photographs, videos and push-button exhibits. There are also educational computer games and displays on exploration and astronomy.

Aquarium ❼

Plantage Kerklaan 38–40. **Map** 6 D3. **Tel** 523 3400. 🚊 9, 14. **Aquarium** ⬜ 9am–5pm daily (Apr–Sep: to 6pm, Jul–Aug: till sunset). **Zoölogisch Museum** ⬜ as above. 📷 ♿ 📹

Perhaps the best feature of the Artis complex is its Aquarium, which opened in 1882 in a grand Neo-Classical building. Mainly housed on the first floor, there are now four separate aquatic systems: one freshwater and three saltwater. Together they hold almost a million litres (220,000 gallons) of water. These tanks, each kept at a different temperature, contain almost 500 species of fish and marine animals that can be viewed at close quarters. They range from simple invertebrates to piranhas, sharks and massive marine turtles. Look out for the vivid coral fish and charming sea horses housed at the far end of the gallery.

The Amfibarium is housed in the basement of the Aquarium building. This hall contains a substantial collection of frogs, toads and salamanders in all shapes, sizes and colours.

The building also houses the small Zoölogisch Museum, which is as old as the park itself. The museum has a more academic flavour, and its exhibition halls hold temporary shows on such themes as the history of the dodo.

Tropical fish at the Aquarium, home to almost 500 marine species

Spout-gable façades of former warehouses along Entrepotdok

Entrepotdok ⑧

Map 6 D2. 🚋 9, 14, 22, 32.

The redevelopment of the old VOC *(see pp28–9)* warehouses at Entrepotdok has revitalized this dockland area. It was once the greatest warehouse area in Europe during the mid-19th century, being a customs-free zone for goods in transit. The quayside buildings of Entrepotdok are now a lively complex of offices, homes and eating places. Some of the original façades of the warehouses have been preserved, unlike the interiors, which have been opened up to provide an attractive inner courtyard. Café tables are often set out alongside the canal. On the other side, brightly coloured houseboats are moored side by side, and herons doze at the water's edge.

Muiderpoort ⑨

Alexanderplein. **Map** 6 E3. 🚋 7, 9, 10, 14. ◐ *to the public.*

Formerly a city gate, the Muiderpoort was designed by Cornelis Rauws in about 1770. The central archway of this Classical structure is topped with a dome and clock tower. Napoleon entered the city through this gate in 1811 and, according to legend forced the citizens to feed and house his ragged troops.

De Gooyer Windmill ⑩

Funenkade 5. **Map** 6 F2. 🚋 7, 10. ◐ *to the public.*

Of the six remaining windmills within the city's boundaries, De Gooyer, also known as the Funenmolen, is the most central. Dominating the view down the Nieuwevaart, the mill was built around 1725, and was the first corn mill in the Netherlands to use streamlined sails.

It first stood to the west of its present site, but the Oranje Nassau barracks, built in 1814, acted as a windbreak, and the

The grand dome and clock tower of the Muiderpoort

mill was then moved piece by piece to the Funenkade. The octagonal wooden structure was rebuilt on the stone foot of an earlier water-pumping mill, demolished in 1812.

By 1925, De Gooyer was in a very poor state of repair and was bought by the city council, which fully restored it. Since then, the lower part of the mill, with its neat thatched roof and tiny windows, has been a private home, though its massive sails still creak into action sometimes. Next to the mill is the IJ brewery *(see p48)*, one of two independent breweries in the city.

Museum 't Kromhout ⑪

Hoogte Kadijk 147. **Map** 6 D1. **Tel** 627 6777. 🚋 9, 10, 14. 🚌 22, 32. 🚢 Oosterdok or Kattenburgergracht. ◐ 10am–3pm Tue. **www**.machinekamer.nl

The Museum 't Kromhout is one of the oldest working shipyards in Amsterdam, and is also a museum. Ships were built here as early as 1757. In the second half of the 19th century, production changed from sailing ships to steamships. As ocean-going ships got bigger, the yard, due to its small size, turned to building lighter craft for inland waterways. It is now used only for restoration and repair work. The museum is largely dedicated to the history of marine engineering, concentrating on work carried out at the shipyard, with engines, maritime photographs and ephemera, and a well-equipped forge.

Werf 't Kromhout Museum and working shipyard

Nederlands Scheepvaartmuseum ⑫

See pp146–7.

Koninklijk Theater Carré ⑬

Amstel 115–125. **Map** 5 B3.
Tel 0900 252 5255. ⊞ 4, 7, 9, 10, 14. M Weesperplein.
Box office ◯ 4–9pm daily.
See **Entertainment** p246.
▨ ▨ 11am Sat (phone in advance). ⊘ ⴺ ⫟
www.theatercarre.nl

During the 19th century, the annual visit of the Carré Circus was a popular event. In 1868, Oscar Carré built wooden premises for the circus on the banks of the Amstel river. The city council considered the structure a fire hazard, so Carré persuaded them to accept a permanent building modelled on his other circus in Cologne. Built in 1887, the new structure included both a circus ring and a stage. The Classical façade is richly decorated with sculpted heads of dancers, jesters and clowns.

The Christmas circus is still one of the annual highlights at the theatre, but for much of the year the enlarged stage is taken over by concerts and big-show musicals, such as *The Sound of Music*, *Chicago* and *Mamma Mia*.

Amstelsluizen ⑭

Map 5 B3. ⊞ 4, 7, 9, 10, 14.
M Weesperplein.

The Amstelsluizen, a row of sturdy wooden sluice gates spanning the Amstel river, form part of a complex system of sluices and pumping stations that ensure Amsterdam's canals do not stagnate. Four times a week in summer the sluices are closed while fresh water from large lakes north of the city is allowed to flow into Amsterdam's canals. Sluices to the west of the city are left open, allowing the old water to flow, or be pumped, into the sea.

The Amstelsluizen date from the 18th century, and were operated manually until 1994, when they were mechanized.

Verzetsmuseum ⑮

Plantage Kerklaan 61. **Map** 6 D2.
Tel 620 2535. ⊞ 9, 14. ◯ 10am–5pm Tue–Fri, 11am–5pm Sat–Mon & public hols. ▨ 1 Jan, 30 Apr, 25 Dec. ▨ ⊙ ⴺ ▨ ▢ ⫟
www.verzetsmuseum.org

Carving on façade of Koninklijk Theater Carré

Previously based in a former synagogue in Nieuw Zuid (New South), now moved to this site in the Plantage, the Resistance Museum holds a fascinating collection of memorabilia recording the activities of Dutch Resistance workers in World War II. It focuses on the courage of the 25,000 people actively involved in the movement. On display are false documents, film clips, slide shows, photographs, weaponry and equipment.

By 1945 there were 300,000 people in hiding in the Netherlands, including Jews and anti-Nazi Dutch. Subsequent events organized by the Resistance, like the February Strike against deportation of the Jews *(see p35)*, are brought to life by exhibits showing where the refugees hid and how food was smuggled in. Voted the best historic museum in 2002 and 2003, it complements the Anne Frank Huis *(see p90)* perfectly.

Hermitage Amsterdam ⑯

Amstel 51. **Map** 8 E5. **Tel** 0900 437 648 243. ⊞ 4, 9, 14. M Waterlooplein. ◘ Muziektheater. ◯ 10am–5pm daily (to 8pm Wed) during exhibitions only. ▨ free for under 16s. ◗ 1 Jan, 30 Apr, 25 Dec. ⴺ ⫟ ▢ ▢ www.hermitage.nl

In the early 1990s the State Hermitage Museum in St Petersburg decided upon Amsterdam as the ideal city to open a branch of the Russian museum. This satellite museum would display rotating temporary exhibitions drawn from the Hermitage's rich collection.

The Hermitage Amsterdam opened in early 2004, in a side wing of the Amstelhof, with a spectacular exhibition of fine Greek gold jewellery from the 6th to the 2nd century BC. Other exhibitions have included the collection of the last Tsars Nicholas and Alexandra. The former old people's home has been fully restored and the Hermitage now occupies the whole complex, with two exhibition wings, an auditorium and a special children's wing.

The Neerlandia building in the Amstelhof, home of the Hermitage Amsterdam, overlooking De Nieuwe Herengracht canal

Nederlands Scheepvaartmuseum ⑫

Once the arsenal of the Dutch Navy, this vast Classical sandstone building was built by Daniel Stalpaert in 1656 round a massive courtyard. It was supported by 18,000 piles driven into the bed of the Oosterdok. The Navy stayed in residence until 1973, when the building was converted into the Netherlands Maritime Museum. The museum is under renovation until 2011, but the VOC ship *Amsterdam*, moored nearby, remains open, and part of the collection is on show at other locations.

Ornate 17th-century brass sextant

Ajax
This figurehead is from a ship built in 1832. It portrays Ajax, a hero of the Trojan War, who killed himself in despair when Achilles' armour was given to Odysseus.

First floor

★ The Orrery of Jan van den Dam *(1750)*
With a copper ball at its centre to represent the Sun, this is the oldest working orrery in the Netherlands.

MUSEUM GUIDE
The museum is currently arranged chronologically. The first floor covers the early maritime history of the Netherlands. The second floor spans merchant shipping from the 19th century to date, including technical developments. The museum is rearranging the exhibition. There will be three main themes aimed at children, families and those interested in naval history.

STAR EXHIBITS
★ Royal Barge

★ The Amsterdam

★ The Orrery of Jan van den Dam

Classical sandstone façade

Map of the World
This map of Asia forms part of a series of five published in the Netherlands in 1780. Too inaccurate for navigation, they were used as wall decorations.

Main entrance

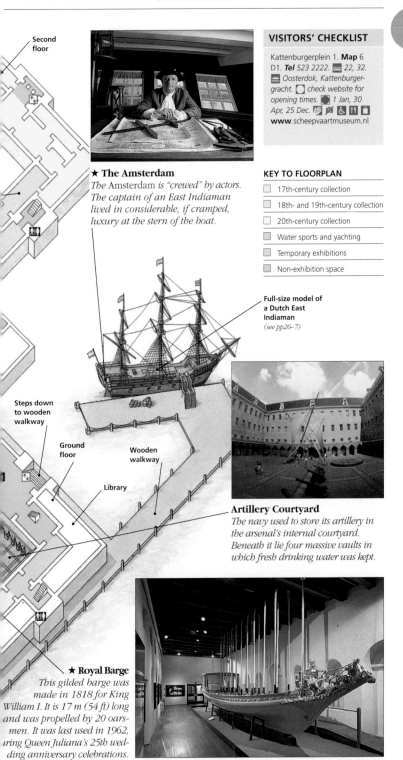

Second floor

VISITORS' CHECKLIST

Kattenburgerplein 1. **Map** 6
D1. **Tel** 523 2222. 🚌 22, 32.
🚊 Oosterdok, Kattenburgergracht. ⬭ check website for
opening times. ● 1 Jan, 30
Apr, 25 Dec. 📷 📵 ♿ 🍴 🛈 📷
www.scheepvaartmuseum.nl

★ The Amsterdam

The Amsterdam is "crewed" by actors.
The captain of an East Indiaman
lived in considerable, if cramped,
luxury at the stern of the boat.

KEY TO FLOORPLAN

☐ 17th-century collection

☐ 18th- and 19th-century collection

☐ 20th-century collection

☐ Water sports and yachting

☐ Temporary exhibitions

☐ Non-exhibition space

Full-size model of
a Dutch East
Indiaman
(see pp26–7)

Steps down
to wooden
walkway

Ground
floor

Wooden
walkway

Library

Artillery Courtyard

The navy used to store its artillery in
the arsenal's internal courtyard.
Beneath it lie four massive vaults in
which fresh drinking water was kept.

★ Royal Barge

This gilded barge was
made in 1818 for King
William I. It is 17 m (54 ft) long
and was propelled by 20 oars-
men. It was last used in 1962,
uring Queen Juliana's 25th wedding anniversary celebrations.

FURTHER AFIELD

Great architecture and good town planning are not confined to central Amsterdam. Parts of the Nieuw Zuid (New South) bear testament to the imagination of the innovative Amsterdam School architects *(see p97)* under the auspices of the Municipal Councils. Many fine buildings can be found in De Dageraad Housing complex and the streets around the Olympic Quarter. If you are seeking old-world charm, the historic small town of Ouderkerk aan de Amstel, nestling on the southern fringes of the

Sculpture on the fountain at Frankendael

city, prides itself on being older than Amsterdam. There are also fine parks just a short tram ride from the city centre, which offer a whole host of leisure activities. Visitors can view the lakes, woods and parkland of the Amsterdamse Bos *(see pp34–5)* from the deck of an antique tram which tours the park from the Electrische Museumtramlijn. The more formal horticulture of the Amstelpark can be viewed aboard a miniature train. There is also a clutch of instructive museums to be found in the suburbs of Amsterdam.

SIGHTS AT A GLANCE

Historic Monuments, Buildings and Districts
De Dageraad Housing **5**
Frankendael **1**
Olympic Quarter **9**
Ouderkerk aan de Amstel **8**

Museums and Exhibition Halls
Amsterdam RAI **6**
Electrische Museumtramlijn **10**

Nemo Science Center Amsterdam **3**
Schiphol Airport **12**
Tropenmuseum see pp152–3 **2**

Parks and Gardens
Amstelpark **7**
Amsterdamse Bos **11**
Westerpark **4**

KEY

▨	Central Amsterdam
▨	Greater Amsterdam
✈	Airport
━	Major road
━	Minor road

0 kilometres   2

0 miles   2

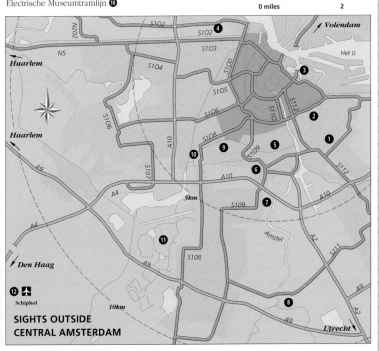

SIGHTS OUTSIDE CENTRAL AMSTERDAM

◁ Moored sailing boat on the river at Ouderkerk aan de Amstel

Frankendael **1**

Middenweg 72. **Map** 6 F5. 🚋 9.
🚌 41. **Restaurant Tel** 665 0880.
🕐 dawn–dusk.

During the early part of the
18th century, many of
Amsterdam's wealthier
citizens built country retreats
south of Plantage Middenlaan
on reclaimed land called the
Watergraafsmeer. The elegant
Louis XIV-style Frankendael is
the last survivor; the best
views of the ornamented
façade are from Middenweg.
This is also the best place to
view the fountain made by Ignatius van Logteren in 1714,
complete with reclining river
gods, in the front garden.

The formal gardens at the
back of the Frankendael are
open to the public. They
have been painstakingly reconstructed over the past few years
and now offer a peaceful refuge of shrubs and ancient
trees. The coach house has a
café-restaurant, Merkelbach.

**Ignatius van Logteren's fountain
in the grounds of the Frankendael**

Tropenmuseum **2**

See pp152–3.

The back of the Frankendael, with its well-tended formal gardens

Nemo Science Center Amsterdam **3**

Oosterdok 2. **Map** 2 F4. **Tel** 531
3233. 🚌 22, 42, 43. 🕐 10am– 5pm
Tue–Sun (daily during public hols).
⬤ 1 Jan, 30 Apr, 25 Dec. 🈳 🔒 📷
♿ 🔧 🚻 **www**.e-nemo.nl

In June 1997 Holland's
national science centre moved
to this dazzling curved building which protrudes 30 m (99
ft) over water. Nemo presents
technological innovations in
a manner which allows visitors' creativity full expression.
You can interact with virtual
reality, operate the latest
industrial equipment under
expert supervision and harness science to produce your
own art. The Centre is divided into five themed zones
(Interactivity, Technology,
Energy, Science and Humanity), each of which is
revamped every three years
to keep pace with scientific
evolution. Visitors – who in
this setting might equally
be termed explorers – can

Striking architecture of Nemo Science and Technology Centre

participate in games, experiments, demonstrations and workshops or take in lectures, films and even educational stage shows.

In July and August the roof is turned into a beach and visitors are welcome to bring picnics and enjoy the views.

Westerpark ❹

Haarlemmerweg 8–10. **Map** 1 A1.
🚊 *10.* 🚌 *21, 22, 46.* **Westergasfabriek** *Tel 586 0710.* **Museum Het Schip** Spaarndammerplantsoen 140. **Map** 1 B1. *Tel 418 2885.* ⬜ *11am–5pm Tue–Sun.* 📷 🎫 *hourly.* 🖥 *www.westergasfabriek.com; www.hetschip.nl*

The wasteland around Amsterdam's former gasworks (Westergasfabriek) was transformed into a 14-hectare park in the early 2000s. Facilities in this green area include playgrounds, bars and restaurants, and several performance spaces.

The gasworks itself has been redeveloped and is being rented out to various associations that organize festivals, performances and exhibitions. The Westergasfabriek is now the city's foremost cultural destination.

Nearby is Het Schip (The Ship), one of the most iconic buildings by the Amsterdam School *(see p97)*. Designed by Michel de Klerk in 1919, this apartment block contains 102 homes and the Museum Het Schip, displaying a restored working-class house.

Het Schip, a standard of the Amsterdam School

De Dageraad Housing ❺

Pieter Lodewijk Takstraat. 🚊 *4, 12, 25.* ⚫ *to the public.*

One of the best examples of Amsterdam School architecture *(see p97)*, De Dageraad housing project was developed for poorer families following the revolutionary Housing Act of 1901 by which the city council was forced to condemn slums and rethink housing policy in Amsterdam.

Socialist architect HP Berlage *(see p79)* drew up ingenious plans for the suburbs, aiming to integrate rich and poor by juxtaposing their housing. After Berlage's death, Piet Kramer and Michel de Klerk of the Amsterdam School adopted his ideas. Between 1918 and 1923, they designed this complex for a housing association known as De Dageraad (the Dawn).

They used a technique called "apron architecture" in which an underlayer of concrete allows for tucks, folds and rolls in the brick exterior, which was then subtly coloured and interspersed with decorative doors and windows. Each house mirrors the one opposite and there is a corner tower at the end of every block. The façades of the buildings were designed to give the impression of horizontal movement, an effect which is produced by the streamlined windows and the undulating roofs.

Amsterdam RAI ❻

Europaplein. *Tel 0900 267 8373.* 🚊 *4.* Ⓜ 🚉 *RAI.* 🚌 *62, 65.* ⬜ *depending on exhibition.* 📷 🚫 ♿ *with assistance.* **www**.rai.nl

Amsterdam RAI is one of the largest exhibition and conference centres in the country. It hosts more than a thousand events annually, from cabaret to horse shows and trade fairs.

The first Amsterdam trade fair was a bicycle exhibition held in 1893. Subsequent shows included cars and became an annual event known as the "RAI" (Rijwiel Automobiel Industrie). The present complex on Europaplein opened in 1961. It has undergone several extensions since then and has 11 exhibition halls, 48 congress halls and seven restaurants. The spectacular Elicium Expo foyer was opened in 2010.

Imposing corner block of De Dageraad public housing

Tropenmuseum ❷

Built to house the Dutch Colonial Institute, this vast complex was finished in 1926 by architects MA and JJ Nieukerken. The exterior is decorated with symbols of imperialism, such as stone friezes of peasants planting rice. When the building's renovation was completed in 1978, the Royal Tropical Institute opened a museum, with a huge central hall and three levels of galleries. The institute's aims are to study and to help improve the lives of the indigenous populations of the tropics. The displays reflect this, focusing on development issues regarding daily life, education and colonization.

Moroccan Bride
The gold embroidery is one of the most remarkable aspects of this Moroccan wedding dress.

★ **Pustaha – Book of Divinations**
Made of wood and tree bark, this volume contains prescriptions applied by the village healer-priest.

Great hall

★ **Bisj Poles**
The roots of massive mangrove trees were used to make these exotic, painted ritual totem poles from New Guinea.

GALLERY GUIDE

Temporary exhibitions are held in the Great hall on the ground floor. On the upper floors, the permanent exhibitions combine static and interactive displays covering diverse topics. The shop on the ground floor has a wide range of gifts and in the basement are a restaurant, café and theatre.

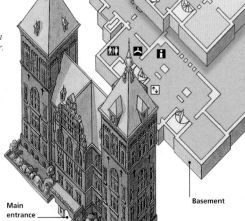

Basement

Main entrance

STAR EXHIBITS

- ★ Bisj Poles
- ★ Diorama
- ★ Pustaha – Book of Divinations

Second floor

Park Hall

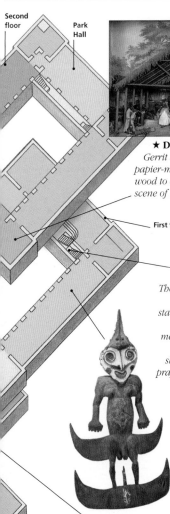

★ **Diorama** (1819)
Gerrit Schouten used papier-mâché and painted wood to create this colourful scene of life in Surinam.

First floor

Javanese Stone Friezes

The stone friezes decorating the main stairs are copies from a Javanese monument from about AD 800. This section shows two Buddhas praying under ornate temple awnings.

Wooden Hook

This wooden hook is carved in the shape of a naked male figure wearing a tribal mask. The item comes from New Guinea, in the South Pacific.

KEY TO FLOORPLAN

- 🟦 SE Asia & Textiles in Indonesia
- 🟦 W Asia & N Africa
- 🟦 Latin America & the Carribean
- 🟦 Man & the Environment
- 🟦 Music, Dance & Theatre
- 🟦 Africa
- 🟦 Dutch Colonialism
- 🟦 Dutch New Guinea
- 🟦 Tropenmuseum Junior
- 🟦 Temporary exhibition space
- 🟦 Non-exhibition space

Jeepney

Old army trucks left behind by the Americans after World War II are used as taxibuses, or jeepneys, in Manila, in the Philippines. The one housed here is a typically colourful example.

Amstelpark's Rieker windmill

Amstelpark ❼

Europaboulevard. 🚋 *4.* Ⓜ 🚉 *RAI.*
🚌 *62.* ⭘ *dawn–dusk.*

Situated in the suburb of Buitenveldert, southwest of Amsterdam, this large park was created in 1972. Among its attractions are a rose garden, rhododendron walk and model garden with nursery.

The park offers good facilities for children, including a playground, pony rides, mini-golf and mini-football. The well-preserved Rieker windmill (1636) stands at the southern tip of the park, and art exhibitions are held in the Glazen Huis (Glass House) and the Papillon Gallery. From Easter to October, you can tour the park in a miniature train.

Ouderkerk aan de Amstel ❽

Ⓜ 🚉 *Bijlmer.* 🚌 *175 & 300 from Bijlmer station.* **Wester Amstel Garden** ⭘ *mid-Apr–mid-Oct: 10am–8pm daily; mid-Oct–mid-Apr: 10am–4pm daily.*

This pretty village at the junction of the Amstel and the Bullewijk rivers has been a favourite with Amsterdammers since the Middle Ages. They had no church of their own until 1330 *(see pp66–7)*, and worshippers had to travel to the 11th-century Ouderkerk that gave the village its name. The Old Church was destroyed in a tremendous storm in 1674, and a fine 18th-century church now stands on its site. Opposite is the Beth Haim Jewish cemetery, where more than 27,000 Jews from Amsterdam have been buried since 1615. The elders of the Jewish community bought this land to use as a burial ground because Jews were forbidden to bury their dead inside the city.

Today Ouderkerk aan de Amstel is popular with cyclists who come to enjoy the ambience of its waterfront cafés and restaurants. The skyline is dominated by the 50-m (160-ft) spire of the Urbanuskerk, a Catholic church designed by PJH Cuypers *(see pp32–3)*

and consecrated in 1867. A short walk upriver along Amsteldijk, there are two 18th-century country houses. There is no access to the first, but the wooded garden of the second, Wester Amstel (built in 1720), is open to the public.

Olympic Quarter ❾

🚋 *16, 24.* 🚌 *15, 62, 142, 144, 170, 172, 197, 370.*

Development of the western side of the Nieuw Zuid (New South) began during the run up to the Olympic Games, held here in 1928. Many of the streets and squares were given Grecian names, like Olympiaplein and Herculesstraat.

The Stadium was designed by J Wils and C van Eesteren. Its stark vertical lines and soaring torch tower recall the work of the American architect Frank Lloyd Wright. Once threatened with demolition, it has now been renovated.

The sturdy bridge across the Noorder Amstel Kanaal at Olympiaplein is typical Amsterdam School design. It is the work of PL Kramer and the sculptor H Krop. Beyond the bridge, the Amsterdams Lyceum (a secondary school) shows the style at its best.

The peaceful waterfront at Oudekerk aan de Amstel, south of Amsterdam

Pedalos on a lake in the Amsterdamse Bos

Electrische Museumtramlijn ⑩

Amstelveenseweg 264. **Tel** 673 7538. 🚋 16. 🚌 15, 62, 142, 145, 170, 172, 197, 370. ⏰ Easter–Oct: 11am–5pm Sun. 🎫 📷 www.museumtramlijn.org

Not a museum, as the name suggests, but a tram ride that operates from Haarlemmermeerstation and the southern tip of the Amsterdamse Bos. The

Classic tram from the Museumtramlijn

tramcars, which date from 1910 to 1950, come from all over the Netherlands, Vienna, Prague and Berlin. The fleet is run by a group of enthusiasts along traditional lines and cars depart regularly from either terminus. A one-way journey takes about 20 minutes and provides a good view of the Olympic Stadium.

Amsterdamse Bos ⑪

Amstelveenseweg. 🚋 Electrische Museumtramlijn (see entry 10). 🚌 142, 166, 170, 171, 172. **Theatre Tel** 643 3286. www.bostheater.nl

This woodland park is the largest recreational area in Amsterdam. It was laid out in the 1930s in a bid to reduce unemployment in the city (see p35). Extensive wooded areas, interspersed with grassy meadows, lakes, waterways

and even a hill, were created on reclaimed land that lies 3 m (13 ft) below sea level. The park was enlarged periodically until 1967, when it reached its present size of more than 800 ha (2,000 acres).

Today, the marshy areas around Nieuwe Meer and the lakes at Amstelveense Poel and Kleine Poel are nature reserves. Other highlights include an animal enclosure, a goat farm, the Vogeleiland botanical gardens and the Bosmuseum, with its exhibits on the natural and social history of the park.

Among the facilities are an extensive network of planned walks, cycle paths and bridle ways, as well as water sports and an open-air theatre (see p245) during the summer.

Schiphol Airport ⑫

Evert van Beekstraat 202. **Tel** 0900 0141. 🚆 Schiphol Airport. www.schiphol.nl

Attracting over 120,000 people each day, this modern, forward-thinking airport (official name: Amsterdam Airport Schiphol) is one of the world's most efficient and user-friendly, with different colour-coded signs to help visitors navigate around this huge area (see pp266–7).

The airport has a wide variety of exciting extras to help pass the time while waiting for a flight. In 2002, an annex of the Rijksmuseum was opened on Holland Boulevard at Schiphol airport, where a small selection of classic works of art are on show. The museum is situated beyond passport control, and entrance is free to everyone with a boarding pass.

The airport also boasts a small casino between gates E and F (open from 6:30am to 7:30pm) to help pass the time, as well as a haven for the sore and weary traveller in the form of a chair massage.

The "Silence Centre", is open between 9am and 5pm. This is a place of worship for all religions, or simply a place for quiet contemplation.

In addition to the vast number of shops, bars and restaurants there is also a Panorama Terrace offering great views of the aircraft.

The entrance to Amsterdam's modern Schiphol Airport

TWO GUIDED WALKS

Many of Amsterdam's most important historical landmarks, and several fine examples of 16th- and 17th-century architecture, can be enjoyed on both of these walks. The first takes the visitor through the streets of the Jordaan, a peaceful quarter known for its narrow, pretty canals, houseboats and traditional architecture. The route winds through to the man-made Western Islands of Bickerseiland, Realeneiland and Prinseneiland, built in the 17th century to accommodate the expansion in Amsterdam's overseas trade. The area, with its rows of warehouses

**Wall plaque at
No. 6 Zandhoek**

and wharves, is a reminder of the city's erstwhile supremacy at sea. The city's maritime heritage is also evident on the second walk, which starts off from the Schreierstoren, where women waved their husbands off to sea in the 17th century, and finishes at the Nederlands Scheepvaart Museum. On the way, the walk passes the original city boundaries, countless converted warehouses and along streets named after the spices brought in by the East India Company (VOC). On any weekday, there is also the opportunity to spend a few pleasurable hours browsing round the Waterlooplein flea market.

**A Two-Hour Walk along the
Historic Waterfront** *(see pp160–61)*

**A Walk around the
Jordaan and Western
Islands** *(see pp158–9)*

**Houses on the Amstel near the
Stopera** *(see pp160–61)*

KEY

• • • Walk route

0 kilometres   1

0 miles   0.5

The Drieharingenbrug across Prinsengracht
(see pp158–9)

◁ View from the tower of the Westerkerk across the Jordaan, with Prinsengracht in the foreground

A Walk around the Jordaan and Western Islands

The Jordaan is a tranquil part of the city, crammed with canal houses, old and new galleries, restaurants, craft shops and pavement cafés. The walk route meanders through narrow streets and along enchanting canals. It starts from the Westerkerk and continues past Brouwersgracht, up to the IJ river and on to the Western Islands. These islands have now been adopted by the bohemian artistic community as a fashionable area to live and work.

Plaque on No. 8 Zandhoek, a former sailors' hostel

Prinsengracht to Westerstraat

Outside Hendrick de Keyser's Westerkerk ① *(see p90)* turn left up Prinsengracht, past the Anne Frank Huis ② *(see p90)*, and cross over the canal. Turn left down the opposite side of Prinsengracht and walk along Bloemgracht – the prettiest canal in the Jordaan. Before crossing the second bridge, look out for the three identical canal houses called the Drie Hendricken (the three Henrys) ③ *(see p91)*. Continue up 3e Leliedwarsstraat, with its cafés and old shops in the first half of the street, turn right and walk past the St Andrieshofje ④, one of the numerous well-preserved almshouses in the city. It is worth pausing to take a look across Egelantiersgracht at No. 360, a rare example of an Art Nouveau canal house.

Follow the bank to the end, turn left on to Prinsengracht, passing the Café't Smalle, and turn left into Egelantiersstraat. In 1e Egelantiersdwarsstraat can be found a group of 17th-century almshouses, known as

the Claes Claeszhofje ⑤ *(see p92)*. Follow this tiny street past several cafés as well as many unusual shops selling clothes, bric-a-brac, pottery and paintings, to Westerstraat.

Simple wooden gable with hoisting hook on Westerstraat

Westerstraat to Bickerseiland

Cross the street – Westerstraat originally bordered a canal, now filled in – and turn right. The gabled houses are typical of the late-17th-century style of the Jordaan. Walk along for one block and take the first left into 1e Boomdwarsstraat, then right to the Noorderkerk ⑥ *(see p92)*. Each Monday morning, a lively flea market takes place in the Noordermarkt *(see p92)*. Continue on to the south side of the

Lindengracht. To the left, at Nos. 149–163, is the Suyckerhofje ⑦, a former refuge for abandoned women. Turn right and you will pass a wall plaque on No. 55 Lindengracht depicting fish swimming in trees and echoing an inverted view of houses reflected in the city's canals. The statue on Lindengracht is of the writer and educationalist, Theo Thijssen. Turn left down Brouwersgracht *(see p93)*, which is lined with colourful houseboats. Cross the first lift bridge and go into Binnen Oranjestraat, then under the railway bridge on to Bickerseiland, which is named after one of the city's most wealthy 17th-century families.

Ornate step gables (1642) at Nos. 89 and 91 Bloemgracht

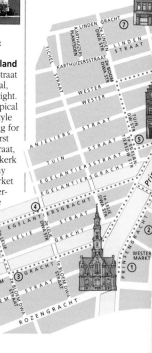

KEY

••• Walk route

0 metres   200

0 yards   200

A view of houseboats and gabled houses from Galgenstraat ⑨

The Western Islands

The Western Islands are made up of Bickers-, Prinsen- and Realeneiland *(see p93)*. They were created in the early 17th century to cope with the city's need for warehouses as a result of Amsterdam's maritime trading success. Their quays were lined with ships, while sailors and dockworkers lived in nearby canal houses.

Cross the Hendrik Jonkerplein ⑧ and go on to Bickersgracht where the boatyards are still operational. The first bridge to the left leads on to Prinseneiland and then into Galgenstraat (gallows street) ⑨, so called because the view from here in the 17th century was of the gallows across the IJ. Turning right, follow the bend and cross the wooden drawbridge on to Realeneiland. Turn right along Realengracht, take the first left, then right into Jan Mensplein and through to Taanstraat, first looking back along Vierwindenstraat where there stands a series of sombre old warehouses, once used for storing grain, hemp and flax. At the end, turn right down Zandhoek (sand corner) ⑩ *(see p93)*, with its rows of charming 17th-century houses. The name originates from the sand market which once took place here.

Follow Zandhoek and cross the wooden bridge (a 1983 replica of the original). Stay on the canal and follow the footpath that runs along Bickersgracht. Keep your eyes on the water and you might see a blue-grey heron looking for fish. Walk along Grote Bickersstraat and you will find yourself back where you started, at the bridge leading on to Prinseneiland. To leave the islands and return to the city centre, retrace your steps to Haarlemerdijk and turn left.

TIPS FOR WALKERS

Starting point: *Outside the Westerkerk on the Prinsengracht.*
Length: *4.5 km (2.8 miles).*
Duration: *One and a half hours.*
Getting there: *Buses 142, 144, 170 and 172. Trams 13 and 17 from Centraal Station.*
Stopping-off points: *The Jordaan is packed with cafés and bars. On the Egelantiersgracht, 't Smalle is particularly atmospheric and there are bars in Noordermarkt, Haarlemmerdijk and Hendrik Jonkerplein. De Gouden Reaal in Zandhoek is ideal to rest in before the trip home.*

The tranquil, tree-lined Egelantiersgracht

A Two-Hour Walk along the Historic Waterfront

Begin the walk at the Schreierstoren *(see p67)*, once a defence tower in the medieval town wall. The route follows the development of Amsterdam as a great trading city, as wharves, warehouses and houses were built to accommodate the boom in overseas trade and in population. The city's expansion was carefully planned; as existing waterfronts became overcrowded, more islands were created to the east, slowly reclaiming the surrounding marshy countryside. The walk takes in a number of reminders of the Dutch East India Company (VOC) *(see pp28–9)*, such as the streets named after spices, and ends up at the imposing Nederlands Scheepvaart Museum.

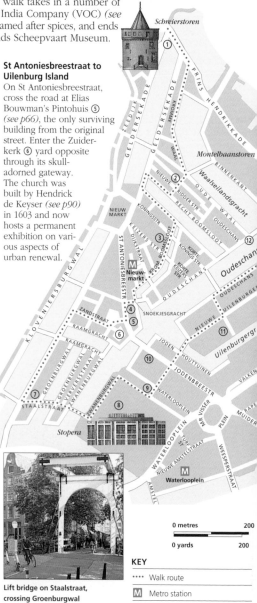

16th-century stone tablet near the main door, Schreierstoren ①

St Antoniesbreestraat to Uilenburg Island

On St Antoniesbreestraat, cross the road at Elias Bouwman's Pintohuis ⑤ *(see p66)*, the only surviving building from the original street. Enter the Zuiderkerk ⑥ yard opposite through its skull-adorned gateway. The church was built by Hendrick de Keyser *(see p90)* in 1603 and now hosts a permanent exhibition on various aspects of urban renewal.

Gables and façades along the right bank of Krommewaal

Schreierstoren to St Antoniesbreestraat

From the Schreierstoren ①, walk along Prins Hendrikkade, turning at Kromme Waal and following the right bank, with its series of rich façades and gables, to Lastageweg ②. Lastage is an area which was developed for trade after the fire of 1452 *(see p23)*. The expansion which followed in the 16th century *(see p25)* brought Lastage within the city walls.

Continue to Rechtboomssloot and turn right and keep going until you reach Geldersekade, one of the town boundaries in the 15th century. Follow along Recht Boomssloot, then along the side of Krom Boomssloot, until you see the Schottenburch warehouses ③ at Nos. 18–20. Built in 1636, these are among the oldest in the city and are now converted into apartments. Next door is an Armenian church, converted from a warehouse in the mid-18th century. Then follow Snoekjesgracht, turning left into St Antoniesbreestraat ④.

Lift bridge on Staalstraat, crossing Groenburgwal

KEY

•••• Walk route

M Metro station

0 metres   200
0 yards   200

Cross the square and continue to Zandstraat. Continue on to Kloveniersburgwal and turn left along the canal on to Staalstraat, where another left turn takes you past the Saaihal ⑦ (the draper's hall), with its unusual trapezoid gable. The first bridge crosses the Groen-burgwal, with splendid views of the Amstel to the right and Zuider-kerk to the left. The next bridge leads to the Stopera ⑧ (see p63), and Water-looplein flea market ⑨ (see p63). Follow the market stalls and half way along turn left towards Jodenbreestraat,

Wall plaque at Museum Het Rembrandthuis

transformed since it was the heart of Jewish Amsterdam. To the left on Jodenbreestraat is the Museum Het Rembrandthuis ⑩ (see p62). Cross the road and continue on to Nieuwe Uilenburgerstraat and on to the island of Uilenburg, built in the late 16th century to take housing for the poor. On the right can be seen the vast Gassan Diamonds factory ⑪, with two syna-gogues in the yard, a reminder of the time when diamond polish-ing was one of the few trades open to Jews (see p64).

Uilenburg to the Eastern Islands

Turn left into Nieuwe Batavierstraat and then right at Oude Schans, a broad canal with former warehouses and quays full of eccentric-looking

The 16th-century Montelbaans-toren, part of the city defences ⑫

reach Peperstraat. Like other streets on these man-made islands, Peperstraat was named after a commodity imported by the VOC (see pp28–9) in the 17th century. From here, turn right on to the main road of Prins Hendrikkade and then into Nieuwe Foeliestraat. Turn left onto Rapenburg, then left again onto Rapenburger Plein. Take the bridge across Nieuwe Herengracht to the gateway of the Entrepotdok ⑬ (see p144). Turn left into Kadijk-splein, continue along Prins-Hendrikkade and across the Nieu-wevaart bridge from which you can see Daniel Stal-paert's Oosterkerk. Con-tinue on to the Eastern Islands, built in 1658 to create more shipyards. The Nederlands Scheepvaart Museum ⑭ (see pp146–7) dominates the Oosterdok to the left. To return to the centre, follow Prins Hendrikkade westwards.

Oosterdok

Oosterdok

Scheepvaart Museum

houseboats. On the opposite bank of the canal is the Mont-elbaanstoren ⑫ (see p66), an old defence tower. At the bend, cross over the Rapenburgwal bridge until you

TIPS FOR WALKERS

Starting point*: The Schreierstore-non Prins Hendrikkade.*
Length*: 6 km (4 miles).*
Duration*: 2 hours.*
Getting there*: Some buses go along Prins Hendrikkade, but it is easier to take a tram to Centraal Station (see p79) and walk along the IJ. To pick up the walk halfway, trams 9 & 14 go to Waterlooplein.*
Stopping-off points*: There are brown cafés (see pp 48 and 236) along the start of the walk and at the Stopera (see p63). There are also bars on Schippersgracht and within the Entrepotdok.*

Antiques and bric-a-brac at Waterlooplein flea market ⑨

Tulips in full bloom in the Bloembollenstreek, near Leiden ▷

BEYOND AMSTERDAM

BEYOND AMSTERDAM

Amsterdam is at the heart of a region known as the Randstad, the economic powerhouse of the Netherlands. The city is a haven for tourists; within easy reach are the ancient towns of Leiden and Utrecht, as well as Den Haag and Haarlem with their exceptional galleries and museums. The Randstad extends south as far as Rotterdam, a thriving modern city full of avant-garde architecture.

Much of the land comprising the Randstad has been reclaimed from the sea during the last 300 years, and the fertile soil is farmed intensively. Production is centred around early season greenhouse crops, like tomatoes and cucumbers and the incomparable Dutch bulbs. Spreading to the southwest in spring, dazzling colours carpet the fields, and the exquisite gardens at Keukenhof *(see p 181)* are the showcase of the bulb industry.

Reclamation continues apace, and Flevoland, the Netherlands' newest province, consists entirely of polder. This flat marshy land, interspersed with drainage channels, has been created since 1950 by draining 1,800 sq km (695 sq miles) of the IJsselmeer. The flat terrain provides shelter for wild birds such as herons, swans and grebes, which nest along the reed-fringed canals. The area beyond Utrecht, to the east of Amsterdam, is much less populated than the Randstad, with vast tracts of unspoilt forest, moorland and peat bog, home to red deer and wild boar.

North of Amsterdam, the traditional fishing communities that depended on the Zuiderzee before it was closed off from the sea in 1932 *(see p170–71)*, have now turned to tourism for their income.

The coast round Zandvoort, lying to the west of Amsterdam, takes the full brunt of vicious North Sea storms in winter, but maritime vegetation and wild birds find shelter among the sandbanks of the exposed coastline.

Lift bridge and canalside café at Enkhuizen – a popular haunt for visitors to the Zuiderzee Museum

◁ Traditional working smock mills *(see p173)* at Zaanse Schans

Exploring the Netherlands

Amsterdam is at the centre of a part of the Netherlands where there are many places of interest within easy reach. Haarlem is just 15 minutes away, and it takes less than half an hour to get to the cheese markets of Edam and Gouda. To the north, the Zuiderzee Museum recreates an old fishing community, and to the south lies historic Utrecht. The east offers the wilderness of the Nationaal Park de Hoge Veluwe, and the stately Paleis Het Loo, a hunting lodge and summer residence of the Dutch royal family since 1692.

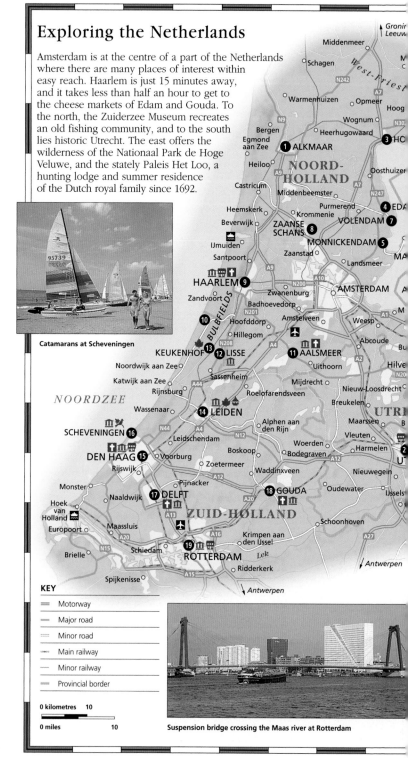

Catamarans at Scheveningen

Gronir
Leeuw
Middenmeer
Schagen
West-Friesl
N242
A7
Warmenhuizen
Opmeer
Hoog
N9
Wognum
N30
Bergen
Heerhugowaard
3 HC
Egmond
aan Zee
1 ALKMAAR
Heiloo
NOORD-
Oosthuizer
A9
HOLLAND
Castricum
Middenbeemster
N247
Heemskerk
Purmerend
4 EDA
Krommenie
Beverwijk
ZAANSE
SCHANS **8**
VOLENDAM **7**
IJmuiden
MONNICKENDAM **5**
Santpoort
Zaanstad
Zaandam
MA
Landsmeer
A10
HAARLEM **9**
Zwanenburg
N200
AMSTERDAM
Zandvoort
Badhoevedorp
Weesp
M
N201
Hoofddorp
Amstelveen
BULBFIELDS
10
Hillegom
Abcoude
Bu
N208
A4
A2
KEUKENHOF **13** **12** LISSE
11 AALSMEER
Hilve
Noordwijk aan Zee
Sassenheim
Uithoorn
N20
Katwijk aan Zee
Mijdrecht
Nieuw-Loosdrecht
A44
Rijnsburg
Roelofarendsveen
Breukelen
NOORDZEE
Wassenaar
UTR
14 LEIDEN
Alphen aan
den Rijn
Maarssen
B
N44
A4
N12
Vleuten
SCHEVENINGEN **16**
Leidschendam
Woerden
Harmelen
DEN HAAG **15**
Voorburg
Boskoop
Bodegraven
A12
Nieuwegein
Rijswijk
Zoetermeer
Waddinxveen
2
Monster
Pijnacker
A20
U
Hoek
van
Naaldwijk
17 DELFT
18 GOUDA
Oudewater
IJssels
Holland
A13
ZUID-HOLLAND
Europoort
Maassluis
Schoonhoven
A16
Brielle
Krimpen aan
A27
N15
den IJssel
Schiedam
19
Lek
Antwerpen
Spijkenisse
ROTTERDAM
Ridderkerk
A15
Antwerpen

KEY

═══	Motorway
───	Major road
┄┄┄	Minor road
╍╍╍	Main railway
───	Minor railway
━━━	Provincial border

0 kilometres 10

0 miles 10

Suspension bridge crossing the Maas river at Rotterdam

For additional map symbols *see back flap*

Traditional wooden fishing boats in the harbour at Hoorn

GETTING AROUND

Amsterdam sits at the hub of the Dutch transport system, with fast road and rail links to towns and cities throughout the Netherlands. The A9 and A7 motorways connect the capital with Alkmaar and Hoorn in Noord Holland, and a network of motorways and first-class roads cuts across the provinces to the south and east. It is not vital to have a car, as regular buses run to all major towns from Amsterdam, and the rail service, using modern double-decker trains, is even better. Cycling is the ideal way to take in the beauty of the spring bulbfields.

(Map showing: huizen, ZUIDERZEE MUSEUM, N302, rmeer, Groningen, Leeuwarden, Lelystad, A6, N302, FLEVOLAND, re-Buiten, Trekkersveld, Zuidelijk-Flevoland, N305, Harderwijk, Zwolle, Vaassen, A50, N301, A28, oten, Putten, PALEIS HET LOO 23, N344, arn, Nijkerk, Voorthuizen, Apeldoorn, Enschede, est, Hoevelaken, A1, GELDERLAND, Beekbergen, oort, A28, N312, Barneveld, Hoenderloo, esterberg, N30, Lunteren, Otterlo, A50, Eerbeek, N226, Scherpenzeel, NATIONALE PARK DE HOGE VELUWE 21, Ede, Dieren, A12, N224, Veenendaal, Bennekom, Velp, Neder Rijn, N225, Wageningen, Oosterbeek, ARNHEM 22, Düsseldorf, k bij stede, Elden, Duiven, A325, Eindhoven, Nijmegen)

**An elaborate
gabled façade in
Monnickendam**

SIGHTS AT A GLANCE

Children in national costume at the Zuiderzee Museum

Renaissance façade and bell tower of Alkmaar's Waaggebouw (1582)

Alkmaar **❶**

40 km (25 miles) NW of Amsterdam.
94,000. 🚉 ℹ️ *Waaggebouw,
Waagplein 2–3. (072) 511 4284.*
📅 🧀 *cheese market: Apr–Sep:
10am–12:30pm Fri; main market: Sat.*
www.vvvalkmaar.nl

Alkmaar is an attractive old
town with tree-lined canals
and an historic centre, scene
of an unsuccessful siege by
the Spanish in 1573. It is one
of the few Dutch towns to
maintain its traditional cheese
market, held every Friday in
summer. Local producers lay
out Gouda cheeses and some
rounds of Edam in the Waagplein, and from here porters
take them off on sledges for
weighing. The porters, who
sport colourful straw hats,
belong to an ancient guild

and indulge in good-natured
rivalry. The streets around the
Waagplein are packed with
stalls that sell everything from
cheese to locally made pottery.

🏛 Waaggebouw
Waagplein 2. **Tel** *(072) 511 4284.*
Hollands Kaasmuseum 🕐 *Easter–
Oct: 10am–4pm Mon–Sat.* 📷 ♿
www.kaasmuseum.nl
The focal point of the cheese
market is the imposing Waaggebouw (weigh house), which
was altered in 1576 from a
14th-century chapel. It
now contains the
Hollandse Kaas-
museum, where local
cheese-making techniques
are revealed. Each day on
the hour, mechanical
knights, under the clock of
the Waaggebouw, stage a
jousting tournament,
while a clarion blower
sounds his trumpet.

🔔 Grote Kerk
Kerkplein, Koorstraat 2.
Tel *(072) 514 0707.*
🕐 *Jun–Aug: 10am–5pm
Tue–Sat, 1–5pm Sun (and
during exhibitions).*
This imposing Gothic church
contains the tomb of Floris V
(see p21), whose body was
exhumed and brought here
when the building was completed in 1520. The 17th-century
organ, built after designs by
Jacob van Campen *(see p74)*
and painted by Cesar van
Everdingen, dominates the
Grote Kerk's nave.

Zuiderzee-museum **❷**

See pp170–71.

Hoorn **❸**

40 km (25 miles) N of Amsterdam.
68,000. 🚉 ℹ️ *Veemarkt 4. (072)
511 4284.* 📅 *Sat; mid-Jun–Aug: Wed
(for tourists).* **www**.vvvhoorn.nl

Hoorn was the capital of the
ancient province of West
Friesland and one of the
great seafaring towns of
the Golden Age *(see
pp26–9)*. The collection
of ornate patrician
houses around Rode
Steen, Hoorn's main
square, attests to the
town's prosperous
history. Several famous
maritime heroes were
born here, including
Willem Schouten
(1580–1625), who
named the tip of
South America
Cape Horn after
his birthplace, and
Abel Tasman *(see
pp28–9)*. A statue in Rode
Steen commemorates Jan
Pieterszu Coen (1587–1629), a
famous explorer who went on
to found Batavia, now known
as Jakarta, the capital of
Indonesia *(see pp28–9)*.

**Painted unicorn,
Westfries Museum**

🏛 Westfries Museum
Rode Steen 1. **Tel** *(0229) 280 022.*
🕐 *11am–5pm Tue–Fri (also Mon
Apr–Oct), 1–5pm Sat & Sun.* 🔴
*1 Jan, 30 Apr, 3rd Mon in Aug, 25
Dec.* 📷 **www**.wfm.nl
The building that houses the
Westfries Museum in Rode
Steen was built in 1632 as a
prison – the square takes its
name, "red stone", from the
blood spilt at executions there.
The three-tiered gable of
the building is decorated with
heraldic figures carrying the
coats of arms of the towns
that made up the province of
West Friesland. Inside the
museum, little has changed
since 1925, when writer Aldous
Huxley affectionately described
it as "filled with mixed rubbish".
There is much to enjoy here,
from archaeological displays to
17th-century rooms filled with
furniture and antique clocks.

Porters carrying cheese on sledges in Alkmaar's traditional market

Wooden clogs outside a restored fisherman's cottage in Monnickendam

Edam ❹

22 km (14 miles) N of Amsterdam.
🏠 7,200. 🚌 ℹ️ Damplein 1.
(0299) 315 125. 🧀 cheese market:
Jul–mid-Aug: 10:30am–12:30pm
Wed; general market: every Wed.
www.vvv-edam.nl

The name of Edam is known throughout the world for its ball-shaped cheeses wrapped in wax – red for export, and yellow for local consumption. In the summer, cheese lovers should head for the *kaasmarkt* (cheese market), held in the main square, which is called Jan van Nieuwenhuizenplein. The *kaasmarkt's* single-gabled weigh house dates from 1592 and has a gaudy painted façade. Cheese-making is now an automated process and some factories around the outskirts of the town offer guided tours for visitors.

Edam itself is exceptionally pretty, full of narrow canals bordered by elegant, gabled Golden Age canal houses and crossed by wooden lift bridges. The imposing Grote Kerk is noted both for its 16th-century carillon, and its outstandingly beautiful stained-glass windows (1606–24). The harbour to the east of the town was built in the 17th century, in the days when Edam was a prominent whaling centre.

🏛 Edams Museum
Damplein 8. **Tel** (0299) 372 644.
🕐 Apr–Oct: 10am–4.30pm
Tue–Sat, noon–4.30pm Sun. 🔵 30
Apr. 🖼 **www**.edamsmuseum.nl
This amazing Gothic building (1530) is home to an eccentric museum of local history. The

timbered interior and steep, narrow stairs look like the inside of a ship. The house is said to have been built for a retired sea captain who could not bear sleeping on dry land. The unusual floating cellar has a floor that rises and falls with fluctuations in the water table. Just as strange are the 17th-century portraits of odd-looking locals, such as Trijntje Kever, who was said to be almost 2.8 m (9 ft) tall.

Monnickendam ❺

16 km (10 miles) N of Amsterdam.
🏠 10,000. 🚌 🚆 Sat.
www.vvv-waterland.nl

Visitors flock to this beautifully preserved port to admire the gabled houses and the renovated fishermen's cottages in the narrow streets around the harbour. Freshly smoked local eel can be bought here, and the fish restaurants are a popular draw for tourists.

The **Museum de Speeltoren** is dedicated to the history of Monnickendam. It is housed in the clock tower of the Stadhuis, with its an ornate 15th-century carillon. When bells chime the hour, the clockwork knights in armour parade around the exterior of the tower.

🏛 Museum de Speeltoren
Noordeinde 4. **Tel** (0299) 652 203.
🔵 for restoration until end 2011.
Check the website for the latest information. 🖼
www.despeeltoren.nl

Lift bridge on one of the canals at Edam

Zuiderzeemuseum ❷

Enkhuizen was one of several villages around the edge of the Zuiderzee whose fishing-based economy was devastated when access to the North Sea was blocked by construction of the Afsluitdijk in 1932 *(see p165)*. The village's fortunes were revived with the opening of this museum complex. The Binnenmuseum (indoor museum) focuses on the Zuiderzee history, including an impressive display of historic boats. The Buitenmuseum (open air museum) consists of rescued buildings, reconstructed to create a typical Zuiderzee village, with demonstrations of local crafts.

★ **Houses from Urk**
Buildings from the little island of Urk have been rebuilt in the open air museum. Daily life on the island in 1905 is recreated by actors in role play.

Smoke-houses from Monnickendam

Reconstruction of Marken harbour

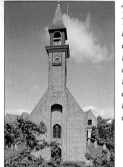

The Church
The builders of this late 19th-century church, from the island of Wieringen, disguised the organ in a cupboard to avoid the tax that was then levied on church organs.

★ **Marine Hall**
Housed in an old ware-house of the Dutch East India Company (see pp28–9), the indoor museum's Marine Hall contains sailing and fishing boats. A small pleasure boat is rigged up for children to play in.

Barges carry visitors to the open air museum.

Main entrance

Lime Kilns
Bottle-shaped kilns were used to burn shells dredged from the sea bed. The resulting quicklime was used as an ingredient in mortar for bricklaying. These kilns are from Akersloot in Noord Holland.

★ **Contemporary Delft blue design**
Modern Dutch culture is presented on traditional Delft blue tiles in this installation by Hugo Kaagman. Icons such as the Internet Explorer sign are scattered throughout the piece.

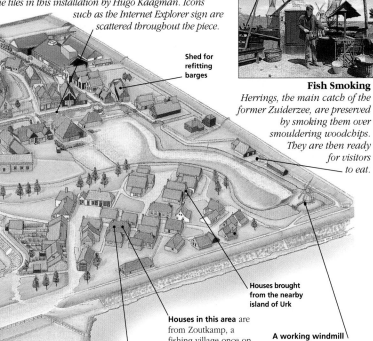

Shed for refitting barges

Fish Smoking
Herrings, the main catch of the former Zuiderzee, are preserved by smoking them over smouldering woodchips. They are then ready for visitors to eat.

Houses brought from the nearby island of Urk

Houses in this area are from Zoutkamp, a fishing village once on the Zuiderzee.

A working windmill shows how excess water was cleared from the dykes to create polders *(see pp24–5).*

```
0 metres        50
0 yards         50
```

Keeping House in 1930
This interactive exhibition allows you to experience Zuiderzee life in the 1930s. A "housewife" sits down with visitors and describes her daily life over a cup of tea.

STAR FEATURES

★ Houses from Urk

★ Marine Hall

★ Contemporary Delft blue design

Marken

16 km (10 miles) NE of Amsterdam.
🚶 *2,000.* 🚌 🚲 ℹ️ *Havenbuurt
19C. 0900 400 4040.* 🛒 *Sat.*
www.vvv-waterland.nl

Marken was once an island fishing community that had changed very little over 200 years. However, the construction of a causeway link between the village and the mainland in 1957 brought an abrupt end to its isolation.

The village is popular with tourists, who are drawn here by its old-world character. The locals sometimes wear traditional dress, and the gabled timber houses are painted in shades of black and green.

Marken's transition from fishing community to tourist centre is neatly symbolized by the **Marker Museum**, which consists of six historical houses, one of which is furnished as a traditional fisherman's abode.

🏛 Marker Museum
Kerkbuurt 44. *Tel (0299) 601 904.*
◻ *Apr–Sep: 10am–5pm daily
(from noon Sun); Oct: 11am–4pm
Mon–Sat, noon–5pm Sun.* 🎫

Yachts and pleasure boats in Volendam's marina

Volendam ❼

18 km (11.5 miles) NE of Amsterdam.
🚶 *21,000.* 🚌 ℹ️ *Zeestraat 37.
(0299) 363747.* 🛒 *Sat.*
www.vvv-volendam.nl

The harbour in Volendam is now overrun with tourists, but the village is still worth exploring for the narrow canals and streets behind the main dykes, an area known as the Doolhof. The residents wear traditional costume: tight bodices, winged lace caps and striped aprons for the women; baggy trousers and jerseys for the men.

Artists flocked to Volendam in the late 19th century to paint views of this pretty town. Many stayed at the Spaander Hotel at No. 15 Haven, and the walls of the hotel's café are covered with paintings accepted by the owners in lieu of payment.

Zaanse Schans ❽

Schansend 7, Zaandam 13 km
(8 miles) N of Amsterdam.
🚉 *Koog-Zaandijk.* 🚶 *50.*
ℹ️ *Zaandam. Tel (075) 681 0000.*
◻ *9am–5pm daily (some attractions
closed during the week in winter).*
🎫 *for some buildings and parking.*
www.zaanseschans.nl

Part of the town of Zaandam, Zaanse Schans was created in 1960 as a monument to village life in the 17th century. Shops, cottages, windmills, houses and historic buildings from all over the Zaan region have been relocated here to create a museum village in which people can live and work.

The local community is dedicated to preserving the traditional Dutch way of life, and Zaanse Schans is run as a piece of living history. The inhabitants operate the carefully restored windmills themselves; these include a mustard mill, the last working oil mill still in existence, and mills that generate power. The energy they produce goes to sawing logs for building timber, and to grinding minerals to make pigments used in paint.

In summer, cruises can be taken in open-topped boats along the surrounding dykes.

A typical 17th-century gabled timber house in Marken

Windmill Technology

Windmills have been a familiar feature of the Dutch landscape since the 13th century. They had many uses, including grinding corn, crushing seed to make oil and driving sawmills. However, as much of the Netherlands lies below sea level, their most vital function was to drain the land of lakes and marshes, and extend the shoreline to create fertile farmland called *polder*. Subsequently, the windmills have had to cope with the constant threat of flooding. To help prevent this, canals were dug to drain water from the soil; the mills then pumped excess water via a series of stepped canals until it drained into the main river system. Today, most land drainage is carried out by electric pumps driven by wind turbines. Of the thousands of windmills that once dotted the Dutch countryside, about 950 survive, many preserved in working order.

Miller in cap and apron

Modern aerogenerators, *or wind turbines, are widely used in the Netherlands. They harness strong gusts of wind to create electricity without the pollution caused by burning fossil fuels such as gas or coal.*

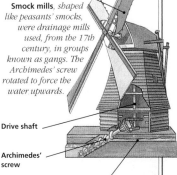

Trelliswork and canvas sail

Smock mills, *shaped like peasants' smocks, were drainage mills used, from the 17th century, in groups known as gangs. The Archimedes' screw rotated to force the water upwards.*

Drive shaft

Archimedes' screw

Upper channel

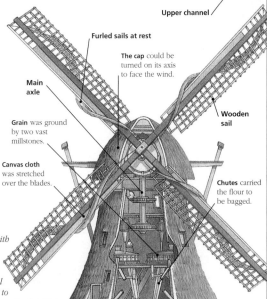

Furled sails at rest

The cap could be turned on its axis to face the wind.

Main axle

Grain was ground by two vast millstones.

Wooden sail

The sails *of this traditional windmill transmit power via mechanical gears. A rotating cog operates an adjacent wheel to drive the water pump.*

Canvas cloth was stretched over the blades.

Chutes carried the flour to be bagged.

Flour mills, *thatched with reeds and shaped like giant pepperpots, were vital to Dutch daily life. Sophisticated internal mechanisms were used to grind the wheat, barley and oats which formed the basis of the community's diet.*

Street-by-Street: Haarlem ❾

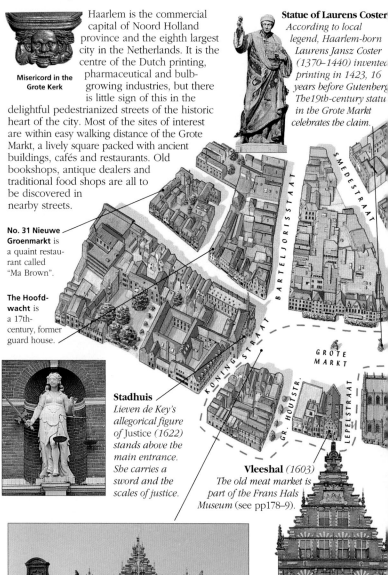

Misericord in the Grote Kerk

Haarlem is the commercial capital of Noord Holland province and the eighth largest city in the Netherlands. It is the centre of the Dutch printing, pharmaceutical and bulb-growing industries, but there is little sign of this in the delightful pedestrianized streets of the historic heart of the city. Most of the sites of interest are within easy walking distance of the Grote Markt, a lively square packed with ancient buildings, cafés and restaurants. Old bookshops, antique dealers and traditional food shops are all to be discovered in nearby streets.

Statue of Laurens Coster
According to local legend, Haarlem-born Laurens Jansz Coster (1370–1440) invented printing in 1423, 16 years before Gutenberg. The 19th-century statue in the Grote Markt celebrates the claim.

No. 31 Nieuwe Groenmarkt is a quaint restaurant called "Ma Brown".

The Hoofdwacht is a 17th-century, former guard house.

Stadhuis
Lieven de Key's allegorical figure of Justice (1622) stands above the main entrance. She carries a sword and the scales of justice.

Vleeshal *(1603)*
The old meat market is part of the Frans Hals Museum (see pp178–9).

Grote Markt
The tree-lined market square is bordered with busy pavement restaurants and cafés. It has been the meeting point for the townspeople for centuries.

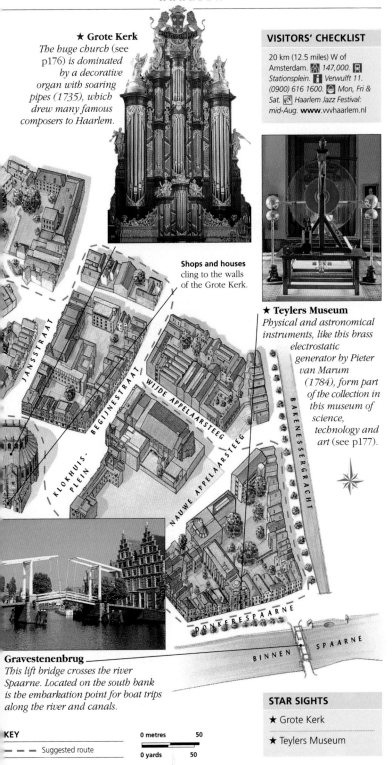

★ Grote Kerk
The huge church (see p176) is dominated by a decorative organ with soaring pipes (1735), which drew many famous composers to Haarlem.

Shops and houses cling to the walls of the Grote Kerk.

VISITORS' CHECKLIST

20 km (12.5 miles) W of Amsterdam. 147,000. Stationsplein. Verwulft 11. (0900) 616 1600. Mon, Fri & Sat. Haarlem Jazz Festival: mid-Aug. **www**.vvvhaarlem.nl

★ Teylers Museum
Physical and astronomical instruments, like this brass electrostatic generator by Pieter van Marum (1784), form part of the collection in this museum of science, technology and art (see p177).

JANSSTRAAT

BEGIJNESTRAAT

WIJDE APPELAARSTEEG

KLOKHUIS-PLEIN

NAUWE APPELAARSTEEG

BAKENESSERGRACHT

DONKERE SPAARNE

BINNEN SPAARNE

Gravestenenbrug
This lift bridge crosses the river Spaarne. Located on the south bank is the embarkation point for boat trips along the river and canals.

STAR SIGHTS

★ Grote Kerk

★ Teylers Museum

KEY

– – – Suggested route

0 metres 50
0 yards 50

Exploring Haarlem

Haarlem became a city in 1245, and had grown into a thriving clothmaking centre by the 15th century. But in the Spanish siege of 1572–3 the city was sacked, and a series of fires wreaked further destruction in 1576. The town's fortunes changed in the 17th century, when industrial expansion ushered in a period of prosperity lasting throughout the Golden Age *(see pp26–9)*. The centre was largely rebuilt by Lieven de Key (1560–1627) and still retains much of its character. The Grote Kerk continues to overlook the city's *hofjes* (almshouses), and the brick-paved lanes around the Grote Markt are little changed.

Grote Markt, Haarlem (c.1668) by Berckheyde, showing the Grote Kerk

🏛 Frans Hals Museum
See pp178–9.

🛉 Grote Kerk
Oude Groenmarkt 23. **Tel** (023) 553 2040. ◯ 10am–4pm Mon–Sat. ◉ 25 Dec–2 Jan, Easter, Whitsun, 5 May, 30 Apr. 🈲 ♿ **www**.bavo.nl
The enormous Gothic edifice of Sint Bavo's great church, often referred to simply as the Grote Kerk, was a favourite subject of the 17th-century Haarlem School artists Pieter Saenredam (1597–1665) and Gerrit Berckheyde (1639–98). Built between 1400 and 1550, the church and its ornate bell tower dominate the market square. Clinging on to the exterior of the south wall is a jumble of 17th-century shops and houses. The rents raised from these ramshackle, untidy buildings contributed to the maintenance of the church.

Today, the entrance to the Grote Kerk is through one of the surviving shops, a tiny ante-chamber that leads straight into the enormous nave. The church has a high, delicately patterned, vaulted cedarwood ceiling, white upper walls, and 28 supporting columns painted in greens, reds and golds. The intricate choir screen, like the magnificent brass lectern in the shape of a preening eagle, was made by master metal worker Jan Fyerens in about 1510. The choirstalls (1512) are painted with coats of arms, and the armrests and misericords are carved with caricatures of animals and human heads. Not far away is the simple stone slab covering the grave of Haarlem's most famous artist, Frans Hals.

The Grote Kerk boasts one of Europe's finest and most flamboyant organs, built in 1738 by Christiaan Müller. In 1740 Handel tried the organ and pronounced it excellent. It also found favour with the infant prodigy Mozart, who shouted for joy when he gave a recital on it in 1766. The organ is still often used for concerts, recordings and teaching.

🏛 Stadhuis
Grote Markt 2. **Tel** (023) 511 5115. ◯ by appt only. ♿
Haarlem's Stadhuis (town hall) has grown rather haphazardly over the centuries and is an odd mixture of architectural styles dating from 1250. The oldest part of the building is the beamed medieval banqueting hall of the counts of Holland *(see p21)*, originally known as the Gravenzaal. Much of this was destroyed in two great fires in 1347 and 1351, but the 15th-century panel portraits of the counts of Holland can still be seen.

The wing of the town hall bordering the Grote Markt was designed by Lieven de Key in 1622. It is typical of Dutch Renaissance architecture, combining elaborate gables, ornate painted detail and Classical features, such as pediments over the windows.

In a niche above the main entrance is a plump allegorical figure of Justice, bearing a sword in one hand and scales in the other as she smiles benignly upon the pavement cafés in the market below. To the left, in Koningstraat, an archway leads to the university buildings behind the Stadhuis, where there is a 13th-century cloister and library.

🏛 De Hallen (Vleeshal and Verweyhal)
Grote Markt 16. **Tel** (023) 511 5775. ◯ as Frans Hals Museum (p179). ◉ 1 Jan, 25 Dec. 🈲 **www**.dehallen.nl
De Hallen (the halls) is the collective name for two buildings in the Grote Markt which are part of the Frans Hals Museum *(see pp178–9)*. The more recent Verweyhal accommodates exhibitions of Dutch Expressionism, the Cobra School, Impressionism and contemporary works. It is named after the painter Kees Verwey, whose Impressionist still lifes are an important feature of the collection. The heavily ornamented Vleeshal (meat market) is situated just to the west of the church

Detail on Vleeshal façade by Lieven de Key

The west gate of the Amsterdamse Poort (1355)

and houses temporary exhibitions of modern art. It was built in 1602 by the city surveyor, Lieven de Key, and has a steep step gable which disguises the roof line. The extravagantly over-decorated miniature gables above each dormer window bristle with pinnacles. A giant painted ox's head on the building's façade signifies its original function.

Amsterdamse Poort

Nr Amsterdamsevaart. *to public.*
The imposing medieval gateway that once helped protect Haarlem lies close to the west bank of the river Spaarne. The Amsterdamse Poort was one of a complex of 12 gates guarding strategic transport routes in and out of Haarlem. The gate was built in 1355,

though much of the elaborate brickwork and tiled gables date from the late 15th century.

The city defences were severely tested in 1573, when the Spanish, led by Frederick of Toledo, besieged Haarlem for seven months during the Dutch Revolt *(see pp24–5)*. The city fathers agreed to surrender the town on terms that included a general amnesty for all its citizens. The Spanish appeared to accept, but once inside they slaughtered nearly 2,000 people – almost the entire population of the city.

Teylers Museum

Spaarne 16. **Tel** *(023) 516 0906.*
10am–5pm Tue–Sat, noon–5pm Sun & holidays. *1 Jan, 25 Dec.*
www.teylersmuseum.nl
This was first major public museum to be founded in the Netherlands. It was established in 1778 by the silk merchant Pieter Teyler van der Hulst to encourage the study of science and art. The museum's eccentric collection of fossils, drawings and scientific paraphernalia is displayed in Neo-Classical splendour in a series of 18th-century rooms. The two-storey Oval Hall was added in 1779, and contains bizarre glass cabinets full

Tiles in Haarlem Station

of minerals and cases of intimating medical instruments. A significant collection of sketches by Dutch and Italian masters are shown a few at a time. There is also a multimedia room.

Historisch Museum Haarlem

Groot Heiligland 47. **Tel** *(023) 542 2427.* *noon–5pm Tue–Sat, 1–5pm Sun.* *1 Jan, Easter, Whitsun, 25 Dec.* **www**.historischmuseum haarlem.nl
Haarlem is well known for its *hofjes* (almshouses) that were set up to minister to the poor and sick *(see p93)*. Almshouses began to appear in the 16th century, and were run by rich guild members, who took over the role traditionally filled by the monasteries until the Alteration of 1578 *(see pp24–5)*.

St Elisabeth's Gasthuis was built in 1610, around a pretty courtyard. A stone plaque carved above the main doorway in 1612 depicts an invalid being carried off to hospital. After extensive restoration, this almshouse was opened as Haarlem's principal historical museum.

Haarlem Station

Stationsplein. **Tel** *0900 92 92.*
The first railway line in the Netherlands opened in 1839 and ran between Haarlem and Amsterdam *(see pp32–3)*. The original station, built in 1842, was reworked in Art Nouveau style between 1905–8. It is a grandiose brick building with an arched façade and square towers. The green and beige interior is decorated with brightly coloured tiles depicting modes of transport. Other highlights include the timberwork of the offices.

17th- and 18th-century gabled houses along the river Spaarne in Haarlem

Frans Hals Museum

Hailed as the first "modern" artist, Frans Hals (c.1582–1666) introduced a new realism into painting. While contemporary painters aimed for an exact likeness, Hals captured the character of his sitters through a more impressionistic technique. In his eighties, he still painted passionate portraits, such as *The Governesses of the Old Men's Home* (1664). The Old Men's Home, one of many in Haarlem, became the Frans Hals Museum in 1913. Besides his work, there is a selection of Dutch painting and applied art from the 16th and 17th centuries.

Mother and Child
Following the Alteration (see pp24–5), artists like Pieter de Grebber (1600–53) often painted secular versions of religious themes. This painting (c.1630) of a woman suckling her baby recalls the Virgin Mary with Jesus.

STAR PAINTINGS

★ Banquet of the Officers by Frans Hals

★ Still Life by Floris van Dijck

★ Mercury by Hendrick Goltzius

KEY TO FLOORPLAN

- [ ] Works by Frans Hals
- [ ] Renaissance Gallery
- [ ] Old Masters
- [ ] History of 17th-century Haarlem
- [ ] Temporary exhibitions
- [ ] Non-exhibition space

Hals's Civic Guard portraits

18th-century doll's house

★ Banquet of the Officers of the Civic Guard of St George *(1616)*
The characteristics of each of the 12 Civic Guards and the opulence of their banqueting hall are superbly portrayed in this formal group portrait by Frans Hals.

Delft Dish *(1662)*
This blue-and-white earthenware dish by M Eems shows the Grote Kerk and Grote Markt in Haarlem (see p176).

Doll's House *(c. 1750)*
This 11 room house, which belonged to Sara Rothé, is made to a scale of 1:10. Its representation is so realistic that it offers a good view into what it was like inside an 18th-century canal-side mansion (see pp30–31).

VISITORS' CHECKLIST

Groot Heiligland 62, Haarlem.
***Tel** (023) 511 5775.*
🚉 *Haarlem.* ⏰ *11am–5pm Tue–Sat (lastadm 4:30pm); noon–5pm Sun & public hols.*
🚫 *1 Jan, 25 Dec.*
🖼 ⓞ ♿ 🅿 🏪 🏛
www.franshalsmuseum.nl

★ **Mercury** *(1611)*
Hendrick Goltzius (1558–1617) painted a lot of biblical and mythological scenes. This canvas was commissioned by a wealthy Haarlem burgomaster as one of a series of three.

MUSEUM GUIDE
The entrance leads into a modern wing with a museum shop. The best route is anti-clockwise; displays of Frans Hals' work, other portraits, still life and many other paintings are usually reordered each year. Exhibits of modern art are held in De Hallen (Vleeshal and Verweyhal) which are in the Grote Markt (see p176).

Small
courtyard

Main
entrance

An Allegory on Tulip Mania *(c. 1640)*
Jan Breughel II's painting ridicules the obsession with tulips that was gripping Holland at the time.

★ **Still Life** *(1613)*
Precise attention to detail and texture was the hallmark of Floris van Dijck (1574–1651). The damask tablecloth shown in the painting was a product of Haarlem's thriving linen industry.

A Tour of the Bulbfields ⓾

Occupying a 30-km (19-mile) strip between Haarlem and Leiden, the Bloembollenstreek is the main bulb-growing area in the Netherlands. From late January, the polders bloom with a series of vividly coloured bulbs, beginning with early crocuses and building to a climax around mid-April when the tulips flower. These are followed by late-blooming flowers like lilies, which extend the season into late May. If you don't have a car, the VVV *(see p259)* has details on a variety of tours. Alternatively, hire a bicycle at Haarlem railway station, cycle to Leiden and take the bike back to Haarlem on the train.

TIPS FOR DRIVERS

Starting point: Haarlem.
Length: Approx 30 km (19 miles).
Stopping-off points: In addition to the places named below, all of which have a selection of restaurants, cafés and bars, it is worth diverting to Noordwijk aan Zee. This lively seaside town, with its lovely dune-backed beach, is a perfect picnic spot. Good viewpoints en route are marked on the map.

De Cruquius Museum ①
The museum cont[ains]
exhibits that expl[ain]
how polders and
dams work a[nd]
how they have
kept sea and floo[d]
water at bay.

Sand dunes lining the coast

Vogelenzang ③
The first nurseries in Vogelenzang were established in 1789 – the Frans Bozen nurseries (sadly they recently went bankrupt).

Linnaeushof ②
Named after an 18th-cent[ury] botanist, this huge park c[on-]tains one of Europe's larg[est] adventure playgrounds.

Keukenhof ④
Visitors to this park are greeted by the heady scents and brilliant colours of millions of bulbs in bloom.

Lisse ⑤
There is a small bulb-museu[m in] Lisse and boat trips are avail[able] on Kager Plassen lake, near[by.]

```
0 kilometres        5
0 miles        2.5
```

KEY

▓▓▓ Tour route

═══ Roads

⁂ Viewpoint

Katwijk ⑦
A rare, early-17th-century lighthouse is situated just to the north of this seaside town, which stands at the mouth of the Oude Rijn.

Sassenheim ⑥
West of the town lie the remains of Burcht Teylingen, an 11th-century castle where Jacoba of Bavaria, the deposed Countess of Holland, died in 1436.

A tulip field in the Bloembollenstreek

ddin tulips

na pink tulips

iti daffodils

nnow daffodils

e jacket hyacinths

An array of bulbs in flower in the wooded Keukenhof park

Aalsmeer ⓫

10 km (6 miles) south of Amsterdam.
🚶 23,000. 🚌 🛈 Driekolommen-
plein 1. (0297) 325 374. 🛒 Tue.
www.aalsmeer.nl

Aalsmeer is home to the largest
flower auction in the world,
the Bloemenveiling (see www.
vba.nl). Visitors can watch the
colourful proceedings from
a viewing gallery above the
trading floors. As the 3.5 billion
cut flowers and 400 million
pot plants sold here annually
all have a short shelf-life,
speed is of the essence. A
clock above the auctioneer's
head shows the prices falling
as the hand sweeps round,
from 100 to 1. When it reaches the price that bidders are
willing to pay, the clock stops.

Lisse ⓬

35 km (22 miles) west of Amsterdam.
🚶 22,000. 🚌 🛈 Grachtweg 53.
(0252) 414 262. www.vvlisse.nl

The best time to visit Lisse
is at the end of April, when
the town mounts a series of
colourful flower parades.
    The **Museum de Zwarte
Tulp** (the Black Tulip Museum) has displays on the
history and life cycle of bulbs.
Imported from Turkey in the

early 17th century, by the mid-
1630s "tulip mania" gripped the
nation (see pp26–7). At the
height of the boom rare bulbs
were sold for their weight in
gold. By February 1637 however, the market had collapsed.

🏛 **Museum de Zwarte Tulp**
Grachtweg 2a. **Tel** (0252) 417 900.
◻ Renovations scheduled; check
website for opening hours. ● 1 Jan,
Easter Sun, last Thu in Sep, 5 Dec,
15 Dec–15 Jan. 🌼

Keukenhof ⓭

Stationsweg, Lisse. **Tel** (0252) 465555.
🚌 54 (Leiden Centraal Station; ask for
the bus & entry deal, or 58 from
Schiphol airport). ◻ late Mar– mid-
May: 8am–7:30pm daily (last adm
6pm). 🌼 www.keukenhof.nl

Set in a wooded park on the
outskirts of Lisse, this spectacular flower garden was set up in
1949 as a showcase for Dutch
bulb growers and is now
planted with some 7 million
bulbs. It is at its most spectacular from late March to late May,
when drifts of daffodils, hyacinths or tulips are in bloom.
The flowers are complemented
by the snowy blossom of
Japanese cherry trees early in
the season, and by splashes of
azaleas and rhododendrons
later in the year.

Street-by-Street: Leiden ⑭

Leiden is a prosperous university town, with its origins in Roman times. It grew due to its position on a branch of the Rijn (Rhine) and is still an important commercial crossroads. During term-time, the streets are crowded with students cycling between lectures or packing the cafés and bookshops. A number of exceptional museums document Leiden's turbulent history, including the Golden Age, when the town was a centre for world-wide trade *(see pp28–9)*. The wall plaque on the façade of Rembrandt's house in Weddesteeg marks his birthplace in June 1606 *(see p62)*.

Statue of Justice on Stadhuis wall

★ **Rijksmuseum van Oudheden**
This squat statue of a kneeling treasury scribe is among the many Egyptian artifacts in the museum.

John Robinson *(see p185)* lived in the Jan Pesijnshofje.

★ **Hortus Botanicus**
The botanical gardens (see p184) are owned by Leiden University, and were laid out initially as a study aid for botany students in 1590.

Oude Rijn
Many of the gabled houses along Leiden's canals have shops and cafés on the ground floor.

Neo-Classical houses on Rapenburg

University library

Het Gravensteen
The university's law faculty lies behind the Classical façade of this complex of buildings, which grew up between the 13th and 17th centuries.

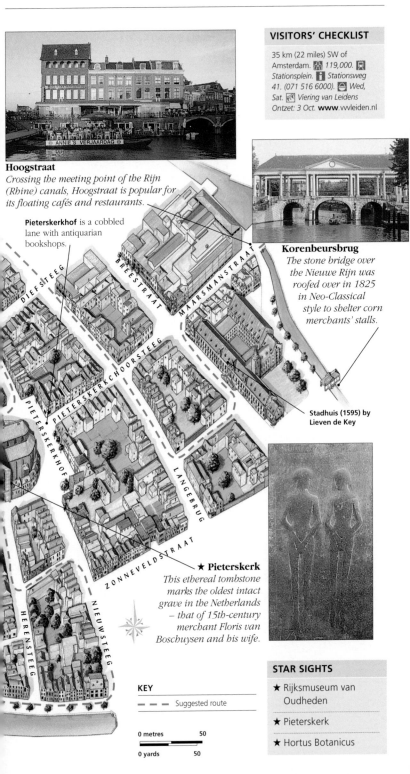

VISITORS' CHECKLIST

35 km (22 miles) SW of
Amsterdam. 119,000.
Stationsplein. Stationsweg
41. (071 516 6000). Wed,
Sat. Viering van Leidens
Ontzet: 3 Oct. www.vvvleiden.nl

Hoogstraat
*Crossing the meeting point of the Rijn
(Rhine) canals, Hoogstraat is popular for
its floating cafés and restaurants.*

Pieterskerkhof is a cobbled
lane with antiquarian
bookshops.

DIEFSTEEG

BREESTRAAT

MAARSMANSTRAAT

Korenbeursbrug
*The stone bridge over
the Nieuwe Rijn was
roofed over in 1825
in Neo-Classical
style to shelter corn
merchants' stalls.*

PIETERSKERKCHOORSTEEG

PIETERSKERKHOF

**Stadhuis (1595) by
Lieven de Key**

LANGEBRUG

ZONNEVELDSTRAAT

★ **Pieterskerk**
*This ethereal tombstone
marks the oldest intact
grave in the Netherlands
– that of 15th-century
merchant Floris van
Boschuysen and his wife.*

HERENSTEEG

NIEUWSTEEG

KEY

– – – Suggested route

0 metres   50

0 yards   50

STAR SIGHTS

★ Rijksmuseum van
Oudheden

★ Pieterskerk

★ Hortus Botanicus

Exploring Leiden

Leiden is famous for its university, the oldest and most prestigious in the Netherlands. It was founded in 1575 by William of Orange, a year after he relieved the town from a year-long siege by the Spanish *(see pp24–5)*. As a reward for their endurance, William offered the citizens of Leiden a choice of the building of a university or the abolition of tax. They chose wisely, and the city's reputation as a centre of intellectual and religious tolerance was firmly established. English Puritan dissidents, victims of persecution in their homeland, were able to settle here in the 17th century before undertaking their epic voyage to the New World.

Arched gazebo within the Clusiustuin in the Hortus Botanicus

🏛 Stedelijk Museum De Lakenhal

Oude Singel 28–32. *Tel (071) 516 5360.* ⬜ *10am–5pm Tue–Fri, noon–5pm Sat & Sun.* ⬤ *1 Jan, 25 Dec.* 🖼 ♿ 📷 🏛 📷 www.lakenhal.nl

The Lakenhal (cloth hall) was the 17th-century headquarters of Leiden's cloth trade. Built in 1640 in Dutch Classical style by Arent van 's Gravesande, it houses the municipal museum, with temporary exhibitions of modern art and furniture from the 16th century onwards.

The pride of the collection is Lucas van Leyden's Renaissance triptych of *The Last Judgment* (1526–7), rescued from the Pieterskerk during the religious struggles of 1566 *(see pp24–5)*. A wing built in the 1920s offers a silver collection, furniture and exhibits covering the local weaving industry. Not to be missed is a big bronze *hutspot*, or

cauldron, allegedly left behind by the Spanish when William of Orange broke the siege in 1574. The cauldron contained a spicy stew which the starving people ate. This meal is now cooked every year on 3 October, to commemorate Dutch victory over the Spanish.

♣ Hortus Botanicus der Rijksuniversiteit Leiden

Rapenburg 73. *Tel (071) 527 7249.* ⬜ *Apr–Nov: 10am–6pm daily; Dec–Mar: 10–4pm Tue–Sun.* ⬤ *3 Oct, 25 Dec–1 Jan.* 🖼 ♿ partial. 📷 🏛 www.hortus.leidenuniv.nl

Leiden's botanical garden was founded in 1590 as part of the university. The varied trees and shrubs include a 350-year-old laburnum. Carolus

Clusius, who was responsible for introducing the tulip to the Netherlands in 1593 *(see pp26–7)*, became the first professor of botany at Leiden University. Today the Hortus Botanicus contains a modern reconstruction of his original walled garden, called the Clusiustuin. Other delights include hothouses full of exotic orchids, rose gardens and colourful beds of tulips planted around ponds.

🏛 Museum Boerhaave

Lange St Agnietenstraat 10. *Tel (071) 521 4224.* ⬜ *10am–5pm Tue–Sat; noon–5pm Sun, pub hols.* ⬤ *1 Jan, 3 Oct, 25 Dec.* 🖼 ♿ 📷 www. museumboerhaave.nl

This museum is named after the great Dutch professor of medicine, botany and chemistry, Herman

Lucas van Leyden's triptych of *The Last Judgment* in the Stedelijk Museum de Lakenhal

Boerhaave (1668–1738). Its collections reflect the development of mathematics, astronomy, physics, chemistry and medicine. They range in time from a magnificent 15th-century astrolabe to the electron-microscope and the surgeon's equipment of yesteryear. It is located in the former Caecilia Hospital.

🏛 Museum Volkenkunde

Steenstraat 1. **Tel** *(071) 516 8800.* ⬜ *10am–5pm Tue–Sun.* ⬤ *1 Jan, 30 Apr, 3 Oct, 4 Oct, 25 Dec.* 📷♿📱🏪 www.volkenkunde.nl

This outstanding ethnological museum, founded in 1837, houses collections from non-western cultures. Individual displays are linked together to create a worldwide cultural journey that shows both the differences and connections between cultures. Temporary exhibitions feature living conditions across the world, from the Arctic wastes to the hills of China, adding to this eclectic museum's wide appeal to people of all age groups.

🏛 Stedelijk Molenmuseum de Valk

2e Binnenvestgracht 1. **Tel** *(071) 5165 353.* ⬜ *10am–5pm Tue–Sat, 1–5pm Sun.* ⬤ *1 Jan, 3 Oct, 25 Dec.* 📷📱 www.molenmuseumdevalk.nl

This towering grain mill, built in 1743, is Leiden's last remaining mill. It is an imposing seven storeys high, and now restored to its original working state. A tour takes in the living quarters on the ground floor, the repair workshop and a retrospective exhibition on the history of Dutch windmills.

🕍 Pieterskerk

Pieterskerkhof 1a. **Tel** *(071) 512 4319.* ⬜ *opening times vary; phone in advance.* ⬤ *3 Oct, 31 Dec.* ♿ www.pieterskerk.com

The magnificent Gothic church was built in the 15th century in rose-pink brick, and stands in a leafy square surrounded by elegant houses. Now a community centre, the church is worth visiting for its austere

---

THE PILGRIM FATHERS

The Netherlands was proudly Protestant by the 17th century, giving refuge to Puritans fleeing persecution in England. Preacher John Robinson (1575–1625) established a church in Leiden in 1609, inspiring his congregation with visions of a new Jerusalem in the New World. The Pilgrim Fathers set sail from Delfshaven in 1620 in the *Speedwell*, which proved unseaworthy. Putting in at Plymouth, England, they crossed the Atlantic in the *Mayflower* to found Plymouth, Massachusetts. Robinson was too ill to travel, dying in Leiden in 1625.

The *Mayflower* crossing the Atlantic Ocean

---

interior and its organ, built by the Hagenbeer brothers in 1642 and enclosed in gilded woodwork. The floor of the nave is covered with worn slabs marking the burial places of 17th-century intellectuals like Puritan leader John Robinson and Golden Age artist Jan Steen *(see p133)*. Parts of the church may be screened off due to restoration.

Heraldic lion at De Burcht

⚓ De Burcht

Nieuwe Rijn. **Battlements** ⬜ *daily.*

De Burcht is an odd 12th-century fortress with crenellated battlements. It sits between two channels of the Rijn (Rhine) atop a grassy, manmade mound, which is thought to be of Saxon origin. The top of the citadel offers superb views over Leiden.

🏛 Rijksmuseum van Oudheden

Rapenburg 28. **Tel** *(071) 516 3163.* ⬜ *10am–5pm Tue–Sun.* ⬤ *1 Jan, 30 Apr, 3 Oct, 25 Dec.* 📷♿📱🏪 www.rmo.nl

The Dutch museum of antiquities, established in 1818, is Leiden's main attraction. The centrepiece of the collection is the Egyptian Temple of Taffeh, reassembled in the main exhibition hall in 1978. It dates from the 1st century AD, and was dedicated to Isis, Egyptian goddess of fertility, from the 4th century AD.

The museum's rich collection of Egyptian artifacts occupies the first two floors. There are also impressive displays of musical instruments, textiles and shoes, expressive Etruscan bronzework and fragments of Roman mosaic and frescoes.

The presentation has been designed with children in mind with interactive media reconstructing daily life in ancient Egypt, Greece and Rome.

A lift bridge across the Oude Rijn in Leiden

Den Haag ⑮

Den Haag ('s-Gravenhage or The Hague) is the political capital of the Netherlands, home to prestigious institutions such as the Dutch Parliament and International Court of Justice, located in the Vredespaleis *(see p190)*. When Den Haag became the seat of government in 1586, it was a small town built around the castle of the counts of Holland. That same castle, much rebuilt, now stands at the heart of a city which is home to half a million people. It is surrounded by public buildings, such as the Mauritshuis *(see pp188–9)*, and protected to the north by the remains of a moat which forms the Hofvijver (lake). To the west is the seaside town of Scheveningen *(see p191)*.

Statue in Binnenhof courtyard

🏛 Mauritshuis
See pp188–9.

🏰 Ridderzaal
Binnenhof 8a. **Tel** (070) 364 6144.
◻ 10am–4pm Mon–Sat. 🔴 Sun & public hols. ▨ 🎫 www. binnenhofbezoek.nl
By the side of the Hofvijver is the Binnenhof courtyard. In the centre of this stands the fairy-tale, double-turreted Gothic Ridderzaal (Hall of the Knights). This was the 13th-century dining hall of Floris V, Count of Holland *(see p21)*. Since 1904, the hall's function has been mostly ceremonial; it is used for the opening of the Dutch Parliament by the monarch (Prinsjesdag, the third Tuesday in September), and for other state occasions. It is open to visitors when parliament is not in session. A tour takes in the two former debating chambers.

🏛 Museum Bredius
Lange Vijverberg 14. **Tel** (070) 362 0729. ◻ 11am–5pm Tue–Sun. 🔴 1 Jan & 25 Dec. ▨ 🎫 www.museumbredius.nl
Dr Abraham Bredius was an art historian and collector as well as director of the Mauritshuis *(see pp188–9)* from 1895 to 1922. On his death in 1946, he bequeathed his vast collection of 17th-century art to the city of Den Haag. This bequest is displayed in a distinguished 18th-century merchant's house on the north side of the Hofvijver, and features around 200 Golden Age paintings – famous works by Dutch Masters such as Rembrandt *(see p66)* and Jan Steen *(see p133)*, and others by lesser-known artists.
The building itself has undergone considerable renovation and boasts a fine collection of antique furniture, delicate porcelain and elaborate silverware.

🔒 Grote Kerk
Rond de Grote Kerk 12. **Tel** (070) 302 8630. ◻ mid-Jul–mid-Aug, or book a guided tour on (070) 345 1298. 🚻 www.grotekerkdenhaag.nl
In its present form, the Grote Kerk dates mainly from 1539, but has undergone major rebuilding between 1985 and 1987. Its most impressive feature is a stained-glass window which depicts Charles V, the Holy Roman Emperor *(see pp24–5)*, kneeling at the feet of the Virgin Mary. The church is at the centre of Den Haag's shopping area.

Coat of arms on façade of Rijksmuseum Gevangenpoort

🏛 Rijksmuseum Gevangenpoort
Buitenhof 33. **Tel** (070) 346 0861. ◻ check opening times on the website. 🔴 1 Jan, 25, 26 Dec. ▨ 🎫 (every hour: obligatory. Last tour: 4pm) 🚻 www.gevangenpoort.nl
The Gevangenpoort (prison gate) was originally the main gateway to the 14th-century castle of the counts of Holland. Later, it was turned into a jail, becoming infamous during a period of violent social unrest in the late 17th century when burgomaster Cornelis de Witt *(see p27)* was confined and tortured here. Both he and his brother Jan were subsequently tried for heresy, and torn limb from limb outside the prison gate by a rioting mob.
Now a prison museum, on display is a unique collection of torture instruments, accompanied by a stereo soundtrack of blood-curdling screams.

The Hofvijver and parliament buildings in Den Haag

Paintings in Galerij Prins Willem V

🏛 **Galerij Prins Willem V**

Buitenhof 33. **Tel** (070) 302 3456.
⬜ check website for opening times.
📷 📷 ♿ www.mauritshuis.nl

In his youth, Prince William V (see p30) was a collector of Golden Age paintings. His collection was opened to the public in 1774, inside this former inn, which the prince had converted for use as his *kabinet* – the 18th-century Dutch word for an art gallery. The Galerij is the oldest art gallery in the Netherlands. The 18th-century fashion for covering every available inch of wall space with paintings has been retained, and so several pictures are hung high and close together. Many of Prince William's original purchases are still to be seen. Old Master paintings by Rembrandt, Jan Steen and Paulus Potter (1625–54) are included in a collection that consists principally of typically Dutch Golden Age landscapes, genre works, "conversation pieces" and recreations of historical events (see p132).

🏛 **Haags Historisch Museum**

Korte Vijverberg 7. **Tel** (070) 364 6940. ⬜ 10am–5pm Tue–Fri, noon–5pm Sat–Sun. ● 1 Jan, 3rd Tue in Sep, 25 Dec. 📷 ♿ 📷 📷
📷 www.haagshistorisch museum.nl

Den Haag's history museum is in the Sebastiaansdoelen, a Dutch Classical mansion built in 1636 and the former headquarters of the Civic Guard of St Sebastian. Exhibitions tell the story of Den Haag's growth since the Middle Ages.

VISITORS' CHECKLIST

56 km (35 miles) SW of Amsterdam. 🚉 446,000. 🚉 Koningin Julianaplein, Centraal Station; Stationsplein, Station Hollands Spoor (HS). 🛈 Hofweg 1 (0900 340 3505). ⬜ 10am–6pm Mon–Sat (to 5pm Sat), noon–5pm Sun. 🚌 Mon, Wed, Fri, Sat. 🎏 Vlaggetjesdag Scheveningen: last Sat in May or first Sat in Jun; Prinsjesdag: 3rd Tue in Sep. www.denhaag.com

The displays are changed periodically and are drawn from the city's collection of landscapes, portraits and genre paintings (see pp132–3) as well as 17th- and 18th-century furnishings.

The 17th-century façade of the Haags Historisch Museum

DEN HAAG CITY CENTRE

Galerij Prins Willem V ③
Grote Kerk ①
Haags Historisch Museum ⑥
Mauritshuis ⑦
Museum Bredius ④
Ridderzaal ⑤
Rijksmuseum Gevangenpoort ②

0 metres 250
0 yards 250

Key to Symbols see back flap

The Mauritshuis

The Count of Nassau, Johann Maurits, commissioned this graceful house while he was the governor of Brazil. It was completed in 1644 by Pieter Post and Jacob van Campen in Dutch Classical style with influences from Italian Renaissance architecture, and enjoys wonderful views across the Hofvijver *(see p186)*. The mansion was bequeathed to the state after Maurits's death in 1679, and has been the home of the Royal Picture Gallery since 1822. The collection is small, but almost every painting is a superb work by one of the Old Masters. This, combined with the exquisite presentation in elegant period rooms, makes the Mauritshuis one of the finest galleries in the Netherlands.

★ **The Anatomy Lesson of Dr Nicolaes Tulp** *(1632)*
Rembrandt's painting of surgeons examining a corpse reflects the burgeoning contemporary interest in anatomy and science.

GALLERY GUIDE

The Mauritshuis is a small gallery set on three floors. The arrangement of the paintings changes frequently in order to cover all aspects of the collection, but you can check the current display on the museum's website. Information sheets and an audio tour are available in English. If in doubt, ask for help from one of the gallery attendants. The permanent collection is subject to changes. The museum will close for renovations from 2012–13.

Vase with Flowers in a Niche *(c.1618)* Ambrosius Bosschaert the Elder captured the beauty of early summer flowers, but the flies buzzing around remind us of mortality.

Ground floor

Offices and administration

Portrait of a Man from the Lespinette Family *(c. 1485–90)* Thought to be a work by Antonello da Messina until the 19th century, this tightly framed portrait has now been attributed to Hans Memling.

Basement

Main stairwell

The Goldfinch *(1654)*
*This tiny, delicate
painting is by Carel
Fabritius (1622–54),
who was a pupil of
Rembrandt.*

Main stairs
first floor)

First floor

VISITORS' CHECKLIST

Korte Vijverberg 8, Den Haag. **Tel**
(070) 302 3456. 🚆 Den Haag
Centraal. ⬜ 10am–5pm Tue–
Sun (from 11 Sun & pub hols) (last
adm 4:30pm) (Apr–Sep: also open
Mon). ⬤ will close in 2012 for
restoration. 🏛 📷 ♿ 🎁 🎧

KEY TO FLOORPLAN

⬜	Portrait Gallery
⬜	15th- and early-16th-century work
⬜	Late-16th- and 17th-century work
⬜	Golden Room
⬜	17th-century painting
⬜	18th-century painting
⬜	Non-exhibition space

**The Way You Hear It is the
Way You Sing It** *(c.1665)*
*A serious moral is implicit
in Jan Steen's allegorical
genre painting (see p131)
warning adults not to
set a bad example to
their offspring.*

★ **Hunting for Lice**
(c.1652–53)
*Gerard ter Borch's painting
is a scene of obsessive
domesticity. It reflects the pre-
occupation of the 17th-century
Dutch with cleanliness and
social respectability.*

Main
entrance

★ **Girl with a Pearl
Earring** *(c.1665)*
*This haunting portrait
was painted during
the most successful
middle period of Jan
Vermeer's career. The
model may have been
his daughter, Maria.*

STAR PAINTINGS

★ Girl with a Pearl Earring
by Jan Vermeer

★ Hunting for Lice by
Gerard ter Borch

★ The Anatomy Lesson
of Dr Nicolaes Tulp
by Rembrandt

♛ Vredespaleis

Carnegieplein 2. **Tel** *(070) 302 4137.*
⬜ *Mon–Fri.* 🔲 *compulsory (phone in advance).* ⬤ *public hols and when court is in session.* 🗝
www.vredespaleis.nl

In 1899, Den Haag played host to the first international peace conference. This then led to the formation of the Permanent Court of Arbitration, which had the aim of maintaining world peace. To provide a suitably august home for the court, the Scottish-born philanthropist, Andrew Carnegie (1835–1919) donated £1 million towards the building of the mock-Gothic Vredespaleis (peace palace), which was designed by French architect Louis Cordonnier.

The enormous palace was completed in 1913, and many of the member nations of the Court of Arbitration contributed to the interior's rich decoration. Today the Vredespaleis is the seat of the United Nations' International Court of Justice, which was formed in 1946 as successor to the Permanent Court of Arbitration.

Vredespaleis, home to the International Court of Justice

♜ Haags Gemeentemuseum

Stadhouderslaan 41. **Tel** *(070) 338 1111.* ⬜ *11am–5pm Tue–Sun.*
⬤ *1 Jan, 25 Dec.* 🗝 ♿ 📷 ⬜
📷 **www**.gemeentemuseum.nl

The Gemeentemuseum is one of the town's finest museums. The building was the last work of HP Berlage, the father of the architectural movement known as the Amsterdam School *(see p97)*. The museum was completed in 1935, a year after his death, and is built in sandy-coloured brick on two storeys round a central courtyard.

The exhibits are displayed in three sections. Highlights of the superb applied arts section include antique Delftware,

Islamic and Oriental porcelain and the world's largest collection of paintings by Piet Mondriaan *(see p136)*.

Costumes and musical instruments dating from the 15th to the 19th centuries are too fragile to be on permanent display, though there are regular exhibitions of selected items from these collections.

The labyrinthine basement is the stage for the "Wonderkamers" – the Wonder Rooms – which hold quirky displays of artworks from all the collections, aimed especially at teenage visitors.

♜ Panorama Mesdag

Zeestraat 65. **Tel** *(070) 364 4544.*
⬜ *10am–5pm Mon–Sat, noon–5pm Sun.* ⬤ *1 Jan, 25 Dec.* 🗝
www.panorama-mesdag.com

This painted cyclorama is important both as a work of Dutch Impressionism and as a rare surviving example of 19th-century entertainment. The vast painting is 120 m (400 ft) around and lines the inside wall of a circular, canopied pavilion. It shows the old fishing village of Scheveningen.

The astonishingly realistic effect of the painting is achieved through the brilliant use of perspective, enhanced by natural daylight from above. It was painted in 1881 by members of the Dutch Impressionist School, led by HW Mesdag (1831–1915) and his wife, Sientje (1834–1909). George Hendrik Breitner (1857–1923) later added a group of cavalry officers charging along the beach on horseback. Renovations will take place until 2012, although the museum will stay open during this time.

Haags Gemeentemuseum (1935), designed by HP Berlage

⬛ Omniversum

President Kennedylaan 5.
Tel (0900) 666 4837. ⬛ daily.
⬛ ⬛ ⬛ www.omniversum.nl
The Omniversum is a cross between a planetarium and a space-age cinema, and is especially appealing to children. It has a high-tech sound system and a massive dome-shaped screen, on to which films and lasers are projected. These are combined to create stunning three-dimensional images of space exploration, volcanic eruptions and life beneath the ocean's surface.

⬛ Madurodam

George Maduroplein 1.
Tel (070) 416 2400. ⬛ daily. ⬛
⬛ ⬛ ⬛ www.madurodam.nl
Madurodam is a model of a composite Dutch city, built to a scale of 1:25. It incorporates replicas of the Vredespaleis and Binnenhof in Den Haag, the canal houses of Amsterdam, Rotterdam's Europoort (see p199) and Schiphol airport, along with windmills, polders, bulbfields and a nudist beach. At night it is illuminated by 50,000 tiny lights.

The model city was opened by Queen Juliana in 1952. It was conceived by JML Maduro as a memorial to his son George, who died at Dachau concentration camp in 1945.

Scale models in the miniature town of Madurodam

Scheveningen ⓰

45 km (28 miles) SW of Amsterdam.
⬛ 17,800. ⬛ ⬛ Thu.
www.denhaag.com

This resort is a 15-minute tram-ride from the centre of Den Haag. Like many Dutch sea-side towns, it had its heyday in the 19th century, and is now a mixture of faded gentility and seediness. Even so, it has retained its popularity as a holiday destination, mainly due to stretches of clean, sandy beaches as well as a pier, built earlier last century, which was recently renovated. There is no shortage of places to eat, including some good seafood restaurants. The imposing French Empire-style Kurhaus, now a luxury hotel with its own casino, was built in 1885 when Scheveningen was still an important spa town.

Modern amenities include the **Sea Life Centre**, nearby, where visitors can walk in see-through tunnels for under-water views of stingrays, sharks and other forms of sea life. It is also a sanctuary for all kinds of wounded marine creatures.

The town has swallowed up the original fishing village of Scheveningen Haven, which has still managed to maintain some of its traditional fishing industry. The south side of the harbour is the departure point for tourists' fishing trips.

Close by is the **MuZee Scheveningen**, which combines exhibits of marine life from around the world with displays on life in the village at the turn of the 20th century.

⬛ MuZee Scheveningen

Neptunusstraat 92. **Tel** (070) 350 0830. ⬛ Tue–Fri & Sun. ⬛ 1 Jan, 25 Dec. ⬛ www.muzee.nl

⬛ Sea Life Centre

Strandweg 13. **Tel** (070) 354 2100.
⬛ daily. ⬛ 25 Dec. ⬛ ⬛ ⬛
⬛ www.sealife.nl

Holiday-makers on Scheveningen's popular sandy beach

Street-by-Street: Delft ⑰

19th-century Delft tile showing a church and barges

The origins of Delft date from 1075 and its prosperity was based on weaving and brewing. However, a massive explosion at the national arsenal destroyed much of the medieval town in October 1645. The centre was rebuilt in the late 17th century and the sleepy old town has changed little since then – gabled Gothic and Renaissance houses still line the tree-shaded canals. Activity centres on the market square, bordered by the landmarks of the Stadhuis and Nieuwe Kerk. Visitors can dip into the scores of shops selling antiques and expensive, hand-painted Delftware. Tours of local factories are available, and their shops are often reasonably priced.

★ **Stedelijk Museum Het Prinsenhof**
Here you can see bullet holes where William of Orange was murdered in 1584.

SCHOOLSTRAAT

ST AGATHA PLEIN

Volkenkundig Museum Nusantara

★ **Oude Kerk**
The 13th-century Oude Kerk contains tombs of eminent Delft citizens like Antonie van Leeuwenhoek, inventor of the microscope.

Oude Delft is lined with Renaissance canal houses.

HIPPOLYTUSBUURT

OUDE DELFT

NIEUWSTRAAT

BOTER BRUG

OUDE DELFT

PEPERSTR

STAR SIGHTS

★ Oude Kerk

★ Nieuwe Kerk

★ Stedelijk Museum Het Prinsenhof

Chapel of St Hippolytus
This simple, red-brick Gothic chapel (1396) was used as an ammunition store during the Alteration (see pp24–5).

0 metres   50

0 yards   50

KEY

– – – Suggested route

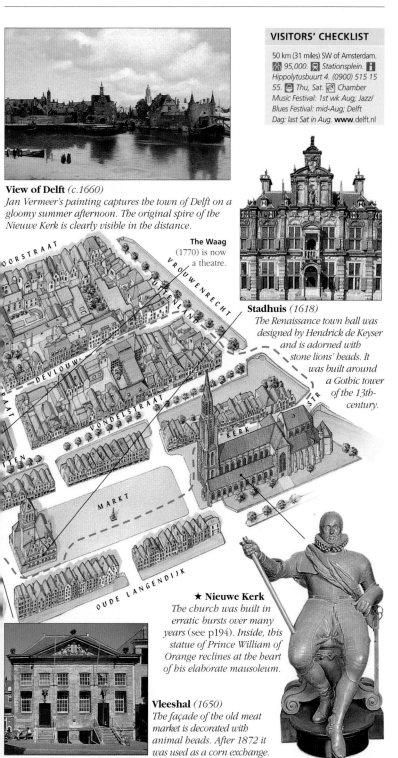

View of Delft (c.1660)
Jan Vermeer's painting captures the town of Delft on a gloomy summer afternoon. The original spire of the Nieuwe Kerk is clearly visible in the distance.

VISITORS' CHECKLIST

50 km (31 miles) SW of Amsterdam.
🚋 95,000. 🚉 *Stationsplein.* ℹ️
*Hippolytusbuurt 4. (0900) 515 15
55.* 🛒 *Thu, Sat.* 🎷 *Chamber
Music Festival: 1st wk Aug; Jazz/
Blues Festival: mid-Aug; Delft
Dag: last Sat in Aug.* **www.**delft.nl

The Waag
(1770) is now
a theatre.

Stadhuis (1618)
*The Renaissance town hall was
designed by Hendrick de Keyser
and is adorned with
stone lions' heads. It
was built around
a Gothic tower
of the 13th-
century.*

★ **Nieuwe Kerk**
*The church was built in
erratic bursts over many
years (see p194). Inside, this
statue of Prince William of
Orange reclines at the heart
of his elaborate mausoleum.*

Vleeshal (1650)
*The façade of the old meat
market is decorated with
animal heads. After 1872 it
was used as a corn exchange.*

Exploring Delft

The charming town of Delft is known the world over for its blue-and-white pottery, but is equally famous as the resting place of William of Orange (1533–84), one of the most celebrated figures in Dutch history. He commanded the Dutch Revolt against Spanish rule from his headquarters in Delft, and his victory resulted in religious freedom and independence for the Dutch people *(see pp24–5)*. Delft was also the birthplace of artist Jan Vermeer (1632–75), whose talent was so underrated during his lifetime that he died in extreme poverty.

The imposing Renaissance pulpit (1548) of the Oude Kerk

🔒 Oude Kerk

Heilige Geestkerkhof. *Tel (015) 212 3015.* ☐ *9am–6pm Mon–Sat (Nov–Jan: 11am–4pm Mon–Fri, 10am–5pm Sat; Feb–Mar: 10am–5pm Mon–Fri).* 📷 ♿ **www**.oudekerk-delft.nl
Although a church has existed on this site since the 13th century, the original building has been added to many times. The ornate, but leaning, clock tower was built in the 14th century, and the flamboyant Gothic north transept was added in the early 16th century. The interior is dominated by the carved wooden pulpit with overhanging canopy. The simple stone tablet at the east end of the north aisle marks the burial place of Jan Vermeer. In the north transept lies Admiral Maarten Tromp (1598–1653), who routed the English fleet in 1652. Admiral Piet Heyn (1577–1629), who captured the Spanish silver fleet in 1628, is in the chancel.

🔒 Nieuwe Kerk

Markt. *Tel (015) 212 3025.* ☐ *9am–6pm Mon–Sat (Feb–Mar: 10am–5pm Mon–Sat ; Nov–Jan: 11am–4pm Mon–Fri, 10am–5pm Sat).* 📷 **www**.nieuwekerk-delft.nl
The Nieuwe Kerk was built between 1383 and 1510, but much of the original structure was restored following a fire in 1536 and an explosion at the national arsenal in 1645. Work on the church continued for many years, and it was not until 1872 that PJH Cuypers *(see pp32–3)* added the statuesque 100-m (320-ft) tower to the Gothic façade.

The burial vaults of the Dutch royal family are in the crypt of this empty, cavernous church, but the most prominent feature is the mausoleum of William of Orange. The richly decorated tomb was designed by Hendrick de Keyser *(see p90)* in 1614 and is carved from black and white marble, with heavy gilded detailing. At its heart is a sculpture of William in his battle dress, and at each corner stand bronze figures representing the Virtues. Close to William is his dog, who died days after him, and at the foot of the tomb is a trumpeting angel – symbol of Fame. From 2011 the church will be restored in phases. It will remain open to the public, but opening times might change temporarily.

The Nieuwe Kerk in Delft's market square

DELFTWARE

The blue-and-white tin-glazed pottery, known as Delftware, was developed from majolica and introduced to the Netherlands by immigrant Italian potters in the 16th century. Settling around Delft and Haarlem, the potters made wall tiles, adopting Dutch motifs such as animals and flowers as decoration. Trade with the east brought samples of delicate Chinese porcelain to the Netherlands, and the market for coarser Dutch majolica crashed. By 1650, local potters had adopted the Chinese model and designed fine plates, vases and bowls decorated with Dutch landscapes, and biblical and genre scenes. In 1652, De Porceleyne Fles was one of 32 thriving potteries in Delft. Today, it is one of two Delftware factories still in production, and is open for guided tours (www.royaldelft.com).

Hand-painted 17th-century Delft tiles

🏛 Koninklijk Nederlands Legermuseum

Korte Geer 1. *Tel* (015) 215 0500. ⬜ 10am–5pm Tue–Fri, noon–5pm Sat–Sun. ● 1 Jan, 30 Apr, 25 Dec. ⬜ 🏠 www.legermuseum.nl

Built in 1692, this army museum is full of weaponry, military uniforms, battle models and armoured vehicles. These exhibits trace developments in Dutch military history since the Middle Ages up to the present peacekeeping role of the Netherlands in the service of the United Nations. At the end of 2012 the museum will move to a new location in Soesterberg, near Utrecht.

Coat of arms on façade of the Legermuseum

🏛 Stedelijk Museum Het Prinsenhof

St Agathaplein 1. *Tel* (015) 260 2358. ⬜ 11am–5pm Tue–Sun. ● 1 Jan, 30 Apr, 25 Dec. 📷 www.prinsenhof-delft.nl

This tranquil Gothic building, formerly a convent, now houses Delft's historical museum but is better known as the place where William of Orange was assassinated. He requisitioned the convent in 1572 for his headquarters during the Dutch Revolt. In 1584, by order of Philip II of Spain *(see pp24–5)*, William was shot by Balthasar Gerards. The bullet holes in the main staircase wall can still be seen.

The museum houses a rare collection of antique Delftware, displayed alongside tapestries, silverware, medieval sculpture and a series of portraits of the Dutch royal family.

🏛 Volkenkundig Museum Nusantara

St Agathaplein 4. *Tel* (015) 260 2358. ⬜ 11am–5pm Tue–Sun. ● 1 Jan, 30 Apr, 25 Dec. 📷 📷 📷 www.nusantara-delft.nl

When William of Orange took over the Prinsenhof in 1572, the nuns moved into one of its wings across the square. This is now the home of the Nusantara ethnological museum. It is small, but has a wonderful collection of masks, carvings, textiles, jewellery and musical instruments brought back from Indonesia by traders working for the Dutch East India Company *(see pp28–9)*. The shop sells unusual modern Indonesian crafts.

🏛 Museum Lambert van Meerten

Oude Delft 199. *Tel* (015) 260 2358. ⬜ 11am–5pm Tue–Sun. ● 1 Jan, 30 Apr, 25 Dec. 📷 www.lambertvanmeerten-delft.nl

This small museum is located in an elegantly furnished 19th-century mansion, with paintings and architectural details salvaged from local 17th- and 18th-century buildings. Its main attraction is the antique hand-painted Delftware tiles and tile pictures.

Fine gabled façades along Binnenwaterslot in the centre of Delft

St Janskerk, Gouda

The original Catholic church of 1485 was rebuilt in Gothic style after it was razed by fire in 1552. Between 1555 and 1571, a series of remarkable stained-glass windows were donated to the church by wealthy Catholic benefactors such as Philip II of Spain. After the Alteration *(see pp24–5)* the church became Protestant, but even the iconoclasts could not bring themselves to destroy the windows – in fact Protestant patrons, such as the aldermen of Rotterdam, continued to donate windows until 1603. Depicting contemporary figures and events, the stained glass is rich in political symbolism, using biblical stories to make coded reference to the conflict between Catholic and Protestant, and Dutch and Spanish that led to the Dutch Revolt in 1572.

Donor's coat of arms (1601)

The Nave
At 123 m (403 ft), the nave is the longest in the Netherlands. Memorial slabs cover the floor.

The Adulterous Woman *(1601)*
Dressed as a Franciscan monk, Jesus begs the people in the temple to forgive the adulterous wife, who is heavily guarded by Spanish soldiers.

Baptism of Christ

North aisle

Visitors' entrance

Purification of the Temple

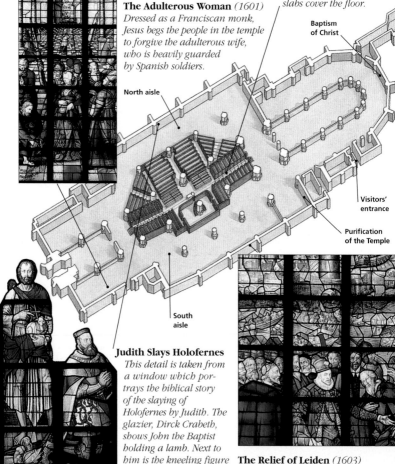

South aisle

Judith Slays Holofernes *(1601)*
This detail is taken from a window which portrays the biblical story of the slaying of Holofernes by Judith. The glazier, Dirck Crabeth, shows John the Baptist holding a lamb. Next to him is the kneeling figure of Jean de Ligne, Count of Aremberg, who commissioned the window.

The Relief of Leiden *(1603)*
William of Orange is pictured here directing Leiden's heroic resistance to the Spanish siege of 1574 (see p184).

VISITORS' CHECKLIST

Achter de Kerk 16. *Tel (0182) 514 119.* ⬜ *9am–5pm Mon–Sat (Nov–Feb: 10–4pm; pub hols 11am–5pm).* ⬤ *1 Jan, 25 & 26 Dec.* ⬜ ⬜ ⬜ **www**.sintjan.com

Purification of the Temple
The window was donated by William of Orange (see p24) in 1567. The detail shows dismayed traders watching Jesus drive the moneylenders from the temple. It represents the Dutch desire to expel the Spanish from their country.

Baptism of Christ *(1555)*
John the Baptist is shown baptizing Christ in the river Jordan. The window was donated by the Bishop of Utrecht.

View over Gouda with St Janskerk in the background

Gouda ⑱

50 km (33 miles) S of Amsterdam. 🏠 *72,000.* 🚉 🛈 *Markt 27. (0900) 468 3288.* 🧀 *cheese market: mid-Jun–Aug: 10am–12.30pm Thu; general market: Thu & Sat; antiques: May–Aug, Wed.* **www**.vvvgouda.nl

Gouda received its charter from Count Floris V *(see p21)* in 1272. Situated at the confluence of two rivers, the town became the centre of a successful brewing industry in the 15th century. The growth of the cheese trade during the 17th century brought more prosperity. Today, the name of Gouda is synonymous with its famous full-bodied cheese. There is a cheese market in summer, and the twice-weekly general market offers local cheeses and crafts. There is also a Candle Festival the second or third Tuesday in December. All these markets take place in the huge square around the Stadhuis which, dating from 1450, is one of the oldest town halls in the Netherlands. The building bristles with pinnacles and miniature spires in Flemish Gothic style. The elaborate façade includes statues of Gouda's former rulers. The principal attraction of the town is the stained-glass windows in St Janskerk.

🏛 Museum Gouda

Achter de Kerk 14. *Tel (0182) 331 000.* ⬜ *10am–5pm Wed–Fri, noon–5pm Sat & Sun.* ⬤ *1 Jan, 25 Dec.* ⬜ **www**.museumgouda.nl
An arched gatehouse (1609) leads into the leafy courtyard of this delightful museum. The Catharina Gasthuis was built in the 14th century as a hospice for travellers, later becoming an almshouse for the elderly. Converted into a museum in 1910, it has a series of Civic Guard portraits and landscapes by Dutch Impressionists.

🏛 Nationaal Farmaceutisch Museum De Moriaan

Westhaven 29. *Tel (0182) 331 000.* ⬜ *noon–5pm Wed–Sun.* ⬤ *1 Jan, 25 Dec.* ⬜ **www**.museumgouda.nl
This little museum was once a sugar refinery and later a coffee and tobacco shop. Since 2007 it has housed the National Pharmaceutical Museum, focusing on the history of the apothecary trade.

Early 17th-century gatehouse of the Museum Gouda

Rotterdam ⑲

Rotterdam occupies a strategic position where the Rijn (Rhine), Europe's most important river, meets the North Sea. Barges from Rotterdam transport goods deep into the continent, and ocean-going ships carry European exports around the world. This made Rotterdam a prime target for aerial bombardment during World War II, and the city's ancient heart was destroyed. Much of the city has been rebuilt in experimental styles, resulting in some of Europe's most original and innovative architecture. The Europoort is now Europe's largest container port, stretching for 40 km (25 miles) along the river banks.

Cabin on the warship *De Buffel*

🏛 **Maritiem Museum Rotterdam**
Leuvehaven 1. *Tel (010) 413 2680.*
☐ 10am– 5pm Tue–Sat, 11–5pm Sun & public hols; Jul & Aug: also Mon.
● 1 Jan, 30 Apr, 25 Dec. 🖾 🖾 ☐
🖾 🗓 www.maritiemmuseum.nl
Prince Hendrik, brother of King William III *(see pp32–3)*, founded this museum in 1873. Its main highlight is an iron-clad warship called *De Buffel*, built in 1868. Recently renovated, it boasts opulent officers' quarters with the atmosphere of a gentleman's club, and a small fleet of barges and steamships.

🏛 **Historisch Museum Rotterdam**
Korte Hoogstraat 31. *Tel (010) 217 6767.* ☐ 11am–5pm Tue–Sun.
● 1 Jan, 30 Apr, 25 Dec. 🖾 🖾
www.hmr.rotterdam.nl
Rotterdam's historical museum is in the Schielandshuis, a town house built in 1665 by Jacob Lois after designs by Pieter Post. The museum charts the development of the city, and the urbane lifestyles of its people, through displays of paintings, silverware and furniture in elegant rooms.

Oudehaven, with the futuristic Kubuswoningen houses in the background

Exploring Rotterdam

Much of Oudehaven, the old harbour area of Rotterdam, was bombed in World War II. It has largely been rebuilt in daring and avant-garde styles. The pencil-shaped **Gemeentebibliotheek** (public library) is in a similar style to the Pompidou Centre in Paris. Kop van Zuid, the former port area on the south bank, now has Renzo Piano's KPN Telecom head office and the Luxor Theater by Australian architect Peter Wilson.

Piet Blom's **Kubuswoningen** (cube houses) of 1982 are extraordinary apartments, set on concrete stilts and tilted at a crazy angle. Residents have specially designed furniture to fit the sloping rooms.

Pavement cafés have sprung up along the harbour quayside, and apartment blocks have now replaced the old wooden warehouses.

In the Golden Age, maritime trade brought wealth to Dutch towns with access to the sea. Delft *(see pp192–5)* lacked a harbour, so its citizens built a 12-km (7.5-mile) canal from the town to the Nieuwe Maas river, and constructed **Delfshaven** – a purpose-built village complete with harbour which remains a pretty corner of the city, with 18th-century warehouses converted into restaurants and cafés.

🏛 **Museum Boijmans Van Beuningen Rotterdam**
See pp200–201.

Peaceful canal houses in a quiet corner of Delfshaven

🏛 Historisch Museum de Dubbelde Palmboom

Voorhaven 12. **Tel** (010) 476 1533. ⏱ 11am–5pm Tue–Sun & public hols. ● 1 Jan, 30 Apr, 25 Dec. 📷 ♿ 🍴 🛈 **www**.hmr.rotterdam.nl

The museum "of the double palm tree" is in a twin-gabled, brick warehouse dating to 1825. Its five storeys are open-plan with vast, beamed rooms. These display arts and crafts, photographs and scale models depicting life at the mouth of the Nieuwe Maas river, from Iron Age fishing settlements to today's industrial port.

🏛 Wereldmuseum Rotterdam

Willemskade 25. **Tel** (010) 270 7172. ⏱ 10am–10pm Tue–Sun. ● 1 Jan, 30 Apr, 25 Dec. 📷 ♿ 🍴 🛈 **www**.wereldmuseum.rotterdam.nl

During the 17th century, the city fathers amassed a superb ethnological collection. The Wereldmuseum displays 1,800 artifacts from Indonesia, the Americas and Asia, and presents audiovisual displays of theatre, film, dance and music. A café-restaurant offers cuisine from around the world, with views of the river.

Euromast against the skyline

🚇 Euromast

Parkhaven 20. **Tel** (010) 436 4811. ⏱ Apr–Sep: 9:30am–11pm daily; Oct–Mar: 10am–11pm daily. 📷 ♿ 🍴 🛈 **www**.euromast.nl

Visitors ride a high-speed lift up the first 100 m (328 ft) of the Euromast to enjoy sweeping views of Rotterdam. This lower section, built in 1960, has a viewing platform with a restaurant and exhibition area.

In 1970 the Space Tower added another 85 m (272 ft) to make this the tallest construction in the Netherlands. A "space cabin" attached to the outside ascends 58 m (190 ft) up from the viewing platform.

Spido

Havenrondvaarten Willemsplein 85. **Tel** (010) 275 9988. **Europoort** ⏱ daily. **Boat tours** ⏱ Apr–Oct: daily; Nov–Mar: Wed–Sun. 📷 **www**.spido.nl

The wharves and quays of the city's port service about 32,000 container ships a year. A boat tour is an ideal way of seeing the port, built between 1958 and 1975. Cyclists and motorists follow the 48-km (30-mile) Haven Route (harbour route) along the Nieuwe Maas.

ROTTERDAM CITY CENTRE

Key to Symbols see back flap

Museum Boijmans Van Beuningen Rotterdam

The museum is named after two art connoisseurs, FJO Boijmans, who bequeathed his paintings to Rotterdam in 1847, and DG van Beuningen, whose heirs donated his collection to the state in 1955. The resulting collection is one of The Netherlands' finest. First displayed in the nearby Schielandshuis, the collection was moved to the present gallery in 1935. Known for its supreme series of Old Master paintings, the collection also covers the whole spectrum of art, from the medieval works of Jan van Eyck to rare glassware, Surrealist paintings and contemporary art.

Thetis Receives Achilles' Armour from Vulcanus
(1630–32)
This oil sketch by Peter Paul Rubens is one of a series inspired by Achilles' life.

Three Marys at the Open Sepulchre *(1430)*
Brothers Jan and Hubert van Eyck collaborated on this colourful work, which shows the three Marys at the tomb of the resurrected Christ.

Nautilus Cup
(1590)
A beautiful example of Dutch Renaissance art, this cup contains ornamental motifs relating to the sea and is crowned with Neptune sitting on a dolphin.

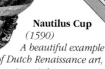

First floor

STAR PAINTINGS

- ★ The Tower of Babel by Pieter Bruegel
- ★ The Pedlar by Hieronymus Bosch
- ★ Titus at his Desk by Rembrandt

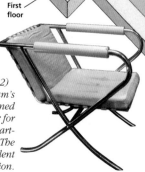

Armchair nr 04 *(1932)*
J J P Oud, Rotterdam's city architect, designed this tubular steel chair for the Amsterdam department store Metz & Co. The museum has an excellent design collection.

MUSEUM GUIDE

The museum is vast and the displays change regularly. Signposting to the museum's main sections is clear, however, and attendants are well adept at directing visitors. For Brueghel and Rembrandt follow signs to the Old Masters Collection, and for Dali and Magritte look for the Modern Art section.

VISITORS' CHECKLIST

Museumpark 18–20, Rotterdam.
Tel *(010) 441 9400.* 🚇 *Centraal Station.* 🕐 *11am–5pm Tue–Sun.* ⬤ *1 Jan, 30 Apr, 25 Dec.* 📷 ♿ 🍴 🛍
www.boijmans.nl

★ **Titus at his Desk** *(1655)*
Rembrandt portrayed his sickly son in introspective mood, bathed in a tender light which heightens the ghostly pallor of his brooding features.

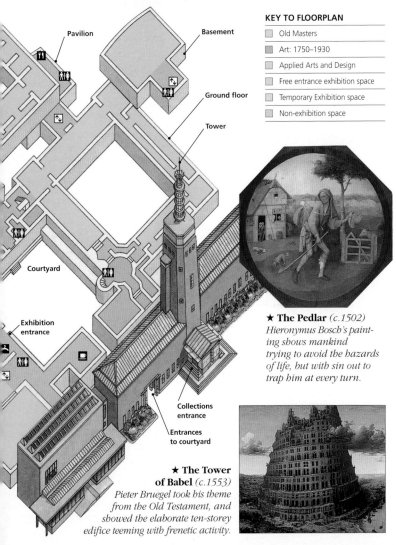

KEY TO FLOORPLAN

- 🔲 Old Masters
- 🔲 Art: 1750–1930
- 🔲 Applied Arts and Design
- 🔲 Free entrance exhibition space
- 🔲 Temporary Exhibition space
- 🔲 Non-exhibition space

Pavilion

Basement

Ground floor

Tower

Courtyard

Exhibition entrance

Collections entrance

Entrances to courtyard

★ **The Pedlar** *(c.1502)*
Hieronymus Bosch's painting shows mankind trying to avoid the hazards of life, but with sin out to trap him at every turn.

★ **The Tower of Babel** *(c.1553)*
Pieter Bruegel took his theme from the Old Testament, and showed the elaborate ten-storey edifice teeming with frenetic activity.

Utrecht ⑳

Utrecht was founded by the Romans in AD 47 to protect an important river crossing on the Rijn (Rhine). The town was among the first in the Netherlands to embrace Christianity. In 700, St Willibrord (658–739), a missionary from northern England, established a bishopric here, known as Het Sticht. Utrecht grew in importance as a religious centre throughout the Middle Ages, extending its control over much of the Netherlands until 1527, when Bishop Hendrik of Bavaria was obliged to sell all his temporal powers to Charles V *(see pp24–5)*. The city centre still retains many of its medieval churches and monasteries, but these now stand alongside modern blocks and a vast undercover shopping complex. The Oudegracht (old canal) threads its way through the city, flowing 5 m (16.5 ft) below ground level to prevent flooding. Today, it is lined with broad quays, cellar bars and cafés.

so it is fitting that the town has a superb railway museum in the restored 19th-century Maliebaan station. Inside there are specialist technical displays, engines and modern rail accessories. Outside, children can explore steam engines, carriages, trams and signal boxes.

The museum includes five new railway "worlds", each with its own theme.

🚩 Domtoren

Via "Rondom", Domplein 9. *Tel (030) 236 0010.* 🕐 *every hour. Apr–Sep: 11am–4pm daily (from noon*

The Gothic Domtoren

Mon, Sun; Oct–Mar: noon, 2pm & 4pm Sun–Fri; 11am–4pm Sat. ⬤ *1 Jan, 25 Dec.* 📷

The soaring Domtoren is a Gothic masterpiece and one of the tallest towers in the Netherlands at 112 m (367 ft) high. It was completed in 1382, on the site of the small, 8th-century church of St Willibrord. In 1674, the tower, which has always stood apart from the Domkerk, survived a massive hurricane that destroyed the nave of the cathedral. The Domtoren continues to dominate Utrecht's skyline.

⛪ Domkerk

Achter den Dom 1. *Tel (030) 231 0403* 🕐 *daily; phone for times.* ♿ 💻 🌐 www.domkerk.nl

Construction of the cathedral began in 1254. Today, only the north and south transepts, two chapels and the choir remain, along with the 15th-century cloisters and a chapter house (1495), now part of the university. It was here that the Union of Utrecht *(see p25)* was signed in 1579 by John, Count of Nassau, brother of William of Orange. Outside the church is a giant boulder, dated 980 and covered with runic symbols. It was presented to Utrecht by the Danish people in 1936, to commemorate Denmark's early conversion to Christianity by missionaries from Utrecht.

🏛 Nederlands Spoorwegmuseum

Maliebaanstation. *Tel (030) 2306 206.* 🕐 *10am–5pm Tue–Sun & public hols.* ⬤ *1 Jan, 30 Apr.* 📷 ♿ 🍴 💻 🌐 www.spoorwegmuseum.nl

The headquarters of the Dutch railways are based in Utrecht,

Organ in the Speelklok museum

🏛 Nationaal Museum van Speelklok tot Pierement

Buurkerk on Steenweg 6. *Tel (030) 2312 789.* 🕐 *10am–5pm Tue–Sun.* ⬤ *1 Jan, 30 Apr, 25 Dec.* 📷 📹 ♿ 💻 🌐 www.museumspeelklok.nl

This magical place – literally "from musical clock to street organ" – is located in the 13th-century Buurkerk, one of Utrecht's oldest churches. It has a collection of mechanical musical instruments from the 18th century to the present day. Fairground organs compete with clocks, carillons, pianolas and automated birds. These instruments are demonstrated on guided tours, during which visitors are encouraged to sing and dance along.

🏛 Centraal Museum

Nicolaaskerkhof 10. *Tel (030) 2362 362.* 🕐 *11am–5pm Tue–Sun (to 9pm Fri).* ⬤ *1 Jan, 30 Apr, 25 Dec.* 📷 📹 💻 🌐 www.centraalmuseum.nl

Housed in an old convent, Centraal Museum is only a ten-minute walk from the city centre. At the heart of the collection is a series of portraits by artist

Steam engine and guard's box, Nederlands Spoorwegmuseum

Gerrit Rietveld's Schröderhuis (1924), part of the Centraal Museum

VISITORS' CHECKLIST

57 km (35 miles) SE of Amsterdam. 🚇 234,000. 🚉 *Hoog Catharijne.* ℹ️ *Domplein 9 (0900 128 8732).* 🛒 *Wed & Sat.* 🎭 *Holland Festival Oude Muziek: end Aug–beg Sep; Netherlands Film Festival: end Sep–beg Oct.* **www**.utrechtyourway.com

Jan van Scorel (1495–1562). On visiting Rome, van Scorel absorbed ideas from Italian Renaissance painting and he became the first Dutch artist to paint group portraits. These established the tradition leading to the superb 16th-century Civic Guard portraits *(see p81)*.

Another of the museum's highlights is Gerrit Rietveld's Schröderhuis, Prins Hendriklaan 50. Designed in 1924 and regarded as the apogee of De Stijl architecture *(see p136)* (tours by appointment).

There is also a display of Dutch interior design from the Middle Ages to the 18th century.

🏠 Pieterskerk

Pieterskerkhof. *Tel (030) 2311 485.* ⏰ noon–4pm 1st & 3rd Sat (Jul–mid-Sep: 11am–4:30pm Tue–Sat). Built of tufa (limestone) with red sandstone columns, the church was completed in 1048. A rare Dutch example of German Romanesque architecture.

🏛 Museum Catharijneconvent

Lange Nieuwstraat 38. *Tel (030) 231 3835.* ⏰ 10am–5pm Tue–Sun (from 11am Sat, Sun & public hols). 🚫 1 Jan, 30 Apr. 🎫 ♿ 📷 ℹ️ **www**.catharijneconvent.nl
The beautiful former convent of St Catherine (1562) is now home to this fascinating

museum. It deals with the troubled history of religion in the Netherlands and owns an award-winning collection of medieval art. Sculptures, gold and silver work, manuscripts, paintings, ecclesiastical clothing and jewel-encrusted miniatures are displayed in rooms round the cloister.

Sculpture in Catharijneconvent

On the upper floors is a series of model church interiors, highlighting the variety of Dutch religious philosophies through the ages. They range from the lavish statues, paintings and altar in a Catholic church to the plain interiors typical of Protestant churches.

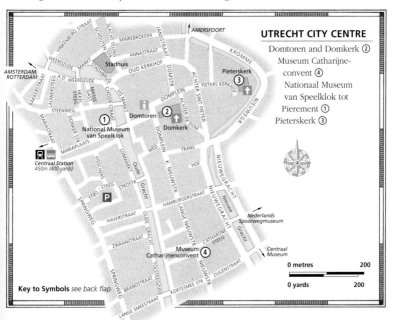

UTRECHT CITY CENTRE

Key to Symbols *see back flap*

0 metres   200
0 yards   200

Het Nationale Park De Hoge Veluwe ㉑

Made up of 5,500 ha (13,750 acres) of woodland, fen, heath and sand drifts, the Netherlands' largest nature reserve is home to thousands of rare plants, wild animals and birds. In order to preserve the natural habitat, cars are banned from large sections of the reserve. Also located in the park are the Museum Kröller-Müller, with more than 250 works by Van Gogh, and an outdoor sculpture garden, the Beeldentuin. Beneath the Visitors' Centre is the Museonder, with audiovisual displays about the earth's sub-surface, including an earthquake simulator.

Jachthuis St Hubertus
This hunting lodge was built in 1920 by HP Berlage (see p79) for the park's wealthy patrons, the Kröller-Müllers.

OTTERLOSE ZAND

De Wetweg

Otterlo entrance

Mouflon

Houtkampweg

Kronkel

Visitors' Centre and Museonder

★ Museum Kröller-Müller

Besides Van Gogh's Café Terrace at Night (1881), the museum has a collection of early Flemish masters and works by modern artists.

Nieuwe Plijmen game observation post

PLIJMEN

★ Beeldentuin

Jean Dubuffet's Jardin d'Emaille, *shown here, is one of the striking modern sculpures on display in this 11-ha (27-acre) sculpture park. The Beeldentuin also provides an elemental setting for works by Auguste Rodin, Alberto Giacometti and Barbara Hepworth.*

Roe Deer

OUD-REEMSTER ZAND

Wild Boar

Reemsterweg

Bosje van Staf game observation post

OUD-REEMS ZAND

Picnicking

Tables are provided near the Visitors' Centre. Picnicking is allowed everywhere except in areas set aside for the animals.

OUD-REEMST

Roe D

For additional map symbols *see back flap*

ee White Bicycles
*the Visitors' Centre bikes are
ailable for exploring the park.*

Camp site

Hoenderloo
entrance

Roe Deer

Koeverbos
game
observation
post

Red Deer

DEELENSE
VELD

ENSE
ND

Game Hides and Observation Points
*Special viewing areas (see map) allow
the wildlife, like red deer, moufflon sheep
and wild boar, to remain undisturbed.*

Schaarsbergen
entrance

ERBERG

VISITORS' CHECKLIST

80 km (50 miles) SE of Amsterdam.
108S from Apeldoorn or Ede-
Wageningen, change to 106 at
Otterlo. **Entrances** *Otterlo, Schaarsbergen, Hoenderloo.* **Nationale
Park Visitors' Centre** *Otterlo.* **Tel**
(0900) 464 3835. Apr: 8am–
8pm; May, Aug: 8am–9pm; Jun,
Jul: 8am–10pm; Sep: 9am–8pm;
Oct: 9am–7pm; Nov–Mar: 9am–
6pm. **Regulations**: *Do
not camp, or disturb the animals.
Vehicles must not leave the road.
Do not light fires outside designated
areas. Keep dogs on a leash.*
Museum Kröller-Müller
Houtkampweg 6, Otterlo. **Tel** *(0318)
591 241.* 10am–5pm Tue–Sun
& public hols. 1 Jan.
www.hogeveluwe.nl

KEY

— Main road

••• Walk route

⸬⸬⸬ Cycle path

▦ Forest

▨ Heath

▧ Sand drifts

▨ No access

0 kilometres 2

0 miles 1

STAR SIGHTS

★ Museum
Kröller-Müller

★ Beeldentuin

Arnhem ㉒

80 km (50 miles) SE of Amsterdam.
141,000. Stationsplein
13. 0900 112 2344.
Sat. www.vvvarnhem.nl

Capital of Gelderland province,
Arnhem was all but destroyed
between 17 and 27 September
1944, in one of the most
famous battles of World War II.
The city still retains a number
of reminders of the conflict,
such as the John Frost Bridge,
scene of some of the heaviest
fighting. The bridge is named
after the commanding officer
of the 2nd Parachute Battalion,
which fought to hold the
bridgehead for four days.

🏛 Airborne Museum
Hartenstein
Utrechtseweg 232, Oosterbeek.
Tel *(026) 3337 710.* check website. 1 Jan, 25 Dec.
www.airbornemuseum.com
The museum traces the course
of the struggle to take Arnhem,
using models, slides, taped
commentaries and original film
footage. The collection is in
Villa Hartenstein near Oosterbeek, used by the Commander
of the 1st British Airborne
Division, General Urquhart.

John Frost Bridge, Arnhem

🏛 Nederlands
Openluchtmuseum
Schelmseweg 89. **Tel** *(026) 357
6100.* 10am–5pm daily; Dec–
mid-Jan: 11am–7pm; mid-Jan–Mar:
11am–4:30pm (park only). 1 Jan,
Nov, 24 Dec. www.
openluchtmuseum.nl
Situated in a wooded park, this
museum recreates the traditional architecture and folklore of
the Netherlands from 1800 to
1950. Founded in 1912, about
100 farmhouses, barns, windmills and workshops have
since been erected here, many
of them furnished in period
style. The museum staff dress
up in traditional costume.

Paleis Het Loo ㉓

Stadholder William III *(see p30)* built Het Loo in 1686 as a royal hunting lodge. Generations of the House of Orange used the lodge as a summer palace. Because of its magnificence, it was regarded as the "Versailles of the Netherlands". The main architect was Jacob Roman (1640–1716); the interior decoration and layout of the gardens were the responsibility of Daniel Marot (1661–1752). The building's Classical façade belies the opulence of its lavish interior; after extensive restoration work was completed on both in 1984, the palace was opened as a museum.

Coat of arms (1690) of William and Mary, future king and queen of England.

King William III's bedroom

★ **Royal Bedroom of Stadholder William III** *(1713)*
Recently refurbished, the wall coverings and draperies in this luxurious bedroom are of rich orange damask and purple silk.

King's Garden

Stadholder William III's Closet *(1690)*
The walls of William's private study are covered in embossed scarlet damask. His favourite paintings and Delftware pieces are exhibited here.

Classic Cars
This 1925 Bentley, nicknamed Min-erva, was owned by Prince Hendrik, husband of Queen Wilhelmina. It is one of the royal family's many vintage cars, which are on display in the stable block (1910).

STAR FEATURES

★ Old Dining Room

★ Royal Bedroom

★ Formal Gardens

VISITORS' CHECKLIST

85 km (53 miles) SE of Amsterdam.
Koninklijk Park 1, Apeldoorn. **Tel**
(055) 577 2400. Apeldoorn,
then bus 102. **Palace & Gardens**
10am–5pm Tue–Sun. 1 Jan.
gardens only.
www.paleishetloo.nl

★ **Old Dining Room** *(1686)*
In 1984, six layers of paint were removed from the marbled walls, now hung with tapestries depicting scenes from Ovid's poems.

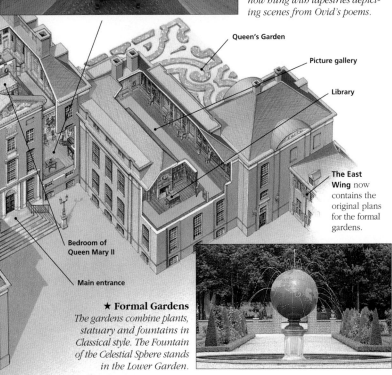

Queen's Garden

Picture gallery

Library

The East Wing now contains the original plans for the formal gardens.

Bedroom of Queen Mary II

Main entrance

★ **Formal Gardens**
The gardens combine plants, statuary and fountains in Classical style. The Fountain of the Celestial Sphere stands in the Lower Garden.

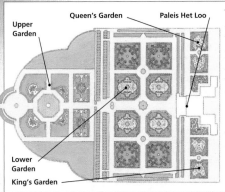

Upper Garden

Queen's Garden

Paleis Het Loo

Lower Garden

King's Garden

THE FORMAL GARDENS

Old prints, records and plans were used as the guidelines for recreating Het Loo's formal gardens, which lie in the vast acres behind the palace. Grass was planted over the original walled and knot gardens in the 18th century, and this was cleared in 1975. By 1983, the intricate floral patterns had been re-established, replanting had begun, the Classical fountains were renovated and the water supply fully restored. The garden reflects the late 17th-century belief that art and nature should operate in harmony.

Layout of the formal section of the gardens

TRAVELLERS' NEEDS

WHERE TO STAY

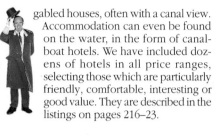

Amsterdam provides top-quality, city-centre accommodation to suit everyone's budget. It ranges from a clutch of luxurious five-star hotels that should impress the most hedonistic traveller to the many cheap hostels for those on a budget. In between there are scores of B&Bs, many occupying pretty gabled houses, often with a canal view. Accommodation can even be found on the water, in the form of canal-boat hotels. We have included dozens of hotels in all price ranges, selecting those which are particularly friendly, comfortable, interesting or good value. They are described in the listings on pages 216–23.

The Van Ostade Bicycle Hotel in southern Amsterdam *(see p223)*

CHOOSING A HOTEL

Most of Amsterdam's hotels are clustered in a few areas: the most popular place to stay, unsurprisingly, is along the scenic canals; the neighbourhood near the museums and Vondelpark is also popular. More suited to the budget traveller is the area around Centraal Station and the Red Light District, where you will find one or two gems studded amongst the general seediness.

Visitors often find accommodation in Amsterdam expensive, while at the same time rooms can be smaller than in other European cities. Hotels which are most beautiful and most typical of Amsterdam are found along the main canal belt, the *Grachtengordel*. Many of these buildings are listed monuments and thus cannot be altered, so you will often come across very steep stairs and no lifts.

Hotels in the Museum Quarter tend to be a little more spacious and are often in elegant villas. This sedate area is away from the bright lights, but near many of Amsterdam's cultural hotspots like the Rijksmuseum and the Concertgebouw.

Hotels which are aimed squarely at the business market are mostly clustered around the RAI exhibition centre in the south, and near the office blocks of Nieuw Zuid (New South).

Arena Hotel *(see p223)*

Wherever a hotel is situated in Amsterdam, however, seems to have little effect on price, so the cost of a hotel in a suburb will differ little from that of one in the same class in the very centre.

The **Amsterdam Tourist Board (VVV)** publishes a comprehensive list of accommodation in the city, available at Schiphol Airport and VVV offices, as well as

NBTC (Netherlands Board of Tourism and Conventions) offices around the world.

ROOM RATES

There are no hard and fast rules as to whether a hotel's advertised rates always include breakfast and the compulsory five per cent City Tax, though the price guide we include in the listings on pages 216–23 does factor all of these additional charges in. Generally, breakfast tends to be included, apart from at those hotels at the very top and bottom ends of the price scale.

If you are staying in the *Grachtengordel*, be aware that rooms with canal views generally cost more, whatever class of hotel you are staying

Hotel de l'Europe, overlooking Muntplein *(see p216)*

◁ **People relaxing on the terrace of De Jaren café, in Nieuwe Zijde**

An airy breakfast room in an Amsterdam hotel

in. Hotels are also increasingly starting to specify that weekend stays must be for a minimum of three nights.

There are a couple of tips that budget-conscious travellers should bear in mind. Firstly, if you are travelling in a group, many hotels have larger rooms for sharing, or will add beds for a fraction of the room price. Secondly, cheaper accommodation is available in budget hotels for those prepared to share sanitation. Lone travellers generally get a bad deal; the maximum reduction on single occupation of a double room is around 20 per cent – if there is any reduction at all, that is. The best option for visitors on their own is to make use of one of the many hostels. Some can be particularly quirky and charming – especially those located in canal boats along the picturesque waterways.

SPECIAL OFFERS

Many hotels – especially private ones – have lower rates between November and March, although they tend to peak again around Christmas and New Year. Some even throw in a complimentary boat trip and/or free museum admissions. When booking, it is always worthwhile making a point of asking about any special offers that might be available when you visit.

Chain hotels, of which there are many, almost always have promotions on, so if you shop around, it is unlikely that you will have to pay the standard rate. You will also find that many chains are aimed at businesses, so weekend rates are often substantially cheaper than weekday prices – **NH Hoteles** and **Best Western** are two of the best in Amsterdam. For good deals in all classes of hotels, whether chain or private, it is worth checking a reputable reservations website like www.hotels.nl or www. booking.com. Other holiday websites, such as lastminute. com, expedia.com and kayak. com also usually have good offers. You can often save money by booking your flight and hotel together.

BOOKING AND PAYING

The busiest times of year for Amsterdam hotels are April to May (as it is tulip season), July and August and the Christmas and New Year period. If you want to visit during these times it is worth bearing in mind that you will have to book your room months in advance to get the best deal. Amsterdam is such a popular city that it is often difficult to book a room last minute at any time of the year, so planning ahead – especially if you intend on staying in a *Grachtengordel* or canalside hotel – is recommended.

Booking a room via telephone, website or email is invariably straightforward, as hotel staff all speak excellent English. All the chains take credit card payments, as do an increasing number of privately-owned hotels.

Many smaller establishments will ask for a deposit in the form of a cheque or postal order, usually for the full amount of the first night's stay, while some of these smaller and/or cheaper hotels are also able to secure room bookings on credit cards. There is, however, no guarantee that the final bill can be settled with a card – often, a cash payment will be necessary when checking out.

If you arrive in Amsterdam without a room already reserved, then the VVV (tourist board) at Schiphol Airport, Centraal Station (two branches) or Leidseplein will book one for you, but this service will incur a small fee. Hotels can also be found and booked through the VVV website, www.iamsterdam.com.

HOTEL GRADINGS

The star system used by Benelux Hotel Classification ranges from one (may have shared sanitation facilities) to five stars (rooms must be of a minimum size and the hotel must have plenty of amenities). These stars relate entirely to facilities and not to location or attractiveness, therefore you may find that a small, cheap hotel on a canal is more charming than a bland, corporate one in the suburbs, but that the more "appealing" of the two will have fewer stars.

The elegant foyer of the Inter-Continental Amstel *(see p223)*

Dining room of the Canal House in the Western Canal Ring *(see p218)*

WHAT TO EXPECT

The only hotels which have restaurants are the larger chains or very expensive hotels, the former are generally middle-of-the-road, the latter among the best in town. On the other hand, quite a few hotels – even the smallest – have bars. The rest provide just bed and breakfast, though bigger places may also have communal lounge areas.

Breakfast itself is a filling buffet which will always include rolls, jam, cheese and meats, a boiled egg and coffee. Only the most expensive hotels will provide hot dishes.

Make sure you get a description of the room when you book, or you may find you do not have that canal vista you had hoped for. Most rooms are on the small side and will come with a TV and telephone. Increasing numbers of hotels – even budget ones – now provide Wi-Fi, though this is not always free of charge. Bathrooms can be tiny, and, as with Amsterdam apartments, bathtubs are a luxury rather than standard.

Wall plaque on the façade of the Radisson Blu *(see p216)*

TRAVELLING WITH CHILDREN

Amsterdam is generally a child-friendly place, and although some of the most exclusive places positively discourage younger travellers, most places welcome them. Many of the chains and bigger hotels allow children (usually up to two) to stay free in parents' rooms and some offer free breakfasts. Other hotels may offer reduced rates or charge a small fee to rent out babies' cots. It is worth shopping around for the best deal. We have indicated which hotels cater for children in the listings on pages 216-23.

GAY HOTELS

Amsterdam is a very gay-friendly city, so you may not even want to stay in a gay hotel. If you do, though, the most popular is the **Golden Bear**, at the heart of the Kerkstraat gay scene. **ITC**, near Rembrandtplein, is also popular with both gay and lesbian travellers. The city lacks women-only accommodation, but many lesbians stay at the **Quentin**, near Leidseplein. *The Bent Guide to Amsterdam* gives a full overview of all things gay and lesbian and is available at **Pink Point** and the **Vrolijk** bookshop, or order the information kit on gay Amsterdam from Gaytic *(see pp257–8).*

DISABLED TRAVELLERS

Cobbled streets, tall, narrow houses and steep stairs are all things that make Amsterdam so charming for able-bodied visitors, but they can cause problems for disabled tourists. As so many hotels on the canal belt have a protected status and cannot be altered, there are few lifts, so wheel-chair access is often only viable in chain hotels or top-price establishments. Our listings on pages 216-23 indicate which hotels have lifts and specially adapted rooms.

HOSTELS

There is a strong hostel scene in Amsterdam, catering to a young backpacking crowd, many of whom are attracted to Amsterdam's liberal attitude to marijuana smoking. Many hostels have cheap, cheerful bars, which are ideal for meeting like-minded people.

Some good hostels are mentioned in our listings. Most hostels are privately owned (except **Stayokay**) and have dorm accommodation, though some may have private rooms as well. There are often curfews and hostels near to Centraal Station are sometimes not as pleasant as elsewhere, so do exercise caution when booking.

CAMPING

Although Amsterdam is well served by campsites, none of them are in the city centre, though there are good public transport links. Open between March and October, **Gaasper Camping** is good for families and there are watersporting opportunities nearby. The **Amsterdamse Bos** site is set in acres of recreational woodland, perfect for children. To the north, **Vliegenbos** is great for exploring pretty Waterland villages, and **Zeeburg** is the nearest of all to the city centre. It has a tram-stop within walking distance, rental huts and is open year-round.

SELF-CATERING

There are few self-catering options in Amsterdam since apartment space is at a premium. The VVV's hotel brochure lists letting agents, who usually stipulate a minimum stay of a week. City Mundo's website (www.citymundo.nl) is also a good place to research possibilities. Of the hotels recommended in this guide, Best Western Eden *(see p219)*, Hotel Acacia *(see p218)* and Sunhead of 1617 *(see p218)* offer the best self-catering options.

STAYING IN PRIVATE HOMES

Owing to the fact real estate is at a premium and Amsterdam flats tend to be tiny, guesthouse stays in people's homes are severely limited and the law also prevents more than four people lodging in a private home at any one time. That said, **Bed and Breakfast Holland** provides an excellent resource for researching and finding those limited rooms that are available.

BEYOND AMSTERDAM

The NBTC's website lists more than 2,000 hotels throughout the Netherlands, with comprehensive information about each of them. Although this guide does not cover hotels outside Amsterdam, the information about booking and paying, hotel gradings, hostels and camping applies throughout the entire country.

The bar of Arena Hotel *(see p223)*, a hostel near Oosterpark

DIRECTORY

INFORMATION

NBTC
Postbus 458, 2260 MG
Leidschendam.
Tel 070 370 5705.
Fax 070 320 1654.
www.holland.com

GAY HOTELS/INFO

Golden Bear
Kerkstraat 37, 1017 GB
Amsterdam. **Map** 1 C3.
Tel 624 4785.
www.goldenbear.nl

ITC
Prinsengracht 1051, 1017
JE Amsterdam. **Map** 5 A3.
Tel 623 0230. Fax 420 4369.
www.itc-hotel.com

Pink Point
Westermarkt, 1016 DH
Amsterdam. **Map** 1 B4.
Tel 428 1070.
www.pinkpoint.org

Quentin
Leidsekade 89, 1017 PN,
Amsterdam. **Map** 4 D1.
Tel 626 2187.
www.quentinhotels.com

Vrolijk
Paleisstraat 135, 1012 ZL
Amsterdam. **Map** 7 B5.
*Tel 623 5142. Fax 638
3807.* www.vrolijk.nu

CHAIN HOTELS

Best Western
Tel 0800 022 1455.
www.bestwestern.com

NH Hoteles
Tel 088 4000 9000.
www.nh-hotels.com

RESERVATIONS

**Amsterdam Tourist
Board (VVV) Offices**
Centraal Station, Stations-
plein 10, Platform 2B.
Map 4 D2.

Leidseplein 26.
Schiphol Airport, Arrivals
Hall 2.
www.iamsterdam.com

HOSTELS

Stayokay
Stadsdoelen (city centre).
Map 7 C4. *Tel 624 6832.*
Vondelpark. **Map** 4 D2.
Tel 589 8996.
www.stayokay.com

CAMPING

Amsterdamse Bos
Kleine Noorddijk 1, 1187
NZ Amstelveen.
*Tel 641 6868. Fax 640
2378.* www.camping
amsterdamsebos.nl

**Gaasper
Camping**
Loosdrechtdreef 7, 1108
AZ Amsterdam.

Tel 696 7326.
Fax 696 9369.
www.gaaspercamping.nl

Vliegenbos
Meeuwenlaan 138, 1022
AM, Amsterdam. *Tel 636
8855. Fax 632 2723.*
www.vliegenbos.com

Zeeburg
Zuider IJdijk 20, 1095 KN,
Amsterdam. *Tel 694
4430. Fax 694 6238.*
www.campingzeeburg.nl

STAYING IN
PRIVATE HOMES

**Bed & Breakfast
Holland**
Tel 615 7527.
www.bedandbreak
fastholland.com

Amsterdam's Best: Hotels

The hotels recommended on these two pages possess an individual charm and character not found in most of their chain-hotel counterparts. All of these recommendations have a typically Dutch atmosphere, ranging from the simple and homely to the ornate, and some have an historical interest. Many of these hotels are impeccably restored 17th-century canal houses offering both canal and garden views, in addition to steep and narrow staircases. So whether you are after a reasonably priced B&B or looking for luxury, there is a huge choice available in Amsterdam.

Canal House
This atmospheric B&B has been restored to create an ambience of past grandeur. (See p218.)

Western Canal Ring

Hotel Pulitzer
This surprising, labyrinthine hotel was created by joining together 24 old canal houses and their gardens. (See p220.)

De Filosoof (Sandton Hotel)
Perhaps the city's most unusual hotel. Rooms are named after the world's greatest thinkers, with thematic decor. (See p222.)

Central Canal Ring

Museum Quarter

Ambassade
This classy B&B is an ideal choice for those who want to stay in a characterful, gabled canal house without forgoing comfort. (See p220.)

NH Grand Hotel Krasnapolsky
This 130-year-old institution has a good choice of restaurants, including the impressive Winter Garden shown left. (See p218.)

The Grand
The newest of Amsterdam's set of luxury hotels has the air of an opulent country house. (See p216.)

Nieuwe Zijde

Seven Bridges
On a pretty canal, this refined B&B is filled with antiques and Persian rugs. (See p220.)

Oude Zijde

Plantage

0 metres	500
0 yards	500

Prinsenhof
The dedicated owners of this charmingly decorated, simple canal-house B&B provide delightful accommodation at a very reasonable price. (See p220.)

Eastern Canal Ring

Intercontinental Amstel
Situated by the side of the Amstel, the city's number one hotel is serene, breathtakingly beautiful and utterly luxurious. (See p223.)

Choosing a Hotel

The hotels listed below have been selected across a wide price range for their excellence of facilities, location or character. The listings start with the central areas and continue with hotels outside of the centre. For map references, see the street finder maps on pp280–87. For restaurant listings, see pp228–35.

PRICE CATEGORIES
The following prices are for a standard double room per night, including breakfast, tax and service.

€ under €100
€€ €100–150
€€€ €150–200
€€€€ €200–250
€€€€€ over €250

OUDE ZIJDE

Stayokay Stadsdoelen   €
Kloveniersburgwal 97, 1011 KB **Tel** *624 6832* **Fax** *639 1035* **Rooms** *8*   **Map** *7 D3*

Aimed at the backpack brigade, Stayokay Stadsdoelen offers packages themed around nature or architecture. In a townhouse near Nieuwmarkt, spartan rooms accommodate eight to 20 people. There is a nice courtyard garden and a simple bar where evening meals are served. **www.stayokay.com**

MISC   €€
Kloveniersburgwal 20, 1012 CV **Tel** *330 6241* **Fax** *330 6242* **Rooms** *6*   **Map** *7 D3*

This funky, small hotel nestled among the cafés and bars of Nieuwmarkt is ideally situated for carousing (breakfast is served until noon) and culture. The bright rooms are decorated individually by theme, such as "Afrika". The owners are very helpful and will organize everything from a walking tour to a boat trip. **www.hotelmisc.nl**

Residence Le Coin   €€€
Nieuwe Doelenstraat 5, 1012 CP **Tel** *524 6800* **Fax** *524 6801* **Rooms** *42*   **Map** *7 C4*

On a pleasant café-lined street near the university, this residence offers spacious apartment-style rooms. They are furnished in a bright, modern style with big windows and equipped with kitchenettes, which makes Le Coin a good bet for families and visitors on longer stays (there are special monthly rates). **www.lecoin.nl**

Grand Hôtel Amrâth Amsterdam   €€€€
Prins Hendrikkade 108–144, 1011 AK **Tel** *552 0000* **Fax** *552 0900* **Rooms** *165*   **Map** *8 E2*

The Grand Hôtel Amrâth Amsterdam opened in 2007 and occupies the Scheepvarthuis *(see pp66–7)*, a 1913 landmark building of the Amsterdam School. Originally constructed as the offices of six shipping companies, the monumental building now houses this luxury hotel overlooking the old harbour. **www.amrathamsterdam.com**

Radisson Blu   €€€€
Rusland 17, 1012 CK **Tel** *623 1231* **Fax** *520 8200* **Rooms** *242*   **Map** *7 C4*

On a beautiful street between two atmospheric canals, this big hotel has a glorious atrium that can be seen from some rooms. Rooms are large by Amsterdam standards, and furnishings are a mixture of classic and funky. There is an in-house fitness room and conference facilities. **www.radissonblu.com**

Hotel de l'Europe   €€€€€
Nieuwe Doelenstraat 2–8, 1012 CP **Tel** *531 1777* **Fax** *531 1778* **Rooms** *109*   **Map** *7 C4*

This landmark hotel with fabulous views over the Amstel has top-of-the-range suites, and these, as well as more workaday rooms, are luxuriously decorated with drapes and chandeliers. Bathrooms are seriously opulent, featuring Bulgari toiletries. There's a separate wing with 23 suites, each inspired by a Dutch master painting. **www.leurope.nl**

The Grand   €€€€€
Oudezijds Voorburgwal 197, 1012 EX **Tel** *555 3111* **Fax** *555 3222* **Rooms** *177*   **Map** *7 C3*

Amsterdam's former town hall abuts the Red Light District but couldn't be further away from the seediness close by. Once inside the courtyard, guests are cocooned in luxury. Everything you expect from a deluxe hotel is here: marble bathrooms, spacious rooms and discreet service. The on-site restaurant (Roux) is also excellent. **www.thegrand.nl**

NIEUWE ZIJDE

Avenue   €€
Nieuwezijds Voorburgwal 33, 1012 RD **Tel** *530 9530* **Fax** *530 9599* **Rooms** *80*   **Map** *7 C1*

Great for exploring Nieuwe Zijde nightlife and, with two lifts, good for those with mobility problems. Avenue consists of nine canal houses, once of which was an East India Company spice warehouse. The rooms are good, but some residents complain of lack of attention to detail (such as running out of coffee at breakfast). **www.embhotels.nl/avenue**

Key to Symbols *see back cover flap*

Rho Hotel
☐ P   €€

Nes 5–23, 1012 KC **Tel** *620 7371* **Fax** *620 7826* **Rooms** *170*   **Map** *7 B3*

Just metres from bustling Dam Square, though tucked down a backstreet bristling with interesting bars, restaurants and theatres, this hotel is well placed and good value. The beautiful Art Nouveau lobby was once part of a theatre built in 1908. Though plain, the rooms are neat and tidy. **www.rhohotel.nl**

Citadel
☐   €€€

Nieuwezijds Voorburgwal 98–100, 1012 SG **Tel** *627 3882* **Fax** *627 4684* **Rooms** *38*   **Map** *7 C1*

A reliable town-centre hotel halfway between the Jordaan and old quarter, the Citadel is ideal for urban explorers. It has been refurbished and though rooms are clean, they are on the plain side. Public spaces like the reception area and bar, however, are decorated in warm wood tones. Staff are helpful. **www.centrehotels.nl**

The Convent Hotel Amsterdam
☐ Ⅱ ⍟ Ⓣ 🛇   €€€

Nieuwezijds Voorburgwal 67, 1012 RE **Tel** *627 5900* **Fax** *623 8932* **Rooms** *148*   **Map** *7 B1*

A good base for sightseeing, dining and shopping, the hotel is furnished with top-of-the-range luxuries: there is a sauna and a restaurant, and the bar is modelled on the Orient Express. The staff are helpful, and the rooms themselves are smart, if somewhat staid, with lots of wood and opulent Regency stripes. **www.accorhotels.com**

Die Port van Cleve
☐ Ⅱ ⍟ 🛇   €€€

Nieuwezijds Voorburgwal 176–180, 1012 SJ **Tel** *718 9013* **Fax** *421 0310* **Rooms** *120*   **Map** *7 B2*

Beer fans will be delighted to stay here, in the very building where Heineken began brewing in the 1870s. Non-drinkers will be equally satisfied with the hotel's big, luxurious rooms and suites. Gourmets enjoy the renowned on-site steak restaurant, as well as the city's restaurant scene on the doorstep. **www.dieportvancleve.com**

Estherea
☐ ⍟ 🛇   €€€

Singel 303–309, 1012 WJ **Tel** *624 5146* **Fax** *623 9001* **Rooms** *92*   **Map** *7 A3*

An elegant, family-run hotel that has been in the same careful hands for more than 60 years. There are 71 rooms spread across six canal houses, all with an emphasis on opulent fabrics and luxury, from DVD players to marble bathrooms. Facilities include an intimate library and a lounge with watery views. **www.estherea.nl**

Hotel des Arts
€€€

Rokin 154–156, 1012 LE **Tel** *620 1558* **Fax** *624 9995* **Rooms** *22*   **Map** *7 B4*

This cosy, family-run place is ideal for shopping addicts, since it is just steps away from from the main consumer thoroughfare, Kalverstraat. There are 18 spacious rooms (pitched at groups and families) and a couple of smaller ones; although on the dark side, they all have glamorous touches such as chandeliers. **www.hoteldesarts.nl**

Hotel Sint Nicolaas
☐   €€€

Spuistraat 1A, 1012 SP **Tel** *626 1384* **Fax** *623 0979* **Rooms** *27*   **Map** *7 C1*

Located near Centraal Station *(see p79)*, this hotel (owned by the same company as Citadel) has quirky touches (an outsized lift and odd-shaped rooms) that reflect its former life as a mattress factory. Rooms are neat and have en-suite facilities – some with baths. Free wireless Internet in every room is a welcome touch. **www.centrehotels.nl**

Kamer 01 Bed & Breakfast
€€€

Singel 416, 1016 AK **Tel** *625 6627* **Rooms** *2*   **Map** *7 B5*

With just two rooms, the warm and plush Red Room and the equally comfortable Blue Room, personal service is never far away. This B&B is housed in a listed building, with lots of authentic details. Both rooms also have modern luxuries like iMacs and rain showers, plus an amazing view over the Singel canal. Breakfast is a feast. **www.kamer01.nl**

Mövenpick Hotel Amsterdam City Centre
☐ Ⅱ Ⓣ 🛇 P   €€€

Piet Heinkade 11, 1019 BR **Tel** *519 1200* **Fax** *519 1239* **Rooms** *408*   **Map** *2 F3*

This hotel has all the comfort you would expect from an upscale chain hotel. The location is perfect for exploring the nearby Eastern Docks architecture or for going to concerts at the next-door Muziekgebouw. There is a tram stop in front of the hotel, or you can rent a bike for easy access to the city centre. **www.moevenpick-amsterdam.com**

Nova
☐   €€€

Nieuwezijds Voorburgwal 276, 1012 RD **Tel** *623 0066* **Fax** *627 2026* **Rooms** *61*   **Map** *7 B2*

A reliable city-centre standard occupying five canal houses. Rooms have up-to-date decor, with red brick walls and blonde-wood furniture; they are comfortable, though bathrooms are rather cramped. It is ideal for all the sights – some rooms have views of the Koninklijk Paleis *(see p74)* – and for exploring nearby nightlife. **www.novahotel.nl**

Singel Hotel
☐ ⍟   €€€

Singel 13–17, 1012 VC **Tel** *626 3108* **Fax** *620 3777* **Rooms** *32*   **Map** *7 B1*

One of the few budget choices in the city, the Singel is good for its proximity to the station and accessibility to canal walks. Once inside the attractive, 17th-century house, things are pretty basic. Rooms are all en suite with showers and, in the main, clean and tidy. Those at the front, however, can get a little noisy. **www.singelhotel.nl**

NH Barbizon Palace
☐ Ⅱ ⍟ Ⓣ 🛇 P   €€€€

Prins Hendrikkade 59–72, 1012 AD **Tel** *556 4564* **Fax** *624 3353* **Rooms** *274*   **Map** *8 D1*

The jewel in the NH crown, this hotel has sleek black-and-white decor in public spaces. Rooms, by contrast, are all dowdy beiges and browns and seem a little tired. Facilities are outstanding: excellent breakfasts, the gourmet Restaurant Vermeer *(see p229)* and a 14th-century chapel as one of the eight conference rooms. **www.nh-hotels.com**

NH Grand Hotel Krasnapolsky

Dam 9, 1012 JS **Tel** *554 9111* **Fax** *622 8607* **Rooms** *468* **Map** *7 C2*

The location of this hotel – on Dam Square, overlooking the Koninklijk Paleis *(see p74)* – is great. Accommodation ranges from utter luxury in the Tower Suite to compact rooms at the back. Facilities are top-notch: restaurants, café, cocktail bar. The Winter Garden is where weekend brunches are consumed. **www.nh-hotels.com**

Renaissance Amsterdam

Kattengat 1, 1012 SZ **Tel** *621 2223* **Fax** *627 5245* **Rooms** *402* **Map** *7 C1*

A large hotel excellent for exploring the Jordaan. Rooms are a touch flowery, but they deliver chain-hotel luxuries like movies, interactive video and PlayStation. Good for business travellers: as well as being close to Centraal Station *(see p79)*, its conference facilities are in the 17th-century domed Koepelkerk, next door. **www.marriott.com**

Swissotel Amsterdam

Damrak 96–98, 1012 LP **Tel** *522 3000* **Fax** *522 3223* **Rooms** *109* **Map** *7 C2*

Rooms here have stylish decor in soothing pastel shades. All are soundproofed, so a good night's sleep is guaranteed. Book the suite for a treat: it overlooks the Dam, and the huge bathroom has a Jacuzzi. Being directly opposite the city's best department store, De Bijenkorf, makes this hotel an ideal base for shopaholics. **www.swissotel.com**

WESTERN CANAL RING

Hotel Acacia

Lindengracht 251, 1015 KH **Tel** *622 1460* **Fax** *638 0748* **Rooms** *14* **Map** *1 B3*

It is back to basics at this functional, if a little care-worn, place in a quiet corner in the farthest reaches of the Jordaan. Rooms are small and completely frill-free, leading some guests to liken Acacia to a seaside B&B. There are also two studios available, each with a kitchenette. **www.hotelacacia.nl**

Hotel van Onna

Bloemgracht 102–108, 1015 TN **Tel** *626 5801* **Rooms** *41* **Map** *1 A4*

On the most scenic canal in Amsterdam, this hotel spread over three canal houses from the 17th to 20th centuries is a few minutes' walk from the Westerkerk *(see p90)* and Anne Frank's house *(see p90)*. It is a non-smoking hotel; rooms are basically furnished and equipped, with reasonable rates for single travellers. **www.hotelvanonna.nl**

Sunhead of 1617

Herengracht 152, 1016 BN **Tel** *626 1809* **Rooms** *2* **Map** *7 A2*

The owners of this cosy bed & breakfast are extremely helpful, cooking up an amazing breakfast and full of information about Amsterdam. The bedrooms, up a narrow winding staircase in the third-floor attic, have exposed beams and a pleasant colour scheme. Magnificent views over the canal at the front. **www.sunhead.com**

Canal House

Keizersgracht 148, 1015 CX **Tel** *622 5182* **Fax** *624 1317* **Rooms** *26* **Map** *7 A1*

An elegant retreat for those who are seeking quiet refuge. Rooms, in classical 17th-century style with heavy wooden furniture, are TV-free, adding further to the serenity. Those without a canal view overlook the pretty inner garden. Excellent breakfasts and well-informed staff. **www.canalhouse.nl**

Chic and Basic

Herengracht 13–19, 1015 BA **Tel** *522 2345* **Fax** *522 2389* **Rooms** *26* **Map** *2 D3*

Located in three adjacent canal houses with a 300-year-old façade, this hotel has a contemporary interior. Wooden floors and white furniture give the rooms a minimalistic touch. There's a breakfast buffet and free espresso machine in the lounge. The more expensive rooms have canal views. **www.chicandbasic.com**

't Hotel

Leliegracht 18, 1015 DE **Tel** *422 2741* **Fax** *626 7873* **Rooms** *8* **Map** *7 A2*

A plain name for a lovely hotel nesting on a beautiful Jordaan canal. Rooms are not full of luxuries, but they are very stylish, painted in neutral tones with 1920s-influenced furniture. They are also spacious and have enormous windows. Room number 8, at the very top, is on a split level and sleeps five. **www.thotel.nl**

Truelove Antiek and Guesthouse

Prinsenstraat 4, 1015 DC **Tel** *320 2500* **Fax** *0847 114 950* **Rooms** *2* **Map** *7 A1*

A dinky, two-roomed romantic bolthole atop an antique shop (also the hotel's reception) at the heart of Amsterdam's most interesting shopping area. It is non-smoking, simple and stylish; although there is no breakfast (you are spoiled for choice nearby), there are considerate touches like wine, water and fresh flowers in the room. **www.truelove.be**

Hotel de Looier

3e Looierdwarsstraat 75, 1016 VD **Tel** *625 1855* **Fax** *627 5320* **Rooms** *27* **Map** *4 D1*

In a previous life, the building was a diamond factory; now it is a comfortable hotel that is a good base for exploring the Jordaan's markets. The De Looier antiques market is directly opposite, and the Noordermarkt *(see p92)* a short stroll away. Although fairly characterless, rooms are en suite, spotless and have in-house movies. **www.hoteldelooier.com**

Key to Price Guide *see p216* **Key to Symbols** *see back cover flap*

The Times Hotel
Herengracht 135–137, 1015 BG **Tel** *330 6030* **Rooms** *33*   €€€   **Map** *7 B1*

The rooms in two adjacent canal houses, dating back to 1650, offer you a mix between modern comfort and old Dutch tradition. Each room is decorated with a huge print of a painting by a famous Dutch artist, such as Vermeer. Situated near most major attractions and one of the few canal house hotels with a lift. **www.thetimeshotel.nl**

The Toren
Keizersgracht 164, 1015 CZ **Tel** *622 6352* **Fax** *626 9705* **Rooms** *96*   €€€€   **Map** *7 A1*

A stylish place decorated in old golds and baroque reds, The Toren boasts a fascinating history: it has been a merchant's house and a university, and it was also used to hide Jews during World War II. On the downside, standard rooms are small, so spend a little extra on a superior: you get extra legroom and a spa bath. **www.thetoren.nl**

The Dylan
Keizersgracht 384, 1016 GB **Tel** *530 2010* **Fax** *530 2030* **Rooms** *41*   €€€€€   **Map** *1 B5*

Staff here will make you feel like a superstar, attending to your every whim. For a dose of chromatherapy, book rooms by colour according to your mood: soothing green, for example. Every detail has been thought through, from the restaurant's East-meets-West menu to the arrangement of the cushions in the bar. **www.dylanamsterdam.com**

CENTRAL CANAL RING

Hotel Brouwer
Singel 83, 1012 VE **Tel** *624 6358* **Fax** *520 6264* **Rooms** *8*   €   **Map** *7 B1*

This hotel has been in the same family's hands since 1917. The eight rooms, all named after Dutch artists, are individually decorated and well maintained, and the canal views are lovely. All rooms are en suite and no-smoking, and there is even a lift, making the Brouwer all-round great value. **www.hotelbrouwer.nl**

Hotel Nadia
Raadhuisstraat 51, 1016 DD **Tel** *620 1550* **Fax** *428 1507* **Rooms** *45*   €   **Map** *7 A2*

Great for culture-vultures on a budget, the centrally located Hotel Nadia offers small and basic rooms near most of the city's major attractions like the Anne Frank Huis. Opt for the more expensive rooms if you want a canal view or a balcony. The steep stairs are not for everyone, but the friendly staff will gladly help with your luggage. **www.nadia.nl**

Agora
Singel 462, 1017 AW **Tel** *627 2200* **Fax** *627 2202* **Rooms** *16*   €€   **Map** *7 A5*

In a lovely house from the 1730s, the Agora is a cosy hotel. Although lacking flourishes, it is a soothing place to stay: rooms without canal views overlook the garden at the back, and breakfast is served in the conservatory. Just steps from the flower market *(see p123)*, this is ideal for flora fans. **www.hotelagora.nl**

Amsterdam Wiechmann
Prinsengracht 328–332, 1016 HX **Tel** *626 3321* **Fax** *626 8962* **Rooms** *37*   €€   **Map** *1 B5*

A cosy little place ideal for exploring the Jordaan, Wiechmann combines its old-fashioned charm with modern touches like (free) Wi-Fi Internet. The comfortable rooms have chintzy decor, and eccentric knick-knacks abound. The teapot-lined breakfast room has huge windows looking on to the canal. **www.hotelwiechmann.nl**

Belga
Hartenstraat 8, 1016 CB **Tel** *624 9080* **Fax** *623 6862* **Rooms** *10*   €€   **Map** *7 A3*

In the middle of a chic shopping street, yet miles from the designer wealth surrounding it, Belga is a straightforward, plain kind of lodging house, so do not expect four-star trimmings. Some rooms sleep five, making this a good destination for budget-savvy families. Staff are helpful and they will gladly organize a baby-sitter. **www.hotelbelga.nl**

Best Western Eden
Amstel 144, 1017 AE **Tel** *530 7878* **Fax** *623 3267* **Rooms** *218*   €€   **Map** *8 D5*

A chain standard situated on the Amstel, close to Rembrandtplein *(see p118)* and the sights. It is handy for travellers with mobility problems: most rooms are wheelchair accessible, and one has full disabled facilities. For individuality, pay extra for an "art room" designed by students from the Rietveld art school. **www.edenhotelgroup.com**

Leydschehof B&B
Leidsegracht 14, 1016 CK **Tel/Fax** *638 2327* **Rooms** *2*   €€   **Map** *7 A5*

On a genteel canal near the Leidseplein nightlife *(see p110)*, this is ideal for relaxing after a fun night out. Run by the Piller family, this B&B has well-equipped en-suite rooms, with fridges and tea-making facilities a welcome touch. All are bright and simple, and overlook the garden. A simple, pleasing place to stay. **www.freewebs.com/leydschehof**

Dikker & Thijs Fenice Hotel
Prinsengracht 444, 1017 KE **Tel** *620 1212* **Fax** *625 8986* **Rooms** *42*   €€   **Map** *4 E1*

Owned by a publisher, this hotel is proud of its literary connections and the authors who stay here. The 18th-century warehouse building is magnificent, and the decor is smart. Although just moments from Leidseplein *(see p110)*, the atmosphere here is resolutely upmarket. All the sights are within walking distance. **www.dtfh.nl**

Mercure Hotel Arthur Frommer

🏢 🍴 🅿️   €€€

Noorderstraat 46, 1017 TV **Tel** *622 0328* **Fax** *620 3208* **Rooms** *93*   **Map** *4 F2*

Within walking distance of the sights, Rembrandtplein (see p118) and restaurant-lined Utrechtsestraat, this is one of the best placed hotels in Amsterdam. It is pleasantly arranged around a courtyard, and rooms look out on to quiet residential streets. Rooms are comfortable, smart and fairly spacious, as well as non-smoking. **www.mercure.com**

Ambassade Hotel

🏢 📺 🛁   €€€€€

Herengracht 341, 1016 AZ **Tel** *555 0222* **Fax** *555 0277* **Rooms** *59*   **Map** *7 A4*

With its long literary associations, this is the bookworm's choice of lodgings: the library is lined with signed copies from the numerous authors who have stayed here. Arranged across ten buildings, rooms are furnished in an unfussy, classic way, and bathrooms, though small, are marbled. Staff are discreet and attentive. **www.ambassade-hotel.nl**

Hotel Pulitzer

🏢 🍴 🛁 🅿️   €€€€€

Prinsengracht 315–331, 1016 GZ **Tel** *523 5235* **Fax** *627 6753* **Rooms** *230*   **Map** *1 B5*

Spread over 25 adjoining canal houses, this hotel is perfect for a luxurious splurge. Rooms are spacious and stylish, with marble bathrooms, and antiques pop up everywhere. The garden is a floral oasis in summer. In August, the Pulitzer hosts the classical music Grachtenfestival, which culminates on the canal outside. **www.hotelpulitzeramsterdam.nl**

EASTERN CANAL RING

Hotel Prinsenhof

🏢   €

Prinsengracht 810, 1017 JL **Tel** *623 1772* **Fax** *638 3368* **Rooms** *11*   **Map** *5 A3*

A small, no-frills hotel with only ten rooms, most of which share facilities, and all of which are clean and well cared for. Single rooms are pretty cramped. Close to the nightlife and restaurant hub, this is a good budget bet for those who will spend most of their stay exploring and just want a base for sleeping. **www.hotelprinsenhof.com**

Armada

🏢   €€

Keizersgracht 713–715, 1017 DX **Tel** *623 2980* **Fax** *623 5829* **Rooms** *26*   **Map** *5 A3*

On a quiet part of Keizersgracht, just near Utrechtsestraat's great shops and restaurants and close to the bright lights of Rembrandtplein *(see p118)*, this hotel has one major selling point: location. Rooms have been renovated and all have en-suite facilities. A good budget bet if you want to save your euros for shopping or clubbing.

Asterisk

🏢   €€

Den Texstraat 16, 1017 ZA **Tel** *624 1768* **Fax** *638 2790* **Rooms** *43*   **Map** *5 A4*

Decorated in chintzy style from breakfast room to bedrooms (the cheapest have shared facilities), this hotel on a pleasant residential street near the museums is also good for exploring De Pijp. There is also a lift, which is a welcome touch, given the traditional, steep stairs. If you pay cash, breakfast is included in the price. **www.asteriskhotel.nl**

Hotel de Munck

🅿️   €€

Achtergracht 3, 1017 WL **Tel** *623 6283* **Fax** *620 6647* **Rooms** *16*   **Map** *5 B3*

Near the Amstel, on the fringes of town, this sea captain's house has a pleasantly ramshackle air. Arranged pell-mell, bedrooms are homely and basic, if a touch tired. The breakfast room, however, is a kitsch treat: lined with pop memorabilia, its centrepiece is a jukebox that plays while you eat. **www.hoteldemunck.com**

Seven Bridges

€€

Reguliersgracht 31, 1017 LK **Tel** *623 1329* **Fax** *624 7652* **Rooms** *11*   **Map** *5 A3*

In a former merchant house dating back to the 1600s, Seven Bridges is one of the city's best-kept hotel secrets and a perfect hide-out for those seeking peace and quiet. There are just 11 rooms, with either garden or canal views; each is furnished with antiques and breakfast is served in the room. **www.sevenbridgeshotel.nl**

NH Schiller

🏢 🍴 👥 🛁   €€€€

Rembrandtplein 26–36, 1017 CV **Tel** *554 0700* **Fax** *624 0098* **Rooms** *92*   **Map** *7 C5*

Fun-seekers should look no further than this hotel, with its commanding view over Rembrandtplein *(see p118)*. The rooms at the back are not so noisy, and all are decorated with standard-issue smart furnishings. Brasserie Schiller is very cosy, while the eponymous next-door bar has Art Deco fittings and attracts a media crowd. **www.nh-hotels.com**

Banks Mansion

🏢   €€€€€

Herengracht 519–525, 1017 BV **Tel** *420 0055* **Fax** *420 0993* **Rooms** *51*   **Map** *7 B5*

In an imposing former bank, this hotel is all-inclusive: everything, from the Internet to movies to the minibar, is free. This is not just a one-gimmick place, either. Rooms are lovely, with Frank Lloyd Wright-inspired decor, plasma TVs and bathrooms kitted out with oversized shower heads. There is even a pillow menu. **http://banksmansion.carlton.nl**

Hotel 717

🏢   €€€€€

Prinsengracht 717, 1017 JW **Tel** *427 0717* **Fax** *423 0717* **Rooms** *8*   **Map** *5 A3*

Small and expensive, this is one of Amsterdam's luxurious secrets. It's popular with antique hunters from the nearby Spiegelkwartier. Each of the eight rooms has the best accoutrements: blankets from Wales, sheets from New York, and DVDs from Bang & Olufsen. Everything is sumptuous, with fresh flowers all over. **www.717hotel.nl**

Key to Price Guide *see p216* **Key to Symbols** *see back cover flap*

MUSEUM QUARTER

Bellington €

PC Hoofstraat 78–80, 1071 CB **Tel** *671 6478* **Fax** *671 8637* **Rooms** *11* **Map** *4 D3*

Although the Bellington is situated in Amsterdam's most glamorous shopping street, do not come here expecting luxury – this is a serviceable budget hotel providing just the basics. Though they are a little tired, rooms are clean, with TVs and minibars. **www.hotel-bellington.com**

Hotel Aalborg €

Sarphatipark 106, 1073 EC **Tel** *676 0310* **Fax** *676 6560* **Rooms** *36* **Map** *5 A5*

Situated in De Pijp, the city's most fashionable quarter, this budget hotel is ideal for those who want to spend their money on things other than accommodation. Nearby are restaurants, numerous lively bars, trendy shops and a daily market. The basic rooms are clean and brightly decorated, and there is a pleasant garden. **www.aalborg.nl**

Stayokay City Hostel Vondelpark €

Zandpad 5, 1054 GA **Tel** *589 8996* **Fax** *589 8955* **Rooms** *105* **Map** *4 D2*

The second Amsterdam outpost of a worthy organisation, this hostel on the edge of the Vondelpark *(see p128)* is ideal for families and nature lovers. Accommodation ranges from double rooms to 20-bed dorms. There is a TV room, and Brasserie Backpackers has a lovely terrace overlooking the park. **www.stayokay.com**

Atlas Hotel €€

Van Eeghenstraat 64, 1071 GK **Tel** *676 6336* **Fax** *671 7633* **Rooms** *23* **Map** *3 C3*

Tucked between consulates, this restful hotel – part of a small chain – is in a beautiful Art Nouveau villa behind Vondelpark *(see p128)*; there are architectural delights, like ornate gables and stained glass, all over. Rooms are plainer, in warm colours and hung with attractive original paintings, with comfortable beds. **www.hotelatlas.nl**

Best Western Apollo Museum Hotel €€

PC Hoofstraat 2, 1071 BX **Tel** *662 1402* **Fax** *673 3918* **Rooms** *117* **Map** *4 E2*

In a handsome corner building on Amsterdam's exclusive shopping thoroughfare, this hotel is minutes from the Rijksmuseum. Rooms are not luxurious, but they are well equipped and light; some are housed in an annexe in a separate building. **www.apollohotelsresorts.com/museum**

Conscious Museum Square Hotel €€

De Lairessestraat 7, 1071 NR **Tel** *671 9596* **Fax** *671 1756* **Rooms** *36* **Map** *4 D4*

This comfortable "green" hotel is part of the Conscious Hotel group. Their aim is to use sustainable and environmentally friendly materials where possible. Bedrooms are eco-luxury, breakfast is healthy, and there's a beautiful garden to relax in. **www.museumsquarehotel.nl**

Hestia €€

Roemer Visscherstraat 7, 1054 EV **Tel** *618 0801* **Fax** *685 1382* **Rooms** *18* **Map** *4 D2*

On an architecturally fascinating street between Leidseplein *(see p110)* and the museums, this small, private hotel is aimed at families and small groups. Rooms, sleeping up to five, offer nothing fancy but are spotlessly clean and have comfy beds. There is a small garden for guest use; room 15 has a balcony overlooking it. **www.hotel-hestia.nl**

Hotel Jupiter €€

2e Helmersstraat 14, 1054 CJ **Tel** *618 7132* **Fax** *616 8838* **Rooms** *20* **Map** *4 D2*

This family-run, two-star place in a residential side street is just a few minutes' stroll from the park and museums and near numerous bars and restaurants on Overtoom. Rooms are smallish and functional, but they are clean, tidy and cosy. The cash-conscious can opt for triples or rooms with shared facilities. **www.jupiterhotel.nl**

Hotel Zandbergen €€

Willemsparkweg 205, 1071 HB **Tel** *676 9321* **Fax** *676 1860* **Rooms** *18* **Map** *3 C4*

Located very close to the Van Gogh Museum and Vondelpark and yet not far from the heart of the city. The spotless rooms are on the first and second floor, and there is a spacious penthouse suite with kitchen on the third. The family room has a patio and the first floor suite a balcony. Very helpful staff. **www.hotel-zandbergen.com**

Memphis €€

De Lairessestraat 87, 1071 NX **Tel** *673 3141* **Fax** *673 7312* **Rooms** *74* **Map** *4 D4*

At the heart of the chic Oud Zuid residential area, this hotel is popular with both package tourists and classical musicians playing at the nearby Concertgebouw (see p128). Public spaces are smart, but room decor, though cared for, does not quite match this standard. The bar offers food throughout the day. **www.embhotels.nl**

Owl €€

Roemer Visscherstraat 1, 1054 EV **Tel** *618 9484* **Fax** *618 9441* **Rooms** *34* **Map** *4 D2*

Close to Leidseplein *(see p110)*, but on a quiet street ensuring a restful sleep, this enduring, family-run favourite is housed in an attractive villa. There is a bar and a relaxing conservatory overlooking a garden. Rooms are not spacious or particularly stylish, but they are well-looked after, as are guests, many of whom come back. **www.owl-hotel.nl**

Piet Hein
Vossiusstraat 52–53, 1071 AK **Tel** *662 7205* **Fax** *662 1526* **Rooms** *36*   **Map** *4 D3*

A stylish hotel that has been refurbished in soothing caramel and cream tones. The rooms are pleasing on the eye and gentle on the wallet, and rather spacious for Amsterdam. The most popular ones overlook Vondelpark *(see p128)*. There is a late-opening bar and relaxing lounge area, and the staff are helpful, too. **www.hotelpiethein.nl**

Sandton Hotel
Anna van der Vondelstraat 6, 1054 GZ **Tel** *683 3013* **Fax** *685 3750* **Rooms** *38*   **Map** *3 C2*

A much-loved hotel on a street off the Vondelpark *(see p128)*. Every room here is individually decorated according to a different philosopher or treatise. Rooms are stylish and modern. It is a favourite of brooding intellectuals, who make use of the lovely garden and, of course, the library. **www.sandton.eu/amsterdam**

Vondel
Vondelstraat 26, 1054 GE **Tel** *515 0455* **Fax** *515 0451* **Rooms** *84*   **Map** *3 C3*

Near the museums and designer shops, this stylish non-smoking place is decorated throughout with art, and it appeals to a chic crowd. Rooms, named after poems by the hotel's namesake, are spacious and decorated in calming creamy tones. Best of all are the suites, nestling in the eaves, with splendid views over Amsterdam. **www.vondelhotels.nl**

Amsterdam Marriott Hotel
Stadhouderskade 12, 1054 ES **Tel** *607 5555* **Fax** *607 5511* **Rooms** *392*   **Map** *4 D2*

With 11 floors, the Marriott is a bit of a red-bricked behemoth, but it does occupy an excellent position bordering the Vondelpark *(see p128)*, with Leidseplein *(see p110)* lying nearby. Rooms are corporate smart, in country clubbish greens and browns. There are plenty of business facilities, including 11 conference rooms. **https://marriott.com**

The College Hotel
Roelof Hartstraat 1, 1071 VE **Tel** *571 1511* **Fax** *571 1512* **Rooms** *40*   **Map** *4 E5*

Stay in this stylish boutique hotel and you will be looked after by students from Amsterdam's hotel and catering school, learning their craft in situ. Do not expect reduced prices, though: the emphasis is on indulgence, from decor through to dinner. The glamorous Van Baerle suite is bigger than most city apartments. **www.collegehotelamsterdam.com**

Fusion Suites 40
Roemer Visscherstraat 40, 1054 EZ **Tel** *618 46 42* **Fax** *618 46 42* **Rooms** *4*   **Map** *4 D2*

Just a stone's throw away from all the major museums, posh shopping streets, Vondelpark and the bustling Leidseplein, this B&B is a great choice. Rooms are large and with four poster beds, decorative wallpaper and antique furnishings. All rooms also have fresh flowers and champagne. **www.fusionsuites.com**

PLANTAGE

Hotel Adolesce
Nieuwe Keizersgracht 26, 1018 DR **Tel** *626 3959* **Fax** *627 4249* **Rooms** *10*   **Map** *8 F5*

At the upper end of the budget category, this hotel is similar to Hermitage, a few doors down. Its unfussy rooms all have their own sanitation and are geared towards family groups. Although the hotel does not provide breakfast, guests can help themselves all day long to drinks and snacks in the lounge. Closed Nov–mid-Mar. **www.adolesce.nl**

Hermitage Hotel
Nieuwe Keizersgracht 16, 1018 DR **Tel** *623 8259* **Fax** *622 3913* **Rooms** *22*   **Map** *5 B3*

A smart choice that is good for culture-seekers on a budget, this hotel is a few doors down from the Hermitage and minutes from Waterlooplein *(see p63)* and the Plantage, at the quiet end of a main canal. Rooms are decorated in shades of grey and silver and are en suite. **www.hotelhermitageamsterdam.nl**

Bridge Hotel
Amstel 107–111, 1018 EM **Tel** *623 7068* **Fax** *624 1565* **Rooms** *51*   **Map** *5 B3*

In a former stonemason's workshop, this hotel stands in splendid isolation right on the river bank, looking towards Rembrandtplein *(see p118)*. All of the rooms are simple and bright, but those looking onto the water cost extra. There are two apartments with kitchenettes for stays of three nights or longer. **www.thebridgehotel.nl**

Hotel Allure
Sarphatistraat 117, 1018 GB **Tel** *428 3707* **Fax** *427 9859* **Rooms** *18*   **Map** *5 C3*

A small hotel with modern interior. All rooms have a TV, a fridge and coffee and tea making facilities. Some rooms have a balcony. Close to the Oosterpark, Rembrandtplein, Waterlooplein and Artis-Zoo and a short tram ride away from the city centre. This hotel also offers paid private parking. **www.hotelallure.com**

Ibis Stopera
Valkenburgerstraat 68, 1011 LZ **Tel** *531 9135* **Fax** *531 9145* **Rooms** *207*   **Map** *8 E4*

One of two central branches of this useful chain, this hotel lies just behind the opera house on a busy thoroughfare. Nevertheless, it is ideally placed for discovering the old Jewish quarter and the Eastern Docklands. The air-conditioned rooms (with Wi-Fi) deliver no surprises, but are none the worse for it. Pets are welcome. **www.ibishotel.com**

Key to Price Guide *see p216* **Key to Symbols** *see back cover flap*

Rembrandt
Plantage Middenlaan 17, 1018 DA **Tel** *627 2714* **Fax** *638 0293* **Rooms** *17*   **Map** *8 F5*

One of the few cheaper options in this area, this hotel is good for families intent on visiting nearby Artis zoo *(see p142)*. Public spaces are covered in flamboyant murals that recall the hotel's namesake, and have dark, wooden furniture. The bedrooms, meanwhile, are brighter and more modern, and all are en suite. **www.hotelrembrandt.nl**

InterContinental Amstel Amsterdam
Professor Tulpplein 1, 1018 GX **Tel** *622 6060* **Fax** *622 5808* **Rooms** *79*   **Map** *5 B4*

This imposing building overlooking the river has been the city's top hotel since 1867. This is the place where royalty and rock stars stay when in town (as hordes outside testify), and its prices reflect its status. The huge rooms are soundproof and have everything you can think of. Restaurant La Rive has a Michelin star. **www.ichotelsgroup.com**

FURTHER AFIELD

Arena
's Gravesandestraat 51, 1092 AA **Tel** *850 2410* **Fax** *850 2415* **Rooms** *116*   **Map** *6 D4*

The restaurant, bar and nightclub are the stars of this former orphanage in a slightly out-of-the-way residential district, so the Arena is ideal for young trendies intent on socialising in situ. Unless you shell out top dollar for one of the extra-large rooms or suites (by leading local designers IDing), rooms may well disappoint. **www.hotelarena.nl**

Between Art and Kitsch
Ruysdaelkade 75–II, 1072 AL **Tel/Fax** *679 0485* **Rooms** *2*   **Map** *4 E4*

A refreshing change from faceless corporate chains. The name of this B&B says it all: one room has pastiche Baroque decoration, the other features Art Deco touches, and there are fun trinkets scattered all over. On a pleasant canal, it is ideal for exploring the nearby museums and enjoying De Pijp. **www.between-art-and-kitsch.com**

Bicycle Hotel
Van Ostadestraat 123, 1072 SV **Tel** *679 3452* **Fax** *671 5213* **Rooms** *16*   **Map** *4 F5*

This cheapish, cheerful place is geared to pedal enthusiasts, though equally welcoming to pedestrians. They rent two-wheelers, there is a bike park and staff are happy to suggest cycle routes. After a hard day's cycling, guests retire to simple yet clean and comfy rooms or enjoy the wide range of restaurants in De Pijp. **www.bicyclehotel.com**

Cake Under My Pillow
Jacob van Campenstraat 66, 1072 BH **Tel** *751 0936* **Fax** *776 4604* **Rooms** *2*   **Map** *4 F4*

Run by – and located above – the city's most outrageous cake shop, this B&B is very gay-friendly. It is a brilliant base for exploring De Pijp. Rooms have white walls and bed linen, and blue Delft plates and colourful china knickknacks. Breakfast usually includes freshly baked treats from downstairs. **www.cakeundermypillow.nl**

CitizenM Hotel Amsterdam City
Prinses Irenestraat 30, 1077 WX **Tel** *811 7090* **Rooms** *215*

Budget, luxury and gadgets come together in this fun and futuristic hotel. Touch-screen check-in, wall-to-wall windows and a mood pad to change the (small) room's light colour is aimed at both business travellers and techie-tourists. The number 5 tram takes you straight to the centre of town. Online reservations only. **www.citizenamsterdamcity.com**

Hotel Savoy Amsterdam
Ferdinand Bolstraat 194, 1072 LW **Tel** *644 7445* **Fax** *644 8989* **Rooms** *42*   **Map** *4 F5*

As good for travellers with business at RAI *(see p151)* as it is for epicures exploring De Pijp, the Savoy is a welcome addition to the area's (limited) hotel scene. Once inside the formidable red-brick building, things are bright, with good-sized rooms and bathrooms. The bar is in soothing shades of beige. **www.savoyhotel.nl**

Lloyd Hotel
Oostelijke Handelskade 34, 1019 BN **Tel** *561 3636* **Fax** *561 3600* **Rooms** *117*

This hotel and "cultural embassy" offers everything from one- to five-star accommodation, and all kinds of arts events. Formerly a borstal, the Lloyd (intentionally) retains an institutional feel, but two restaurants, an intimate bar and attentive staff add to an unusual experience in the up-and-coming Eastern Docklands. **www.lloydhotel.com**

Bilderberg Garden
Dijsselhofplantsoen 7, 1077 BJ **Tel** *570 5600* **Fax** *570 5654* **Rooms** *124*   **Map** *3 C5*

On a quiet canal in an upmarket residential area, this hotel (with a highly rated restaurant) feels deliciously isolated, yet it is just a short walk from Museumplein *(see p126–7)*. Rooms are a little staid, but they are spacious and many have whirlpool baths. Extensive conference facilities make it popular with business travellers. **www.gardenhotel.nl**

Amsterdam Hilton
Apollolaan 138, 1077 BG **Tel** *710 6000* **Fax** *710 6080* **Rooms** *271*   **Map** *3 C5*

Still famous after all these years for being the place where John Lennon and Yoko Ono had their bed-in, this luxury chain standard is now geared mainly towards the business market. Very close to Schiphol airport *(see p155)*, it is also near the financial district and, naturally, it has the full complement of business amenities. **www.hilton.com**

RESTAURANTS, CAFES AND BARS

Although the Netherlands does not enjoy the gastronomic reputation of France or Italy, the chances of finding good food at a reasonable price in Amsterdam are high. Many cafés and bars serve tempting snacks, and some, known as *eetcafés*, provide full three-course menus at exceptionally good prices *(see pp236–7)*. In addition to the city's selection of Dutch restaurants, where portions are invariably generous, there are also hundreds of other places to try, offering a range of culinary delights from around the world. The following pages will help you locate the best quality food and most exciting cuisine in all price categories. Detailed reviews on each of the selected restaurants are provided on pages 228–35 and this introduction gives a few practical tips to help you enjoy eating out in Amsterdam.

A typically cosy, atmospheric restaurant, Amsterdam

WHERE TO EAT

Amsterdam is a small city, and most of the restaurants listed in this guide are fairly central. The highest concentrations of restaurants are along Van Baerlestraat in the Museum Quarter, in the Red Light District and along Spuistraat in the Nieuwe Zijde, on Reguliers-dwarsstraat and Utrechtstraat in the Eastern Canal Ring and in the Jordaan. Cheap meals can also be enjoyed in any of the city's *eetcafés*.

WHAT TO EAT

In the past, Dutch home cooking and snacks were traditionally offered in *eetcafés*, and Indonesian-based cuisine was the main cheap alternative. French food was served in more expensive restaurants. Today, there is a much greater choice of international cuisine available and many of the city's restaurants combine French cooking techniques with seasonal Dutch ingredients.

Since Indonesia was once a Dutch colony, Amsterdam is one of the best places in Europe to sample its diverse flavours. Much of the cooking may lean too heavily towards the Chinese style for purists, but it is possible to sample genuine Indonesian recipes. Japanese and Thai food is also popular and affordable. Italian cooking is another favourite and the standard is improving. Indian, Mexican and African food can also be found, but the quality is variable.

On the whole, vegetarians are very well catered for here. Vegan and vegetarian eateries are particularly prolific on the canalsides of the Jordaan area.

WHAT TO DRINK

Beer is the drink of preference in most Dutch cafés and bars, and all have a wide selection of local and imported brews *(see p48–9)*. Wine is widely available and nearly all restaurants in Amsterdam offer a good choice, with emphasis on French wines. Most Spanish and Italian restaurants also have an interesting range of their own local wines. A special symbol is awarded to

Amsterdam's famous floating Chinese restaurant, the Sea Palace *(see p235)*

those restaurants listed in this guide that offer an exceptionally good choice of wines.

Restaurants specializing in traditional cuisine tend to have the best selection of *jenevers* (Dutch gin) (*see p48–9*).

HOW MUCH TO PAY

Dutch people like to know exactly how much they are going to pay for a meal, so almost all restaurants display a menu in the window. This gives the prices, which include VAT (BTW) and service. Prices vary markedly in the city and a meal at a luxurious restaurant can cost more than €80 per head. However, if you are on a budget, Amsterdam has a wide choice of places serving meals at under €45 per head. The cost of drinks is invariably extra and the mark-up levied by a restaurant, especially on cheap wine, can be high.

Enjoying attentive service – a feature of eating out in Amsterdam

OPENING TIMES

Since the Dutch don't view lunch as the main meal of the day, few restaurants are open during the day. However, many designer bars and brown cafés (*see pp236–7*) serve lunch from around noon to 2pm. In most restaurants, dinner is served from 6pm onwards, and last orders are often taken as early as 10pm. Nowadays, however, some kitchens are deciding to stay open longer. Some restaurants, particularly those in the central areas, now take orders until 11pm, and a few remain open considerably later. Traditionally, many do not open at all on a Monday,

Outdoor café life near the Waag in Nieuwmarkt

although this is also changing. For details of café and bar opening times, see *Light Meals and Snacks* on pages 236–7.

MAKING A RESERVATION

When visiting one of the city's more celebrated restaurants, it is always wise to book in advance. The listings on pages 228–35 indicate where booking is advisable.

Popular brown cafés and designer bars can also become crowded in the evening, but few of them take reservations.

READING THE MENU

The menus at many tourist restaurants are written in Dutch, French and English. However, as most waiters and waitresses in the city speak good English, and often another European language, it is rarely a problem ordering a meal anywhere in Amsterdam. For more details on what to order, see pages 226–7.

ETIQUETTE

Most restaurants in Amsterdam are relaxed, so smart casual or semi-formal dress is suitable almost everywhere. Although there is nothing to stop you dressing up for special occasions, nowhere insists on a tie. For details of eating out with children, see page 253.

SMOKING

In 2005 the Dutch government embarked upon an anti-smoking campaign. Indeed, in line with many other

European countries, since July 2008 smoking has been banned in all Dutch cafés, restaurants, hotels and other public areas. The ban also includes "smoking" coffee-shops (*see p49*) where, in theory, owners must provide special rooms for their smoking clientele.

DISABILITIES

Disabled visitors will be able to get into the majority of ground-floor restaurants in the city. However, toilets can be difficult to get to as access to them is often via steep stairs.

TIPPING

A service charge of 15 percent is automatically included on bills in restaurants, cafés and bars. This rarely goes to the server, however, so most Amsterdammers leave a gratuity of about 10 per cent. This is left as change rather than included on a credit card payslip.

The picturesque terrace at the ever-popular De Jaren café (*see p228*)

The Flavours of Amsterdam

From its street-corner fish-stalls to its cafés and top-flight gourmet restaurants, eating out in Amsterdam can be full of surprises. Traditional Dutch cuisine may be simple, wholesome and hearty, but the variety of food on offer in the city is huge and influenced by culinary styles from across the globe. Holland was once a major colonial power and its trading ships brought back exotic ingredients, ideas and people from former colonies to settle. Dutch chefs branched out and tried new flavours, and as such, "fusion" food has long been a feature of Amsterdam's menus.

Edam cheese

Sampling pickled herring at one of Amsterdam's many fish-stalls

HOME-GROWN STAPLES

The typical Dutch menu offers good, solid fare. Plainly prepared fish or meat is served with well-cooked vegetables. Pork, hams and all kinds of sausages are popular. The North Sea provides plenty of fresh fish, especially cod, herring and mackerel, as well as its own variety of tiny brown

shrimps. Leafy green vegetables, such as cabbage, endive (chicory) and curly kale make regular appearances, frequently mashed with the ubiquitous potato. Sauerkraut arrived from Germany long ago and is now considered a native dish, as are French fries dowsed in mayonnaise, which are a Belgian import. The world famous Gouda and Edam cheeses are sold

at various stages of maturity, and with flavourings such as cloves, cumin or herbs.

THE MELTING POT

Amsterdam has long had a reputation for religious and political tolerance. Refugees who found a safe haven there brought along their own styles of cooking. In the 16th century, Jews fleeing persecution in Portugal and

Selection of typical *rijsttafel* dishes

Fried tofu with sambal oelek (chilli sauce)

Bami goreng (fried noodles with chicken and shrimp)

Steamed rice

Prawn crackers

Satay ayam (chicken satay)

Gado gado (vegetable salad with peanut sauce)

LOCAL DISHES AND SPECIALITIES

Dining out in Amsterdam is almost guaranteed to come up with some curious quirks. Cheese, ham and bread are standards at breakfast, but you may also find *ontbijtkoek* (gingerbread) and *hagelslag* (grains of chocolate) to sprinkle over bread. Ham and cheese are also lunchtime staples, often served in a bread roll

Brown shrimp

with a glass of milk, though more adventurous sandwiches and salads are creeping in. Numerous pancake houses provide both sweet and savoury snacks throughout the day. The evening is the time when Amsterdam's eateries have the most to offer. The soups and mashed vegetables of Dutch farmhouse cooking sit alongside spicy Indonesian delights, as well as innovative cuisine from some of Amsterdam's fine chefs.

Erwtensoep *is a thick pea and smoked sausage soup, which is often served with rye bread and slices of ham.*

Baskets of wild mushrooms at an organic market

Antwerp were some of the first foreigners to make their home in the city. Today, Amsterdammers count as their own such Jewish specialities as *pekelvlees* (salt beef), pickled vegetables (often served as salad) and a variety of sticky cakes, now found mostly in the more old-fashioned tea-rooms.

The 20th century saw an influx of immigrants from Turkey and several North African countries. Large Arab and Turkish communities have become established in Amsterdam. As a result, restaurants with menus that feature Middle-Eastern style stuffed vegetables, succulent stews and couscous, are almost everywhere. *Falafel* (fried chickpea balls) are readily available from road-side take-aways and are now

one of the city's favourite late-night snacks. Ethiopians, Greeks, Thais, Italians and Japanese are among other waves of immigrants to make their culinary mark, and most recently traditional British fare has become popular.

Gouda on offer in an Amsterdam cheese shop

INDONESIAN LEGACY

The Dutch began colonizing Indonesia in the 17th century and ruled the south-east Asian archipelago right up until 1949. Indonesian cuisine has had a marked influence on eating habits in Holland. Ingredients once regarded as exotic have crept into Dutch dishes. It is now common-place to spice up apple pies and biscuits with cinnamon, which is sometimes even used to flavour vegetables. Coconut and chillis are very popular flavourings, too, and sampling a *rijsttafel* (see below) is considered one of the highlights of any trip to Amsterdam.

THE RIJSTTAFEL

Dutch colonialists in Indonesia often found that the modest local portions failed to satisfy their hunger. To match their larger appetites, they created the *rijsttafel* (literally "rice-table"). It consists of around 20 small spicy dishes, served up with a shared bowl of rice or noodles. Pork or chicken *satay* (mini kebabs with peanut sauce) and *kroepoek* (prawn crackers) usually arrive first. A selection of curried meat and vegetable dishes follows, with perhaps a plate of fried tofu and various salads, all more or less served together. A sweet treat, such as bananas fried in batter, rounds it all off.

Shrimp croquettes *are shrimps in a creamy sauce, coated in breadcrumbs and deep-fried until golden.*

Stamppot *is a hearty dish of curly kale, endive (chicory) and crispy bacon mixed with mashed potato.*

Nasi goreng, *an Indonesian-style dish of egg-fried rice with pork and mushrooms, is also popular for a* rijsttafel.

Choosing a Restaurant

The restaurants in this guide have been selected for their good value, exceptional food and interesting locations. The restaurants are listed by area; entries are alphabetical within each price category. Information on cafés and bars can be found on pp236–7. Smoking is banned in all the city's restaurants, cafés and bars.

PRICE CATEGORIES
The following price ranges are for a three-course meal for one, including half a bottle of wine, plus all unavoidable extra charges, such as cover, service and tax.
€ under €30
€€ €30–45
€€€ €45–55
€€€€ €55–65
€€€€€ over €65

OUDE ZIJDE

A-Fusion
€

Zeedijk 130, 1012 BC **Tel** *330 4068*
Map 8 D2

In the heart of Amsterdam's Chinatown, A-Fusion revives fusion food's reputation: dishes combine influences from across Asia, but they are served in small, tapas-sized, sharing portions. The decor is a little Spartan, but the service is efficient and friendly. Try the steamed oysters and the fresh soy beans. Open over Christmas.

Bird
€

Zeedijk 72–74, 1011 HB **Tel** *620 1442*
Map 8 D2

The best Thai eatery in town is spacious, with authentic decor and impeccable service from the mainly Thai staff. Renowned for its sublime red- and green-curry sauces – which are combined with fish, beef, chicken, pork and tofu – Bird is also great value for money. Alternatively, pop over to the tiny, typically Thai snack bar opposite. Closed lunch.

Café Bern
€

Nieuwmarkt 9, 1011 JR **Tel** *622 0034*
Map 8 D3

A stone's throw from the Red Light District, this cheap and cheerful brown bar/restaurant specializes in Swiss cheese fondues, served alongside simple salads and desserts. It is particularly popular with locals (many of whom eat at the bar), so advance reservations are recommended. A wide range of spirits and house wines is available. Closed lunch.

De Jaren
€€

Nieuwe Doelenstraat 20–22, 1012 CP **Tel** *625 5771*
Map 7 C4

This huge, high-ceilinged grand café serves simple soups and sandwiches on the ground floor, and heartier meat, fish and vegetarian dishes in the first-floor restaurant (which also features a large salad bar). Both areas have pleasant outdoor terraces. On the downside, when things can get busy (and they often do), service can be slow.

Éenvistwéévis
€€

Schippersgracht 6, 1011 TR **Tel** *623 2894*
Map 5 C1

Located near Kilimanjaro *(see above)*, this small, charming restaurant is a paradise for fish lovers. The chef transforms the catch of the day – be it plaice, sea bass, oysters or tuna – into simple, no-frills dishes where the flavours are not drowned in unnecessary sauces. A modest pavement terrace allows *al fresco* eating in summer. Closed lunch; Mon.

Hemelse Modder
€€

Oude Waal 11, 1011 BZ **Tel** *624 3203*
Map 8 E2

This spacious, modern and gay-friendly restaurant, on one of the city's oldest canals, offers international cuisine with strong French and Italian influences, and an eclectic wine list. The *pièce de résistance,* however, is its charming terrace at the back. It is wise to book outdoor tables in advance during the warmer months. Closed lunch; Mon.

Kilimanjaro
€€

Rapenburgerplein 6, 1011 VB **Tel** *622 3485*
Map 5 C1

An absolute gem, this warm and friendly pan-African restaurant specializes in dishes from across the vast continent. Additional delights include the Alligator cocktail, Mongozo beer (served in a bowl) and Ethiopian coffee, which comes with popcorn. In warm weather, they also set up a charming outdoor terrace. Closed lunch; Mon.

Me Naam Naan
€€

Koningsstraat 29, 1011 ET **Tel** *423 33 44*
Map 8 D3

Just off the bustling Nieuwmarkt, Me Naam Naan is a tranquil yet authentic Thai restaurant down a quiet side street. The service is polite and the decor exotic though not kitsch. Dishes include classic Thai specialities like noodles and curries, though even those marked as "hot" are not overly spicy.

In De Waag
€€€

Nieuwmarkt 4, 1012 CR **Tel** *422 7772*
Map 8 D3

In De Waag is set in a castle-like building dating from 1488 *(see p60)*. Above the restaurant, which is lit entirely by candles, is where Rembrandt made sketches for *The Anatomy Lesson of Dr Tulp,* his first group portrait. On the menu are eclectic (if a tad expensive) meat and fish dishes and vegetarian options. Desserts are also divine. Book ahead.

Key to Symbols *see back cover flap*

Blauw aan de Wal ▦ €€€€
Oudezijds Achterburgwal 99, 1012 DD **Tel** *330 2257* **Map** *8 D3*

One of the Red Light District's best-kept secrets is this stylish restaurant hidden at the end of a tiny alley. Refined palates will enjoy the imaginative Mediterranean fusion delights and excellent wine list. Blauw's reputation means that advance reservations are necessary (especially to eat on its peaceful terrace in summer). Closed lunch; Sun, Mon.

Vermeer (NH Barbizon Palace Hotel) ♿ €€€€
Prins Hendrikkade 59–72, 1012 AD **Tel** *556 4885* **Map** *8 D1*

Set within four adjoining 17th-century buildings, this excellent restaurant produces rich gastronomic delights from France. Start the adventure in the intimate cocktail lounge, where you can enjoy options such as lobster with cranberries and turnips flavoured with lemon verbena, or Anjou pigeon with celeriac. Inspired wine list. Closed Sat lunch, Sun.

NIEUWE ZIJDE

Brasserie Harkema ♿ ⚥ €
Nes 67, 1012 KD **Tel** *428 2222* **Map** *7 B4*

A classic Parisian brasserie with a stylish New York sensibility, Harkema serves *haute cuisine* at affordable prices. It is immensely popular, especially in the evenings, so it is wise to book ahead. Feast on delights such as pan-fried sea bream with Roseval potatoes, pomodori and basil, followed by limoncello jelly with lime sorbet.

Català ▦ ▦ €
Spuistraat 299, 1012 VS **Tel** *623 1141* **Map** *7 A4*

A tapas bar, Català serves all the classic Spanish dishes you'd expect. The interior is rustic and authentic, but a seat on the pavement terrace in summer is a great spot for people-watching. It's also practically next door to Harry's – one of the finest cocktail bars in Amsterdam.

Keuken van 1870 ▦ ♿ ⚥ ▦ €
Spuistraat 4, 1012 TS **Tel** *620 4018* **Map** *7 C1*

Something of an Amsterdam institution, this former soup kitchen (dating from 1870) still maintains its policy of providing cheap meals – though its patrons these days are office workers, students and pensioners. There is a set daily changing menu of "homely Dutch cooking" (meat and veg dishes). Closed lunch; Sun.

Tibet ⚥ ▦ €
Lange Niezel 24, 1012 GT **Tel** *624 1137* **Map** *8 D2*

A marvellous find, and veritable haven, in the bowels of the bustling Red Light District – not least because it serves food until 1am. The menu offers an overwhelming choice of mostly Chinese Szechuan dishes, alongside staple Tibetan fare like *momo* (dumplings). Eclectic Tibetan decor, and relaxed, friendly, attentive service. Closed Tue.

Kapitein Zeppos ♿ ⚥ ▦ €€
Gebed Zonder End 5, 1012 HS **Tel** *624 2057* **Map** *7 B4*

Tucked down a tiny alley, lit by fairy-lights, this bar-restaurant (with Belgian ceramic-tile tables and eclectic ornaments) was once a coach stable, then a cigar factory. The kitchen turns out delicious French-Mediterranean cuisine, with Italian, Moroccan and Spanish influences. Ideal for a romantic evening. Occasional live music.

Van Kerkwijk ▦ €€
Nes 41, 1012 KC **Tel** *620 3316* **Map** *Map 7 B3*

Tucked away to the south of the Dam square, Van Kerkwijk is an *eetcafé* with a difference. The atmosphere is definitely Dutch, but the food is cosmopolitan, with dishes from Indonesia, Morocco, France and Italy. Van Kerkwijk is always busy with locals and tourists alike, but reservations are not possible so arrive early to guarantee a table.

1e Klas ⚥ €€€
Stationsplein 15, 1012 AB **Tel** *625 0131* **Map** *8 D1*

The former first-class waiting room on platform 2B of Centraal Station *(see p79)* is now a grand café/restaurant exuding Art Nouveau elegance throughout its stunning interior. On the menu, everything from standard fare, such as soup and salads, to first-class fare in the form of traditional French dishes. Breakfast is served from 8:30am.

De Compagnon ▦ €€€€
Guldehandsteeg 17, 1012 RA **Tel** *620 4225* **Map** *8 D1*

This small restaurant, hidden down a little alleyway, can be hard to find, but persistence will be rewarded. De Compagnon's Burgundian kitchen produces meat, fish and vegetarian dishes, made with mostly organic ingredients. It is the ideal place for intimate dinners: book a table by the window. Exceptional wine list. Closed Sat lunch, Sun.

Supperclub ⚥ €€€€€
Jonge Roelensteeg 21, 1012 PL **Tel** *344 6400* **Map** *7 B3*

Remove your shoes and recline on cushioned beds at this spacious restaurant-club. DJs spin upbeat lounge as you graze on culinary delights from the open kitchen – all spread out over five courses. Fine wines, video art, massage and offbeat performances complete this assault on the senses. There is also a lounge bar downstairs. Closed lunch.

WESTERN CANAL RING

De Bolhoed   €
Prinsengracht 60–62, 1015 DX **Tel** *626 1803*   **Map** *1 B3*

A charming vegetarian restaurant with a delightful canalside terrace, great for sunny afternoons and balmy evenings. Chefs whip up imaginative international dishes – the daily vegan dish is superb – from mostly organic ingredients. Plates overflow, but be sure to leave room for the delicious desserts. Service can be slow. Reservations recommended.

Foodism   €
Oude Leliestraat 8, 1015 AW **Tel** *627 6424*   **Map** *7 A2*

Hidden down a small street in the Jordaan, five minutes' walk from the Dam, this bright and endearing restaurant serves anything from New York-style breakfasts to hearty soup/sandwiches for lunch and wild-basil pasta for dinner. Or simply pop in for a mid-afternoon coffee and cake. No alcohol. Opens 11:30am (12:30pm Sun). Closed for dinner Mon and Tue.

Semhar   €
Marnixstraat 259–261, 1015 WH **Tel** *638 1634*   **Map** *1 A4*

The friendly Ethiopian owners of this spacious restaurant (ideal for groups) create sublime traditional dishes from their homeland and neighbouring Eritrea. Their *injera* (pancake) dishes are a must – especially for vegetarians. An absolute gem despite its location on a rather unattractive street (albeit on the edge of the Jordaan). Open from 4pm. Closed Mon.

Chez Georges   €€
Herenstraat 3, 1015 BX **Tel** *626 3332*   **Map** *7 A1*

Small and seductive, this restaurant is a veritable tour de force of Burgundian cuisine. It is a must for gourmands, who will delight in owner/chef Georges' superb meat and fish dishes (opt for the five-course or seven-course menus). It is also great value for money, though the fine wines could push up the price. Book ahead. Closed lunch; Wed, Sun.

De Gouden Reael   €€
Zandhoek 14, 1013 KT **Tel** *623 3883*   **Map** *1 C1*

This 1648 building used to be a herring warehouse and then a 19th-century *jenever* (Dutch gin) bar. Located in one of the most picturesque parts of Amsterdam, this low-key bar-restaurant is popular with lovers of French and Alsatian cuisine. A good wine list complements the food, and there are great waterfront views from the small terrace. Closed lunch.

Spanjer & Van Twist   €€
Leliegracht 60, 1015 DJ **Tel** *639 0109*   **Map** *7 A2*

Less than a minute's walk from the Anne Frank Huis *(see p90)*, this split-level café-restaurant opens at 10am for breakfast and has a seasonally changing menu of soups, sandwiches and main dishes. It features a reading table and a charming canalside terrace. The kitchen shuts at 10:30pm, but light snacks are served until closing time.

Stout!   €€
Haarlemmerstraat 73, 1013 EL **Tel** *616 3664*   **Map** *2 D3*

A hip, yet unpretentious, restaurant offering creative international fusion fare, with inspired combinations of flavours. The speciality dish (Plateau Stout; for a minimum of two people) allows you to sample ten small, varied dishes. Stout! is also renowned for its wine list.

Assaggi   €€€
Tweede Egelantiersdwarsstraat 4–6, 1015 SC **Tel** *420 5589*   **Map** *1 B4*

Assaggi is a modern, elegant Italian restaurant run by knowledgeable staff. The restaurant serves high-quality *antipasti*, pasta and rice dishes, as well as traditional main courses like *osso bucco* (braised veal shank). Its location in the maze of tiny streets unofficially known as Little Italy makes it a little hard to find, but well worth it. Closed lunch.

Bordewijk   €€€
Noordermarkt 7, 1015 MV **Tel** *624 3899*   **Map** *1 C3*

Renowned for its superb French international cuisine and for service that will make you feel truly pampered, Bordewijk is one of the best restaurants in town. The chef will come to your table in person to describe the day's menu. As it fills up, the acoustics can sometimes make the place quite loud. Book ahead. Closed lunch; Mon, Sun.

La Oliva   €€€
Egelantiersstraat 122, 1015 PR **Tel** *320 4316*   **Map** *1 B4*

La Oliva sits on the corner of two of the Jordaan area's labyrinthine streets, with small wooden tables dotted along the pavement. The restaurant has a great wine list and specializes in *pintxos* – the Northern Spanish, bread-based appetizers that are great for sharing. Closed Mon.

Lof   €€€
Haarlemmerstraat 62, 1013 ES **Tel** *620 2997*   **Map** *2 D3*

Despite its rather innocuous appearance, Lof is a firm favourite of many of the city's most discerning diners. The daily changing offerings revolve around seasonal fish, meat and game. There is no menu: the staff come to your table and simply describe what is on offer to you. For intimate, lingering dining, book the small backroom. Closed lunch; Mon.

Key to Price Guide *see p228* **Key to Symbols** *see back cover flap*

Toscanini 🏃 🍴 €€€

Lindengracht 75, 1015 KD **Tel** *623 2813* **Map** *1 C3*

Despite its huge size, this Italian restaurant gets booked up quickly. Formerly a coach house, then a blacksmith's forge, the venue retains its original 19th-century glass roof. Chefs create authentic regional dishes in the open kitchen, while the wine list affords the chance to drink both classic and lesser-known wines from Italy. Closed lunch; Sun.

Christophe 🍴 €€€€€

Leliegracht 46, 1015 DH **Tel** *625 0807* **Map** *7 A2*

This canalside establishment, named after former owner and chef Christophe Royer, has been taken over by his sous chef Jean Joel Bonsens and sommelier Ellen Mansfield. They continue creating inventive and full-flavoured dishes that have earned the restaurant a string of well-deserved Michelin stars. Closed lunch; Sun, Mon.

CENTRAL CANAL RING

Stoop en Stoop 🏃 🍴 €

Lange Leidsedwarsstraat 82, 1017 NM **Tel** *620 0982* **Map** *4 E2*

The Leidseplein may not be the most salubrious of Amsterdam's many squares, but at Stoop en Stoop you can get away from the tourists for some hearty, basic *eetcafé* fare. Meat lovers will appreciate the mountains of marinated ribs, chicken satay skewers, pork escalopes and grilled steaks, though fish and pasta dishes are also on offer.

Balthazar's Keuken 🏃 🍴 €€

Elandsgracht 108, 1016 VA **Tel** *420 2114* **Map** *1 B5*

A clutter of pots and pans hangs from the open kitchen here. In fact, it is so cosy, you will feel as though you're eating at the home of owners Karin and Alain, not least because there is no menu: guests are simply given a weekly changing, three-course international meal. Closed lunch; Mon, Tue, Sat, Sun (on these days large groups can rent it).

Brix 🍴 €€

Wolvenstraat 16, 1016 EP **Tel** *639 0351* **Map** *1 C5*

The interior at Brix combines cosy warmth with funky freshness – there's even live jazz on Sunday nights. The food is international in its influences, and everything is served in starter-sized portions, making it easy to order a range of dishes to share. A good night out, especially with a small group of friends. Closed lunch.

Café George 🚹 🍴 €€

Leidsegracht 84, 1016 CR **Tel** *626 0802* **Map** *4 E1*

Rub shoulders with the Dutch hip and famous at the Café George. This New York brasserie serves uncomplicated dishes like steak and French fries or eggs benedict, as well as more sophisticated fare such as oysters and lobster. Close to the shopping streets and Leidseplein nightspots, so perfect for a late lunch or pre-club dinner.

Los Pilones 🍴 €€

Kerkstraat 63, 1017 GC **Tel** *320 4651* **Map** *7 A5*

A small and warm cantina run by two Mexican brothers who serve authentic dishes from their country. This is some of the best Mexican food in the whole of Amsterdam. Expect the occasional unusual combination such as enchiladas with a chocolate sauce. The *pièce de résistance* is their huge range of tequilas (around 35 brands). Closed lunch; Mon.

Mayur 🚹 🏃 🍴 €€

Korte Leidsedwarsstraat 203, 1017 RB **Tel** *623 2142* **Map** *4 E2*

Authentic tandoori dishes cooked in a wood-fired clay oven are the speciality of this spacious restaurant just off the Leidseplein *(see p110)*. Preparation of food is also given special attention: meats are marinated for 24 hours in yogurt and spices, resulting in dishes that are spicy but not eye-wateringly hot. Closed lunch.

Struisvogel €€

Keizersgracht 312, 1016 EX **Tel** *423 3817* **Map** *1 B5*

A cosy restaurant housed in the cellar of a traditional canal house, the Struisvogel serves a simple three-course menu for €23.50. The name of the restaurant means ostrich, and if you're a meat eater, be sure to try their signature ostrich dish. A great spot in winter for proper comfort food. Closed lunch.

Nomads €€€

Rozengracht 133, 1016 LV **Tel** *344 6401* **Map** *1 A5*

The ultimate treat for decadent diners is this first-floor restaurant inspired by Arabic nomad culture. Kick off your shoes and lounge on beds in a scene straight out of *Arabian Nights*, while Eastern food is served from bronze platters. DJs at weekends. Late-opening kitchen (11:30pm) and bar (1am weekdays; 3am weekends). Closed lunch; Mon.

Proeverij 274 🏃 🍴 €€€

Prinsengracht 274, 1016 HH **Tel** *421 1848* **Map** *1 B5*

Popular with both locals and visitors to the city, this warm and romantic two-floored restaurant serves classic international dishes using predominantly organic ingredients. Book the round table by the door for a delightful view over the canal. Groups of up to 25 people can be catered for in the downstairs basement. Closed lunch.

Blue Pepper
€€€€

Nassaukade 366, 1054 AB **Tel** *489 7039*
Map *4 D1*

Flawless and inspired contemporary Indonesian cuisine (with Chinese and Filipino influences), with extraordinary combinations of flavours. The *rijsttafel (see p226)* created by the Javanese chef is utterly unique. No wonder this small, chic restaurant is adored by foodies, despite the rather ordinary location. Impressive wine list. Closed lunch, Tue.

Restaurant Vinkeles
€€€€€

Keizersgracht 384, 1016 GB **Tel** *530 2010*
Map *4 E1*

The intimate gourmet restaurant at this stunning boutique hotel offers international cuisine with an inspired choice of traditional and contemporary dishes. Service is attentive and the wine menu eclectic. Outdoor dining is on offer in the beautiful courtyard when the weather is good. A must for the discerning diner. Dinner only. Closed Sunday.

EASTERN CANAL RING

Bazar
€

Albert Cuypstraat 182, 1073 BL **Tel** *675 0544*
Map *5 A5*

A terrific Eastern-style restaurant within a former church located halfway up the bustling Albert Cuyp street market *(see p122)*. On the menu is a mouth-watering choice of North African, Moroccan, Iranian and Turkish dishes for breakfast, lunch or dinner (during the week, it opens at 8am; 9am till midnight at weekends). Great for vegetarians.

Zushi
€

Amstel 20, 1017 AA **Tel** *330 6882*
Map *7 C5*

A large, bright, high-ceilinged modern sushi restaurant where you can take your sushi straight from the oval conveyor belt, while chefs in the middle of the belt prepare additional goodies. Each plate is colour-coded according to price. Wash the wasabi down with Japanese beers like Sapporo, Kirin or Asahi.

Bouchon du Centre
€€

Falckstraat 3, 1017 VV **Tel** *330 1128*
Map *5 A4*

You will feel like you are having dinner at a friend's house at Bouchon du Centre. Hostess/chef Hanneke Schouten creates a fixed three-course meal using produce she has bought fresh from the market and specialist shops. The cuisine is traditional French. Organic wines are carefully chosen to match the food. Last dinner orders at 6:30pm. Closed Sun–Tue.

De Waaghals
€€

Frans Halsstraat 29, 1072 BK **Tel** *679 9609*
Map *4 F3*

A superb vegetarian restaurant that will leave even the most hardened of carnivores sated. Each month, the menu focuses on a different country, and organic produce is used wherever possible; even the beer is locally brewed and the wines organic. In summer, ask for a table in the charming garden at the back. Book ahead. Closed lunch, Mon.

Rose's Cantina
€€

Reguliersdwarsstraat 38–40, 1017 BM **Tel** *625 9797*
Map *7 B5*

A sprawling, long-established Mexican restaurant with a terrific atmosphere and delicious food (though a limited choice for vegetarians). Its success is due to a combination of friendly service, great value and classic menu: choose fillings for your taco, enchilada or quesadilla. Great cocktails, too. Small patio terrace in summer at rear. Closed lunch.

Take Thai
€€

Utrechtsestraat 87, 1017 VK **Tel** *622 0577*
Map *5 A3*

Take Thai couples elegant, minimalist decor with well-executed, reasonably priced Thai food. Classics like green and red curries and lamb *massaman* (southern-style Thai curry) are on offer, as well as less spicy dishes like chicken roasted with garlic and peppercorns. The staff is also attentive. Closed lunch.

Vamos A Ver
€€

Govert Flinckstraat 308, 1073 CJ **Tel** *673 6992*
Map *5 A5*

The best Spanish restaurant in town is found in the neighbourhood of De Pijp. Although the interior might be a little tacky, the food served is no-nonsense, authentic Spanish fare – and it is outstanding. Service is very friendly, but do not come here if you're after a hip and trendy tapas bar. Closed lunch; Tue.

Coffee & Jazz
€€€

Utrechtsestraat 113, 1017 VL **Tel** *624 5851*
Map *5 A3*

While Coffee & Jazz may sound like a haunt for coffee-lovers, it's actually an Indonesian restaurant, overseen by a rather eccentric proprietor. The decor and ambience make for a relaxed experience, while the menu includes chicken satay and beef *rendang* (spicy stew). Alternatively, you can give the chef free rein to surprise you. Closed Sat–Mon.

Le Zinc... et les Autres
€€€

Prinsengracht 999, 1017 KM **Tel** *622 9044*
Map *5 A3*

Creative and hearty French-international cuisine is on offer here. Le Zinc has a formal, classic interior complemented by wooden beams and rustic furniture, and is located over two floors of a beautifully restored warehouse. Other perks include an excellent wine list, a canalside terrace for balmy nights and no mobile phones. Closed lunch; Sun.

Key to Price Guide *see p228* **Key to Symbols** *see back cover flap*

Van de Kaart

€€€

Prinsengracht 512, 1017 KH **Tel** *625 9232*

Map *4 E2*

Do not be fooled by the smart, yet unremarkable, interior of this restaurant: a quick perusal of the exciting French-Mediterranean menu will provoke a much stronger reaction. Starters alone include delights such as mushroom, truffle and Jerusalem artichoke vol-au-vent; lobster and veal ravioli with goat's cheese. Closed lunch; Sun.

Beddington's

€€€€

Utrechtsedwarsstraat 141, 1017 WE **Tel** *620 7393*

Map *5 B3*

One for discerning taste buds and those in search of slow-paced dining in sober, stylish surroundings. From the open kitchen, British owner/chef Jean Beddington produces seamless French and Asian fusion, with a sprinkling of British sensibility. Delightful desserts and friendly service; vegetarians are also well catered for. Closed lunch; Sun, Mon.

De Utrechtsedwarstafel

€€€€

Utrechtsedwarsstraat 107, 1017 WD **Tel** *625 4189*

Map *5 A3*

This modern French-oriented restaurant is a must for indecisive diners: you do not choose the food itself but only the number of courses (three to five) and menu type ("simple" to "gastronomic"). The details are left to the owner of this establishment. Exclusive wines from all over the world are matched to your food. Closed Sun, Mon, Tue; Jan.

Gorgeous

€€€€

Tweede van der Helststraat 16, 1072 PD **Tel** *379 1400*

Map *5 A5*

A relatively new addition to Amsterdam, this small yet stylish, modern French restaurant offers a variety of adventurous "gastronomic tapas" (which live up to their name). Alternatively, choose from the (rather limited) à la carte menu. The small pavement terrace is conducive to people-watching on this bustling street. Closed lunch; Sun, Mon.

In de Keuken

€€€€

Utrechtsestraat 114, 1017 VT **Tel** *616 7414*

Map *5 A3*

In de Keuken deserves its reputation as one of the city's fine-dining establishments. But it's refreshingly unpretentious, with the kitchen in full-view of the diners and an informal style of service. The tasting menu comprises several small courses, and changes every two weeks. Closed Sun and Mon.

Segugio

€€€€€

Utrechtsestraat 96, 1017 VS **Tel** *330 1503*

Map *5 A3*

The simple yet smart interior of this intimate, split-level restaurant belies the exquisite menu, offering classic and modern Italian dishes. Delicacies include gnocchi with wine-cured cheese, or pheasant breast in filo pastry; the risotto is also divine. Superb wine list. Closed lunch; Sun; Christmas/New Year.

MUSEUM QUARTER

Arabic Lounge

€€

Spiegelgracht 27, 1017 JP **Tel** *627 9657*

Map *4 F2*

Housed on the first floor of an old canal house, Arabic Lounge combines Dutch antiquity with North African exoticism. Moroccan tagine, *bastilla* (chicken pie) and other traditional fare is served at informal, low tables. If you time your visit right, you'll also be treated to a performance by a professional belly dancer. Closed lunch.

Café Toussaint

€€

Bosboom Toussaintstraat 26, 1054 AS **Tel** *685 0737*

Map *4 D1*

This absolute gem is well worth the five-minute stroll from the busy Leidseplein *(see p110)* across to this quiet street. It is a small but charming café with an open kitchen where healthy international fare, such as sandwiches, soups and tapas (with plenty for vegetarians), is created. Cosy and romantic at night, with a peaceful terrace and no mobiles.

Pompa

€€

Willemsparkweg 6, 1017 HD **Tel** *662 6206*

Map *4 D3*

In an area short of restaurants – let alone inexpensive ones – this tapas bar is a real find, especially after an evening at the nearby Concertgebouw *(see p128)*, when most restaurants are filled to the brim. Split-level, warm and friendly, this eatery has a broad, value-for-money menu offering Mediterranean dishes and tapas; great salads, too.

Pulpo

€€

Willemsparkweg 87, 1071 GT **Tel** *676 0700*

Map *4 D3*

Just east of the Vondelpark *(see p128)*, near the Museumplein, is this popular, relaxed and unpretentious restaurant. The Mediterranean cuisine is occasionally imbued with subtle African and Middle Eastern hints, such as marinated chicken kebabs with *taboulleh* and lime harissa. Closed lunch and Sun.

Vertigo

€€

Vondelpark 3, 1071 AA **Tel** *612 3021*

Map *4 D2*

Resembling a wine cellar, this spacious and comfortable international restaurant is within Amsterdam's historic Filmmuseum *(see p129)*, at the top of the Vondelpark *(see p128)*. Warm and candlelit in the winter, it has one of the city's most popular terraces in summer, when they also sell picnics that you can take into the park.

Brasserie van Baerle   €€€

Van Baerlestraat 158, 1071 BG **Tel** *679 1532*   **Map** 4 E4

This French-style brasserie is particularly popular with Dutch celebrities, especially for lunch and Sunday brunch (when it opens at 10am). Mouth-watering dishes include grilled turbot with a citrus-fennel salad and shellfish risotto. Exceptional wine list and gorgeous garden terrace. Reservations recommended. Closed Sat lunch.

The College Hotel   €€€

Roelof Hartstraat 1, 1071 VE **Tel** *571 1511*   **Map** 4 E5

Head to this training hotel for catering students before or after a day's shopping on nearby PC Hooftstraat. The renovated gymnasium of an 1895 school building is home to an elegant gourmet restaurant where classic Dutch dishes are given a contemporary twist. Open for breakfast. Closed Sun.

Le Garage   €€€€

Ruysdaelstraat 54–56, 1071 XE **Tel** *679 71 76*   **Map** 4 E4

A favourite haunt of Dutch celebs is this elegant bistro with red plush seating and mirrors. The food is French-international, and organic ingredients are used whenever possible. Le Garage is renowned for its three-course menu and superb wine list featuring classic and lesser-known wines from all over the world. Closed Sat & Sun lunch.

PLANTAGE

Meneer Nilsson   €€

Plantage Kerklaan 41, 1018 CV **Tel** *624 4846*   **Map** 6 D2

This is a tapas restaurant with a difference: dishes are broadly Mediterranean, but they don't stop at Spain. Duck *rillettes* and smoked mozzarella are as likely to appear on the menu as manchego cheese and *patatas bravas* (spicy, tomato potatoes). The organic wines are a perfect accompaniment to the tapas.

Plancius   €€

Plantage Kerklaan 61, 1018 CX **Tel** *330 9469*   **Map** 6 D2

A gay-friendly restaurant in a former fire station opposite the main entrance to Artis Zoo *(see p142)*. Although the designer decor is stark, it is comfortable and friendly. The menu is French-oriented, with an accent on meat and fish, but there are also tempting vegetarian options. On Saturdays and Sundays they also serve breakfast.

La Rive (Amstel Hotel)   €€€€€

Professor Tulpplein 1, 1018 GX **Tel** *520 3264*   **Map** 5 B4

This Michelin-starred restaurant within the Amstel Hotel is one for connoisseurs. Outstanding cuisine from its modern French-Mediterranean kitchen is matched by an excellent wine list. Reserve the chef's table in the kitchen (four to eight people) for an unusual twist to your dining experience. Dress code is elegant. Closed Sat lunch, Sun.

FURTHER AFIELD

Azmarino   €

Tweede Zweelinckstraat 6, 1073 EH **Tel** *671 7587*   **Map** 5 A5

East African food is still relatively hard to come by in Amsterdam, but it's worth going off the beaten track to find Azmarino, just south of the Sarphatipark. Spicy vegetarian and meat options come on huge sharing platters with piles of the sour, spongy pancakes characteristic of the region. Closed lunch.

Amsterdam   €€

Watertorenplein 6, 1051 PA **Tel** *682 2666*

Within a former water-pumping house dating from 1897, this huge, industrial-style restaurant near the Westerpark serves simple, well-priced European food – from steak and fries to grilled wild-boar cutlets. There is a relaxing grass terrace at the back, which makes it great for families. The kitchen is open until 11:30pm on Friday and Saturday.

De Odessa   €€

Veemkade 259, 1019 CZ **Tel** *419 3010*

Head to this enchanting Ukrainian fishing boat as the sun sets and enjoy cocktails on the deck, while snacking on oysters. De Odessa's international menu (predominantly fish and meat) is well presented and reasonable – but the draw is the experience itself. DJs play on the lounge-style deck below. Closed lunch; Mon, Sun–Tue.

Gare de L'Est   €€

Cruquiusweg 9, 1019 AT **Tel** *463 0620*

Within the former coffee house built in 1901 (and an old railway station), this unique, romantic restaurant is hugely popular with locals and those who have wandered through the redeveloped Eastern Docklands area, where Gare de L'Est is located. Reservations for the daily changing, four-course global dinners are a must. Closed lunch.

Key to Price Guide *see p228* **Key to Symbols** *see back cover flap*

Sea Palace
Oosterdokskade 3, 1011 AD **Tel** *626 4777*
€€
Map *8 F2*

This floating, pagoda-style Chinese restaurant is an impressive sight on a small dock, five minutes from Centraal Station *(see p79)* en route to the Muziekgebouw aan 't IJ. The huge menu offers Cantonese staples such as won ton soup, alongside more unusual Pekingese and Szechuan dishes.

Star Ferry
Piet Heinkade 1, 1019 BR **Tel** *788 2090*
€€

Named after the Hong Kong ferry company, and located within the architecturally stunning Muziekgebouw aan 't IJ, this spacious, glass-walled café-restaurant specializes in Asian-influenced international cuisine. There are incredible views across the busy waterfront behind Centraal Station *(see p79)*, but avoid the unshaded terrace on hot days.

Wilhelmina-Dok
Noordwal 1, 1021 PX **Tel** *632 3701*
€€
Map *2 F2*

Take the ferry from behind Centraal Station across the River IJ to this spacious 1950s-style restaurant with a waterfront terrace offering splendid views of Amsterdam's skyline. With its great-value Mediterranean food, reasonable wine list and extensive bar, it is ideal for groups and informal business lunches, and it can get packed when the sun is out.

Blauw
Amstelveenseweg 158, 1075 XN **Tel** *675 5000*
€€€
Map *3 A5*

Amsterdam is famed for its Indonesian restaurants, and Blauw is certainly one worth visiting. Order one of its enormous *rijsttafels* (selection of Indonesian dishes). The decor is stylish and intimate, without a hint of the kitsch, faux exoticism that afflicts many of the city's other Indonesian establishments. Closed lunch.

Fifteen
Jollemanhof 9, 1019 GW **Tel** *0900 343 8336*
€€€

British celebrity chef Jamie Oliver's open-plan restaurant is situated within a renovated, waterfront warehouse. Book ahead for the set four-course modern Italian tasting menu (with a vegetarian alternative), or just turn up and eat pasta, risotto and ravioli in the cheaper trattoria. Waiting staff and sommelier are very attentive. Closed Sun lunch.

De Kas
Kamerlingh Onneslaan 3, 1097 DE **Tel** *462 4562*
€€€€

An upmarket, organic Mediterranean restaurant set within a 1926 greenhouse (ingredients are picked fresh from the adjacent nursery or their own land elsewhere). Although popular for business lunches, De Kas becomes a romantic destination in the evening. Reserve the chef's table in the kitchen and the terrace in summer. Closed Sat lunch, Sun.

Mangerie de Kersentuin (Garden Hotel)
Dijsselhofplantsoen 7, 1077 BJ **Tel** *570 5600*
€€€€
Map *4 D5*

Experience the pure tastes of unpretentious French-Mediterranean cuisine within the enjoyable, informal atmosphere of this long-established restaurant. The menu changes frequently, the comprehensive wine list is well chosen, and there is a terrace for outdoor dining. No mobile phones. Closed Sat lunch, Sun.

Marius
Barentszstraat 243, 1013 NM **Tel** *422 7880*
€€€€
Map *1 C1*

With just four hard-to-reserve tables, Marius has a cosy, living-room feel to it. The chef offers a daily changing "market menu", comprising of whatever is in season at the local markets, with a leaning towards Mediterranean dishes. Paired wines are also available with each course. Closed Sun and Mon and lunch.

Visaandeschelde
Scheldeplein 4, 1078 GR **Tel** *675 1583*
€€€€

This spacious, white-linen seafood restaurant opposite the RAI *(see p151)* is popular with well-heeled fish lovers. Creative dishes based on Mediterranean cuisine, with a nod to Japanese, use fresh fish from the market (pick your lobster from the tank). Signature dishes are *bouillabaisse* and *fruits* de mer. No mobiles. Closed Sat & Sun lunch.

Ciel Bleu (Okura Hotel)
Ferdinand Bolstraat 333, 1072 LH **Tel** *678 7450*
€€€€€
Map *4 F5*

A Michelin-starred French restaurant on the 23rd floor of the Okura Hotel renowned for its creative, innovative dishes, and terrific views of Amsterdam. A must for impressive dinners – or dates. The adjacent cocktail bar opens at 6pm, half an hour before the restaurant. Closed lunch.

Supperclub Cruise
Pier 14 (Behind Centraal Station), 1012 AB **Tel** *344 6403*
€€€€€
Map *2 E3*

Fancy dining on a 1960 ship, once used by the late Queen Juliana to entertain visiting dignitaries? On Fridays and Saturdays, fashionistas catch the sun on the top deck, sip champagne and cocktails in the bar below, then retire to dinner on the lower deck as the boat sails along the River IJ. Booking necessary. Board at 7:30pm.

Yamazato (Okura Hotel)
Ferdinand Bolstraat 333, 1072 LH **Tel** *678 8351*
€€€€€
Map *4 F5*

This Michelin-starred restaurant serves traditional Japanese specialities. For less adventurous palates, its sushi bar has more than 20 types of freshly prepared sushi and sashimi. Authenticity extends throughout – from the food to the tatami room, private-dining spaces and kimono-clad Japanese waiting staff. Also open 7:30–9:30am for breakfast.

Light Meals and Snacks

In addition to the normal assortment of burger joints, pizzerias and the like, most Dutch cafés and bars serve food ranging from simple bar snacks to a three-course meal. Those that offer lunch-time snacks and an evening meal are generally known as *eetcafés*. While the choice of dishes tends to be limited, the quality is generally high and prices are often very reasonable. Some *eetcafés* have started serving more adventurous dishes and generally offer a good vegetarian selection. However, café and bar kitchens close early and it is difficult to get a meal after 9pm. For more information on cafés and bars, including a selection of the top ten in Amsterdam, see pages 46–7.

BARS AND STREET STALLS

Almost all bars serve a range of snacks. The standard selection of nibbles includes olives, chunks of Dutch cheese served with mustard and *borrelnoten* (nuts with a savoury coating). More substantial tapas-like snacks include *bitterballen* (deep-fried meatballs), *vlammetjes* (deep-fried batter envelopes similar to meat and vegetable spring rolls) and *osseworst* (a spicy mince-beef sausage).

Given the maritime tradition of the Netherlands, it is worth trying the fish dishes available in bars and from stalls on the street, such as herring served with onion or gherkins. Pizza, sandwiches and hamburgers are also commonly available from stalls. However, the most popular snack from street stalls is french fries or *patat frites*, which are served with mayonnaise in a plastic tray or a paper cone (*see p226*).

PANCAKE HOUSES

Pancakes (*pannenkoeken*) are a popular, value-for-money light meal in Amsterdam. The French-style *crêpe* is believed to have been adopted in the Netherlands during the Napoleonic occupation (*see pp30–31*) as a way of using up leftovers.

These days there is nothing penny-pinching about the wide range of sweet and savoury toppings available at most pancake houses in Amsterdam. It is not uncommon to find up to 70 varieties on offer and you can usually combine any of these to create the pancake of your choice. The best places include **De Carrousel**, **Boerderij Meerzicht**, **The Pancake Bakery** and **Upstairs**. Portions may seem small, but they are deceptively filling. Pancakes and waffles served with syrup are also available as the staple snack at smoking coffeeshops (*see p49*).

BROWN CAFÉS AND BARS

The term *eetcafés* is usually applied to traditional brown cafés (*see also p48*). These often offer much better value and a more relaxed ambience than many small restaurants. Outstanding brown cafés include **De Prins**, **Het Molenpad**, **Café du Lac**, **Stof**, **De Reiger**, and **Blincker**, which have extensive and appealing menus. Not surprisingly, they often get crowded and it can be hard to find a free table.

The majority of basic *eetcafés* just offer filling home-made fare, such as sandwiches, soups, salads, omelettes and chips. The only unfamiliar dishes you are likely to come across are *uitsmijter* (a large open sandwich with roast beef or ham, topped with fried eggs) and *erwtensoep* (a thick pea soup with pork). Of the cheaper, more down-to-earth varieties of *eetcafés*, **De Doffer** serves filling food that is excellent value. **BIHP** combines international cuisine with an art gallery in the basement. De Doffer has the attraction of a billiard room. Both places attract a young, lively crowd and are popular with students. **Van Puffelen** offers more formal French-style dishes. All meals are served in the back extension, and adjacent building, of this intimate brown café, which has an impressive 19th-century interior. For the best French fries in the city, head to **Vleminckx Vlaamse Friteshuis**.

DESIGNER BARS

An extensive range of food is offered in some of the more up-market designer bars (*see p49*). This type of bar is invariably more expensive than other types of cafés and bars in the city and in most cases the quality of the fare does not justify such inflated prices. **Café Schiller**, housed in a beautiful Art Deco building on Rembrandtplein, is an honourable exception. Amid portraits of 1930s cabaret stars painted by Frits Schiller, you can enjoy a value-for-money selection of snacks and meals in an evocative period bar. Both **Het Land van Walem** and **De Balie** also serve tasty food in a stylish setting. **Morlang**, next door to Het Land van Walem, is less chic, but the food definitely is better value, and the trendy **Caffé Esprit** is very popular with Kalverstraat shoppers.

SPECIALIST CAFÉS

If you feel like trying something different, sample the delicious food at the Flemish cultural centre **De Brakke Grond**, where international dishes with a Belgian twist are served in both the café and the restaurant. **De Zotte** also serves down-to-earth Flemish food and stocks a huge variety of Belgian beers. While the quality of the food may not be that exceptional, the portions certainly are large enough to soak up the strongest of beers. Café-restaurant **Stanislavski** occupies almost the entire ground floor of the Stadsschouwburg (*see p111*). Named after the famous Russian theatre director, it has an atmosphere reminiscent of Paris or Berlin. Here, you can while away your day from breakfast until the small hours, enjoying the food and mingling with the theatre crowd.

DIRECTORY

PANCAKE HOUSES

Boerderij Meerzicht
Koenenkade 56.
Amsterdamse Bos.
Tel 679 2744.

De Carrousel
Tweede
Weteringplantsoen 1.
Map 4 F3.
Tel 625 8002.

The Pancake Bakery
Prinsengracht 191.
Map 1 B4.
Tel 625 1333.

Upstairs
Grimburgwal 2.
Map 7 B4.
Tel 626 5603.

BROWN CAFÉS AND BARS

BIHP
Keizersgracht 335.
Map 1 B5.
Tel 622 4511.

Blincker
St Barberenstraat 7.
Map 7 B4.
Tel 627 1938.

Café du Lac
Haarlemmerstraat 118.
Map 1 C3.
Tel 624 4265.

De Doffer
Runstraat 12–14.
Map 4 E1.
Tel 622 6686.

't Doktertje
Rozenboomsteeg 4.
Map 7 B4.
Tel 626 4427.

Molenpad
Prinsengracht 653.
Map 4 E1.
Tel 625 9680.

Pieper
Prinsengracht 424.
Map 4 E1.
Tel 626 4775.

De Prins
Prinsengracht 124.
Map 1 B4.
Tel 624 9382.

Van Puffelen
Prinsengracht 375–377.
Map 1 B4.
Tel 624 6270.

De Reiger
Nieuwe Leliestraat 34.
Map 1 B4.
Tel 624 7426.

De Tuin
2e Tuindwarsstraat 13
(near Westerstraat).
Map 1 B3.
Tel 624 4559.

Stof
Van der Helstplein 9.
Tel 364 0354.

Vleminckx Vlaamse Friteshuis
Voetboogstraat 33.
Map 7 B4.
Tel 624 6075.

PROEFLOKALEN AND MODERN TASTING BARS

De Drie Fleschjes
Gravenstraat 18.
Map 7 B2.
Tel 624 8443.

In De Wildeman
Kolksteeg 3.
Map 7 C1.
Tel 638 2348.

Mulliner's Wijnlokaal
Lijnbaansgracht
266–267.
Map 4 E2.
Tel 627 9782.

Whisky Café L&B Limited
Korte Leidsedwarsstraat
82–84.
Map 4 E2.
Tel 625 2387.

GRAND CAFÉS AND DESIGNER BARS

De Balie
Kleine Gartman-
plantsoen 10.
Map 4 E2.
Tel 553 5151.

Café Americain
American Hotel,
Leidsekade 97.
Map 4 E2.
Tel 556 3000.

Caffè Esprit
Spui 10.
Map 7 B4.
Tel 622 1967.

Café Luxembourg
Spui 22–24.
Map 7 B4.
Tel 620 6264.

Café Schiller
Rembrandtplein 26.
Map 7 C5.
Tel 624 9846.

De Jaren
Nieuwe Doelenstraat
20–22. **Map** 7 C4.
Tel 625 5771.

De Kroon
Rembrandtplein 17.
Map 7 C5.
Tel 625 2011.

Het Land van Walem
Keizersgracht 449.
Map 7 A5.
Tel 625 3544.

Morlang
Keizersgracht 451.
Map 7 A5.
Tel 625 2681.

Vertigo
Nederlands Filmmuseum,
Vondelpark 3.
Map 4 D2.
Tel 612 3021.

SMOKING COFFEESHOPS

Abraxas
Jonge Roelensteeg 12.
Map 7 B3.
Tel 625 5763.

The Bulldog
Leidseplein 15.
Map 4 E2.
Tel 627 1908.

Global Chillage
Kerkstraat 51.
Map 4 E1.
Tel 777 9777.

The Grasshopper
Nieuwezijds Voorburgwal
59. **Map** 7 A4.
Tel 624 6753.

Rusland
Rusland 16.
Map 7 C4.
Tel 627 9468.

Siberië
Brouwersgracht 11.
Map 1 C3.
Tel 623 5909.

COFFEESHOPS AND SALONS DE THÉ

Arnold Cornelis
Elandsgracht 78.
Map 1 B5.
Tel 625 8585.

Backstage
Utrechtsedwarsstraat 67.
Map 5 A3.
Tel 622 3638.

Bagels & Beans
Ferdinand Bolstraat 70.
Map 4 F4.
Tel 672 1610.

Coffee Company
Haarlemmerdijk 62.
Map 1 C2.
Tel 624 4278.

Metz & Co
Leidsestraat 34–36.
Map 4 F1.
Tel 520 7020.

Pompadour
Huidenstraat 12.
Map 7 A4.
Tel 623 9554.

Tazzina
Brouwersgracht 139.
Map 1 B2.
Tel 330 4649.

SPECIALIST CAFÉS

De Brakke Grond
Nes 43.
Map 7 B3.
Tel 626 0044.

De Zotte
Raamstraat 29.
Map 4 E1.
Tel 626 8694.

Stanislavski
Leidseplein 25.
Map 4 E2.
Tel 495 9995.

SHOPS AND MARKETS

Amsterdam has a huge range of shops and markets, so if you are present-hunting, you will find no shortage of ideas. Most of the large clothing and department stores are to be found in the Nieuwe Zijde, especially along Kalverstraat *(see p72)*, but there are many other shopping areas to discover. The narrow streets which cross the Canal Ring, such as Herenstraat and Hartenstraat, contain a diverse array of specialist shops selling everything from ethnic fabrics and beads to unusual games and handmade dolls. The best luxury fashion is to be found on the classy PC Hooftstraat and Van Baerlestraat. However, if you are looking for a bargain, take time to explore the street markets and numerous second-hand shops. Here you can pick up recent fashion items and worn leather jackets cheaply.

Atrium of the Magna Plaza in the former Postkantoor

OPENING HOURS

Shops are usually open from 9am or 10am to 6pm Tuesday to Saturday and from 1pm to 6pm on Monday *(see p257)*. Many shops are now also open on Sundays. In the city centre, shops stay open until 9pm on Thursdays. However, legislation does allow shopkeepers in the city centre to remain open between 7am and 10pm seven days a week. Retailers are most likely to take advantage of this law in the run up to Sinterklaas *(see p53)* and during Christmas.

HOW TO PAY

Cash is the most popular method of payment, so if you intend to use a credit card, ask if they are accepted before buying. Although cards are becoming more widely accepted, department stores often require purchases to be paid for at a special till, and smaller shops may only accept them for non-sale items and goods costing more than €45. Travellers' cheques are accepted in most shops and, if you have a bank account in the Netherlands, direct debits are popular. Some tourist shops take foreign currency, but offer a poor rate of exchange.

VAT EXEMPTION

Most Dutch goods are subject to value added tax (BTW) of either 19 per cent for clothes and other goods, or 6 per cent for books. Non-EU residents are entitled to a refund, subject to certain conditions. Shops which stock the relevant forms will have a sign saying "Tax free for tourists". On leaving the country, present your goods, receipt and the form at customs who will refund you 10 per cent of the purchase price of your goods. Refunds are only made on purchases above €50.

Stoeltie Diamonds (see p242)

SALES

Sales take place mainly in January and July but smaller shops and boutiques may offer discount items at any time. *Uitverkoop* describes anything from a closing-down sale to a stock-clearance sale, while *korting* merely indicates that discounts are being offered.

Towards the end of a sale, further discounts, which will be calculated at the till, are often subtracted from the marked-down price. Beware of clothes rails marked, for example, *VA 40* or *Vanaf 40* as this sign means "From 40" – the items cost €40 or more, rather than exactly €40.

DEPARTMENT STORES AND MALLS

Perhaps Amsterdam's best-known department store is **De Bijenkorf** on Dam square, often described as the Dutch Harrods. It has a huge perfumery, and stocks a wide range of men's and women's clothing, plus toys, soft furnishings and household goods. At Christmas it devotes a whole floor to decorations. Both **Maison de Bonneterie** and **Metz & Co** are more exclusive. Among the less expensive stores, **Hema** is very popular for household goods, children's clothes and underwear. Also popular for basic items is **Vroom & Dreesmann**. The only shopping malls in central Amsterdam are the Kalvertoren (Kalverstraat, near Singel) and Magna Plaza, which is housed in the old Postkantoor building *(see p78)*. The impressive, vaulted interior of this former head post office now contains a huge assortment of upmarket boutiques and shops.

MARKETS

Amsterdammers' love of street trading is most graphically illustrated on 30 April during Queen's Day *(see p50)*, when Amsterdam turns into the biggest flea market in the world, as local people crowd the city to sell off all their unwanted junk. Such is the crush of eager bargain-hunters that the entire city centre is closed to traffic during the festivities.

As Amsterdam still resembles a collection of small villages, every district has its own local market. The best-known of these, because of its size, is the Albert Cuypmarkt *(see p122)* in the Pijp district, which sells a wide assortment of food, both Dutch and ethnic. This market is also good for cheap clothes and reasonably priced flowers.

Apart from the local markets, Amsterdam has a wide range of specialist markets. Seasonal flowers are on sale at the Bloemenmarkt *(see p123)*. Another market popular with tourists is Waterlooplein flea market *(see p63)*. Despite the crowds, vigilant collectors can still seek out the odd bargain among the bric-a-brac; there is also a selection of new and second-hand clothes for sale.

Browsers will be fascinated by the hundreds of stalls at the Looier Kunst Antiekcentrum *(see p113)*, which sell anything from antique dolls to egg cups. Every Wednesday and Saturday on the Nieuwezijds Voorburgwal there is a specialist market for stamp and coin collectors. On Fridays there is a second-hand bookmarket on Spui. Gourmets should head for the Noordermarkt *(see p92)*, which holds an organic food market on Saturdays. The best prices, however, are to be found about 25 km (16 miles) northwest of Amsterdam in the port town of

MEXX, a smart boutique on PC Hooftstraat *(see p126)*

Beverwijk, where the **Beverwijkse Bazaar**, open weekends, is one of Europe's largest indoor flea markets. Next door the market continues with a cross-section of Oriental merchandise, including rugs, carpets, pottery, crafts and food.

Smoked fish on display at the Albert Cuypmarkt

SPECIALIST SHOPS

Dotted throughout Amsterdam are dozens of small specialist shops. One of the more unusual is **Condomerie Het Gulden Vlies**, located in a former squat, which sells condoms from all over the world. Equally unusual is **Christmas**

Palace, which sells festive adornments all year round, and **Party House**, which has a vast collection of paper decorations. **Capsicum Natuurstoffen** has a huge selection of exotic silks and linens, while **Coppenhagen 1001 Kralen** has more than 1,000 different types of beads. It is also worth making time to explore **Joe's Vliegerwinkel** for its wide range of kites, **Simon Levelt** for tea and coffee, or **Hooy & Co.** for an array of wonderful-smelling herbs.

BOOKS, NEWSPAPERS AND MAGAZINES

As books are subject to Value-Added tax in the Netherlands, you may find them slightly more expensive than at home. English-language books are generally available, particularly at **The American Book Center**, **Waterstone's** and **The English Bookshop**. Holiday reading can be picked up very cheaply at second-hand bookshops, such as **De Slegte**. Collectors of comics should not miss a visit to **Lambiek**. Most city-centre newsagents stock foreign papers. *Het Financieel Dagblad* has a daily business update in English and publishes a weekly English-language edition. *Day by Day* is a useful listings magazine, as is the monthly *Time Out* magazine.

A selection of seasonal flowers, including sunflowers, roses and lilies

What to Buy in Amsterdam

Traditional wooden clogs

Amsterdam has hundreds of tourist shops selling souvenirs, but those looking for something different will find a better selection of genuine Dutch items in one of the city's specialist shops or even at an ordinary supermarket. Authentic Delftware is only found at a handful of licensed dealers, but there are still many jewellers selling anything from uncut stones to second-hand diamond rings. Dutch cheese, chocolate and locally produced beers and *jenevers* offer a flavour of the city, while a bunch of flowers is always appreciated.

Ceramics
Finely detailed model canal houses can be be bought singly or by the row.

Droste chocolate pastilles

Sweet and salty varieties of drop liquorice

Dutch Sweets
Handmade Belgian chocolates and Droste pastilles are both delicious, but salty liquorice is an acquired taste.

Handmade Belgian chocolates

Flowers
Bulbs and cut flowers are a colourful reminder of the city and, due to greenhouse production, many blooms are available all year round.

Tulip bulbs

A bunch of fresh tulips

Gouda Cheese
There are many types of Gouda of different maturity (see p242). Any shop will be happy to let you try a slice before making a purchase.

Two popular brands of beer

Beer in Amsterdam
A huge variety of imported, bottled beers are sold in Amsterdam as well as many local brews (see p242).

Sturdy stone flagons of *jonge* and *oude jenever (see pp48–9) – also available in flavoured varieties

Dutch windmill prints

Old Maps and Prints
Historically famous for cartography, Amsterdam has a good selection of new and old maps, and many second-hand bookshops stock etchings.

Reproductions of old maps of Amsterdam and Russia

Diamond brooch

Chain-link, diamond-encrusted bracelet

Diamonds
Diamond-cutting was first established in Amsterdam during the 16th century. The city is still one of the major diamond centres.

Different coloured brilliant-cut diamonds

ROYAL DELFT
In response to the demand for Chinese design, more than 30 factories sprang up in Delft in the 17th century, producing distinctive blue-and-white ceramics *(see p195)*. Today, only De Porceleyne Fles still makes real Delftware. Items from this factory are sold with a certificate of authenticity.

Polychrome jug painted in colours used on 17th-century majolica

Pynaker tobacco jar influenced by Japanese Imari ware

Plate painted in traditional Delft blue

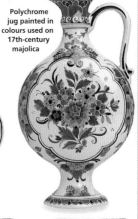

Painter's initials

Year code – DB means 1982

Trademark since 1876

Item number

Genuine De Porceleyne Fles marks

Delft-blue vase

17th-century plate made for rich family

Decorative 17th-century fireplace tile

Antique Delft
Old Delftware is highly sought after and expensive, but Delft fireplace tiles can be picked up more cheaply.

Where to Shop in Amsterdam

The Netherlands is justly famous for its flowers, beer and cheese. A wide choice of these indigenous products is available in Amsterdam, which has also long been regarded as the world centre for diamonds. Owing to the large numbers of overseas settlers living in Amsterdam and the cosmopolitan outlook of its residents, it is easy to find a selection of foreign goods in the city. These range from Indonesian beads to French designer wear.

FASHION AND CLOTHES

Van Baerlestraat and PC Hooftstraat contain numerous designer boutiques such as **MEXX**, offering top names like Katharine Hamnet and the leading French and Italian designer labels. The smart set from the Canal Ring haunt the stylish **The People of the Labyrinths** and **Pauw** for their timeless clothes and accessories.

Boutiques in the Nieuwe Zijde offer less pricey items. The French designer **Agnès B** has her own shop along Rokin selling classic designer wear. If leather's your thing, try **Robin & Rik** on Runstraat for handmade leather clothes and accessories. Along Kalverstraat, **Sissy Boy** specializes in refined classic suits as well as eye-catching designs.

Fanatics of second-hand clothes will find well-priced and stylish selections at shops such as **Zipper**. For the widest choice of fashionable boots and shoes, **Dr Adams** is almost a Dutch institution.

ANTIQUES AND FURNISHINGS

While you can pick up the odd bargain on Waterlooplein (see p63) and at the Noordermarkt (see p92), the best place for antiques is around Spiegelgracht. A wide selection of shops sells everything from 17th-century tiles to icons. The **EH Ariëns Kappers** has a comprehensive collection of old prints, maps and graphic art. It is also interesting to visit an auction house. Both **Sotheby's** and **Christie's** have branches in Amsterdam. Looier Kunst en Antiekcentrum (see p113), has a potpourri of odds and ends, while **Fanous Ramadan** has a colourful collection of

Arabic lampshades, pottery and furniture. **De Looier Kunst en Antiekcentrum** (see p113) is a good place for antiques.

FLOWERS AND BULBS

No Dutch person would dream of visiting a friend without a bunch of flowers, so Amsterdam is crowded with flower shops. Worth visiting are **Madelief**, for a vast assortment of colourful domestic blooms, and **Gerda's Bloemen en Planten**, for its stock of tropical flowers.

Cut flowers are cheapest at Albert Cuypmarkt (see p122), but Bloemenmarkt (see p123) has a better selection, as well as hundreds of bulbs and tubers. It also sells potted plants, but due to customs regulations, these usually can't be exported.

DIAMONDS

Amsterdam has a long tradition of cutting and polishing diamonds (see p32). It is still possible to purchase loose stones and diamonds in a new setting at one of the city's many diamond-cutting centres, such as **Gassan Diamonds** or Coster Diamonds (see p128). The city is also well stocked with jewellers, several specializing in diamonds. The best second-hand jewellery can be found in the fascinating antique shops around Spiegelgracht.

CHEESE

You can buy a good selection of cheese at street markets and specialist shops such as **Wout Arxhoek** or **De Kaaskamer**. Instead of buying the red-wax-covered Edam, try one of the many varieties of Gouda. Mature Gouda (overjarige kaas) has a rich, salty taste and crumbly

texture, while young Gouda is softer and more buttery. This cheese is also sold with cummin (leidsekaas) or cloves (nagelkaas) (see p226).

CHOCOLATES

Verkade and Droste are the best-known makes of chocolate in the Netherlands. For a treat, visit **Pompadour**, for its delicious hand-made chocolates, or another Amsterdam favourite, **Puccini Bomboni**.

BEERS AND SPIRITS

The Dutch are knowledgeable beer drinkers. Along with brand-name lagers like Heineken, Grolsch and Amstel, there is also a huge range of bottled beers on offer. Local specialities include Zatte, a rare, bottle-fermented beer and Wieckse Witte, a white beer. Specialist shops like **De Bierkoning** offer the widest choice and best advice.

The Dutch spirit jenever, the "father" of gin, is often sold in stone bottles and flavoured with herbs or fruit (see p48).

POTTERY AND GLASSWARE

Blue-and-white pottery is stocked by most shops, but only items with a certificate are real Delftware. **Rinascimento** sells the real thing from De Porceleyne Fles, one of the original Delft potteries.

The Jordaan is the best place to hunt for modern pottery, while **Glasgalerie Kuhler** has a stunning range of modern glass, and **Het Klei Kollektief** offers an ever-changing choice of bright ceramics.

POSTERS AND PRINTS

The best places to find good reproductions of paintings are in museum shops. **Art Unlimited** offers an excellent selection of the less famous Dutch scenes.

A range of old etchings can be found at **Hoogkamp Old Prints** and among the stalls at the Oudemanshuispoort in the Oude Zijde (see p61).

DIRECTORY

DEPARTMENT STORES

De Bijenkorf
Dam 1.
Map 7 B2.
Tel 0900 0919.

Hema
Kalvertoren, Kalverstraat.
Map 7 B4.
Tel 422 8988.
Nieuwendijk 174–176.
Map 7 B2.
Tel 623 4176.

Maison de Bonneterie
Rokin 140–142.
Map 7 B4.
Tel 531 3400.

Metz & Co
Leidsestraat 34-36.
Map 7 A5.
Tel 520 7020.

Vroom & Dreesmann
Kalverstraat 203.
Map 7 B5.
Tel 0900 235 8363.

MARKETS OUTSIDE THE CITY

De Beverwijkse Bazaar
Montageweg 35
Beverwijk.
Tel 0251 262666.

SPECIALIST SHOPS

Capsicum Natuurstoffen
Oude Hoogstraat 1.
Map 7 C3.
Tel 623 1016.

Christmas Palace
Singel 508.
Map 7 B5.
Tel 421 0155.

Condomerie Het Gulden Vlies
Warmoesstraat 141.
Map 7 C2.
Tel 627 4174.

Coppenhagen 1001 Kralen
Rozengracht 54.
Map 1 B4.
Tel 624 3681.

Jacob Hooy & Co
Kloveniersburgwal 12.
Map 8 D3.
Tel 624 3041.

Joe's Vliegerwinkel
Nieuwe Hoogstraat 19.
Map 8 D3.
Tel 625 0139.

Party House
Rozengracht 92b.
Map 1 B4.
Tel 624 7851.

Simon Levelt
Prinsengracht 180.
Map 1 B4.
Tel 624 0823.

BOOKS, NEWSPAPERS AND MAGAZINES

The American Book Center
Spui 12. **Map** 7 A4.
Tel 625 5537.

The English Bookshop
Lauriergracht 71.
Map 1 B5.
Tel 626 4230.

Lambiek
Kerkstraat 132.
Map 4 F2.
Tel 626 7543.

De Slegte
Kalverstraat 48–52.
Map 7 B3.
Tel 622 5933.

Waterstone's Bookseller
Kalverstraat 152.
Map 7 B4. **Tel** 638 3821.

FASHION AND CLOTHES

Agnès B
Rokin 126. **Map** 7 B4.
Tel 627 1465.

Dr Adams
Oude Doelenstraat 5–7.
Map 7 C3.
Tel 622 3734.

MEXX
PC Hooftstraat 118–120.
Map 4 D3.
Tel 675 0171.

Pauw
Van Baerlestraat 48.
Map 4 D3.
Tel 673 1665.

The People of the Labyrinths
Van Baerlestraat 44.
Map 4 D3.
Tel 664 0779.

Robin & Rik
Runstraat 30. **Map** 7 B4.
Tel 627 8924.

Sissy Boy
Kalverstraat 210.
Map 7 B4.
Tel 626 0088.

Zipper
Huidenstraat 7.
Map 7 A4.
Tel 623 7302.

ANTIQUES AND FURNISHINGS

Christie's
Cornelis Schuytstraat 57.
Map 3 C4.
Tel 575 5255.

EH Ariëns Kappers
Nieuwe Spiegelstraat 32.
Map 4 F2.
Tel 623 5356.

Fanous Ramadan
Runstraat 33.
Map 4 E1.
Tel 423 2350.

Kitsch Kitchen
Rozengracht 8–12.
Map 1 B4.
Tel 622 8261.

De Looier
Elandsgracht 109.
Map 1 A5.
Tel 624 9038.

Sotheby's
De Boelelaan 30.
Map 7 B4.
Tel 550 2200.

FLOWERS AND BULBS

Gerda's Bloemen en Planten
Runstraat 16.
Map 4 E1.
Tel 624 2912.

Madelief
Haarlemmerdijk 93.
Map 1 C2.
Tel 625 3239.

DIAMONDS

Gassan Diamonds
Nieuwe Uilenburgerstraat
173–175. **Map** 8 E4.
Tel 622 5333.

CHEESE

De Kaaskamer
Runstraat 7. **Map** 4 E1.
Tel 623 3483.

Wout Arxhoek
Damstraat 19. **Map** 7 C3.
Tel 622 9118.

CHOCOLATES

Pompadour
Huidenstraat 12. **Map** 7
A4. **Tel** 623 9554.

Puccini Bomboni
Staalstraat 17. **Map** 8 D4.
Tel 626 5474.

BEERS AND SPIRITS

De Bierkoning
Paleisstraat 125.
Map 7 B3.
Tel 625 2336.

POTTERY AND GLASSWARE

Fleur de Lys
Beethovenstraat 41.
Map 4 D5. **Tel** 662 1737.

Galleria d'Arte Rinascimento
Prinsengracht 170.
Map 1 B4.
Tel 622 7509.

Glasgalerie Kuhler
Prinsengracht 134.
Map 1 B4.
Tel 638 0230.

Het Kleikollektief
Hartenstraat 19.
Map 7 A3.
Tel 622 5727.

POSTERS AND PRINTS

Art Unlimited
Keizersgracht 510.
Map 7 A5. **Tel** 624 8419.

Hoogkamp Old Prints
Spiegelgracht 27.
Map 4 F2. **Tel** 625 8852.

ENTERTAINMENT IN AMSTERDAM

Amsterdam offers a diverse array of world-class entertainment. A variety of performances are staged in hundreds of venues throughout the city, ranging from the century-old Concertgebouw *(see p128)* to the 17th-century IJsbreker café on the Amstel *(see p248)*. The Dutch passion for American jazz draws many international greats such as BB King and Pharaoh Sanders to annual events such as the Blues Festival and Drum Rhythm Festival *(see p50)*. The city's most popular events take place in the summer, and include the Holland Festival *(see p51)* and the Amsterdam Roots Festival *(see p51)*. There is a huge choice of multilingual plays and films throughout the year. There is also plenty of free entertainment to be enjoyed from the multitude of street performers and live bands in late-night bars and cafés.

ENTERTAINMENT INFORMATION

One of the most useful sources of entertainment information is *Uitkrant*, a free listings magazine *(see p265)*. It is printed monthly and available, as are a variety of other Dutch-language listings, from theatres, cafés and bars, libraries and tourist offices.

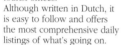

Late-night bar in the Red Light District

Although written in Dutch, it is easy to follow and offers the most comprehensive daily listings of what's going on.

The **Amsterdam Tourist Board** *(see also p259)* publishes an English-language listings magazine every two weeks called *Day by Day*. It can be picked up for a nominal price at Tourist Board offices and some newsagents, or free

issues can be found in selected hotels and restaurants; or check out the monthly *Time Out* magazine. For music listings look out for the *Pop & Jazz Uitlijst* published by the **AUB** (Amsterdam Uitburo). Daily newspapers including *De Volkskrant, Het Parool, NRC Handelsblad* and *De Telegraaf* publish a selection of listings on Wednesdays, although they are mainly excerpts from *Uitkrant*.

BOOKING TICKETS

Amsterdam's major classical music, opera and dance performances, such as those by the Dutch National Ballet, are likely to be sold out weeks ahead of time. It is advisable to book tickets in advance to

ensure the day, time and seats of your choice. For most other events, it is possible to buy tickets on the day. The AUB has a last-minute window (noon–7:30pm daily) selling tickets for same-day shows.

The main reservations office for entertainment and all cultural activities is the AUB, which is located next to the Stadsschouwburg *(see p111)* in Leidseplein. You can make reservations, pick up tickets in advance (a booking fee is charged) and obtain information in person or over the telephone. You can also make bookings at the venue itself, or through Tourist Board offices. Tickets to major rock concerts can be obtained at the Tourist Board, AUB and at some of the large record shops in the city centre. Although some of the most popular club dates need to be booked in

The Stopera complex, home to the Dutch national opera and ballet companies

The Neo-Classical-style pediment of the Concertgebouw *(see p128)*

advance, entrance to clubs like the Paradiso and De Melkweg *(see pp110–11)* can usually be bought at the door. Going to the cinema is very popular with Amsterdammers, so it is advisable to book tickets in the afternoon for evening performances during a film's opening week. Most multi-screen cinemas provide a Dutch-speaking automated booking service. All booking offices are usually open from Monday to Saturday, between 9am and 6pm, or later. Credit cards are usually not accepted and it is important to collect reserved tickets at least an hour before the show starts, or the tickets may be resold.

*atre sign
on Nes
ee p74)*

REDUCED-PRICE TICKETS

Entry to some performances can be obtained at bargain prices for holders of the Cultureel Jongeren Passport (CJP). Valid for one year, it is available to anyone under the age of 26 for €15. Some hotels include reduced-price entry to certain events as part of their package deals – check details with your travel agent. Half-price last-minute tickets can be bought at the AUB last-minute ticket office. Several venues, such as the Concert-gebouw *(see p128)* and the Westerkerk *(see p90)*, have free lunchtime concerts throughout the year.

FACILITIES FOR THE DISABLED

Most major theatres, cinemas and concert halls in Amsterdam have unrestricted wheelchair access, and assistance is always available. A number of the city's smaller venues, however, are housed in old buildings not designed with the disabled in mind. Venues like De Kleine Komedie *(see p246)* will make special arrangements if they are notified beforehand. Cinemas also provide facilities for the hard of hearing and visually impaired. Always telephone the box office a couple of days before your visit and specify what you require.

OPEN-AIR ENTERTAINMENT

Since Amsterdammers are avid supporters of theatre and of all sorts of music, there are plenty of open-air venues operating throughout the summer. In the heart of the city, the Vondelpark

open-air theatre *(see p128)* stages a wide variety of free concerts and theatre performances. The restored turn-of-the-century Nederlands Filmmuseum *(see p129)* is housed in a pavilion in the park. During the summer, free screenings and documentaries are shown, as well as silent films that are sometimes accompanied by live music.

The Prinsengracht classical music concert *(see p51)* is performed in August on a group of canal barges. On the outskirts of the city, the scenic Amsterdamse Bos *(see p155)* is the setting for productions of Shakespeare, Chekhov and other classical dramatists, staged in the open-air theatre. In the south, Amstelpark *(see p154)* is the venue for De Parade at the end of July *(see p246)*. Amsterdammers also enjoy rowing on the Amstel, with rowing clubs operate from a boathouse near Amstelpark.

USEFUL ADDRESSES

AUB/Last-Minute Ticket Office
Leidseplein 26. **Map** 4 E2.
Tel 795 9950.
www.amsterdamsuitboro.nl

Amsterdam Tourist Board
Centraal Station, Platform 2.
Map 2 E3. *Tel* 0900 400 4040.
Stationsplein 10. **Map** 8 D1.
Tel 0900 400 4040.
Leidseplein 26. **Map** 4 E2.
Tel 0900 400 4040.
www.visitamsterdam.nl
www.amsterdamtourist.nl
www.iamsterdam.nl

Customers enjoying café life in the popular Thorbeckeplein

Theatre, Dance and Film

Theatre and dance are important aspects of cultural life in Amsterdam, and performances take place throughout the year in dozens of venues all over the city. Experimental theatre can be found in one of the oldest streets in the city, along the Nes *(see p74)*. Theatres on the Nes, such as De Brakke Grond, are also popular venues for radical theatre productions. The city's main locations for dance include the Felix Meritis, Meervaart, Muziektheater, Stadsschouwburg and the Dutch Dance Laboratory, for experimental productions. The Dutch love cinema and, though Amsterdam has only a few large cinema complexes, there is a surprising number of venues that show a variety of films, from first-run, mainstream and art, to foreign-language, revival and gay.

THEATRE AND CABARET

Amsterdam has more than 50 theatre venues and boasts a number of English-speaking companies. The Toneelgroep Amsterdam is the resident theatre company at the **Stadsschouwburg**, and the **Felix Meritis** *(see p113)*, **Westergasfabriek** and **Bellevue** are important venues for many touring theatre companies.

Experimental theatre can be found at a range of locations throughout Amsterdam, including the **Westergasfabriek**. The **Theatercompagnie** is a small company that specializes in translating and staging the classics, as well as promoting works by young playwrights. The Orkater musical theatre company often holds performances at Stadsschouwburg and the Theater Bellevue.

The annual Holland Festival *(see p51)* in June offers a prestigious series of opera, theatre and dance performances. It features international talent such as Peter Brook, Peter Zadek and John Jesurum. The International Theatre School Festival presents innovative performances at **De Brakke Grond**, **Frascati** and other venues on the Nes *(see p74)* at the end of June.

The **Tropentheater** has a packed programme of lively productions from all over the world. Downriver from the Muziek-theater, near the smart Amstel Inter-Continental *(see p223)*, the **Koninklijk Theater Carré** plays host to long-running international musicals

such as *Les Misérables* and *Cyrano*. The **Koninklijk Theater Carré** is often the setting for elegant premières attended by members of the Dutch royal family. Closer to the Muziektheater and also facing the Amstel is the charming 17th-century **De Kleine Komedie**. It can seat an audience of up to 500 and offers a perfect setting for cabaret. It also features stand-up comedy and occasionally has English-language theatre productions. Although De Kleine Komedie is closed throughout the summer, such is its reputation throughout Europe that bookings must be made at least three months in advance. Stand-up comedy (in English) also can be found at the **Leidseplein Theater. Panama** is one of the latest venues to offer cabaret shows.

Summer outdoor theatre can be seen at the **Vondelpark** open-air theatre *(see p128)* and at the Amsterdamse Bos *(see p155)*, a woodland park on the edge of town. Here, a pathway lined with Classical Greek statuary leads to a 1,800-seat amphitheatre, the venue for performances of Shakespeare and Chekhov plays. In the south of Amsterdam, the Amstelpark *(see p154)* is the venue for De Parade, a tent city erected each summer in late July and early August where international dance, theatre and circus acts perform before a rapturous audience. Merry-making often carries on into the early morning hours.

DANCE

The Netherlands possesses two world-class ballet companies, the Dutch National Ballet and the Nederlands Dans Theater (NDT). The Dutch National Ballet is housed in the 1,600-seat **Muziektheater** *(see p63)*, which provides magnificent views along the Amstel river, and is renowned for its classical and modern repertoire.

The Nederlands Dans Theater (NDT) regularly performs in venues throughout the city. Ballets from the Czech artistic director, Jiri Kylian, form the majority of the programming. In addition to the core company, the NDT also has one other group, the Nederlands Dans Theater II, a younger company made up of dancers aged 18–21 who perform the work of established choreographers such as Hans van Manen. The company also performs the works of younger choreographers such as Lionel Hoche and Paul Lightfoot.

Dance is often performed at Stadsschouwburg and at the Felix Meritis, Amsterdam's 18th-century concert hall and one of its earliest performancevenues. Westergasfabriek, the former gasworks, also holds dance performances.

Amsterdam is a laboratory for experimental dance, and many innovative performances can be seen throughout the city. They are not confined to any one venue though, so it is best to check the entertainment listings, such as *Uitkrant* *(see p265)*, for full details. Experimental dance can be enjoyed regularly at top venues like the Stadsschouwburg and the **De Meervaart**. Companies to look out for include Introdans, who combine jazz with flamenco alongside other varieties of ethnic dance, and Opus One, who mix jazz, classical ballet and tap. Needless to say, the Nederlands Dans Theater's repertoire also includes experimental dance routines.

During the first two weeks of July the Stadsschouwburg and surrounding theatres host The Julidans International Festival for Contemporary Dance. Young and established choreographers and dance groups give daring and often ground-breaking performances, to great acclaim. The programme can be found on www.julidans.nl. The Holland Festival in June *(see p51)* is used as the principal platform for premières of shows by top choreographers from both the Nederlands Dans Theater and the Dutch National Ballet. The International Thetre School Festival, also in June, focuses increasingly on dance, with performances taking place in the historic street of Nes *(see p74)*, which is one of the very oldest parts of the city.

FILM

Amsterdammers love the cinema, and there are more than 45 venues in the city. All films are screened in the original language with subtitles. Movie lovers should not miss the plush Art Deco Tuschinski Theater *(see p123)*. Built between 1918 and 1921, this cinema features a luxurious foyer, stained-glass windows, tables, sofas and lamps. First-run films often open at the Tuschinski, and this is often the place to catch public appearances by film stars.

It is easy to find out which films are showing where, as each cinema has a listing at its entrance, and details are also posted in bars and cafés.

Programmes change on a Thursday, and most new film listings, carried in the daily newspapers, are printed on the Wednesday. *De Filmkrant* is a free monthly film magazine that carries complete listings; these are written in Dutch but very easy to understand. It is also possible to check online at www.filmladder.nl.

Ticket prices vary from around €7 to €10, depending on whether it is a matinée or an evening screening, although some longer films can command a slightly higher admission price.

Some of the larger cinema complexes carry afternoon matinées during the week and these usually begin at 2pm. At the weekend the schedule varies. Some of the cinemas, such as the mainstream **City** and the arthouse **Kriterion**, often schedule several showings of children's films at the weekend. For adults, the Kriterion offers a great selection of arthouse and mainstream films, with late-night screenings of cult and erotic movies.

Evening shows usually begin at either 6:30pm or 7pm, and there is a second showing at 9pm or 9:30pm, although a few cinemas also have an 8pm screening. Some cinemas have an intermission, known as the "pauze". This is a 15-minute obligatory break that is usually scheduled to coincide exactly with the most exciting scene of the film.

If you suddenly get the urge to see a film and don't particularly mind what it is, check out Leidseplein *(see p110)*, one of the biggest gathering areas in the city, where cinemas, cafés, restaurants and bars abound.

One first-run and art-house cinema that can be found within a two-minute walk of Leidseplein is the recently renovated eight-screen **City** theatre.

The Movies near Haarlemmerpoort *(see p93)* specializes in films with a psychological connection. The theatre also houses a pleasant pub and restaurant. For arthouse films there is also the **Cinecenter**, situated on a side street just off the main square across from De Melkweg *(see p110)*; and for a real treat, **Filmtheater de Uitkijk**, which is a short walk along Leidsestraat to Prinsengracht. This small, venerable 158-seat venue specializes in movie classics and, best of all, refuses to indulge in the dreaded "pauze". Dating from 1913, De Uitkijk is Amsterdam's oldest operational cinema.

DIRECTORY

THEATRE/CABARET

De Brakke Grond
Vlaams Cultureel Centrum, Nes 45. **Map** 7 C3.
Tel 626 6866.
www.brakkegrond.nl

De Kleine Komedie
Amstel 56–58. **Map** 5 B3.
Tel 624 0534.
www.dekleinekomedie.nl

Felix Meritis
Keizersgracht 324.
Map 1 B5. *Tel 623 1311.*
www.felix.meritis.nl

Frascati
Nes 63. **Map** 7 B4.
Tel 626 6866.
www.frascati.nl

Koninklijk Theater Carré
Amstel 115–125. **Map** 5 B3. *Tel 0900 252 5255.*
www.theatercarre.nl

Leidseplein Theater
Leidseplein 12. **Map** 4 E2.
Tel 423 0101.
www.boomchicago.nl

Panama
Oostelijke Handelskade 4.
Tel 311 8689.
www.panama.nl

Stadsschouwburg
Leidseplein 26. **Map** 4 E2.
Tel 624 2311.
www.sssba.nl

Theater Bellevue
Leidsekade 90. **Map** 4 D1.
Tel 530 5301.
www.theaterbellevue.nl

Theatercompagnie
Kloveniersburgwal 50.
Map 7 C3. *Tel 520 5320.*
www.theatercompagnie.nl

Tropentheater
Linnaeusstraat 2.
Map 6 E3. *Tel 568 8500.*
www.tropentheater.nl

Westergasfabriek
Haarlemmerweg 8–10.
Map 1 A1. *Tel 586 0710.*
www.westergasfabriek.com

DANCE

De Meervaart
Meer en Vaart 300. *Tel 410 7777.* www.meervaart.nl

Het Muziektheater
Amstel 3. **Map** 7 C5.
Tel 625 5455.
www.muziektheater.nl

See also venues under **Theatre/Cabaret**

FILM

Cinecenter
Lijnbaansgracht 236.
Map 4 E2. *Tel 623 6615.*

City Theater
Kleine Gartmanplantsoen 15–19. **Map** 4 E2.
Tel 0900 1458.

Filmtheater de Uitkijk
Prinsengracht 452.
Map 4 E2. *Tel 623 7460.*

Kriterion
Roetersstraat 170
Map 5 C3. *Tel 623 1708*

The Movies
Haarlemmerdijk 161.
Map 1 B2. *Tel 638 6016.*

Classical Music and Opera

Amsterdam is a city with a long and rich tradition in classical music and opera. The principal orchestral venues house some of the world's finest musical events. The city has also acquired a reputation as a centre for early music and organ recitals, with performances in traditional settings such as the English Reformed Church or the Oude Kerk. In summer, concerts can be enjoyed as you relax in one of the city's beautiful parks.

ORCHESTRAL, CHAMBER AND CHORAL MUSIC

Amsterdam's music centre-piece is the **Concertgebouw**, renowned for its acoustics and home to the celebrated Royal Concertgebouw Orchestra. International orchestras and soloists come here regularly, and each summer it hosts Robeco Groep concerts, which are famous for showcasing young talent. Early music is also performed here, often by the world-famous Amsterdam Baroque Orchestra and the Orchestra of the Eighteenth Century.

The **Beurs van Berlage** *(see p79)* was originally the city's stock and commodities exchange and is now used as a concert venue. Many international orchestras and chamber choirs perform here. The **RAI** *(see p151)* is principally a convention centre, but is often the setting for classical music and opera events. The **Tropentheater** *(see pp152–3)* often features traditional music from all over the world. Modern classical music, opera and choirs can also be heard at De Melkweg *(see*

pp110–11) multimedia centre and the Paradiso *(see p251)*.

The **Bethaniënklooster**, near the Nieuwmarkt, is host to varied and interesting concerts. Leading international chamber groups and soloists perform in the intimate setting of the old refectory of this former convent, where the oak wood ceiling contributes to the extraordinary acoustics.

The **Muziekgebouw aan de IJ**, a 15-minute walk from Centraal Station, is Amsterdam's new grand location for innovative modern music concerts, festivals and multimedia events.

MUSIC IN CHURCHES

Churches in Amsterdam offer concerts throughout the year. The historic church organs in the **Oude Kerk** *(see pp68–9)*, **Nieuwe Kerk** *(see pp76–7)* and **Waalse Kerk** are particularly magnificent.

Carillon concerts are often held in the Oude Kerk and at lunch time on Tuesdays in the **Westerkerk** *(see p90)*. This church also hosts free organ concerts on Fridays at 1pm, April to October. The

17th-century **English Reformed Church** holds concerts that range from Baroque to modern. In the summer, free lunch-time concerts are given by new ensembles and young musicians. The **Thomaskerk**, built a few decades ago, holds a free lunch-time concert every other Tuesday (except in July and August). Concerts are also held in the **Waalse Kerk** and **Noorderkerk** *(see p92)*.

OPERA

Built in 1988, the **Muziektheater** houses the Stadhuis (town hall) and the Dutch National Opera. Its nickname, the Stopera, is a combination of both names *(see p63)*. It is one of Europe's most up-to-date theatres and features an internationally famous repertoire, as well as lesser-known and some experimental works. Opera can also be seen at the Stadsschouwburg *(see p111)* on Leidseplein. More experimental opera is performed at nightclubs such as the Paradiso and De Melkweg *(see p251)*. Also, check the Holland Festival listings for world premières *(see p51)*.

OPEN-AIR CONCERTS

The Prinsengracht concert *(see p51)* takes place in late August. Musicians perform on barges on the canal in front of the Pulitzer Hotel *(see p220)*. In summer, concerts also take place in the Vondelpark open-air theatre and the Amsterdamse Bos *(see p155)*.

DIRECTORY

ORCHESTRAL, CHAMBER AND CHORAL MUSIC

Bethaniënklooster
Barndesteeg 6. **Map** 8 D3.
Tel 625 0078.
www.bethanienklooster.nl

Beurs van Berlage
Damrak 243. **Map** 7 C2.
Tel 521 7575.
www.beursvanberlage.nl

Concertgebouw
Concertgebouwplein 2–6.
Map 4 D4.

Tel 0900 671 8345.
www.concertgebouw.nl

Muziekgebouw aan 't IJ
Piet Heinkade 1.
Tel 788 2000.
www.muziekgebouw.nl

RAI
Europaplein 8. **Tel** 0900 267 8373. www.rai.nl

Tropentheater
Linnaeusstraat 2.
Map 6 E3. **Tel** 568 8500.
www.tropentheater.nl

MUSIC IN CHURCHES

English Reformed Church
Begijnhof 48. **Map** 7 B4.
Tel 624 9665.

Nieuwe Kerk
Dam. **Map** 7 B2.
Tel 638 6909.

Oude Kerk
Oudezijds Achterburgwal 23.
Map 7 C2. **Tel** 625 8284.

Thomaskerk
Prinses Irenestraat 36.
Tel 622 5170.

Waalse Kerk
Oudezijds Achterburgwal 159. **Map** 7 C3.
Tel 623 2074.

Westerkerk
Prinsengracht 281.
Map 1 B4. **Tel** 624 7766.
www.westerkerk.nl

OPERA

Muziektheater
Amstel 3. **Map** 7 C5.
Tel 625 5455.
www.muziektheater.nl

Pop, Rock and Nightclubs

Amsterdam is bursting with live music. From the omnipresent street entertainers to a whole variety of music venues and nightclubs, as well as countless music cafés, it is hard to avoid the city's rock and pop and club scene. Concerts and clubs tend to be cheap and relaxed, with few venues having a strict door policy or dress code. Local bands and musicians are encouraged, and many venues receive subsidies from the local council, so tickets, with the exception of the big-name concerts, rarely cost more than €8. Some of the best bands can be enjoyed for the price of a drink. Fierce competition means that venues and clubs come and go. For the latest information and gig guides, consult the free *Pop & Jazz Uitlijst*, available from cafés and libraries as well as the AUB ticket service and Tourist Board offices *(see p245)*. Both AUB and tourist offices sell advance tickets for major concerts. The free magazine *Uitkrant* and English-language *Day by Day* also carry concert listings *(see p244)*.

POP AND ROCK

Many big names tend to by-pass Amsterdam and head for Rotterdam's Ahoy and Utrecht's Vredenburg stadiums instead. However, mainstream pop and rock concerts are held at the RAI *(see p151)*, Amsterdam Arena (home to Ajax football club) and the **Heineken Music Hall**. Middle-of-the-road artists tend to play in large theatres, such as the Theater Carré *(see p145)* and the Theater Bellevue *(see p247)*. The Marcanti Plaza and Escape nightclubs *(see p251)* host a variety of hot dance and soul acts.

For most Amsterdammers, rock and pop are synonymous with two venues – **Paradiso** and **De Melkweg**. Paradiso, housed in a converted church just off Leidseplein, is more prestigious. De Melkweg is housed in a former dairy, hence the name, the "Milky Way" *(see pp110–11)*.

Both the Paradiso and De Melkweg offer an extremely varied and entertaining programme: rock, pop, dance, rap and world music. The standards range from chart-toppers and cult heroes to local hopefuls trying their luck at one of the regular talent nights. Big-name bands which come to play in Amsterdam invariably turn up at one of these two places.

The seventh floor of a former newspaper office is home to **Canvas**, a grungy café-restaurant, where you can enjoy a mix of musical styles played by local DJs. Followers of rock'n'roll should visit the **Cruise-Inn**. The **Arena** is part of the well-known hotel *(see p223)*, where tourists and locals cram in to dance to the latest music played by live DJs. **The Waterhole**, located near Leidseplein, features live rock nightly.

Blues music alternates with rock at the loud and crowded **Maloe Melo**. Sweaty and beer-soaked, this place may not seem particularly inviting, but the atmosphere is convivial. From May to September, free concerts are held every Sunday afternoon in the Vondelpark open-air theatre *(see pp128–9)*, often featuring some of the country's top pop acts. The Drum Rhythm Festival *(see p50)*, held annually at the end of May, is a high-spirited celebration of the sheer diversity of popular music. Cutting edge musicians from around the world come to Amsterdam for a weekend extravaganza featuring drum-and-bass, asian underground, jungle, hiphop, R&B, soul, triphop, world music and more. Every Saturday afternoon, the **Media Café de Plantage** hosts a live radio programme which plays pop, jazz and world music.

JAZZ

There may well be more jazz venues in Amsterdam than anywhere else in the world. The relaxing rhythms of jazz music are perfectly suited to the mood of the brown cafés and bars *(see pp46–9)*.

The city's jazz flagship is the **Bimhuis**, a venue that takes its music seriously. Commonly known as the "Bim", it is the best venue in Amsterdam for contemporary jazz and has an international reputation. In late 2005, Bimhuis moved next to the Muziekgebouw, Piet Heinkade 1.

Café-restaurant **Casablanca**, in the Red Light District on the Zeedijk, offers live jazz three or four times a week (always on Friday, Saturday and Sunday). More traditional than the Bimhuis, the music here is played by both veterans and newcomers alike.

The many jazz cafés dotted around the city are very popular. Most of them are small brown cafés where local bands perform. Late opening and free entry boost their appeal, although drinks cost a little above average. Most cafés hold weekly jam sessions, when anyone can take the stage.

Around Leidseplein are the **Alto Jazz Café** and the **Bourbon Street**. Alto is best on Wednesday evenings when Hans Dulfer, the so-called "father" of the Amsterdam jazz scene, is in residence. His daughter Candy is a regular attraction at the **De Heeren van Aemstel**. **De Engelbewaarder** has popular jam sessions on Sunday afternoons. The Vondelpark *(see pp128–9)* is also a popular jazz venue in the summer, when free open-air concerts are held here.

The Dutch passion for jazz turns to frenzy in the summer, when there is a festival held in almost every town. In July, the North Sea Jazz Festival *(see p51)*, held in Rotterdam, attracts some of the biggest names in the world of jazz.

WORLD MUSIC AND FOLK

In the Netherlands the world-music scene has been heavily influenced by its many immigrant communities. The West Indian, Indonesian, Maghreb, West African, Surinamese and Turkish traditions are thriving, and are actively encouraged by the city's authorities. A high-brow programme of ethnic, classical and popular concerts is on offer at the Tropentheater *(see p246)*. Groups from around the world appear there on a regular basis, with a strong emphasis on Asian music.

The **Akhnaton** is a multi-cultural centre. Its main strengths are Caribbean, African and Arabic music. In addition, there are regular performances by reggae, rap, and salsa artists. These styles are also features of the dance nights.

De Melkweg, and to a lesser extent the Paradiso and Panama, also schedule world music – De Melkweg hosts a colourful Amsterdam Roots Festival *(see p51)* in June. **De Badcuyp**, in the lively Pijp neighbourhood, swings with salsa, tango, African music and dance options. The venue often holds free workshops highlighting Cuban dance and salsa traditions.

The indigenous folk music of the Netherlands is an acquired taste. It sounds like a mix of traditional German folk music, French *chanson* and old sea shanties. Large cafés around Rembrandtplein, including **Jantjes Verjaardag** and **Café Tante Roosje**, provide folk music for tourist consumption. For a more authentic experience, head for the Jordaan. In bars like **De Twee Zwaantjes** and **Café Nol** regulars sometimes burst into joyous song.

Many of Amsterdam's Irish pubs feature live music. Some of the best include **Mulligan's**, **The Blarney Stone** and the huge and extremely popular **O'Donnells**, where you can hear authentic fiddle playing almost every weekend.

CLUBS AND DISCOS

Amsterdam is well-known for its lively nightclub scene. There is little pretension here, and the mood is relaxed and carefree. Most clubs open at 11pm but don't really get going before 1am. They usually close at 4am during the week, and 5am on Friday and Saturday nights. Entrance prices are relatively low and drinks are reasonably priced. Few clubs enforce a strict dress code, but they do reserve the right to refuse admission. It is an established custom to tip the doormen on the way out.

Amsterdam was one of the very first cities to embrace house music during the late 1980s. It still dominates most clubs, but there is now more variety on offer. DJs and music vary from one night to the next, so check listings for details.

Club Rose is presented as the successor of the exclusive Roxy which, before it burned down, was where the beautiful people of Amsterdam gathered to rub shoulders with whichever stars were in town. More has a members-only policy, though it often only applies during busy times.

Even harder to get into is **Jimmy Woo**, famous for its tough door policy. Inside it's Hong-Kong hip, with plenty of black leather and a great sound system. The **Westergasfabriek**, to the north of the Jordaan, is a huge former gasworks. Its buildings now house a collection of music and dance spaces.

Amsterdam's students have established their own club, called **Dansen Bij Jansen**. The two sweaty dance floors in this rambling club are always packed at weekends. You will need a student card to get in, but provided you look the part there should not be a problem.

The leading non-house club in town is **The Sugar Factory**, with its varied and enjoyable menu of soul, funk and jazz-dance. The **Odeon** has been recently renovated. Here, you can party your way up from the brasserie in the basement to the dance palace on the first floor.

The city's biggest dance hall is **Escape Lounge**, attracting a predominantly young crowd who usually come from out of town each weekend. The discos around Leidseplein are basically just extended bars with only small dance floors, catering for tourists and attracting a much wider age range of people. On the whole, mainstream and chart music tend to be played. **Bitterzoet** attracts a more alternative crowd and often stages live music from a wider variety of music genres.

GAY AND LESBIAN CLUBS

Clubbing is at the heart of Amsterdam's gay scene. The techno sounds and floor shows at many venues attract a trendy clientele. Crowds are often mixed and most gay clubs will rarely turn away women or straight men.

Exit, in Reguliersdwarsstraat, is a slick bar with three levels and a balcony for viewing the dance scene below. Practically next door, **ARC** is a combination of bar and grand café. Drop in for a drink during the day or join the dance crowd later. Up the road, café **Reality**, also in the Reguliersdwarsstraat, attracts a Surinamese crowd, and offers a mix of disco and salsa.

Prik, near the Dam, is a straight-friendly gay bar, and gets pretty busy almost every night. **De Trut** is housed in the basement of a famous former squat and packs in a mixed crowd on Sunday nights. The decor is seedy, but the dance floor is big and the drinks are cheap.

If you're interested in a mixed lesbian/gay disco head to **Club Roque**, with music from the Top 40. Details of other events are available from the **Gay and Lesbian Switchboard** and the Pink Point kiosk. **Gayforcing** organizes gay and lesbian bridge afternoons. The decor is imaginative and the atmosphere friendly. **Saarein II** is frequented by lesbians and gays and offers a friendly, relaxed atmosphere.

DIRECTORY

POP AND ROCK

Arena
's-Gravesandestraat 51.
Map 6 D4.
Tel 850 2400.
www.hotelarena.nl

Canvas
Wibautstraat 150
(7th floor).
Map 5 C5.
Tel 716 3817.
http://canvas.audive.nl

Cruise-Inn
Zuiderzeeweg 29
(Amsterdam-Noord).
Tel 692 7188.
www.cruise-inn.com

Heineken Music Hall
Arena Boulevard 590.
Tel 0900 687 424255.
www.heineken-music-hall.nl

Maloe Melo
Lijnbaansgracht 163.
Map 4 D1.
Tel 420 4592.
www.maloemelo.nl

De Melkweg
Lijnbaansgracht 234a.
Map 4 E2.
Tel 531 8181.
www.melkweg.nl

Paradiso
Weteringschans 6–8.
Map 4 E2.
Tel 626 4521.
www.paradiso.nl

The Waterhole
Korte Leidsedwarsstraaat
49. **Map** 4 E2.
Tel 620 8904.
www.waterhole.nl

Winston International
Warmoesstraat 123–9.
Map 7 C2.
Tel 623 1380.
www.winston.nl

JAZZ

Alto Jazz Café
Korte Leidsedwarsstraat
115.
Map 4 E2.
Tel 626 3249.
www.jazz-cafe-alto.nl

Bimhuis
Piet Heinkade 3.
Tel 788 2188.
www.bimhuis.nl

Bourbon Street
Leidsekruisstraat 6–8.
Map 4 E2.
Tel 623 3440.
www.bourbonstreet.nl

Brix
Wolvenstraat 16.
Map 7 A3.
Tel 639 0351.
www.cafebrix.nl

Casablanca
Zeedijk 26E.
Map 8 D2.
Tel 06 122 0519.
www.casablanca-amsterdam.nl

De Engelbewaarder
Kloveniersburgwal 59.
Map 8 D3.
Tel 625 3772.

De Heeren van Aemstel
Thorbeckeplein 5.
Map 7 C5.
Tel 620 2173.
www.deheeren
vanaemstel.nl

Media Café de Plantage
Plantage Kerklaan 36.
Map 5 C2.
Tel 638 3646.
www.mediacafe
plantage.nl

WORLD MUSIC AND FOLK

Akhnaton
Nieuwezijds Kolk 25.
Map 7 C1.
Tel 624 3396.
www.akhnaton.nl

De Badcuyp
Sweelinckstraat 10.
Map 5 A5.
Tel 675 9669.
www.badcuyp.nl

The Blarney Stone
Nieuwendijk 29.
Map 7 C1.
Tel 623 3830.

Café Nol
Westerstraat 109.
Map 1 B3.
Tel 624 5380.

Café Tante Roosje
Rembrandtplein 5.
Map 7 C5.
Tel 820 8257.
www.tanteroosje.nl

Jantjes Verjaardag
Reguliersdwarsstraat 108–
114. **Map** 6 F4.
Tel 627 2710.
www.jantjesverjaardag.nl

Mulligan's
Amstel 100.
Map 7 C5.
Tel 622 1330.
www.mulligans.nl

O' Donnell's
Ferdinand Bolstraat 5.
Map 4 F5.
Tel 676 7786.
www.odonnellsirish
pub.com

De Twee Zwaantjes
Prinsengracht 114.
Map 1 C3.
Tel 625 2729.
www.detwee
zwaantjes.nl

CLUBS AND DISCOS

Bitterzoet
Spuistraat 2.
Map 7 C1.
Tel 521 3001.
www.bitterzoet.com

Club Home
Wagenstraat 3–7.
Map 8 D5.
Tel 620 1375.
www.clubhome.nl

Club Rose
Rozengracht 133.
Map 1 A5.
Tel 624 2330.

Dansen Bij Jansen
Handboogstraat 11.
Map 7 B4.
Tel 620 1779.
www.dansenbijjansen.nl

Escape
Rembrandtplein 11–15.
Map 7 C5.
Tel 622 1111.
www.escape.nl

Jimmy Woo
Korte Leidsedwarsstraat 18.
Map 4 E2. *Tel 626 3150.*
www.www.jimmy
woo.com

Odeon
Singel 460.
Map 7 C5.
Tel 521 8555.
www.odeontheater.nl

Sugar Factory
Lijnbaansgracht 238.
Map 4 E2.
Tel 627 0008.
www.sugarfactory.nl

TWSTD
Weteringschans 157.
Map 4 F3.
www.twstd.nl

GAY AND LESBIAN CLUBS

ARC
Reguliersdwarsstraat 44.
Map 7 B5.
Tel 689 7070.
www.bararc.eu

Club Roque
Amstel 178.
Map 7 C5.
www.clubroque.nl

Exit
Reguliersdwarsstraat 42.
Map 7 B5.
Tel 625 8788.
www.clubexit.eu

Gayforcing
Gay & lesbian bridge club.
Tel 625 7809.
www.gayforcing.nl

Gay and Lesbian Switchboard
Tel 623 6565.
www.switchboard.nl

Prik
Spuistraat 109.
Map 7 B2.
Tel 320 0002.
www.prikamsterdam.nl

Reality
Reguliersdwarsstraat 129.
Map 7 C5.
Tel 639 3012.

Saarein II
Elandsstraat 119.
Map 1 B5.
Tel 623 4901.

De Trut
Bilderdijkstraat 165.
Map 3 C1.
www.trutfonds.nl

CHILDREN'S AMSTERDAM

As a lively, cultural city, Amsterdam can be a fascinating place to visit with children. Its network of canals is fun to explore and many of the squares are alive with street musicians and performers. The city's many parks offer a wide range of outdoor activities and the streets are lined with tempting shops, restaurants, cafés and food stalls. Even in summer, there is no guarantee of good weather, but you can always find something to do on wet days. Some theatres and museums are geared for children and there is nearly always an English-language film showing that is suitable for children.

PRACTICAL ADVICE

If you are visiting Amsterdam with a very young child, a baby sling or pouch is essential. While the city centre is small enough to be covered on foot, manoeuvring a heavy pushchair around the cobbled streets can be tough going. Negotiating one of the city's notoriously steep flights of stairs or getting on a crowded tram or canal boat with a pushchair is virtually impossible, and they are actually banned in some of the museums.

For sightseeing, it is worth taking a boat trip. Details of the options available are given on pages 276–7. Most of the operators offer discounts to children under 12 and allow toddlers to travel free. Trams are another entertaining and efficient way to get around (see p272), although they tend to be crowded at peak periods. Like all other forms of public transport in the city, children under four go for free and under-12s travel at half-price.

Children are welcome at the majority of hotels in Amsterdam (see p212). Some of the bigger ones even provide babysitting facilities. If your hotel does not offer this,

Babysit Centrale Kriterion provides reliable, cheap child care. The service is 24-hour, but bookings must be made daily from 4:30–8pm.

BABYSITTING SERVICE

Babysit Centrale Kriterion
Roetersstraat 170.
Tel 624 5848.
www.kriterionoppas.org

THEATRES AND MUSEUMS

Many theatres, such as the **Circus Elleboog** and **De Krakeling**, hold children's shows on Wednesdays or Sundays and the Vondelpark (see p128) stages weekly open-air shows in summer.

Seasonal attractions include the Christmas circus at the Koninklijk Theater Carré (see p145). The Amsterdam Tourist Board's monthly publication, *Uitkrant*, contains a complete listing, which is easy to understand, despite being written in Dutch (see p265).

Rangda witch from Bali at the Kindermuseum

A number of Amsterdam's museums have sections which are geared for children. Nemo (see p150) is one of the best for older children, with its wide range of hands-on exhibits and buttons to press. Adventurous 6- to 12-year-olds will like the exhibitions at Tropenmuseum Junior (see pp152–3), which brings to life the cultures and traditions of the developing world. Would-be pirates love climbing aboard the *Amsterdam*, a full size replica of an 18th-century East Indiaman moored outside the Nederlands Scheepvaart Museum (see pp146–7).

The waxworks at Madame Tussauds Scenerama (see p74) are also worth a visit, although small children may be upset by a few of the more gruesome exhibits. The **Ajax Museum** and World of Ajax Tour are popular with football fans. Most of Amsterdam's museums offer substantial discounts to children, and toddlers under four normally get in free.

CHILDREN'S THEATRES AND MUSEUMS

Ajax Museum
Arena Boulevard 1.
Tel 311 1336.
www.amsterdamarena.nl

Circus Elleboog
Passeerdersgracht 32. **Map** 4 E1.
Tel 626 9370. **www**.elleboog.nl

De Krakeling
Nieuwe Passeerdersstraat 1. **Map** 4 D1. **Tel** 624 5123. **www**.krakeling.nl

Crocodiles basking in the Reptile House of Artis zoo (see pp142–3)

The full-size replica of the *Amsterdam*, outside the Scheepvaart Museum

ZOOS AND CITY FARMS

Artis zoo *(see pp142–3)* incorporates both covered and open-air animal pens, along with a Planetarium and the Geologisch Museum. Cheaper, but less extensive, animal-viewing options in and around the city include the animal enclosure in the Amsterdamse Bos *(see p155)*, donkeys and llamas in the Vondelpark *(see p128)* and free-roaming Highland cattle in the Amstelpark *(see p154)*.

SPORTS AND RECREATION

Amsterdam's parks provide a whole range of activities for children. The Vondelpark *(see p128)* has well-maintained playgrounds, free puppet shows and face-painting sessions at the Milk Bar in summer. The Amstelpark *(see p154)* and Amsterdamse Bos *(see p155)* also have a range of activities. The Electrische Museumtramlijn *(see p155)* runs regular round trips to and from the Amsterdamse Bos in vintage trams. You can also camp in designated sites in this park *(see p213)*. On a rainy day, head to **TunFun**, an indoor recreation centre for children aged up to 12.

There are a number of indoor swimming pools around Amsterdam. The best is **Miranda Bad**, a tropical paradise with water chutes, a beach and a wave machine. Indoor pools tend to close in the summer and are replaced by open-air pools, like the municipal one in Twiske, a rural park north of the IJ. The seaside, which is only a short train ride away, has miles of clean, sandy coastline.

Perhaps the most fun can be had simply exploring Amsterdam's network of canals by hiring canal bikes *(see p277)*. When the canals are frozen during a hard winter, your children will enjoy the thrill of skating around the city.

RECREATION CENTRES

Miranda Bad
De Mirandalaan 9. **Tel** 546 4444.
www.mirandabad.nl

TunFun
Mr Visserplein 7. **Map** 8 E4.
Tel 689 4300.
www.tunfun.nl

EATING OUT

Children may not be welcome in some of the more expensive restaurants, but most places are tolerant, and many cafés and cheaper places have a children's menu such as chicken, chips and *appelmoes* (apple purée). At the **Kinderkookkafé** the food is cooked and served by children. Advance dinner reservations (at least a month) are essential, both for eating and for kids who want to cook.

Amsterdam also has a good selection of pancake houses *(see p236)*. Other treats include *poffertjes*, which are tiny pancakes loaded with butter and icing sugar.

CHILDREN'S CAFÉS

Kinderkookkafé
Kattenlaantje, Vondelpark 6 (path at Overtoom 333). **Map** 3 B3.
Tel 625 3257. ☐ 10am–5pm daily.
www.kinderkookkafe.nl

SHOPPING

Alongside an assortment of large toyshops, there are also a few small shops that sell traditional wooden and handcrafted toys. Look out for the exquisite dolls'-house furniture at **De Kleine Eland**.

For something out of the ordinary in the way of children's clothes, go to **'t Schooltje**.

SHOPS FOR CHILDREN

De Kleine Eland
Elandsgracht 58. **Map** 1 B5.
Tel 620 9001.

't Schooltje
Overtoom 87. **Map** 4 D2.
Tel 683 0444.

Children resting weary legs after a hard day's play

SURVIVAL GUIDE

PRACTICAL INFORMATION

Amsterdam is a cosmopolitan city, and visitors should find its citizens helpful, friendly and often multilingual. The official networks for helping tourists are efficient and straightforward. Telephones, parking meters and cash dispensers may seem familiar to European visitors, but other tourists will need to follow instructions closely. One

The logo of the Amsterdam Tourist Board

of the particular pleasures of visiting the city is to enjoy the relatively car-free environment, which leaves more room for alternative forms of travel. Trams, water transport, bicycles and pedestrians are all given a much higher priority in the centre than motor vehicles. Indeed, the ideal way to explore the city is on foot *(see p270)* or by bicycle *(see pp274–5)*.

I amsterdam sign in the Museumplein

WHEN TO GO

High season for tourists runs from April to September, with another peak around New Year. During school summer holidays (June to August), it can be hot and humid; hotels and travel prices are also more expensive, and many tourist sights are overcrowded. For the annual national holiday, Queen's Day (April 30), it is often difficult to find hotel rooms unless you book well in advance. In winter there can be heavy snow or ice. Early spring and late autumn are the quietest times, but the weather can be rather cool.

VISAS AND PASSPORTS

For a stay lasting up to three months for the purpose of tourism, EU, US, Canadian, Australian and New Zealand nationals need only a valid passport. Other nationalities should check with the Netherlands embassy in their home country. Under the Schengen visa open-borders agreement, a visitor from a Schengen country can travel

freely throughout the Schengen zone with only a valid form of ID and no passport. Immigration procedures have tightened and you may have to prove that you have sufficient funds for your stay and a return ticket. In the Netherlands, everyone over the age of 14 is required to carry ID, and this includes tourists. You can be fined for not having the correct ID. As a visitor, you will be asked to show a stamped passport.

CUSTOMS INFORMATION

EU nationals over the age of 17 are entitled to import unlimited goods for personal use, except for tobacco and alcohol on which duty has already been paid. The limits are: 800 cigarettes, 400 cigars, 1 kg of tobacco, 10 litres of spirits, 20 litres of fortified wine, 90 litres of wine and 110 litres of beer. Duty-free tobacco and alcohol are no longer available to EU citizens. However, some other duty-free goods are available at Schiphol airport after passport control. Citizens of non-EU countries must abide

by the following restrictions: 200 cigarettes, 50 cigars or 250g of tobacco; 1 litre of spirits, 2 litres of non-sparkling wine or 2 litres of fortified wine; other goods or gifts up to the value of €430 per adult.

Bulbs bought in Amsterdam must have a certificate of inspection from the Plant Protection Service if being taken to the USA or Canada.

Non-EU members can reclaim VAT on returning home, or at the Departure Lounge at the airport. Phone the **Customs Information** line, or see www.vatfree.nl.

If you are leaving the EU with more than €10,000, this must be declared.

TOURIST INFORMATION

Amsterdam prides itself on its accessibility to visitors, and has a comprehensive network of tourist information centres. In 2009, I amsterdam was launched, which brought together the Amsterdam

The neo-Gothic façade of the Rijksmuseum *(see pp130–33)*

◁ Illuminated bridge with pretty gabled houses on Herengracht

Tourism and Convention Board (ATCB), the Tourist Board Offices VVV and other tourist services and businesses under one cooperative organization. I amsterdam's main office is in **Centraal Station** on Platform 2B. The state-run Tourist Board, the VVV, which is pronounced, "fay-fay-fay", has three branches and offers multilingual information on sights, entertainment, events, transport and tours. They will also book hotels, plays, shows, excursions and concerts (for a small fee). Tourist Board leaflets and maps are also available from museums. The **AUB Uitboro** can provide information and tickets to cultural events.

For information before you travel, the **NBTC** (Netherlands Board of Tourism and Conventions) produces their own brochures and maps.

Be wary of using agencies unrelated to the Tourist Board or I amsterdam: the accommodation they offer can often be unnecessarily expensive or of poor quality.

Taking a break outside Café 't Smalle

I amsterdam Card

LANGUAGE AND SMOKING ETIQUETTE

The Dutch have been linguists for centuries, and most students learn English, some German and French. However, it's appreciated if you can handle a few niceties, such as saying *Dag* (Good day) before asking a Dutch person whether they speak English. The Dutch are quite liberal in many ways, but they retain a few conventions. Expect to shake hands often, and if you are out with a crowd it's polite to introduce yourself. When eating out in a group, the Dutch tend to pay for their share of the bill, unless it has been made clear that you are being treated.

The Netherlands has a smoking ban in all public places, including bars, cafés, restaurants and hotels for smoking tobacco. Some clubs and cafés do turn a blind eye, especially in coffeeshops, where you may smoke cannabis, but not with tobacco. You are not allowed to smoke in any area serviced by employees. If drinking alcohol, it is best to do so on the premises of a café or bar.

ADMISSION PRICES

Many of the art museums in Amsterdam are free to those under the age of 18. They do not offer discounts for international students or seniors *(see p258)*. Nemo, a favourite family-orientated museum, charges the same price for all visitors above the age of three.

The three main discount cards are the I amsterdam Card, the Museum Card (*Museumkaart*) and the CJP *(see p258)*.

The I amsterdam Card offers free travel on all public transport and canal trips, free access to most museums, a 50 per cent discount on the Park and Ride lots and 40 free and 50 discounted offers. The card is available from all tourist offices and online, and is valid for 24 (€38), 48 (€48) or 72 (€58) hours.

The Museum Card costs €35 for adults and €17.50 for under 25s (plus a €4.95 admin fee) and provides admission to more than 400 museums throughout the Netherlands. This includes 29 museums in Amsterdam, excluding special exhibitions. The card is valid for a year, and you will recoup the cost after three visits. The card can be bought from all tourist offices, online and at museums.

OPENING HOURS

Opening times vary enormously, but each shop has its hours of business posted on the door. In the city centre, shops are open 9am–6pm Monday to Wednesday and Friday; 9am–9pm Thursday, until 5pm Saturday and noon–5pm Sunday. Most of the national museums are closed on Monday, and open from 10am to 5pm, Tuesday to Saturday and 1–5pm on Sunday. Many museums also open on Friday evenings to 10pm and adopt Sunday hours on national holidays. Bank and post office hours tend to be weekdays only, between 9am and 4 or 5pm, although some big-city banks are open Saturday morning. The main post office on the Singel is also open Saturday 10am–1:30pm.

PUBLIC CONVENIENCES

For such a practical nation, Amsterdam is short on public conveniences, and visitors more often use department stores, hotels, museums and cafés. In clubs, cafés and concert venues with attendants you will pay a minimum of 50c, with large stores charging 30c upwards and a similar fee for using baby-changing rooms.

TAXES AND TIPPING

Value-Added (or Sales) Tax is 19 per cent in the Netherlands and will usually be included in the price quoted. The exceptions to this are electronic and computer goods. Non-EU residents can shop tax free in two ways: either shop at places affiliated to the **Global Blue** scheme, or shop anywhere and ask for a tax receipt, then claim the tax back *(see p256)*.

Service is always included in bars and restaurants. It is usual though to tip taxis and in restaurants, mostly between 5–10% to round up the bill.

The Pink Point next to the Homomonument

TRAVELLERS WITH SPECIAL NEEDS

Information and assistance are available for disabled travellers to Amsterdam. One of the most useful websites is run by the **Amsterdam Foundation for People with a Disability** *(Stichting Gehandicapten Overleg Amsterdam)*. The site reviews the accessibility of restaurants, hotels, cafés, public buildings and public toilets.

At Schiphol airport, help is available through **IHD** (International Help to the Disabled). The service is free but must be booked at the same time as your flight. The main train stations have also improved the ease of travel for passengers with special needs. Tactile guidance lines assist visually impaired travellers, mobile ramps make it easier for wheelchair-users to get on and off trains and those with a functional disability can arrange free travel for a travelling companion. Many trains have wheelchair-access doors, and most new double-decker trains have wheelchair-accessible toilets.

All main pedestrian crossings are equipped with sound for the blind. Most foreign Disabled Parking Disks from recognized organizations are valid in the city, but if the parking sign has a licence number on it, it is reserved.

SENIOR TRAVELLERS

Senior travellers will enjoy the relatively easy pace of Amsterdam. Those wishing to avoid loud, drunken crowds in the evenings should choose a hotel either in the canal district or the Museum Quarter, and avoid areas with high concentrations of bars and clubs (such as the Leidseplein or Rembrandtsplein). New Year's Eve can be a problem for anyone who cannot move quickly or easily, as locals tend to go crazy with fireworks on the streets, especially around the Nieuwmarket area.

There are discounts on public transport (trams, buses, metro) for seniors. To be eligible for travel discounts, take your passport to a GVB office *(see p273)* when purchasing your ticket. There are no senior discounts on offer for either the Museum Card or the I amsterdam Card *(see p275)*.

GAY AND LESBIAN TRAVELLERS

Few other cities are better oriented towards gay and lesbian tourism than Amsterdam. Most listings magazines include a special section for gay and/or lesbian events *(see p265)*, and the Pink Point of Presence, next to the unique Homomonument at the Westerkerk, is a great place to pick up tourist information. Around the corner, **COC** (the national gay and lesbian organization) provides general information on gay and lesbian life in the city.

GAYtic is another tourist information service specifically oriented to gay and lesbian visitors. They offer an information kit that can be ordered in advance of your journey and collected when you arrive. The kit contains maps, magazines, discounts and information on parties and events. They also sell tickets to special events, and the I amsterdam Card.

TRAVELLING ON A BUDGET

Amsterdam is not a drastically expensive city to visit, but keep in mind that eating out and entertainment can be more costly than in other European countries.

The I amsterdam website and some magazines list free events and festivals in the city. In summer you can enjoy a picnic in the Vondelpark, outside the Filmmuseum, watching an old classic film projected on the side of the building.

The I amsterdam Card and the Museum Card do not offer discounts for kids, and there are no discounts for children on public transport, except for children under four, who travel free. For students, the ISIC (International Student Card) offers discounts in youth hostels, theatres, restaurants, some museums, shops and a few travel agencies, but not on local transport. The European Youth Card (CJP) is a good alternative for travellers under the age of 30 who are not students. It offers similar discounts in 38 countries in Europe.

RESPONSIBLE TRAVEL

The Dutch take environmental issues very seriously and are constantly striving to improve sustainability on a variety of levels. Amsterdam has a growing awareness of eco-tourism, with a few companies offering eco-tours, like Wetlands Safari, which provides canoe tours through the reed lands north of Amsterdam *(see p271)*.

There is a steadily increasing number of choices for the environmentally aware visitor. The Conscious Hotel group has two eco-friendly hotels in the city centre *(see p221)*. There is an excellent organic

De Kas restaurant

farmers' market on Saturdays at the Noordermarket in the Jordaan, where a dazzling array of local organic produce, bakery goods, meat, fish, cheese and other dairy products are beautifully displayed. This market is a favourite with locals and often crowded. Be sure to explore the array of farmers' cheeses to discover what Dutch cheese should taste like.

Another organic market is held on the Haarlemmerplein on Wednesday afternoons, although it is very small.

Amsterdam's most famous organic restaurant, **De Kas**, is housed in a beautiful old greenhouse saved from demolition by its chef, Gert Jan Hageman. Here, they serve the fruits of their own labours, using herbs and vegetables from the greenhouse, combined with locally sourced organic meat and fish. **Brouwerij 't IJ**, housed in an old windmill, is a small microbrewery producing organic beer. For an unusual local souvenir, visit the shop **La Savonnerie**, with soaps made from organic products.

TIME

The Netherlands is on Central European Time, which means Amsterdam is 1 hour ahead of Greenwich Mean Time. From late March to late October clocks are set forward 1 hour. Australia is 10 hours ahead in winter (8 in summer); while New York is 6 hours behind Central European Time.

ELECTRICITY

The voltage in the Netherlands is 220, 50-cycle AC, and compatible with British equipment, but since the Dutch use two-pin continental plugs you will need an adaptor.

American visitors need to convert their equipment or buy a transformer. Dutch wall sockets require a larger plug than those used in the USA.

DIRECTORY

EMBASSIES AND CONSULATES

Ireland
Scheveningseweg 112,
2584 AE Den Haag.
Tel (070) 363 0993.
www.irishembassy.nl

UK Consulate
Koningslaan 44.
Map 3 B4.
General enquiries:
Tel 676 4343.
www.britain.nl

UK Embassy Den Haag
Tel (070) 427 0427.
www.britain.nl

US Consulate
Museumplein 19.
Map 4 E3.
Tel 5755309.
http://amsterdam.
usconsulate.gov

US Embassy Den Haag
Tel (070) 310 2209.
http://netherlands.
usembassy.gov

CUSTOMS INFORMATION

Tel 0800 0143
(free-phone).
www.douane.nl
www.vatfree.nl (online
refund service)
www.global-blue.com

TOURIST INFORMATION

AUB Uitburo
Leisdeplein 26. **Map** 4 E2.
Tel 020-795 9950.
www.amsterdams
uitburo.nl

Tourist Board (VVV) Offices
Leidseplein 26. **Map** 4 E2.
Schiphol Airport Arrivals
Hall 2. *Tel 0900 400
4040.* www.holland.com

Centraal Station
Platform 2 and in front of
station, Stationsplein 10.
Map 8 D1.
Tel 0900 400 4040.

Netherlands Board of Tourism and Conventions (NBTC)
PO Box 458,
Leidschendam, 2260 MG.
Tel 070 3705 705.
www.nbtc.nl
www.holland.com

UK
PO Box 30783,
London WC2B 6DH.
Tel 020 7539 7950.
Fax 020 7539 7953.

USA
215 Park Ave South, suite
2005, New York, NY
10003.
Tel (1) 212-370 7360.

TRAVELLERS WITH SPECIAL NEEDS

Amsterdam Foundation for People with a Disability
www.toegankelijk
amsterdam.nl

IHD Schiphol Service
Departure Passage 114.
Tel 020 316 1417.
*Fax 020 316 1418 (for
the deaf or hearing
impaired).*

NS Bureau Assistentiever lening Gehandicapten (NS Disabled Assistance Office)
Tel 030 235 7822.
*Fax 030 2353935 (for the
deaf or hearing impaired).*
www.ns.nl

Amsterdam Thuiszorg
Tel 020 886 0000.
www.amsterdam
thuiszorg.nl

Staatsbosbeheer
Tel 030 692 6111.
www.staatsbosbeheer.nl
(under "Organisation";
English section)

De Zeeland
Tel 0900 235 3337.
www.zeilenalacarte.nl

Beach Wheelchairs at Zandvoort
Tel 023 571 6119.

GAY AND LESBIAN TRAVELLERS

COC
Rozenstraat 4.
Map 1 B4.
Tel 020 6263087.
www.cocamsterdam.nl

GAYtic
Spuistraat 44.
Map 7 B1.
Tel 020 330 1461.
www.gaytic.nl

RESPONSIBLE TRAVEL

De Kas
Kamerlingh Onneslaan 3.
Tel 0202 462 4562.
www.restaurantdekas.nl

Brouwerij 't IJ
Funenkade 7.
Map 6 F2.
Tel 020 622 8325.
www.brouwerijhetij.nl

La Savonnerie
Prinsengracht 294.
Tel 020 428 1139.
www.savonnerie.nl

Personal Security and Health

Amsterdam is one of the safest cities in Europe – there are few "no go" areas, and violent crime is rare. However, petty theft is rife, and pickpockets do haunt tourist areas and public transport. Sadly, there has also been a change in attitude towards "tolerance", most noticeably in that there have been attacks on gay clubs. For the most part, this should not impact tourists, but for those who do find themselves in trouble, the city has efficient emergency services and facilities, including a Tourist Assistance service.

Policeman on wheels

Members of the armed Dutch police force

POLICE

If you have been the victim of a serious crime, call **112**. If the crime is petty theft or of a less serious nature, use the general number listed in the Directory box, or simply go to the nearest police station. Almost all police officers will speak some English. If your property has been stolen, or you have been in an incident that has required medical treatment, you will need to file a police report for insurance purposes. It is important to have all information regarding the incident with you when you go to the police station. If you require any help ask the police to contact the **ATAS**, Amsterdam Tourist Assistance Service, on your behalf.

Fire engine

Police cars

Ambulance

WHAT TO BE AWARE OF

Theft is the main problem for visitors to Amsterdam, (*see Lost and Stolen Property*), but you should also be aware that bar and club areas like Leidseplein and Rembrandtsplein, the Red Light District and city parks can be dangerous for lone tourists in the very early morning hours. In general, wandering at night in most Amsterdam neighbourhoods is safe, and women are fine to walk about on their own.

The Red Light District was once a very busy, bustling area that had a real sense of community and, due to a constant stream of people, felt quite safe. Now, after several measures to "clean up" the area, the number of visitors has dropped, and some streets can be very seedy. Keep in mind that you are not allowed to photograph prostitutes in the Red Light District without their permission, and you may be asked to pay a fee to do so.

You are required to have your ID on you at all times, and can be fined if found without it. It is illegal to carry a weapon; consume alcohol in most public places; buy, sell or use hard drugs; buy cannabis outside of coffee-shops; urinate on the street and cycle in pedestrian areas. Uniformed police may perform on-the-spot

body searches, or ask for ID.

Attracted by the canals, mosquitoes can be an irritant during summer. Repellent sprays, antihistamine creams, mosquito nets and plug-in devices are available from large pharmacies.

IN AN EMERGENCY

For serious emergencies, dial 112; this will put you through to a general number for the police, ambulance and the fire brigade. An operator will answer (most speak English) and you will be asked which service you need, and where you are calling from. If the operator decides it is not an emergency that requires immediate intervention, they may direct you to call the **Central Medical Service**, or report to a hospital with a first aid department, or in the case of a crime, to report to the nearest police station. If you feel you need extra support, call the ATAS or **GAYtic**, (*see pp255–9*) who provide a similar service but for gay and lesbian travellers.

LOST AND STOLEN PROPERTY

While Amsterdam is safer than most American and European cities, theft is still some cause for concern. Pickpockets work crowded tourist areas, trams and the train between the city centre and Schiphol airport, especially in summer. Use your common sense and, as in any big city, be alert to your surroundings.

Bicycle and car theft, particularly of foreign vehicles, is also a problem. You must report lost or stolen property in order to claim on your insurance. Local police stations hold recovered items for a day or so before sending them to the **Central Lost Property Office**. For anything lost on the train, try **Centraal Station**. If found, it can be sent to your hotel or home address.

Pharmacy sign

Bus and tram drivers check their vehicles after every journey, and any items found are handed in at the depot. From there they are sent to the Central Lost Property Office, who can tell you if your belongings have been found 48 hours after the day you lost them. If you happen to lose your passport, inform your embassy *(see p259)*. Lost credit or debit cards should be reported to the card issuer *(see p262)*.

HOSPITALS AND PHARMACIES

Minor problems can be dealt with by a chemist *(drogist)*. For medicine on prescription, go to a pharmacy *(apotheek)*. These are open from 8:30am to 5:30pm Monday to Friday. Details of pharmacies open

outside normal hours are posted in all pharmacy windows and in the afternoon newspaper *Het Parool*. The Central Medical Service *(Centrale Doktersdienst)* can also direct you to the nearest pharmacy, and can refer you to a duty GP or supply the name of a dentist. Minor accidents can be treated in hospital outpatient clinics, open 24 hours a day; the VVV or I amsterdam *(see p256)* can advise on these. In an emergency, go to a hospital with a casualty unit, or call an ambulance (112).

TRAVEL AND HEALTH INSURANCE

Travel insurance is available through most travel agents and insurance companies, with a wide variety of policy options, and is highly recommended in case of loss, theft or medical emergencies that require repatriation help.

All EU members can receive medical and dental treatment in the Netherlands at a reduced charge. Before travelling, British visitors should obtain the European Health

Insurance Card (EHIC) – the form is available from all post offices – and seek a refund for any non-private treatment on their return home. You will never be turned away by a doctor even if you do not have an EHIC with you, however, you may have to pay more for treatment.

DRUGS

Soft drugs, such as hashish and cannabis, are part of a very Dutch solution: they are decriminalized, but not legal. This allows the government control over the coffeeshops (where you can buy cannabis), while it earns money through the businesses. You are allowed to possess up to 5 grams of soft drugs at any one time. Smoking on the streets is discouraged, but with the new smoking ban in place, some coffeeshops now have outside areas to smoke *(see p257)*. Hard drugs are a very different matter, and anyone caught with them by the police will certainly be prosecuted. Paddos, or magic mushrooms, were banned in 2009. Never try to take drugs out of Amsterdam or the Netherlands: penalties are stiff.

DIRECTORY

POLICE

Ambulance, Fire and Police
Tel 112 (emergency only).

Amsterdam Tourist Assistance Service (ATAS)
Nieuwezijds Voorburgwal 104-108.
Tel 020 6253246.
www.stichtingatas.nl

Police General Number
Tel 0900 8844.

Main Police Stations
Lijnbaansgracht 219.
Map 4 E2.
Beursstraat 33. **Map** 7 C2.
Nieuwezijds Voorburgwal.
104. **Map** 7 A4.

IN AN EMERGENCY

Central Medical Service (Centrale Doktersdienst)
Tel 08800 30600.

GAYtic
Spuistraat 44.
Tel 020 330 1461.

HOSPITALS

Academisch Medisch Centrum (AMC)
Miebergdreef 9.
Tel 020 566 9111.

Onze Lieve Vrouwe Gasthuis (casualty unit)
1e Oosterparkstraat 279.
Map 6 D4.
Tel 020 599 9111.

Sint Lucas Andreas Ziekenhuis
Jan Tooropstraat 164.
Tel 020 510 89 11.

VU Medisch Centrum
De Boelelaan 1117.
Tel 444 4444.
24-hour first aid:
Tel 444 3636.

LOST PROPERTY

Central Lost Property Office
NS Lost Property Information
Stationsplein 15.
Map 8 D1.
Tel 0900 321 2100.

Centraal Station
Stationsplein.
Map 2 E3.

PHARMACIES

Dam
Damstraat 2.
Map 7 C3.
Tel 020 624 4331.

Jordaan
Westerstraat 180.
Map 1 B3.
Tel 020 624 9252.

Koek, Schaeffer & Van Tijen
Vijzelgracht 19.
Map 4 F3.
Tel 020 623 5949.

Medicijnman
Utrechtsestraat 86.
Map 5 A3.
Tel 020 624 4333.

Het Witte Kruis
Rozengracht 57.
Map 1 A5.
Tel 020 623 1051.

Banking and Currency

Amsterdammers are still partial to cash transactions, although the banking system has started encouraging more use of debit cards to pay for all transactions, including small amounts. Surprisingly, credit cards are not as universally accepted in the Netherlands as in many other countries. The larger hotels, shops and most restaurants will take the major cards, but the golden rule is to ask first if in doubt, or check the front door for logos. Amsterdam has an excellent foreign exchange network, and transactions are virtually hassle-free for visitors, particularly English-speakers. There is no limit to the amount of currency you can bring into the country.

GWK exchange counter at Schiphol airport

BANKS AND BUREAUX DE CHANGE

You can change currency in offices such as **GWK** (*grenswisselkantoren*). In general, the GWK gives the best overall rates. Their offices are found in the airport, main train stations and some tourist areas. The only bank in the Netherlands that still offers an exchange service for tourists is the **ING** bank (formerly the Postbank); American Express also offer this service. All of the above charge a commission for the service. Independent bureaux de change charge an exorbitant commission and give a poor exchange rate. However, they can be the best option if you are exchanging small amounts, as at the official GWK offices the commission rates go down as the amount exchanged goes up. If you arrive by ferry, don't change any money on the boat and visit the GWK just after disembarkation. This stays open for night arrivals. Avoid changing money in hotels, as their charges can be high.

ATM for cash withdrawal

ATMS

Most ATMs will handle cards from the main international banks and many credit cards. Your withdrawal limit may be lower than from your own bank, and there can be an extra service charge. Check on the machine itself if it accepts the same system as your card (for example, **American Express**, **MasterCard**, **Diner's Club**, Cirrus, **Visa** or Maestro). When a foreign card is inserted, most ATMs will offer you a choice of language; after requesting English, it should be simple to follow the directions. This is the easiest method to withdraw cash on a credit card. ATMs are plentiful and can be found outside post offices, banks and GWK offices, and in the main train stations. They can be identified by the small sign above them showing the name of the bank that services them.

TRAVELLER'S CHEQUES AND CREDIT CARDS

Traveller's cheques are being used less and less. No banks will exchange them for cash, and many shops and restaurants do not like to take them. While they may be useful for paying hotel bills, remember that management is not obliged to pay you the change if the cheque is larger than the bill. Pick a well-known name such as American Express, and instead exchange the cheques for cash at an American Express office.The GWK will also accept traveller's cheques.

Banks will not advance you cash against credit cards, but most ATMs accept the major cards. Some restaurants require a minimum purchase to use a credit card. Carry some cash just in case.

DIRECTORY

BANKS AND BUREAUX DE CHANGE

American Express
Postbus 7319, 1007JH.
Tel 020 204 8504.

ING
Singel 250–256.
Map 7 A2.

GWK
Tel 0900 0566 (general number).
Centraal Station. **Map** 8 D1.
Dam 23–25. **Map** 7 B3.
Damrak 1–5. **Map** 7 C1.
Leidsestraat 103. **Map** 4 E2.
Schiphol Airport Station.
Amstel Station.

LOST OR STOLEN CARDS AND CHEQUES

American Express
Tel (001) 336 393 1111
(US – collect).
Tel (+44) 1273 696 933 (UK).
Tel 0900 0566 (traveller's cheques).

Diner's Club
Tel 020 654 5511.

MasterCard
Tel 0800 0225821.

Visa
Tel 0800 022 3110.

THE EURO

The Euro (€) is the common currency of the European Union. It went into general circulation on 1 January 2002, initially for 12 participating countries. The Netherlands was one of those 12 countries.

EU members using the Euro as sole official currency are known as the Eurozone. Several EU members have opted out of joining this common currency.

Euro notes are identical throughout the Eurozone countries, each one including designs of fictional architectural structures and monuments. The coins, however, have one side identical (the value side) and one side with an image unique to each country. Both notes and coins are exchangeable in each of the participating Euro countries.

Bank Notes

Euro bank notes have seven denominations. The €5 note (grey in colour) is the smallest, followed by the €10 note (pink), €20 note (blue), €50 note (orange), €100 note (green), €200 note (yellow) and €500 note (purple).

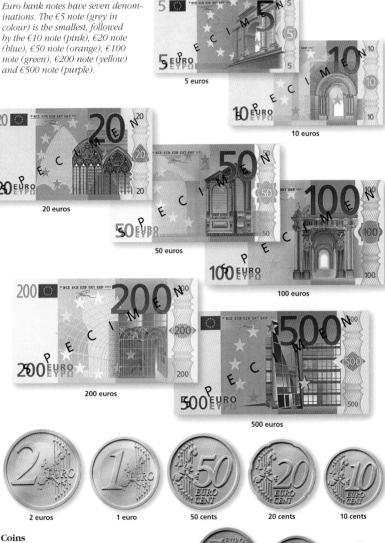

5 euros

10 euros

20 euros

50 euros

100 euros

200 euros

500 euros

2 euros

1 euro

50 cents

20 cents

10 cents

Coins

The euro has eight coin denominations: €1 and €2; 50 cents, 20 cents, 10 cents, 5 cents, 2 cents and 1 cent. The €2 and €1 coins are both silver and gold in colour. The 50-, 20- and 10-cent coins are gold. The 5-, 2- and 1-cent coins are bronze.

5 cents

2 cents

1 cent

Communications and Media

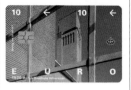

KPN telecoms logo

Amsterdam, and its citizens, are plugged in, logged on and wired up, so there are plenty of options for visitors to check their emails or surf the net when visiting the city. For more traditional communication methods, KPN Telecom and TNT Post handle telephone and postal services, respectively. Both companies are among the most forward-thinking in Europe. With the exception of children's programmes, most Dutch television stations do not dub programmes or films, and several listings magazine are bilingual or exist in English.

REACHING THE RIGHT NUMBER

- National directory inquiries, dial 1888 or visit www.detelefoongids.com
- Local operator, dial 1888. International operator, dial 0900 8418 Mon–Fri.
- To phone the USA or Canada, dial 001 followed by the number.
- To phone the UK, dial 0044 followed by the number, omitting the 0 from the area code.
- To phone Australia, dial 0061 followed by the number.
- To phone New Zealand, dial 0064 followed by the number.
- To phone the Irish Republic, dial 00353 followed by the number.

INTERNATIONAL AND LOCAL TELEPHONE CALLS

The advent of Skype and VoIP has had a huge effect on the public telephone system. More and more homes are switching over and choosing to save money by relinquishing more traditional land lines, especially for international calls. There are also Internet/telephone businesses that offer such low rates for international calls that it can be cheaper than phoning home from a hotel, or from your mobile.

The Dutch White Pages (*Telefoongids*), www.detelefoongids.nl, and the Yellow Pages (*Gouden Gids*), www.goudengids.nl, both have websites available in English. Names are listed in alphabetical order. However, if the last name begins with a de, van, van der, etc you must look under the name that follows these articles. IJ is read as a "y" and comes at the end of the alphabet, not in the "i" section. 0800 numbers are free, 0900 numbers are charged a per-minute or per-call rate.

MOBILE PHONES

There are four main GSM (Global System for Mobile Communications) frequencies in use, so if you want to ensure your phone will work while you are away you should have a quad-band phone. Tri-band phones from the EU will usually work in the Netherlands, but US mobile phones may not. Contact your service provider.

To use your mobile phone abroad, you may need to

enable the "roaming" function on your phone. It is also more expensive to make and receive calls while abroad, despite efforts to decrease roaming charges.

A cheaper option is often to purchase a local SIM card to use in your phone. You can only do this if your handset is "sim free" or unlocked. Some of the local/international networks are **Hi (KPN)**, **T-Mobile**, **Vodafone**, **Telfort**, **Orange** and **Ben**. KPN Hotspots gives you Internet access for smart phones; simply send an SMS to: HOTSPOTS, number 4222, and you can log on for 15 minutes for a small fee, which is charged to your phone.

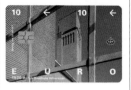

Colourful Dutch pictorial phonecard

PUBLIC TELEPHONES

Public telephones can be found on main streets out of the city centre and at train stations and post offices, but they are starting to disappear in cafés and bars. The city's payphones take phonecards, and some take credit cards, but there can be heavy charges for this form of payment. Phonecards can be bought at post offices, supermarkets, newsagents and train stations. Instructions for using the telephones are in English and Dutch. When you phone popular numbers such as airports,

you may be offered a choice of languages, or encounter an electronic voice that announces how many people are in the queue before you. Most hotels have IDD (International Direct Dialling) units, but be aware that the telephone costs are likely to be inflated.

INTERNET

Amsterdam is the first major European city to offer Wi-Fi access through a network that covers the whole city. KPN provides the Hotspots Wi-Fi system (for a fee), while free public Wi-Fi is available, on request, outdoors. There is a good range of free options to log on in some cafes, within your hotel or the library, and out in the parks.

There are many Internet cafés in Amsterdam where, for a modest fee, you can check your email account and get online. Opening hours vary, but some are open until late at night. Many cafés and some coffeeshops also offer free Wi-Fi. The **Coffee Company**, found on main streets in the centre, is one such option. Some hotels have free Wi-Fi, others have closed circuit systems where you have to pay a fee, or log on through a modem in your room.

Internet access at OBA (Amsterdam Public Library)

The main branch of the **OBA (Amsterdam Public Library)**, near Centraal Station, is Holland's largest library and offers free Internet access at all its 600 computer terminals.

POSTAL SERVICES

Amsterdam's post offices are distinguished by the TNT Post logo. In some neighbourhoods, there are small post offices *(postagentschap)* inside shops, newsagents or tobacconists. Stamps *(postzegels)* can be bought in all of the above places, and in larger supermarkets and souvenir shops. If you send mail outside the Netherlands you will have a choice of Priority or Standard Post. Letters up to 20g can be sent anywhere in Europe – not just within the EU – for a universal flat rate, while destinations further afield cost slightly more. It is worth sending important documents by registered mail.

Postboxes are scattered throughout the city. On the postbox there are two slots *(see illustration below)*. A sign on the post box indicates when the next collection will take place.

Slot for all other destinations

Slot for local destinations

Dutch TNT postbox

NEWSPAPERS AND MAGAZINES

Most foreign newspapers reach the city centre by lunchtime on publication day. The *Het Parool* is the Amsterdam paper that is read throughout the Netherlands, and the *de Volkskrant* and *NRC Handelsblad* are the most respected national newspapers.

Listings can be found in all of the above Dutch newspapers, but posters and listings in the city's bars and cafés may be a quicker, easier guide to entertainment in Amsterdam. *NL 20* and the *Uitkrant* (published by the AUB Uitburo, *see p259*) are free, easily available and have excellent listings, but both are in Dutch. The Tourist Board also produces a number of free English-language leaflets providing details of festivals and cultural highlights *(see p244)*. Amsterdam gay and lesbian magazines *Gay&Night* and *Gay News* (bilingual English/Dutch) and *Time Out Amsterdam* can be bought from most newsagents.

TELEVISION AND RADIO

The main TV channels serve standard European and US fare, but all hotels and homes have cable TV, with 30 or so channels available, including British, French, German, Belgian and Italian stations. British and American shows are subtitled on the Dutch and Belgian channels but are dubbed on the French, Italian and German channels.

English-language stations include BBC1, BBC2, BBC World, Discovery Channel, CNN and CNBC. Comedy Central and MTV both have

some Dutch programming. News is broadcast on Dutch Radio 1 (98.9MHz), pop music on Radio 3 (96.8MHz) and classical music on Radio 4 (94.3MHz). It is also possible to pick up BBC Radio 4 on 198kHzAM and the World Service on 648kHzAM.

DIRECTORY

MOBILE PHONES

Ben
www.ben.nl

Hi (KPN)
www.hi.nl

Orange
www.orange.com

Telfort
Rokin 32. **Map** 7 B3.
www.telfort.nl

T-Mobile
Rokin 64a. **Map** 7 B3.
www.t-mobile.nl

Vodafone
Rokin 32. **Map** 7 B3.
www.vodafone.nl

INTERNET

A Internet
2e van der Helststraat 17.

Amsterdam Internet City
Nieuwendijk 76.
Tel 020 6201292.

Coffee Company
Leidsestraat 60.
Tel 020 4218275.

Internet Café Freeworld
Nieuwendijk 30.
Map 7 C2.
Tel 020 620 0902.

OBA (Amsterdam Public Library)
Oosterdokskade 143.
Map 8 F2.
Tel 0900 242 5468.

POSTAL SERVICES

Main Post Office
Hoofdpostkantoor TNT Post,
Singel 250–256, 1016 AB.
Map 7 A2.
Tel 0582 333 333.

Postal Information
Tel 058 2333 333.
www.tntpost.nl

GETTING TO AMSTERDAM

Amsterdam is one of Europe's most popular destinations. As you would expect of a cosmopolitan city of this size, it is easily accessible by plane, coach, car, ferry and train. In addition, travellers from the UK are able to reach Amsterdam via the Channel Tunnel, although passengers must change train at Brussels. Each method of travel has its own benefits and disadvantages, and the choice will largely depend on whether time, money or comfort is the main priority. Whichever method of transport you choose, it is always worth making a few inquiries to find the best deal. Not only is there an ever-increasing selection of "packages" and special-interest holidays on offer, but also prices can fluctuate widely depending on the time of year you travel (new operators and ventures will emerge all the time).

Entrance to Amsterdam's Schiphol airport

AIRPORTS

Amsterdam's **Schiphol** airport, the fourth largest in Europe, is a major international transport hub and one of the world's most modern, efficient, clean and user-friendly airports. Schiphol has one terminal hub consisting of three departure halls and four arrival halls, which stream into Schiphol Plaza. In the Plaza you will find a tourist information desk, two bureau de change desks, a bank, the national rail service NS office and left-luggage facilities. All signs are posted in both Dutch and in English. Also in the Plaza are dozens of high street shops, fast food restaurants, bars, cafés, newsagents and a fully stocked grocery store. For passengers leaving Amsterdam, the facilities after passport control contain one of the largest tax-free shopping centres in Europe, a museum, a casino, a masseuse, and dozens of restaurants and bars, not to forget a wedding

service called "Say Yes and Go", www.schiphol weddings.nl. For business people and those in transit, there is an amazing range of facilities available, from phone, post and fax services, to business centres and conference rooms. Wireless LAN gives you Internet access throughout the airport.

TICKETS AND FARES

There is an immense choice of flights to Amsterdam from the UK and the Republic of Ireland, with at least eight carriers operating direct flights. These include the airlines **Aer Lingus**, **British Airways**, **bmi** and **KLM**. Cheap flights are advertised in national newspapers, listings magazines and on the Internet, and are also available through discount agencies. Smaller operators, such as **EasyJet**, **Transavia**, **Cityjet** and **Jet2**, can be less expensive than the national airlines. Watch out for flight prices that do not include

airport and security taxes and associated surcharges, such as fuel, as these can be expensive. Dozens of inclusive package deals are available, and if organized through a reliable agency, they can be far cheaper than booking a flight or ferry and separate accommodation.

Amsterdam is also a popular staging post for overseas visitors to Europe. You can fly from many US cities to Schiphol, and operators running non-stop services on scheduled flights include the Dutch company **Martinair**, **Delta/KLM**, **United Airlines** and **American Airlines**. Other operators fly via the major European capital cities, such as Paris and Rome, but London is probably the cheapest transatlantic destination, with uniquely varied connections. Fare prices vary according to season, but APEX (which must be bought a least 2 weeks in advance) is the cheapest year-round option. The leader in the field of charter flights from the USA is Martinair, which offers mid-range prices on non-stop flights from a number of

Self-service check-in at Schiphol airport

cities. Cheaper still are the fares of the "seat consolidators" and "last minute" websites, which buy up unsold seats from the major carriers and sell them off at a huge reduction. For bargain flights, check out the free weeklies and travel sections of newspapers. Several companies offer excellent-value package tours. KLM has the widest range of options, but can be expensive, so it's well worth shopping around.

The cheapest route for visitors from Australia and New Zealand will also usually require a London stopover, as scheduled flights direct to Amsterdam are expensive. **STA Travel** and Flight Centre, which has offices in Australia, New Zealand and the USA, is a source of expert advice for independent travellers.

ON ARRIVAL

Arrival and Exit signs will direct passengers arriving from Schengen countries: to baggage carousels and Customs. All other passengers will be streamed into the huge, central shopping and amenities area of the "Schiphol World Avenue", and should follow the Arrivals and Passport Control signs to the ground floor. After passport control is a hall with baggage carousels and Customs. If you have nothing to declare, simply walk through the doors marked Exit to enter Schiphol Plaza. There are sometimes spot checks at Customs, and this can take some time. Bringing food produce, such as raw meats, cheeses and other dairy products into the country is banned. Additionally, you must declare any of the following: merchandise imports, protected animal and plant species, works of art and antiques, narcotics, arms and ammunition you may be bringing with you. Failure to do so may result in heavy fines, and in some cases, arrest.

A KLM flight departing from Schiphol airport

TRANSPORT FROM THE AIRPORT TO TOWN

There are several ways of getting into the centre of Amsterdam, 18 km (11 miles) to the northeast. These include car rental (although driving in Amsterdam is not recommended), taxis, buses and trains. Car rental firms are arranged around the edge of Schiphol Plaza, by the exits. Once you have arranged the rental, there are courtesy buses to the parking lots. There are two forms of taxi available: the TCA *(see p271)* and private taxis at the rank just outside the Plaza. A taxi to the city centre will cost anywhere from €40 to €60,

Sign showing departure gates

depending on where you are going. You also have the option of the Schiphol Travel Taxi, which must be reserved in advance and can be booked online as either a private taxi or, for a lower fare, shared. A shared fare starts at around €20 for a single trip, and €35 for a return, and private rates start at €40 for a single and €75 for a return. Keep in mind that a shared taxi may take a longer time than expected, as it may make several stops before your destination.

Two buses travel into the centre of Amsterdam from just outside of Schiphol Plaza: the Interliner 370 and 197. Both will take you into Leidseplein, from where you can transfer to the tram system, in about 30 minutes. Single tickets cost €3.80 and can be bought on the bus, or you can also use

the *OV-chipkaart (see p273)*. The most popular way to get to the city centre, however, is by train, and it costs about the same price. The Schiphol NS station is located directly below the airport, and tickets for the airport train as well as other domestic train travel are available from the yellow ticket machines in Schiphol Plaza. Some of the machines take change, and some will also take credit cards (with an extra fee for use).

Trolleys, which are free of charge, can be taken right on to the platform via the lifts. Trains run four to seven times an hour between 6am and midnight, after which they run hourly. The journey takes about 20 minutes, and the fare is either the same as the bus at €3.80, or slightly higher at €5.80 for the high speed FYRA train, which takes 15 minutes. There are also rail connections from Schiphol to most stations in the Netherlands. Rail services are clearly signposted. Tickets for international travel can also be bought from the ticket offices at one end of the Plaza. A small handling fee of 50c is charged.

Railway platform at Schiphol Plaza, destination Amsterdam

A high-speed Thalys train

ARRIVING BY TRAIN

All trains arrive at Amsterdam Centraal Station, including those from Schiphol airport. The **Eurostar** runs to and from London via the Channel Tunnel. Passengers for Amsterdam must change at Brussels. The journey time is about 7 hours, and there are a range of comfort classes, discounts for seniors and children, special tickets for bicycles and combination packages which includes the cost of a hotel and/or car rentals.

Thalys runs a high-speed service between Paris, Brussels and Amsterdam, ten times a day, with a variety of special offers, package deals and half-price last-minute deals. The new FYRA high-speed train, www.nshispeed.nl, is scheduled to run between Brussels and Amsterdam in the near future; the train is currently being tested between Rotterdam and Amsterdam.

Students and those under 26 can benefit from discount rail travel both to and within the Netherlands. The Interrail Global pass allows travel for up to one month, and the Interrail One Country pass allows three–eight days of unlimited travel in the Netherlands. For more information, contact **Rail Europe**; you don't even have to be a student to qualify for some deals.

Amsterdam Centraal Station has all the amenities of a big terminus, but can be very crowded with commuters during peak hours and is a magnet for pickpockets. Most tram and bus routes start here *(see pp272–3)*; head for Stationsplein by the main entrance, following signs to the Amsterdam Tourist Board (VVV). The tram stops are only a few metres from the entrance, and the bus stops are across the bridge, in front of the station. The Tourist Board office and the GVB municipal transport authority office are located in the white pavilion building found on the water in front of the station.

Centraal Station is being extensively reorganized until 2017. Parts of the station may be closed and stops moved.

ARRIVING BY FERRY

The Dutch railways, Nederlands Spoorwegen (NS), in conjunction with **Stena Line** and **One Railway**, operate a boat-train service called the Dutch Flyer which runs from London to Amsterdam via Harwich and the Hook of Holland. The total journey time is about 7 hours 30 minutes, and a variety of deals are offered, including combined packages that include hotels and day trips and short stays. **P&O Ferries** operates an overnight service from Hull to Zeebrugge or Rotterdam, a 10-hour journey. **DFDS Seaways** run an overnight service from Newcastle to IJmuiden (note that the ticket price does not include the journey from IJmuiden to Amsterdam, which is a bus ticket that must be booked separately), and ferry trips can also be booked as a three-day mini-cruise.

ARRIVING BY CAR

An ever-expanding motorway system makes it easy to reach the Netherlands from countries in western, central and southern Europe.

A valid driver's licence is sufficient for driving in the Netherlands, although many car-hire firms and the motoring organization **ANWB (Royal Dutch Touring Club)** favour an international driver's licence. To take your own car into the Netherlands, you will need proof of registration, valid insurance documents, a road safety certificate from the vehicle's country of origin and an international identification disc. Major roads (marked N) are well maintained, but Dutch motorways (labelled A) have narrow lanes, traffic lights and sometimes no hard shoulder. European routes are labelled E.

There are four levels of speed limit: 100 km/h (60 mph)

Stena Line's Dutch Flyer on the London–Amsterdam route

or 120 km/h (75 mph) on motorways, 80 km/h (50 mph) outside cities and 50 km/h (30 mph) in urban areas. From the A10 ring road, the S-routes (marked by blue signs) will take you to the centre of Amsterdam.

ANWB logo

The ANWB provides a breakdown service for members of foreign motoring organizations. A non-member can pay for the ANWB's services, or become a temporary ANWB member for the duration of your stay.

If you break down on a major road or motorway, use the yellow telephone pillars. Once in the city, be careful of cyclists and trams (see p270). Trams take precedence and cyclists need ample space. Take care when turning, and allow cyclists priority. Much of the city centre is one-way, and when driving in the canal area, remember that the water should be to

your left. Pavements in the are usually very narrow, so keep an eye out for people walking in the streets. Main roads, with priority, are marked by a white diamond with a yellow centre; otherwise assume priority is from the right.

ARRIVING BY BUS AND COACH

Long-distance bus or coach travel can be a cheap, if sometimes tiresome, option for those visiting Amsterdam. The **Eurolines** bus service offers routes either through the Channel Tunnel or by ferry from Dover to Calais. There are three daily services in summer from London Victoria station to Amstel Station (from where there is a Metro connection to Centraal Station), and at least one service a day in winter. Eurolines also offers cheap deals the further in advance you book, and some package

deals. Fares can start for as little as £19 one way. There are also discounts for students, children and seniors. One advantage of coach travel is that you are allowed to take two medium suitcases in the hold. Folding bikes are accepted only on the Eurolines coach service to Amsterdam.

Coaches travelling to Europe offer comfortable services, such as reclining seats, air conditioning, toilet facilities and DVD entertainment. The super-long coaches also offer increased legroom.

A Eurolines bus

DIRECTORY

GETTING AROUND AMSTERDAM

The best way to see Amsterdam is on foot or bicycle. Almost everything of interest is within comfortable walking distance or a short cycle away. The city's layout is quite simple, with its concentric canals (*grachten*) and interlocking roads, but it can seem confusing at first. Remember that starting from the innermost canal, the Singel, the main canals after that are

Street sign indicating district

arranged in the alphabetical sequence of Herengracht, Keizersgracht and Prinsengracht (on the outside). If walking or cycling are not your style, there is a range of other options: an excellent public transport system, scooters, water taxis, canal boats – but don't drive. Amsterdam can be a nightmare for even the most experienced local drivers, and there are very limited parking facilities.

GREEN TRAVEL

The Dutch are experts at "greening" their travel options: trams are electric, families are much more likely to travel by bicycle or use a local car-share scheme rather than own a car and buses are fitted with special exhaust filters. The city's infrastructure is oriented to bicycle traffic, and public transport is frequent.

Amsterbike offers electric scooters as a quiet, clean way to explore, and **Wielertaxis** are electrically assisted bike taxi. The bike taxi can carry up to two people and cost less than conventional taxis. **Amsterdamboatguide** and **Canal Motorboats** offer eco-friendly electric boats to rent and **Wetlands Safari** offer canoe tours.

WALKING

Make sure that you are wearing sensible shoes – the brick-cobbled streets can be tiring, as well as hazardous. One main drawback to a stroll around town used to be dog mess, but this has improved a lot since the late 1990s. Local traffic remains a hazard to

tourists – trams have their own path in the middle of the road; buses and taxis zip down, sometimes moving between tram lanes; and traffic lanes and bicycles are everywhere, often going in every direction. Therefore, it is important that pedestrians look both ways when crossing tram routes (trams can be almost silent), and keep off the cycle paths. Cars won't stop at pedestrian crossings without lights.

GUIDED TOURS

Organized group tours offer many options to learn more about the city, and are led by a number of operators.

Amsterdam City Walks organizes guided walks in English that focus on the history and archaeology of Amsterdam and also take in the Red Light District.

Guided tours from **Mee in Mokum** take you around the historic parts of the city and have some of the best, most informed and most entertaining guides. For more extensive Red Light tours, with a choice of day or evening, try **Zoom Tours**. They meet at the historic VOC Café (*see p67*), walk you through the district and take you to a wine cellar/bar in the area.

Amsterdam City Tours offers three main tourist routes, combining a walking tour with a hop-on, hop-off bus and one- or two-day pass system, with

the Canalbus Day Pass. **Bink Original Sightseeing** is a popular touring company which offers group day trips, city walks covering all major sights, sailing trips, and pub crawls; they also organize stag and hen nights.

Green Wheels car-sharing hire cars

DRIVING IN AMSTERDAM

The small inner city streets and canals, the plethora of all sorts of traffic, not to mention the serious parking shortages and high charges, all make Amsterdam unsuited to driving. However, if you do choose to drive, be careful of cyclists and trams in the city. Trams take precedence; take care when turning; and allow cyclists priority. Much of the city centre is one-way, and when driving in the canal area, remember that the water should be to your left. The **ANWB** provides a breakdown service for members of foreign motoring organizations (*see pp268–9*). The car-sharing scheme **Green Wheels** offers a "pay-as-you-go" plan, cheaper than owning your own vehicle. Rentals are charged by the hour. To sign up you need to have an international licence.

Pedestrian crossing, Dam square

PARKING

Although the city is ill-suited to motor traffic, provision is made for drivers. However, parking is difficult, and theft rife, so if you're staying in a hotel, it's better to book with a secure parking facility and leave your car there while in the city. If you are visiting the city from outside, park on the outskirts in a "P&R" (park and ride) and use public transport into the centre. In town use a car park rather than a meter or roadside space. If you do park in a public place, remove your car radio and all other valuables.

Parking space is at a premium in the city, especially on-street parking in the centre, and many outlying neighbourhoods. In the city centre, meters are limited to 2 hours and are in use until midnight.

A pay-and-display parking sign

In the areas outside the canal ring/centre, all-day passes can be bought. Most meters take coins and/or parking cards, but in some of the more residential areas, the meters only take a local bank debit card. Avoid out-of-order meters as you could get fined; you will have to pay your fine in cash at the **Stadstoezicht** or **Service Centres**. If you use a car park, you must obtain a ticket by putting money in the ticket machine, which can be some way from the parking place. Illegally parked cars will be fined, but you won't get clamped until you have five unpaid parking fines. There are now several 24-hour covered car parks, such as **Q-Park** and Byzantium. All car parks located within the city are denoted by a white P on a square blue background.

TAXIS

There have been a lot of problems in Amsterdam with small, unregulated taxi firms and dishonest or aggressive drivers, especially around Centraal Station. As a result, the municipality has introduced regulated taxi stands (*kwaliteitstaxisstandplatsen*) that can only be used by taxis with a seal of approval, known as *kwaliteitstaxi's* (quality taxis), with their registration number displayed on the windscreen. The rules are posted at Centraal Station and most large taxi ranks. The best ways to find a cab are to pick one up at a main taxi rank or phone **TCA Taxicentrale**, which runs a 24-hour service. You will find that the response is fast, apart from Friday and Saturday nights. Rates are quite high, so give only a small tip, unless your driver has been particularly helpful. Other firms include **Sneltaxi** or **Amsterdam Online Taxi**.

DIRECTORY

GREEN TRAVEL

Amsterbike
Piet Heinkade 11A.
Tel 020 419 9063.
www.amsterbike.nl

Amsterdamboat guide
Tel 020 423 3006.
www.amsterdamboat guide.com

Canal Motorboats
Zandhoek 10a.
Tel 020 422 70 07.
www.canalmotorboats. com

Wetlands Safari
Tel 020 686 3445.
www.wetlandssafari.nl

Wielertaxi (bike taxis)
Tel 06 282 47550.
www.wielertaxi.nl

GUIDED TOURS

Amsterdam City Tours
Tel 0299 770799.
www.amsterdamcity tours.com

Amsterdam City Walks
Tel 06 1825 7014.
www.amsterdamcity walks.com

Bink Original Sightseeing
B. Floriszstraat 39.
Tel 020 679 5415.

Mee in Mokum
Tel: 020 625 1390.

Zoom Tours
Tel 020 623 6302.
www.zoomamsterdam. com

PARKING

Parking Amsterdam Centraal
Prins Hendrikkade 20a.
Map 2 D3.

Q-Park
Tesselschadestraat 1g.
Map 4 D2.
Marnixstraat 250. **Map** 4 D1, Waterlooplein 28.
Map 8 D5, Raamplein.
Map 4 D1.
Tel 0900 446 6880.

BREAKDOWN

ANWB Contact Center
Tel (088) 269 22 22.

ANWB Alarm Center
Tel (088) 269 28 88.

PARKING PASS

Service Centres
Karel du Jardinstraat 61.
De Clercqstraat 44.
Map 6 D5.
Daniël Goedkoopstraat 7, Overamstel (metro 50, 53, 54 to Spaklerweg).
Open 24 hours.

Stadstoezicht
Tel 251 2222 (24 hours).
www.stadstoezicht. amsterdam.nl

CAR RENTAL

Adams Rent-a-Car
Nassaukade 346.
Map 4 D1.
Tel 020 685 0111.

Avis
Nassaukade 380.
Map 4 D1.
Tel 020 683 6061.

Green Wheels
Tel 088 210 0100.
www.greenwheels.nl
(Dutch)

Hertz
Overtoom 333.
Map 3 A3.
Tel 020 612 2441.

TAXIS

Amsterdam Online Taxi
Tel 06 19632963.
www.amsterdamtaxi-online.com

Schiphol Taxicentrale
Tel 0900 770 0000.
www.nstc.nl

Sneltaxi
Tel 036 536 3200.
www.sneltaxi.nl

TCA Taxicentrale
Tel 020 777 7777.
www.tcataxi.nl

Using Public Transport

Amsterdam's integrated public transport system (GVB), for which Centraal Station is the central hub, is very efficient. The only way to travel on the Metro, trams and buses is with an *OV-chipkaart*, a smartcard that is reusable and can be topped up electronically. The OV9292, the national public transport information office, provides information via phone or its website on all public transport within the city and the rest of the Netherlands, but does not make reservations.

One of Amsterdam's modern blue-and-white trams

TRAMS

Amsterdam's trams are the most common form of public transport in the city. Routes are shown on a free transport map obtainable from the **GVB** office. The most useful routes go south from Centraal Station along Damrak or NZ Voorburgwal (Nos 1, 2, 4, 5, 7, 9 and 16), diverging after the Singel. Lines 13, 14 and 17 are also useful if you need to travel west into Jordaan. Trams start operating at 6am on weekdays and 7am at weekends. They finish just after midnight, when night buses take over. Blue boards above the tram and bus stops give the name of the stop and the route numbers it serves. Information inside the shelters shows the stops and approximate times. Many, but not all, are wheelchair accessible.

To enter, choose either the front door, or the door two-thirds of the way towards the back, where the conductor sits. On entering the tram you will need to hold your *OV-chipkaart* in

front of the grey machine to calculate your fare, or buy a disposable *OV-chipkaart (see p273)*, good for 1 or 2 hours. If you have a young child or heavy suitcase, you may need to keep one foot on the entrance strip when you board to make sure the door stays open until you have boarded safely.

Tram stops will generally be announced, but if you're not sure where to get off, don't be afraid to ask for guidance. Press a button inside the tram to open the doors. You may leave through any but the conductor's or driver's door. Remember that many stops are in the middle of the road, so take care when you get off. You will need to swipe your *OV-chipkaart* again on leaving the tram so that the correct fare can be

deducted from your card automatically, or – with the disposable ones – so that you can transfer to another tram and continue to use it for the full time period.

BUSES

Like the trams, the majority of Amsterdam's buses set out from Centraal Station, but they soon branch out from the city centre and largely complement the tram network. They have the same stops and *OV-chipkaart* ticketing system as the trams, but you must board by the front door. A minibus, the "Stop/Go" service, leaves daily every 12 minutes from Oosterdokskade near Centraal Station and travels along Prinsengracht to Waterlooplein and back, close to many sights, museums and shopping areas. It connects with other bus and tram routes, and to be as flexible as possible, there are no fixed stops – simply hold out your hand and the driver will stop. Let the driver know where you want to get off. Stop/Go tickets, bought on board, cost €1 per hour, but both the GVB day cards and the *OV-chipkaart* can also be used.

Night-bus stops have a black square with the number on it; night buses are

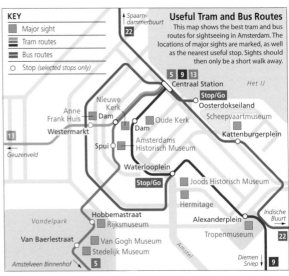

KEY

■	Major sight
═	Tram routes
▬	Bus routes
O	Stop (selected stops only)

Useful Tram and Bus Routes

This map shows the best tram and bus routes for sightseeing in Amsterdam. The locations of major sights are marked, as well as the nearest useful stop. Sights should then only be a short walk away.

Spaarndammerbuurt **22**

5 9 13 Centraal Station   Het IJ

Stop/Go

Oosterdokseiland

Scheepvaartmuseum

Nieuwe Kerk

Anne Frank Huis   Dam

Westermarkt   Oude Kerk

Dam

13   Kattenburgerplein

Geuzenveld

Spui   Amsterdams Historisch Museum

Waterlooplein

Stop/Go   Joods Historisch Museum

Hermitage

Hobbemastraat   Alexanderplein   Indische Buurt

Vondelpark   Rijksmuseum   Tropenmuseum   **22**

Van Baerlestraat   Van Gogh Museum

Stedelijk Museum

Amstelveen Binnenhof   Amstel   Diemen Sniep   **9**

5

A bus serving the north of the city from Centraal Station

numbered from 348 to 392. Night buses run all night, but the service is every hour (every half-hour from Friday to Sunday), so be prepared for a wait, or take a taxi. Note that night buses are more expensive than trams or buses, starting at €3.50 per ride.

METRO

Amsterdam's underground system comprises only four lines, three of which start from and terminate at Centraal Station. Mainly used by commuters, the Metro is not particularly useful for tourists as it only covers four stations in the centre, all on the eastern side – Amsterdam CS, Nieuwmarkt, Waterlooplein and Weesperplein.

The Metro runs for around half an hour longer than trams on weekdays, and uses the same *OV-chipkaart* ticketing system as trams and buses. Take care late at night, when some inner-city stations may have drug dealers.

The North–South line, the fourth Metro line, is currently being constructed to link the area of the city north of the river IJ with the city centre on the southern shore, and eventually run all the way to Schiphol airport. The project is impressive, digging through an unstable substratum directly under the historic centre of Amsterdam, athough this has caused subsidence of up to 23cm (9 inches) deep in some houses. It is planned to open in 2017, with a cost of €1.4 billion.

Distinctive sign for a Metro station

TRAINS

The Dutch national railway company, **Nederlandse Spoorwegen**, or simply **NS**, runs a busy network which is considered one of the best in the world. It is reliable, clean and reasonably priced. Both the **OV9292** (Openbaar Vervoer Reisinformatie) office, and the NS Service Centre, located in the western hall of Centraal Station, can provide information on rail trips. Special fares are also available, for example Family Rovers, which allows you to stop off en route to your destination, or Railrunners, which are cheap tickets for kids aged between 4 and 11. OV9292 does not sell tickets, but the NS Service Centre and national ticket offices do. Tickets can also be bought from the yellow machines at the front and back of Centraal Station. There is a button for English, and machines take credit cards (some also accept cash). Information and bookings for rail travel abroad is available from the NS Service Centre.

TRAM, BUS, METRO AND TRAIN TICKETS

You can buy an *OV-chipkaart* from the GVB, Tourist Board offices and newsagents, as well as disposable cards on the trams, buses or Metro. The size of a credit card, this smartcard works much like a rechargeable telephone card, with each trip being deducted from the credit available. There are two kinds: a disposable, one-time use card for durations of either 1 (€2.60) or 2 hours (€5) or one to seven days (€7–29), and a reloadable pass (€7.50, usable for five years), which allows users to top up the balance (up to €30). *OV-chipkaarts* can be topped up at any of the ticket vending machines and "add value" machines located at all Metro stations and stops, Centraal Station and some super-

markets. In order to validate a journey, users need to hold the *OV-chipkaart* in front of the grey card readers on entering and leaving a Metro or train station, or when getting on and off trams and buses. On all forms of transport, you will be charged a distance fee, so there are no differences in terms of one form of transport being cheaper. Children under 4 travel free, and seniors and 4–11 year olds have to purchase their discounted cards in advance at a GVB office. The "Amsterdam All in One Travel Pass" includes a return train ticket to Schiphol airport and a 24/46/72/96-hour pass (including night buses) that can be bought at the GVB or at Schiphol airport Tourist Information. The All Amsterdam Transport Pass includes all forms of public transport (except trains) and a one-day ticket for the Canalbus (*see p270*), plus discounts for sights and museums.

Always swipe your *OV-chipkaart* to validate your journey

(*see p270*)

DIRECTORY

GVB (Gemeente Vervoer Bedrijf)
Stationsplein 14.
Map 2 E3.
Tel 0900 8011 (GVB info).
Tel 0900 9292 (national info).
www.gvb.nl/english

NS (Nederlandse Spoorwegen)
Centraal Station.
Map 2 E3.
Tel 0900 9292 (national).
Tel 0900 9296 (international).
www.ns.nl (national)
www.nshispeed.nl (international)

OV9292 (Openbaar Vervoer Reisinformatie)
Tel 0900 9292.
www.9292ov.nl

Getting Around by Bicycle

Bicycle safety helmet

The bicycle is the ideal form of transport in Amsterdam. More than half a million people cycle to school or work, and use a bicycle to do the shopping or go out in the evening. The city's traffic system is biased in favour of bicycles, with an excellent network of integrated cycle lanes (*fietspaden*), dedicated traffic lights and road signs, and special routes linking different parts of the city. More and more tourists, too, are adopting this way of exploring Amsterdam and its environs.

A row of bicycles for hire

Amsterdam is the ideal place to explore by bicycle

RULES OF THE ROAD

Amsterdam's traffic is composed of a chaotic mix of trams, buses, taxis, cars and bicycles, often split into their own lanes. Remember to always ride on the right and that other road users will not necessarily recognize you as an inexperienced tourist and may assume you know how to avoid them. If you are unsure or unsteady, it is worth heading to one of the inner city parks for a bit of practice first. Motorists and other cyclists have priority when entering the road from the right, unless otherwise stated. Trams have priority,

so stay well clear. Many novices dismount at busy junctions and cross on foot; if you choose to do this, be sure to switch to the pedestrian section of the crossing. Do not walk with your bike in a bike lane. You will need to be aware of pedestrians who are clearly tourists and tend to wander into the bike paths. Dutch cyclists often ride through red lights and zigzag through traffic, but don't follow their example. Don't use the part of the road with tramlines, but if you have to move inside the tracks to pass a stationary vehicle, do so at an angle, otherwise your front wheel may get stuck in the tramlines. Also watch out for taxis, people emerging from parked

cars and foreign coaches whose drivers may be unsympathetic to cyclists. Don't carry passengers on your bike, or ride on footpaths or pavements, or you could be fined. Be aware that you are legally obliged to have or wear a clear light on the front, and a red, reflective light on the back and could be fined if you don't.

Although the locals don't bother, it is a wise precaution to wear a helmet.

HIRING A BICYCLE

Bicycle hire shops abound in Amsterdam. Rental costs start at around €7.50 per day for a basic, back-pedal brake bike, with costs decreasing per day for longer rental periods and increasing for bikes with gears and/or hand brakes. Tandems are more expensive and may be difficult to manoeuvre on some narrow streets.

Deposits are handled in one of two ways: either a cash deposit, varying from €30 to €100, with a valid, original passport (or in the case of EU citizens, a valid driver's licence), which must be left behind for the duration of the rental, or a credit card imprint.

As well as a range of bicycles and brake systems, **Macbike** and **Orange Bike** also offer extras such as children's seats, saddlebags and even rain gear for those classic Dutch grey and wet days. For those wanting someone or something else to provide the pedal power, many of the bicycle hire firms also rent scooters (some will require a driver's licence), or for the more green oriented, check information on bike taxis and electric scooter rentals (*see pp270–1*).

Traffic lights for bicycles

Bicycles allowed

No entry except to bicycles and mopeds

uitgezonderd

TAKING YOUR OWN BICYCLE

The easiest way to take your own bicycle to the Netherlands is strapped to a bike rack on your car. Your bike travels for free if you are a walk-on passenger on the ferry to the Netherlands; when you book your ticket, simply inform the clerk. On your arrival in the Netherlands, if you want the cycle to go with you by train you are required to buy a ticket for it and enter the train at the doors marked for bicycles.

To take your bicycle by air, you must make a cargo booking with the airline at least a week in advance. It will have to be included in your 20 kg (44 lb) luggage allowance, and you must pay any excess baggage or handling costs.

BUYING A BICYCLE

Be careful when buying a bicycle that it is not listed as stolen, as you will be held responsible for buying stolen goods and will have a hard time selling it at the end of your holiday. A cheap bike for sale on the street will almost certainly have been stolen, and an expensive one from a specialist shop will probably end up being stolen too. It is worth buying a second-hand bargain if you are staying for a few weeks. There are a number of reputable second-hand dealers that will also buy back used bikes. Some of the hire companies also buy and sell used bikes.

BICYCLE SECURITY

Bicycle theft is rife, so it's essential to secure your bike even when parking for just a few minutes. Fasten both front wheel and frame to a post or railings with a metal U-shaped lock or chain. Locals recommend a lock on the back wheel as well. Hire shops are happy to advise on security matters, and will normally provide a lock in the rental price.

BICYCLE TOURS

Guided bicycle tours are a popular way to discover the city and its environs at a sedate pace. The price of the tours usually includes bicycle hire, and they tend to run from March through November. **Mike's Bike Tours** City tour includes canals and houseboats, the Red Light District, Vondelpark and the Jordaan, while their Countryside tour visits a windmill and a cheese farm or clog factory. **Yellowbike**'s City tour includes all of the above, as well as the Museum district and the harbour. The Countryside tour is a 35-km (22-mile) route through the Waterland district north of Amsterdam, and almost exclusively uses paths through a nature reserve, passing small brooks and waterways and tiny, old villages along the way. Orange Bike offers the most extensive range of inner city tours. **Cycletours Holland** only offers countryside trips.

If you want to go it alone, both the Tourist Board and NS Information *(see p259)* provide maps with routes, cycle lanes and refreshment stops. The Arena Hotel *(see p223)* produces information with suggestions and maps for cycle trips around and outside the city. City tours can take 3 hours, and country trips around 7 hours. For an alternative scenic route, take the tram to the Amsterdamse Bos (Amsterdam Woods) and hire a bicycle or scooter once you are there.

Cycle tours a popular way to see the city

DIRECTORY

BICYCLE HIRE

Amsterdamse Bos Fietsverhuur
Amstelveenseweg 88.
Tel 020 644 5473.

Bike City
Bloemgracht 70.
Map 1 A4.
Tel 020 626 3721.
www.bikecity.nl

Damstraat Rent-a-Bike
Damstraat 20-22.
Map 7 C3.
Tel 020 625 5029.
www.bikes.nl

Holland Rent-a-Bike
Damrak 247.
Map 7 C2.
Tel 020 622 3207.

MacBike
Centraal Station Oost,
Stationsplein 12.
Map 8 D1.
Tel 020 428 5778.
Nieuwe Uilenburgerstr 116.
Map 8 E4.
Weteringschans 2.
Map 4 E2.
www.macbike.nl

Orange Bike
Singel 233.
Map 7 A3.
Tel 020 528 9990.

Rent A Bike
Fredericbrouwersgracht
78. **Map** 1 B2.
Tel 020 624 5509.

Star Bike Rental
De Ruyterkade 127.
Map 8 F1.
Tel 020 620 3215.

BICYCLE TOURS

Cycletours Holland
Buiksloterweg 7A. **Map** 2
F2. *Tel 020 521 8490.*
www.cycletours.com

Mike's Bike Tours
Kerkstraat 134.
Map 4 F2.
Tel 020 622 7970.

Yellow Bike
Nieuwezijds Kolk 29.
Map 7 C1.
Tel 020 620 6940.
www.yellowbike.nl

SECOND-HAND BICYCLES

Groeno
2e H de Grootstraat 12.
Map 1 A4.
Tel 020 684 4270.
www.groeno.nl

MacBike
Marnixstraat 220.
Map 4 D1.
Tel 020 428 5778.
www.macbike.nl

Getting Around on the Canal

The name Amsterdam evolved from the 13th-century dam on the Amstel that was built to allow the city to grow and develop into a working system of 165 canals and 1,300 bridges, earning it the name the "Venice of the North". Today, the inner canals are used more for pleasure boating and living than transport or trading, but firms like courier company DHL are rediscovering the ease and speed of using the canals. Canal boats offer a variety of tours, and boat trips are particularly well suited to those without the time to explore on foot or by tram, or to the elderly and families with children.

Embarkation point for P. Kooij

CANAL TOURS

There are many operators in Amsterdam offering canal tours with foreign-language commentaries. Boats depart from a number of embarkation points, mainly from opposite Centraal Station along Prins Hendrikkade, the Damrak and along the Rokin. Many *rondvaartboten* (tour boats) have glass tops, some of which can be opened in fine weather. It is not always necessary to book seats for tours, but it is wise to do so for lunchtime, evening and dinner cruises, especially during the peak tourist season.

Night cruises can feature cheese-and-wine refreshments, a stop at a pub or a romantic candlelit dinner. **Lovers** offers a comprehensive selection of such cruises in addition to its daytime trips. Besides city-centre tours, **Artis Express** operates a special service from Centraal Station to Artis *(see pp142–3)*, the Scheepvaart Museum *(see pp146–7)*, Tropenmuseum

(see pp152–3) and the Hortus Botanicus *(see p142)*. On hot days, try **P. Kooij**, as it has the most open-topped boats. Or, instead of the stag do or hen party, why not get married while you cruise? **Blue Boat Company** offers to arrange everything from the tour and reception to the actual wedding. If you are looking for a sailing trip out of the city, try Bink Original Sightseeing *(see p271)*.

CANALBUS

The **Canalbus** service runs every 30 minutes along four routes, with 19 stops located near the major museums, shopping areas and other attractions. You can embark or alight at any of the stops along the routes, and it is claimed that the Canalbus is the first boat of its kind in Europe to run on gas.

Tickets for a one-, two- or three-day pass can be purchased, and the Canalbus operates a pizza cruise on Saturday evenings, from April to November starting from outside the Rijksmuseum at 7pm. It is generally advisable to reserve a place beforehand at a Canalbus kiosk, as they are very popular and can get fully booked very quickly, especially in summer. You can also find out more information about other ticket offers.

You can purchase an All Amsterdam Transport Pass from the Canalbus kiosks, which, among other discounts, entitles you to a one-day travel pass on both the Canalbus and the public transport system in Amsterdam. A basic one-day pass costs €28. Other combination tickets include entrance to one of the main museums with a day ticket: the Rijksmuseum (€35.50), Van Gogh Museum (€35) and the new Hermitage on the Amstel (€36). The same company also runs Canal Hopper (a sloop hire), and **Canal Bike** services *(see p277)*.

MUSEUM BOAT

Amsterdam's **Hop On, Hop Off Museum Line** is less of a tour and more of a way to get around easily and in style to all the major city sights and shopping areas. Boats run every 20 minutes daily, between 10am and 6:45pm (to 5pm November to March), from opposite Centraal Station. You can buy a day ticket, which allows unlimited use for one day and includes a 50 per cent discount on museum admission prices. Tickets can be bought at the Centraal Station embarkation stage or any landing points. An adult day ticket costs €17, and a child's day ticket is €13. Details of landing stages are on the transport map on this guide's inside back cover.

Canal tour on the Oude Schans, the Montelbaanstoren in the background

A pleasant canal-side café

WATER TAXIS

Water taxis are more convenient than canal boats for sightseeing as they work just like a land taxi; they take you exactly where you want to go and charge per minute. They are also expensive – for an 8-seater, the tariff has a starting cost of €7.50, and €1.75 per minute, per person in the inner city. They also offer tours as part of their "VIP Experience", including food, drink and a guide, which must be booked in advance. Among the itineraries offered are an "Architecture" cruise, a "Hidden City" cruise, a "Candlelight Pub" cruise, and a tailor-made "After Dinner" cruise. If you want to use one of these boats you will need to book in advance from **Water Taxi**. VIP cruises range in price from €26.50 per person (pub cruise) up to €107.50 per person (dinner cruise, only bookable for groups of eight). If you want a more romantic experience, book a private "Honeymoon" cruise for €119.50 for half an hour.

BOAT HIRE AND WATER RULES

If you fancy being captain, both Amsterdam Boat Guide and Canal Motorboats offer a variety of eco-friendly electric boats to rent, with no navigation licence required *(see p271)*, or you can use your legs for pedal power *(see Canal Bikes)* or rent a sloop. Either way, there are some basic rules. In general, you

may cruise on the canals and in the harbour, with some exceptions. Port control and police patrol boats can give both warnings and fines if you stray into a zone not accessible for pleasure or pedal boats. Keep to the right (starboard) side. Maximum speed is 18 km (5 miles) per hour; cruise ships and vessels longer than 20 m (65 ft) always have right of way. Pedal boats must not enter the harbour and are banned from the western port.

Sightseeing by canal bike

CANAL BIKES

Canal bikes are two- or four-seater pedal-boats. Propelling them requires considerable energy, but when you've had enough, you can stop for a drink. You can pick up or leave a pedal-boat at any of the canal-bike moorings in the city: Prinsengracht at the Westerkerk, Keizersgracht near Leidsestraat, Leidseplein between the Marriott and American hotels, and along the Singelgracht just outside the Rijksmuseum. There is a €50 deposit and costs €8 per person, per hour. Between November and March, only the Singelgracht, Prinsengracht and Leidseplein moorings are open.

DIRECTORY

CANAL TOURS

Amsterdam Canal Cruises
Nicolaas Witsenkade 1a.
Map 4 F2. *Tel* 020 626 5636.
www.amsterdamcanalcruises.nl

Artis Express
opposite Centraal Station.
Map 8 D1. *Tel* 020 530 1090.
www.lovers.nl

Blue Boat Company
Stadhouderskade 30.
Tel 020 679 1370.
www.blueboat.nl

Canalbus & Canal Bike
Weteringschans 24. **Map** 4 E2.
Tel 020 623 9886 *(canalbus).*
Tel 020 626 5574 *(canal bike).*
www.canal.nl

Holland International
Prins Hendrikkade 33a,
opposite Centraal Station.
Map 8 D1.
Tel 020 625 3035.
www.hir.nl

Hop On, Hop Off Museum Line
Stationsplein 8.
Map 8 D1.
Tel 020 530 1090.
www.lovers.nl

Lindbergh
Damrak 26.
Map 8 D1.
Tel 020 622 2766.
www.lindbergh.nl

Lovers
Opposite Prins Hendrikkade 25–27.
Map 8 D1.
Tel 020 530 1090.
www.lovers.nl

Meyers
Jetty 4-5, Damrak.
Map 8 D1.
Tel 020 623 4208.
www.meyersrondvaarten.nl

P. Kooij
Opposite Rokin 125.
Map 7 B4.
Tel 020 623 3810.
www.rederijkooij.nl

Tours and Tickets
Tel 020 420 4000.
www.tours-tickets.com

Water Taxi
Stationsplein 8.
Map 8 D1.
Tel 020 535 6363.
www.water-taxi.nl

STREET FINDER

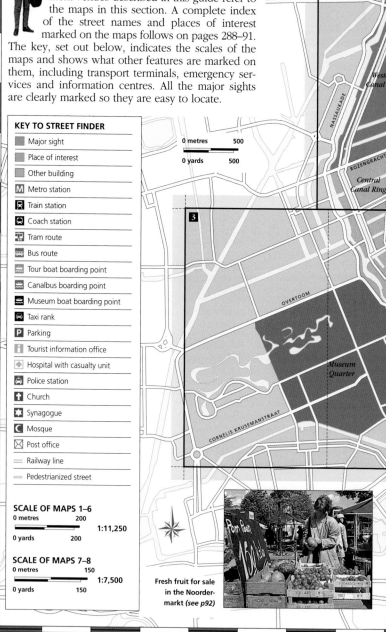

The page grid superimposed on the *Area by Area* map below shows which parts of Amsterdam are covered in this *Street Finder*. The map references given for all sights, hotels, restaurants, shopping and entertainment venues described in this guide refer to the maps in this section. A complete index of the street names and places of interest marked on the maps follows on pages 288–91. The key, set out below, indicates the scales of the maps and shows what other features are marked on them, including transport terminals, emergency services and information centres. All the major sights are clearly marked so they are easy to locate.

KEY TO STREET FINDER

▮	Major sight
▮	Place of interest
▮	Other building
Ⓜ	Metro station
🚉	Train station
🚌	Coach station
🚊	Tram route
🚍	Bus route
⛴	Tour boat boarding point
⛴	Canalbus boarding point
⛴	Museum boat boarding point
🚕	Taxi rank
P	Parking
ℹ	Tourist information office
✚	Hospital with casualty unit
🚓	Police station
✝	Church
✡	Synagogue
☪	Mosque
⊠	Post office
═	Railway line
▬	Pedestrianized street

0 metres 500
0 yards 500

SCALE OF MAPS 1–6

0 metres 200
0 yards 200
1:11,250

SCALE OF MAPS 7–8

0 metres 150
0 yards 150
1:7,500

Fresh fruit for sale in the Noorder-markt *(see p92)*

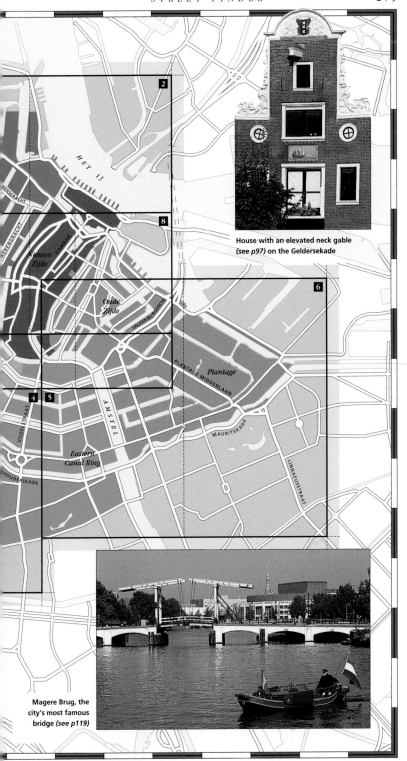

House with an elevated neck gable
(see p97) on the Geldersekade

Magere Brug, the
city's most famous
bridge *(see p119)*

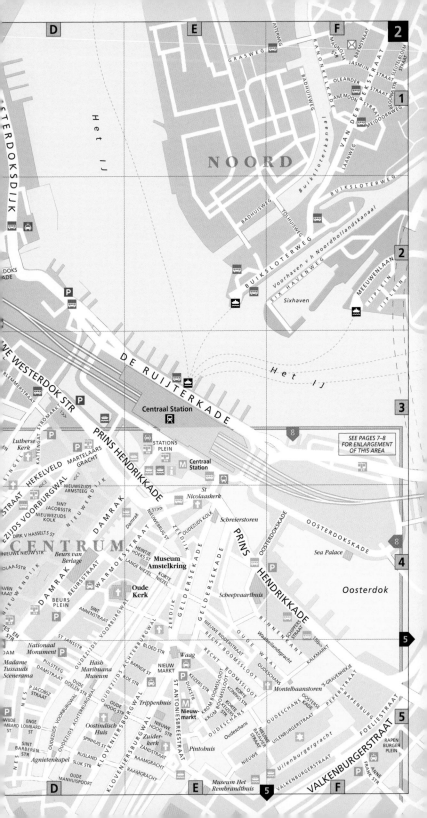

D **E** **F** **2**

GRASWEG

BADHUISWEG

ASTERWEG

RANONKELKADE

MAGNOLIA
BREMSTRAAT
SLEUTELBLOM STR

JASMIJN STRAAT

OLEANDER STRAAT
ANEMOON STRAAT
VAN DER PEKSTRAAT
BEGONIA STR

1

MEIDOORNWEG
LANWEG

Het IJ

N O O R D

Buiksloterkanaal

BUIKSLOTERWEG

BADHUISWEG
TOLHUISWEG

BUIKSLOTERWEG

2

MEEUWENLAAN
IJPLEIN
IJPLEIN

BUIKSLOTERWEG

Voorhaven v h Noordhollandskanaal

SIX HAVENWEG

Sixhaven

OSTERDOKSDIJK

DOKS KADE

Het IJ

D E   R U I J T E R K A D E

NE WESTERDOK STR

P

PRINS HENDRIKKADE

3

Centraal Station

🚂 Centraal Station

SEE PAGES 7–8
FOR ENLARGEMENT
OF THIS AREA

8

KLEMMERSTRAAT

P

Lutherse
Kerk

HEKELVELD
MARTELAARS
GRACHT

KATTENGAT STROMARKT

SINGEL

P

STATIONS
PLEIN

EN

SINT
JACOBSSTR

DIRK V HASSELTS ST

NIEUWEZIJDS
ARMSTEEG

NIEUWEZIJDS
KOLK

St Nicolaaskerk

Schreierstoren

OOSTERDOKSKADE

OOSTERDOKSKADE

Straat

NIEUWEZIJDS VOORBURGWAL

C E N T R U M

Beurs van
Berlage

DAMRAK

NIEUWENDIJK

Damrak

WARMOESSTRAAT

HEINTJE
HOEKS ST

NIEUWEBRUG ST

ZEEDIJK

OUDEZIJDS KOLK

PRINS
HENDRIKKADE

Sea Palace

4

NIEUWE NIEUW STR

OLAASSTR

P

BEURSSTRAAT

Museum
Amstelkring

LANGE NIEZEL
KORTE
NIEZEL

GELDERSEKADE

Oosterdok

8

AVEN
RAAT

DAMRAK

Beurs
PLEIN

SINT
ANNENSTRAAT

ZEEDIJK

GELDERSEKADE

P

Oude
Kerk

Scheepvaarthuis

5

ES
STR

P

NIEUWE RIDDERSTRAAT

RECHT BOOMSSLOOT

O U D E
W A A L

BINNENKANT

SCHIPPERS
STR

1556

KALKMARKT

EN
STR

Nationaal
Monument

DAM

P

ST JANSSTR

OUDEZIJDS VOORBURGWAL

ACHTERBURGWAL

SINT
BARNDE ST

KOE STR

NIEUWE
HOOG STR

BLOED STR

Waag

NIEUW
MARKT

RECHT BOOMSSLOOT

KROM BOOMSSLOOT

KONINGS
STR

KORTE
KONINGS
STR

OUDESCHANS

'S-GRAVENHEKJE

OOSTERSE
PEPERSTRAAT
RAPENBURG

5

Madame
Tussauds
Scenerama

PULSTEEG

P JACOBSZ
STRAAT

P

DAMSTRAAT

Hash
Marihuana
Museum

OUDE
DOELEN ST

ST ANTONIESBREESTRAAT

Trippenhuis

KEIZERS STR

KROM BOOMSSLOOT

OUDESCHANS

Montelbaanstoren

OUDESCHANS
KADE

FOELIESTRAAT

P

WIJDE
MBARD
ST

ENGE
LOMBARD
ST

SINT
BARBEREN
ST

OUDEZIJDS VOORBURGWAL

OUDEZIJDS ACHTERBURGWAL

SPINHUIS STR

Oostindisch
Huis

Zuider-
kerk

NIEUWE
HOOG STR

DIJKSTR

Nieuw-
markt

NIEUWE
BATAVIER
STRAAT

NIEUWE UILENBURGERGRACHT

RAPEN
BURGER
PLEIN

ANNE
FRANK STR

RUSLAND

SLIJK STR

KLOVENIERSBURGWAL

ZANDSTRAAT

Pintohuis

OUDESCHANS

VALKENBURGERSTRAAT

Agnietenkapel

RAAMGRACHT

RAAMGRACHT

Uilenburgergracht

VALKENBURGERGRACHT

VALKENBURGERSTRAAT

OUDE
MANHUISPOORT

D **E** **5** **F**

Museum Het
Rembrandthuis

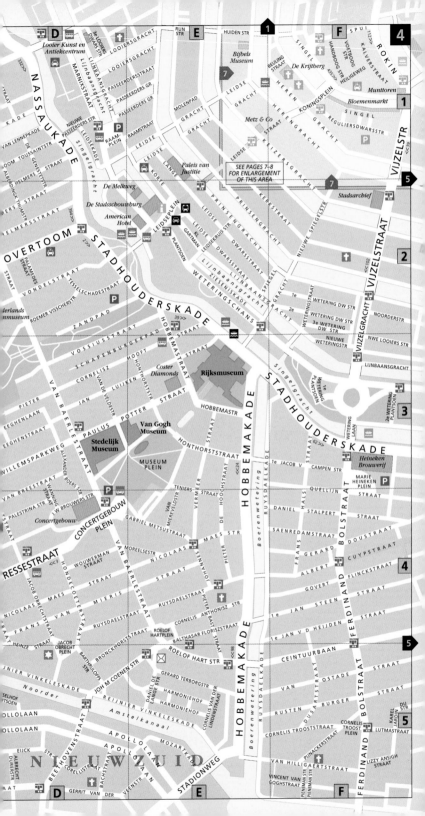

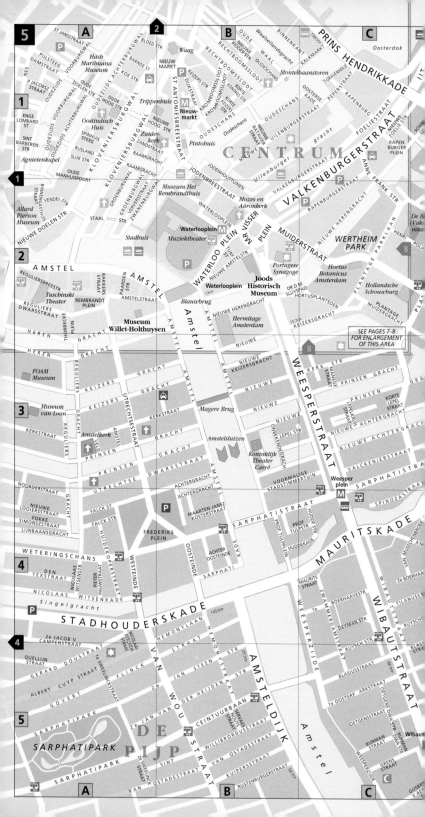

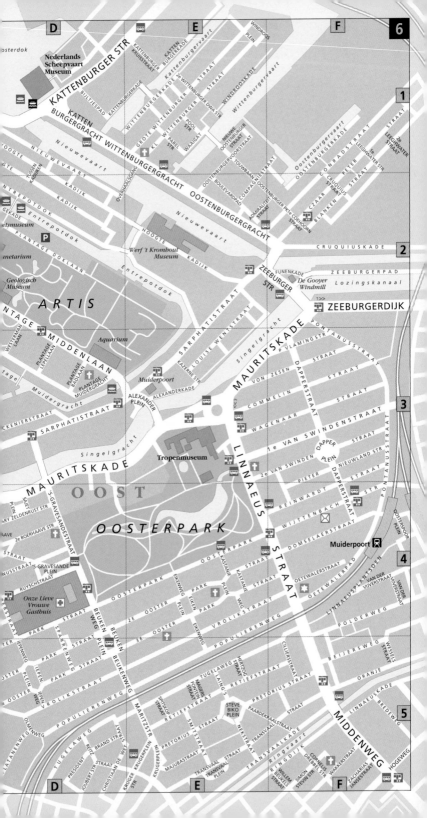

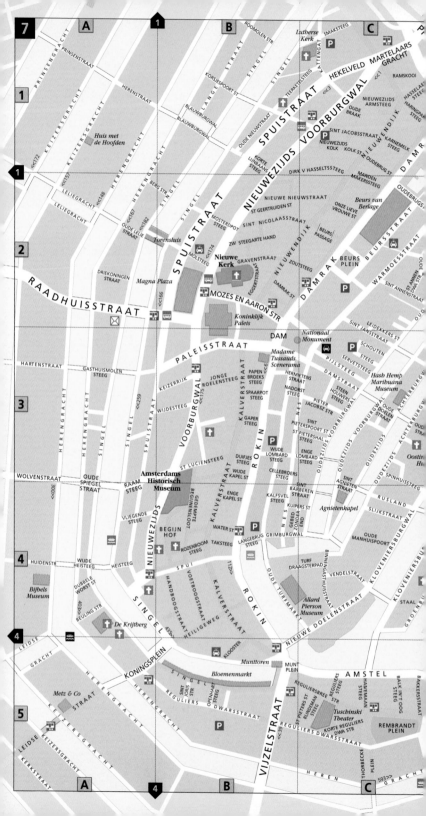

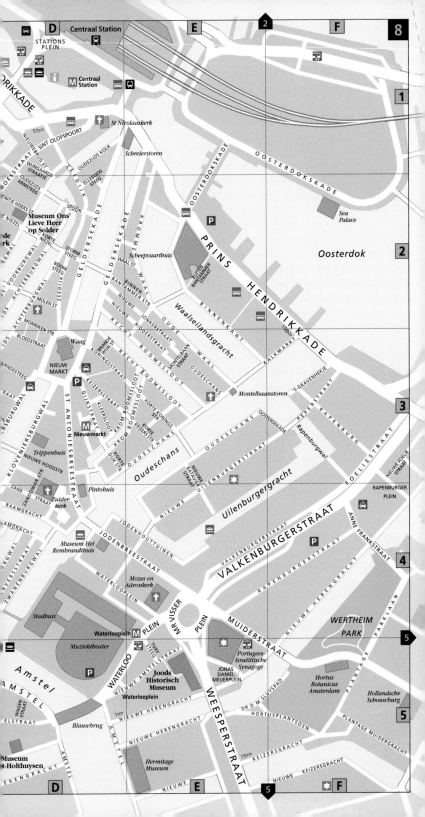

Street Finder Index

General Index

Page numbers in **bold** type refer to
main entries

Acknowledgments

Dorling Kindersley would like to thank the following people whose help and assistance contributed to the preparation of this book.

Main Contributor

Robin Pascoe has lived in Amsterdam since the 1980s. She is a freelance journalist and writes for various Dutch newspapers. She also works for the Dutch national news agency ANP, the international development news agency IPS, and the BBC.

Christopher Catling has been visiting the Netherlands for two decades, since writing his first guide for business travellers in 1984. He has since written a further four guides to Amsterdam and the Netherlands. Besides this guide, he has contributed to four *Dorling Kindersley Travel Guides:* Florence and Tuscany, Venice and the Veneto, Great Britain and Italy.

Additional Photography

Steve Gorton, Ian O'Leary, Neil Lukas, Rough Guides/Neil Setchfield, Tony Souter, Clive Streeter, Gerard van Vuuren

Additional Illustrations

Arcana (Graham Bell), Richard Bonson, Stephen Conlin, Roy Flooks, Mick Gillah, Kevin Goold, Stephen Gyapay, Chris Orr, Ian Henderson, Philip Winton, John Woodcock

Editorial and Design

Managing Editors Vivien Crump, Helen Partington
Managing Art Editor Steve Knowlden
Senior Editor Peter Casterton
Deputy Editorial Director Douglas Amrine
Deputy Art Director Gaye Allen
Production David Proffit
Picture Research Lorna Ainger
DTP Designer Siri Lowe
Emma Anacootee, Claire Baranowski, Hilary Bird, Willem de Blaauw, Johan Blom, Susan Churchill, Lucinda Cooke, Seán O'Connell, Martin Cropper, Karlien van Dam, Russell Davies, Simon Davis, Gadi Farfour, Emer Fitzgerald, Anthea Forlee, Fay Franklin, Anna Freiberger, Robin Gauldie, Vicky Hampton, Annette Jacobs, Gail Jones, Nancy Jones, Maite Lantaron, David Lindsey, Carly Madden, Iris Maher, Sam Merrell, Rebecca Milner, Sonal Modha, Marianne Petrou, Caroline Radula-Scott, Mindy Ran, Sands Publishing Solutions, Simon Ryder, Debbie Scholes, Sadie Smith, Gerard van Vuuren
Hotel listings: Kim Renfrew
Restaurant listings: Pip Farquharson

Cartography

Jane Hanson, Phil Rose, Jennifer Skelley
(Lovell Johns Limited)
MAP CO-ORDINATORS Michael Ellis, David Pugh

Special Assistance

Greet Tuinman, Charlotte van Beurden, Poppy

Photography Permissions

Dorling Kindersley would like to thank the following for their kind permission to photograph at their establishments: Airborne Museum, Arnhem; Allard Pierson Museum; Amstelkring Museum; Amsterdams Historisch Museum/Willet-Holthuysen Museum; Artis Zoo; Aviodrome; Beurs van Berlage; Boerhaave Museum, Leiden; Carré Theater; Concertgebouw; Coster Diamonds; Domkerk, Utrecht; Electrische Museumtramlijn; Europoort, Rotterdam; Filmmuseum; Frankendael; Anne Frankhuis; Grote Kerk, Alkmaar; Grote Kerk, Edam; Hash Marihuana Museum; Heineken Museum; Hollandse Schouwburg; Hortus Botanicus, Leiden; Joods Historisch Museum; Justitie Hall; Koninklijk Paleis; Krijtberg; Kröller-Müller Museum and National Park, Otterlo; Nederlands Scheepvaart Museum; Madurodam, Den Haag; Maritime Museum, Rotterdam; Monnickendam; Nieuwe Kerk; Nieuwe Kerk and Oude Kerk, Delft; Oude Kerk; Paleis Het Loo, Apeldoorn; Peace Palace, Den Haag; Portugese Synagogue; Prince William V Gallery, Den Haag; Prinsenhof, Leiden; Prison Gate Museum, Den Haag; RAI International Exhibition Centre; Rijksmuseum; Rijksmuseum, Utrecht; Rijksmuseum van Oudheden, Leiden; Rijksmuseum van SpeelklokTot Pierement, Utrecht; St Bavo, Haarlem; St Nicolaaskerk; SAS Hotel; Scheveningen Sea Life Centre; Sint Janskerk, Gouda; Stadhuis-Muziektheater; Stedelijk Museum; Stedelijk Molenmuseum, Leiden; Technologie Museum; Teylers Museum, Haarlem; Theater Museum; Tropenmuseum; Vakbonds Museum; Van Gogh Museum; Van Loon Museum; Verzetsmuseum; Werf 't Kromhout Museum; Westerkerk; Westfries Museum, Hoorn; Zuiderzee Museum.

Picture Credits

t = top; tl = top left; tc = top centre; tr = top right; trc = top right centre; cla = centre left above; ca = centre above; cra = centre right above; cl = centre left; c = centre; cr = centre right; clb = centre left below; cb = centre below; crb = centre right below; bl = bottom left; b = bottom; bc = bottom centre; br = bottom right; (d) = detail.

Every effort has been made to trace the copyright holders, and we apologize in advance for any unintentional omissions. We would be pleased to insert the appropriate acknowledgments in any subsequent edition of this publication.

Works of art have been reproduced with the permission of the following copyright holders: © ABC/MONDRIAAN ESTATE/HOLTZMAN TRUST, LICENSED BY ILP 1995: 136br; © ADAGP, PARIS AND DACS, LONDON 1995: 136cl, 200br, 204cb; © DACS, LONDON 1995: 40bl, 136bl; © JASPER JOHNS/DACS LONDON/VAGA NEW YORK: 137cb.

The Publishers are grateful to the following museums, photographers and picture libraries for permission to reproduce their photographs:

AKG, LONDON: 22clb, 24cl, 25c, 26cl, 28br, 29t, 101tr, 130tc, 185tr, 209c; Niklaus Strauss 137br; ALAMY IMAGES: Bertrand Collet 227tl; David R. Frazier Photolibrary, Inc 270bl; Warren Kovach 10br; Frans Lemmens 260tr; Sergio Pitamitz 16tl; Richard Wareham Fotografie 208-9; Stuwdamdorp 270cr, 271cl; MAX ALEXANDER 127bl; AMSTELKRING MUSEUM: 84bl, 85cr, 85br; Image courtesy of

WWW.AMSTERDAM.INFO: 225br; AMSTERDAMS HISTORISCH MUSEUM: 18, 23bc, 24–5c, 25tc, 25crb, 25bl, 26–7c, 27clb, 30cl, 31t, 31cb, 32cl, 33cr, 40cl, 81t, 81tr, 81cr, 81br, 82b, 83t, 83b, 90b, 94, 120cl, 120c, 120bl, 121cr; AMSTERDAM TOERISME & CONGRES BUREAU: 51b, 51cr, 89 br, 256cla, 256tc, 257cl, 273tr, 275crb; ANP PHOTO: 37tc, 37crb, 37bl; ANWB (ROYAL DUTCH TOURING CLUB): 269cl. B&U INTERNATIONAL PICTURE SERVICE: 37tl, 53b, 101bl, 105br, 180cl, 203t; BGB – The travel and PR representation specialists: 268br; BRANDWEER NL: 260cl; BRIDGEMAN ART LIBRARY: Christie's London *The Groote Market Haarlem with the Church of St Bavo* Gerrit Berckheyde c.1668 176t; Giraudon/ Musée Crozatier Le Puy-en-Velay France *King Louis XIV* 27br; Kremlin Museums Moscow 30bl; Private Collection *Self-Portrait Kazimir Malevich* 137cr; Stapleton Collection Delft tile 19th century 192tl; BUREAU MOMUMENTEN & ARCHEOLOGIE (BMA): 117cr. CAMERA PRESS: Karsh of Ottawa 137tr; JEAN-LOUP CHARMET: Musée de l'Armée 28br; COLORSPORT: 36cla; CORBIS: Dave Bartruff 226cl; Owen Franken 227c. DE KAS RESTAURANT: 258br; JAN DERWIG: 99tr, 151b, 224b; DRENTS MUSEUM, ASSEN: 20bl. MARY EVANS PICTURE LIBRARY: 9c, 21cra, 21bc, 23bl, 25br, 26bl, 27br, 29bl, 31br, 32cb, 32bc, 33bl, 35crb 55c, 163c; Louis Raemaehois 34bc; Jean Veber 33br; EYE UBIQUITOUS: T RAFFERTY 263br. THE FLIGHT COLLECTION: Ian Loasby 155br; FOTO NATURA: Fred Hazelhoff 205cb. GAUGUIN RESTAURANT: 224cl; GEMEENTEARCHIEF, AMSTERDAM: 21tl, 23ca, 23cb, 24tl, 24bc, 31cr, 99tl, 99cl, 100clb, 101br, 102bl, 103tr, 103cr, 104tr, 105tr, 105cr; GEMEENTEARCHIEF, KAMPEN: 23tl; GETTY IMAGES: Hulton Archive/Anne Frank Fonds - Basel/Anne Frank House 90tr; GVB AMSTERDAM: 272cl; 273tl; GWK TRAVELEX: 266br. FRANS HALS MUSEUM, HAARLEM: 27tl, 30–31c, 178t, 178bl, 178br,179tl, 179tr, 179bl, 179br; VANESSA HAMILTON: 97tl, 101cr, 104cl; ROBERT HARDING PICTURE LIBRARY: 58tr; Peter Scholey 116c; Adam Woolfitt 11br; HERMITAGE AMSTERDAM: Luuk Kramer 145br; HOLLANDSE HOOGTE: Adrie Mouthaan 150tr; Co de Kruijf 11br; Emile Luider 10cl; Peter Hilz 11tr; HULTON-DEUTSCH COLLECTION: 40t. ICONOGRAFISCH BUREAU: 103tl; THE IMAGE BANK: Bernard van Berg 52cr; Fotoworld 50b; ING GROUP: 37cra; INTERNATIONAL FLOWER BULB CENTRE: 26bc, 180bc, 181tl, 181cla, 181cl, 181clb, 181bl; INTERNATIONAL INSTITUTE OF SOCIAL HISTORY: 34tl; ISTOCKPHOTO.COM: Rob Bouwman 267br. JAMES DAVIS TRAVEL PHOTOGRAPHY: 225tr; COLLECTION JEWISH HISTORICAL MUSEUM, AMSTERDAM: *Mahzor*, Illuminated Manuscript on Parchment, Cologne area, c. 1250 64crb; Liselore Kamping 64cl; *Hanukah Lamp* Peter Robol II, silver, Amsterdam (1753) on loan from NIHS, Amsterdam 65tl. KLM ROYAL DUTCH AIRLINES: 267tr; KONINKLIJKE TPG POST BV: 262tl, 262ca, 262cb; KPN: 264tl; KRÖLLER-MÜLLER MUSEUM: 204tl; MAURITSHUIS, DEN HAAG: 188t, 188cl, 188bl, 189t, 189cr, 189br, 189bl, 193tl; MGM CINEMAS BV: 35cr; MUNICIPAL MUSEUM DE LAKENHAL, LEIDEN: 184b; MUSEUM BOIJMANS VAN BEUNINGEN, ROTTERDAM: 200–1 all; Designer J.J.P Oud / Production Metz & Co 200br; MUSEUM HET SCHIP: 151tr; MUSEUM HUIS LAMBERT VAN MEERTEN, COLLECTION RBK: 195t. NATIONAL EXPRESS LTD:

269cra; NATIONAL FIETSMUSEUM VELORAMA, NIJMEGEN: 33tl; NETHERLANDS ARCHITECTURE INSTITUTE ARCHIVE: 98cl; Isaac Gosschalk 105cl; De Klerk 35t, 97cra; NEMO SCIENCE AND TECHNOLOGY CENTER: 150b. ORANGE BIKE: 274tr; OPENBARE BIBLIOTHEEK AMSTERDAM: Annetje van Praag Sigaar 263tl. PICTURE BOX: Lee Auteur 156; © PHOTO RMN, PARIS: 8–9; PINK POINT: 258tl; POLITIE AMSTERDAM-AMSTELLAND: Nick Hoegeveen 260 clb; PRENTENKABINET DER RIJKSUNIVERSITEIT, LEIDEN: 32br. RANGE PICTURES: 28tr; MUSEUM HET REMBRANDTHUIS: 59b; RETROGRAPH ARCHIVE LTD: Martin Breese 32tl; RIJKSMUSEUM-FOUNDATION, AMSTERDAM: 26tl, 28tl, 30cla, 40c, 42b, 130cl, 130b, 131t, 131c, 131br, 132t, 132b, 133t, 133b; RIJKSMUSEUM PALEIS HET LOO, APELDOORN: F. Boeijinga 206tr, 207tl, R Mulder 206cl; AAW Meine Jansen 206bl; R Mulder 206clb; ROYAL PALACE, AMSTERDAM: Erik Hemsmerg 27tr, 39cr, 70, 74t. SCHEEPVART MUSEUM: 19b, 28cr, 29c, 146tl, 146ca, 146cb, 147c; SCHIPHOL AIRPORT: 266cla, 267cl; SCIENCE PHOTO LIBRARY/Earth Satellite Corporation: 12cl; HARRY SMITH HORTICULTURAL COLLECTION: 36b; SPAARNESTAD FOTOARCHIEF: 35c, 97tr, 99cb; STEDELIJK MUSEUM, ALKMAAR: 34c; STEDELIJK MUSEUM, AMSTERDAM: 136tr, 137tl, 137tc; © ABC/ Mondriaan Estate/Holtzmann Trust, licenced by ILP 1995 *Composition in Red, Black, Blue, Yellow and Grey* Piet Mondriaan 1920 136br; © ADAGP Paris and DACS London 1995 *Portrait of Artist with Seven Fingers* Marc Chagall 1912–13 136cl; © DACS London 1995 *Red Blue Chair* Gerrit Rietveld 1918 136bl; © DACS London 1995 *Stelman Chair* Gerrit Rietveld 1963 40bl; © Jasper Johns/DACS London/VAGA New York 1995 *Untitled* Jasper Johns 1965 137cb; STEDELIJK MUSEUM DE LAKENHAL, LEIDEN: 104br; THALYS INTERNATIONAL SCRL/CVBA: 268tl; TONY STONE IMAGES: 173cl; Kim Blaxland 181tr; John Lamb 2–3; Manfred Mehlig 162–3; Rohan 100t. TNT POST: 263bc, 265bl; TROPENMUSEUM: 152tr, 152ca, 152cl, 153tc, 153cl, 153br; HANS TULLENERS: 99cr, 100cr, 102c. UNIVERSITEITSBIBLIOTHEEK VAN AMSTERDAM: 96tr; VINCENT VAN GOGH (FOUNDATION), VAN GOGH MUSEUM, AMSTERDAM: 40br, 134t, 134c, 134bl, 134br, 135t, 135cr, 135crb; VZA AMBULANCE SERVICE AMSTERDAM: 260bl. WESTERN AUSTRALIAN MARITIME MUSEUM: 28ca; WORLD PICTURES: 95cr. YELLOW BIKE: 274tr. ZEFA: CPA 52b; Steenmans 53c. ZUIDERZEEMUSEUM: 171bc; *The Blue Fishvendor* 2008 (stencils and spraypaint) ©Hugo Kaagman see www.kaagman.nl, photo Petra Stavast 171tl.

Front Endpaper: All special photography except ROYAL PALACE AMSTERDAM Erik Hemsmerg trc.

Map Cover: PHOTOLIBRARY: Hemis/Jean-Baptiste Rabouan.

JACKET: Front: PHOTOLIBRARY: Hemis/Jean-Baptiste Rabouan. Back: ALAMY IMAGES: Yadid Levy bl; AWL IMAGES: Danita Delimont Stock tl; FAN Travel Stock clb; DORLING KINDERSLEY: Rupert Horrox cla. Spine: PHOTOLIBRARY: Hemis/Jean-Baptiste Rabouan. All other images © Dorling Kindersley. For further information see: www.dkimages.com

---

SPECIAL EDITIONS OF DK TRAVEL GUIDES

DK Travel Guides can be purchased in bulk quantities at discounted prices for use in promotions or as premiums. We are also able to offer special editions and personalized jackets, corporate imprints, and excerpts from all of our books, tailored specifically to meet your own needs.

To find out more, please contact:
(in the United States) **SpecialSales@dk.com**
(in the UK) **TravelSpecialSales@uk.dk.com**
(in Canada) DK Special Sales at **general@tourmaline.ca**
(in Australia) **business.development@pearson.com.au**

Phrase Book

In Emergency

Help!	**Help!**	Help
Stop!	**Stop!**	Stop
Call a doctor	**Haal een dokter**	Haal uhn **dok**-tur
Call an ambulance	**Bel een ambulance**	Bell uhn ahm-bew-**luhns**-uh
Call the police	**Roep de politie**	Roop duh poe-**leet**-see
Call the fire brigade	**Roep de brandweer**	Roop duh **brahnt**-vheer
Where is the nearest telephone?	**Waar is de dichtstbijzijnde telefoon?**	Vhaar iss duh **dikhst**-baiy-zaiyn-duh tay-luh-**foan**
Where is the nearest telephone?	**Waar is het dichtstbijzijnde ziekenhuis?**	Vhaar iss het **dikhst**-baiy-zaiyn-duh **zee**-kuh-houws

Communication Essentials

Yes	**Ja**	Yaa
No	**Nee**	Nay
Please	**Alstublieft**	Ahls-tew-**bleeft**
Thank you	**Dank u**	Dahnk-ew
Excuse me	**Pardon**	Pahr-**don**
Hello	**Hallo**	Hallo
Goodbye	**Dag**	Dahgh
Good night	**Slaap lekker**	Slaap **lek**-kah
morning	**Morgen**	**Mor**-ghuh
afternoon	**Middag**	**Mid**-dahgh
evening	**Avond**	**Ah**-vohnd
yesterday	**Gisteren**	**Ghis**-tern
today	**Vandaag**	Vahn-**daagh**
tomorrow	**Morgen**	**Mor**-ghuh
here	**Hier**	Heer
there	**Daar**	Daar
What?	**Wat?**	Vhat
When?	**Wanneer?**	Vhan-**eer**
Why?	**Waarom?**	Vhaar-**om**
Where?	**Waar?**	Vhaar
How?	**Hoe?**	Hoo

Useful Phrases

How are you?	**Hoe gaat het ermee?**	Hoo ghaat het er-**may**
Very well, thank you	**Heel goed, dank u**	Hayl ghoot, dahnk ew
How do you do?	**Hoe maakt u het?**	Hoo maakt ew het
See you soon	**Tot ziens**	Tot zeens
That's fine	**Prima**	**Pree**-mah
Where is/are?	**Waar is/zijn?**	Vhaar iss/zayn…
How far is it to…?	**Hoe ver is het naar…?**	Hoo vehr iss het naar…
How do I get to …?	**Hoe kom ik naar…?**	Hoo kom ik naar…
Do you speak English?	**Spreekt u engels?**	Spraykt ew **eng**-uhls
I don't understand	**Ik snap het niet**	Ik snahp het neet
Could you speak slowly?	**Kunt u langzamer praten?**	Kuhnt ew **lahng**-zahmer praa-tuh
I'm sorry	**Sorry**	Sorry

Useful Words

big	**groot**	ghroaht
small	**klein**	klaiyn
hot	**warm**	vharm
cold	**koud**	khowt
good	**goed**	ghoot
bad	**slecht**	slekht
enough	**genoeg**	ghuh-**noohkh**
well	**goed**	ghoot
open	**open**	open
closed	**gesloten**	ghuh-**slow**-tuh
left	**links**	links
right	**rechts**	rekhts
straight on	**rechtdoor**	rehkht dohr
near	**dichtbij**	dikht baiy
far	**ver weg**	vehr vhekh
up	**omhoog**	om-**hoakh**
down	**naar beneden**	naar buh-**nay**-duh
early	**vroeg**	vroohkh
late	**laat**	laat
entrance	**ingang**	**in**-ghahng
exit	**uitgang**	**ouht**-ghang
toilet	**wc**	vhay say
occupied	**bezet**	buh-**zett**
free (unoccupied)	**vrij**	vraiy
free (no charge)	**gratis**	**ghraah**-tiss

Making a Telephone Call

I'd like to place a long distance call	**Ik wil graag interlokaal telefoneren**	Ik vhil ghraakh **inter**-loh-kaahl tay-luh-foe-**neh**-ruh
I'd like to call collect	**Ik wil 'collect call' bellen**	Ik vhil 'collect call' **bel**-luh
I'll try again later	**Ik probeer het later nog wel eens**	Ik pro-**beer** het later nokh vhel ayns
Can I leave a message?	**Kunt u een boodschap doorgeven?**	Kuhnt ew uhn **boat**-skhahp **dohr**-ghay-vuh
Could you speak up a little please?	**Wilt u wat harder praten?**	Vhilt ew vhat **hahr**-der **praah**-tuh
Local call	**Lokaal gesprek**	Low-**kaahl** ghuh-**sprek**

Shopping

How much does this cost?	**Hoeveel kost dit?**	Hoo-**vayl** kost dit
I would like	**Ik wil graag**	Ik vhil ghraakh
Do you have…?	**Heeft u…?**	Hayft ew…
I'm just looking	**Ik kijk alleen even**	Ik kaiyk alleyn **ay**-vuh
Do you take credit cards?	**Neemt u credit cards aan?**	Naymt ew credit cards aan
Do you take traveller's cheques?	**Neemt u reischeques aan?**	Naymt ew **raiys**-sheks aan
What time do you open?	**Hoe laat gaat u open?**	Hoo laat ghaat ew opuh
What time do you close?	**Hoe laat gaat u dicht?**	Hoo laat ghaat ew dikht
This one	**Deze**	**Day**-zuh
That one	**Die**	Dee
expensive	**duur**	dewr
cheap	**goedkoop**	ghoot-**koap**
size	**maat**	maat
white	**wit**	vhit
black	**zwart**	zvhahrt
red	**rood**	roat
yellow	**geel**	ghayl
green	**groen**	ghroon
blue	**blauw**	blah-ew

Types of Shops

antique shop	**antiekwinkel**	ahn-**teek**-vhin-kul
bakery	**bakker**	**bah**-ker
bank	**bank**	bahnk
bookshop	**boekwinkel**	**book**-vhin-kul
butcher	**slager**	slaakh-er
cake shop	**banketbakkerij**	bahnk-**et**-bahk-er-aiy
cheese shop	**kaaswinkel**	**kaas**-vhin-kul
chip shop	**patatzaak**	pah-**taht**-zaak
chemist (dispensing)	**apotheek**	ah-poe-**taiyk**
delicatessen	**delicatessen**	daylee-kah-**tes**-suh
department store	**warenhuis**	**vhaar**-uh-houws
fishmonger	**viswinkel**	viss-vhin-kul
greengrocer	**groenteboer**	**ghroon**-tuh-boor
hairdresser	**kapper**	**kah**-per
market	**markt**	mahrkt
newsagent	**krantenwinkel**	**krahn**-tuh-vhin-kul
post office	**postkantoor**	**pohst**-kahn-tor
shoe shop	**schoenenwinkel**	**sghoo**-nuh-vhin-kul
supermarket	**supermarkt**	**sew**-per-mahrkt
tobacconist	**sigarenwinkel**	see-**ghaa**-ruh-vhin-kul
travel agent	**reisburo**	**raiys**-bew-roa

Sightseeing

art gallery	**galerie**	ghaller-ee
bus station	**busstation**	**buhs**-stah-shown
cathedral	**kathedraal**	kah-tuh-**draal**
church	**kerk**	kehrk
closed on public holidays	**op feestdagen gesloten**	op **fayst**-daa-ghuh ghuh-**slow**-tuh
day return	**dagretour**	**dahgh**-ruh-tour
garden	**tuin**	touwn
library	**bibliotheek**	bee-bee-yo-**tayk**
museum	**museum**	mew-**zay**-uhm
railway station	**station**	stah-**shown**
return ticket	**retourtje**	ruh-**tour**-tyuh
single journey	**enkeltje**	**eng**-kuhl-tyuh
tourist information	**VVV**	fay fay fay
town hall	**stadhuis**	staht-**houws**
train	**trein**	traiyn
travel pass	**Ov-chipkaart**	oh-**vay**-chip-kaahrt

Staying in a Hotel

Do you have a vacant room?	Zijn er nog kamers vrij?	Zaiyn er nokh **kaa**-mers vray
double room with double bed	een twee persoonskamer met een twee persoonsbed	uhn **tvhay**-per **soans**-kaa-mer met uhn **tvhay**-per **soans** beht
twin room	een kamer met een lits-jumeaux	uhn **kaa**-mer met uhn lee-zjoo-**moh**
single room	eenpersoons-kamer	ayn-per-**soans**-kaa-mer
room with a bath	kamer met bad	**kaa**-mer met baht
shower	douche	doosh
porter	kruier	**krouw**-yuh
I have a reservation	Ik heb gereserveerd	Ik hehp ghuh-ray-sehr-**veert**

Eating Out

Have you got a table?	Is er een tafel vrij?	Iss ehr uhn **tah**-fuhl vraiy
I want to reserve a table	Ik wil een tafel reserveren	Ik vhil uhn **tah**-fuhl ray-sehr-**veer**-uh
The bill, please	Mag ik afrekenen	Mukh ik **ahf**-ray-kuh-nuh
I am a vegetarian	Ik ben vegetariër	Ik ben fay-ghuh-**taahr**-ee-er
waitress/waiter	meneer/merrouw	Sehr-**veer**-ster/**oh**-ber
menu	de kaart	duh kaahrt
cover charge	het couvert	het koo-**vehr**
wine list	de wijnkaart	duh **vhaiyn**-kaart
glass	het glas	het ghlahss
bottle	de fles	duh fless
knife	het mes	het mess
fork	de vork	duh fork
spoon	de lepel	duh **lay**-pul
breakfast	het ontbijt	het ont-**baiyt**
lunch	de lunch	duh lernsh
dinner	het diner	het dee-**nay**
main course	het hoofdgerecht	het **hoaft**-ghuh-rekht
starter, first course	het voorgerecht	het **vohr**-ghuh-rekht
dessert	het nagerecht	het **naa**-ghuh-rekht
dish of the day	het dagmenu	het **dahgh**-munh-ew
bar	het cafe	het kaa-**fay**
café	het eetcafe	het **ayt**-kaa-**fay**
rare	rare	'rare'
medium	medium	'medium'
well done	doorbakken	dohr-**bah**-kuh

Menu Decoder

aardappels	**aard**-uppuhls	potatoes
azijn	aah-**zaiyn**	vinegar
biefstuk	**beef**-stuhk	steak
bier, pils	beer, pilss	beer
boter	boater	butter
brood/broodje	broat/**broat**-yuh	bread/roll
cake, taart, gebak	'cake', taahrt, ghuh-**bahk**	cake, pastry
carbonade	kahr-bow-**naa**-duh	pork chop
chocola	show-coa-**laa**	chocolate
citroen	see-**troon**	lemon
cocktail	cocktail	cocktail
droog	droakh	dry
eend	aynt	duck
ei	aiy	egg
garnalen	ghahr-**naah**-luh	prawns
gebakken	ghuh-**bah**-ken	fried
gegrild	ghuh-**ghrillt**	grilled
gekookt	ghuh-**koakt**	boiled
gepocheerd	ghuh-posh-**eert**	poached
gerookt	ghuh-**roakt**	smoked
geroosterd brood	ghuh-**roas**-tert broat	toast
groenten	**ghroon**-tuh	vegetables
ham	hahm	ham
haring	**haa**-ring	herring
hutspot	huht-spot	hot pot
ijs	aiyss	ice, ice cream
jenever	yuh-**nay**-vhur	gin
kaas	kaas	cheese
kabeljauw	kah-buhl-**youw**	cod
kip	kip	chicken
knoflook	**knoff**-loak	garlic
koffie	coffee	coffee
kool, rode of witte	coal, **roe**-duh off **vhit**-uh	cabbage, red or white
kreeft	krayft	lobster
kroket	crow-**ket**	ragout in bread-crumbs, deep fried
lamsvlees	**lahms**-flayss	lamb
lekkerbekje	**lek**-kah-bek-yuh	fried fillet of haddock
mineraalwater	meener-**aahl**-vhaater	mineral water
mosterd	**moss**-tehrt	mustard
niet scherp	neet skehrp	mild
olie	**oh**-lee	oil
paling	**paa**-ling	eel
pannenkoek	**pah**-nuh-kook	pancake
patat frites	pa-**taht** freet	chips
peper	**pay**-per	pepper
poffertjes	**poffer**-tyuhs	tiny buckwheat pancakes
rijst	raiyst	rice
rijsttafel	**raiys**-tah-ful	Indonesian meal
rode wijn	**roe**-duh vhaiyn	red wine
rookworst	**roak**-vhorst	smoked sausage
rundvlees	**ruhnt**-flayss	beef
saus	souwss	sauce
schaaldieren	**skaahl**-deeh-ruh	shellfish
scherp	skehrp	hot (spicy)
schol	sghol	plaice
soep	soup	soup
stamppot	**stahm**-pot	sausage stew
suiker	**souw**-ker	sugar
thee	tay	tea
tosti	**toss**-tee	cheese on toast
uien	**ouw**-yuh	onions
uitsmijter	**ouht**-smaiy-ter	fried egg on bread with ham
varkensvlees	**vahr**-kuhns-flayss	pork
vers fruit	fehrss frouwt	fresh fruit
verse jus	**vehr**-suh zjhew	fresh orange juice
vis	fiss	fish/seafood
vlees	flayss	meat
water	**vhaa**-ter	water
witte wijn	**vhih**-tuh vhaiyn	white wine
worst	vhorst	sausage
zout	zouwt	salt

Numbers

1	een	ayn
2	twee	tvhay
3	drie	dree
4	vier	feer
5	vijf	faiyf
6	zes	zess
7	zeven	**zay**-vuh
8	acht	ahkht
9	negen	**nay**-guh
10	tien	teen
11	elf	elf
12	twaalf	tvhaalf
13	dertien	**dehr**-teen
14	veertien	**feer**-teen
15	vijftien	**faiyf**-teen
16	zestien	**zess**-teen
17	zeventien	**zayvuh**-teen
18	achttien	**ahkh**-teen
19	negentien	**nay-ghuh**-teen
20	twintig	**tvhin**-tukh
21	eenentwintig	aynuh-**tvhin**-tukh
30	dertig	**dehr**-tukh
40	veertig	**feer**-tukh
50	vijftig	**faiyf**-tukh
60	zestig	**zess**-tukh
70	zeventig	**zay**-vuh-tukh
80	tachtig	**tahkh**-tukh
90	negentig	**nayguh**-tukh
100	honderd	**hohn**-durt
1000	duizend	**douw**-zuhnt
1,000,000	miljoen	mill-**yoon**

Time

one minute	een minuut	uhn meen-**ewt**
one hour	een uur	uhn ewr
half an hour	een half uur	uhn hahlf ewr
half past one	half twee	hahlf tvhay
a day	een dag	uhn dahgh
a week	een week	uhn vhayk
a month	een maand	uhn maant
a year	een jaar	uhn jaar
Monday	maandag	**maan**-dahgh
Tuesday	dinsdag	**dins**-dahgh
Wednesday	woensdag	**vhoons**-dahgh
Thursday	donderdag	**donder**-dahgh
Friday	vrijdag	**vraiy**-dahgh
Saturday	zaterdag	**zaater**-dahgh
Sunday	zondag	**zon**-dahgh

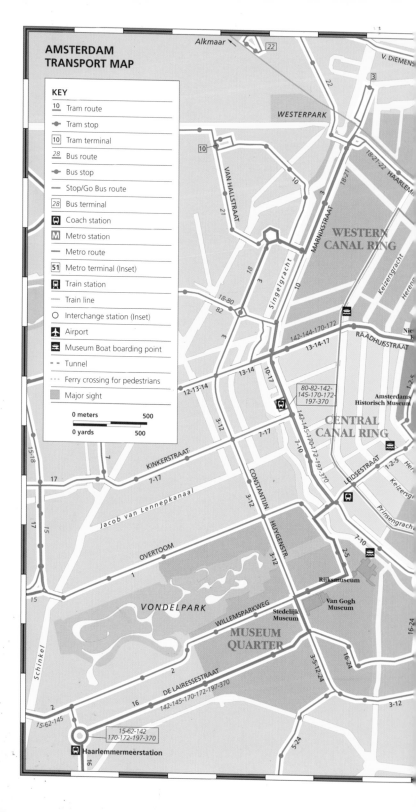

AMSTERDAM TRANSPORT MAP

KEY

10	Tram route
◆	Tram stop
10	Tram terminal
28	Bus route
◆	Bus stop
—	Stop/Go Bus route
28	Bus terminal
🚌	Coach station
M	Metro station
—	Metro route
51	Metro terminal (Inset)
🚆	Train station
—	Train line
O	Interchange station (Inset)
✈	Airport
🚤	Museum Boat boarding point
- -	Tunnel
⋯	Ferry crossing for pedestrians
▨	Major sight

0 meters 500

0 yards 500

Alkmaar

22

3

V. DIEMENS

WESTERPARK

WESTERN CANAL RING

18-21-22 HAARLEM

18-21

MARNIXSTRAAT

VAN HALLSTRAAT

Keizersgracht

Heren

Singelgracht

RAADHUISSTRAAT

Nie K

142-144-170-172

13-14-17

13-14

10-17

1-2-5

80-82-142-145-170-172-197-370

Amsterdams Historisch Museum

12-13-14

142-145-170-172-197-370

CENTRAL CANAL RING

3-12

7-17

7-10

KINKERSTRAAT

LEIDSESTRAAT

1-2-5 Hei

7-17

CONSTANTIN

Keizersgr

3-12

Jacob van Lennepkanaal

Prinsengrach

15-18

17

7

17

15

OVERTOOM

HUYGENSTR.

3-12

7-10

2-5

1

Rijksmuseum

15

VONDELPARK

WILLEMSPARKWEG

Stedelijk Museum

Van Gogh Museum

Schinkel

MUSEUM QUARTER

3-5-12-24

16-24

2

DE LAIRESSESTRAAT

142-145-170-172-197-370

16-24

75-62-145

2

16

15-62-142-170-172-197-370

5-24

3-12

🚆 Haarlemmermeerstation

16